DRIVING FROM JAPAN

# DRIVING FROM JAPAN

## Japanese Cars
## in America

Wanda James

McFarland & Company, Inc., Publishers
*Jefferson, North Carolina, and London*

Library of Congress Cataloguing-in-Publication Data

James, Wanda, 1959–
Driving from Japan : Japanese
cars in America / Wanda James
p.    cm.
Includes bibliographical references and index.

ISBN 0-7864-1734-X (illustrated case binding : 50# alkaline paper) ∞

1. Automobiles—Japan.
2. Automobiles, Foreign—United States.
I. Title.
TL105.J36    2005          629.222'0952—dc22          2004023954

British Library cataloguing data are available

Cover art ©2005 Artville

Manufactured in the United States of America

 *McFarland & Company, Inc., Publishers*
*Box 611, Jefferson, North Carolina 28640*
*www.mcfarlandpub.com*

For L.A.B.

# Acknowledgments

I have often marveled over acknowledgments that run to multiple pages. Now I understand why. So many people have helped bring this book about that they deserve recognition. Thanks go to Marion Adams of the Bookworm — keeper of jewels, and to Doug Stroud — source of vintage magazines and interesting tidbits.

Particularly helpful in direct relation to the manuscript were Masayori Hattori of the Toyota Motor Company's Nagoya, Japan, office, who very kindly sent me chapters of the unpublished Toyota story and directed me to further sources; Jay Springer, Lead Archivist at Toyota Motor Sales USA, who set aside valuable time to assemble a stunning array of photographic material; Robert and Matthew Krause of Krause Toyota in Schnecksville, Pennsylvania, for their input and historical photographs; Fred King of Hamer Toyota for sharing another bit of Toyota's American dealership history; Mike Sullivan of Toyota of Hollywood for speaking to me about the early days of his dealership; Andy Keown of Nissan USA for his patience and for showing me I *can* receive large files by email; Bob Hayes of Melloy Nissan, New Mexico, for his continued input, efforts, and interest; Karen Savolt and Andy Boyd of the American Honda Company for the photographs, and to Jon Fitzsimmons, who scanned them; Greg Young of Mazda Canada, who came through as promised; Kevin Twer of Mazda USA who acted with great alacrity; to Rob Moran and Maryanne McClintic of Subaru of America who entrusted me with the company's slides; Leslie Holm of American Suzuki for the enormous scan; and to Chip Letzgus of Isuzu America for all his efforts.

Many of these people would not be on this list but for one person — the wonderful Jeannine Fallon, of Edmunds, who held out a branch when it was most needed and also directed me to her colleague, Mike Benavides.

Falling under the category of the "kindness of strangers" are Peter Havey with his beautiful 810; Edgar Gonzales for offering his SP212 (photograph); Eric Hall for his contributions; "Merlin" of Datsun.org; Ian Kennedy for his continued interest; Brad Bowling just for taking precious time away from his own deadline to get back to me; Jeff Reich of *The Writer* magazine and Andrew Lilienthal of *Scale Auto* magazine for their strategic assistance.

Much closer to home, I could not have survived this process without the vital help of Peter Gamble, whose constant generosity, limitless technical knowledge, and endless patience cannot have been more appreciated. My thanks also go to Alexandra Reshetnikov-Gamble for always being there, no matter what; to the Bajraktari family — Annette, Lule, Patricia, and Leza — who have helped in so many ways; and to my family for their continued love and support. Not to be forgotten is my beloved cat Scooter, who followed my progress for 17 years but passed away during the writing of this book.

# Contents

# Introduction

The very first Japanese car I ever laid eyes on was a brand-new, grass-green 1969 Datsun 510 that belonged to a relative. I was only ten years old at the time so I don't remember many details of the occasion, but I do remember the adults calling it a "good little car." As my interest in cars was well-developed even at that age, I was fascinated by the Datsun, so much smaller than anything I'd ever seen, other than a VW Beetle. Back then German cars had just begun to be accepted and Japanese cars were considered something of an oddity, especially in a rural area of Canada.

By the time I was in college Toyotas and Datsuns were everywhere, enjoying a huge surge in popularity during the middle to late seventies. I knew nothing of their history either in Japan or in North America. I did know that after my first ride in a 1974 Corolla I was entranced and impressed. Their success, it seemed to me, was well deserved. Like many others I assumed that Japanese cars and trucks were something of an overnight success—but that was definitely not the case.

When the Japanese automakers chose a landing spot in America, they wisely targeted the West Coast, where a Japanese community had already been established. It was also as far away from Michigan's "Motor City" as could be. Yet perhaps it wouldn't have mattered considering that almost no one took them seriously, least of all American automakers. By the time they did realize that here was a force to be reckoned with it was too late to respond effectively. Their first response had been to produce the Chevrolet Corvair, the Ford Falcon, and the Plymouth Valiant, circa 1960, but even while those were in production the Japanese had already improved and kept moving while Detroit rested on its laurels, as it were. As the Japanese shed their image as producers of substandard goods, their sales rocketed, eventually becoming a juggernaut hurtling toward the heartland of America.

How did they do it? The answer is both simple and complex. Hard work, perseverance, sacrifice, clever strategy, luck, wisdom, philosophy, government support (although some would say interference), and sheer determination are all words that apply to Japan's success. Others in certain American boardrooms would probably add unfair policies and trade practices as well. A few might even call it serendipity. But there is no question that however it happened, Japan literally took over America's automobile industry. It certainly was an industry vulnerable to infiltration and one that seemed to many to be already derailing — its navigators apparently dozing at the wheel. Their awakening was not a gentle one. Tolerance and yawning amusement at the sight of a Toyopet Crown or a Subaru 360 turned to glaring hostility as Detroit's once-monopolized market shattered into shards around them.

As America faced major hurdles, such as the oil crisis of the 1970s and the recession of the 1980s, consumers eagerly snapped up the reliable and economical little Japanese cars. Most buyers did not consider the impact on the American auto industry. Those within the industry could not ignore it, nor would they forget it. A few of those who relied on Detroit for their living harbored such hatred that a Chinese worker mistaken for a Japanese was beaten to death in retaliation for lost American jobs. There were many other incidents, not as tragic, that went unnoticed and unreported.

When Honda, Nissan, and Toyota commenced to build their plants on American soil they faced taunts and verbal abuse, as well as violence and work stoppages.

Yet these were not enough to deter the stoic and determined Japanese, who felt the American demand for their products should be met to the best of their abilities, despite obstacles. They saw a lucrative and willing market and thought "why not." American automakers knew "why not" — and they were extremely vocal in their opposition. The American government interceded and the Voluntary Export Restraints were implemented, but frustratingly these only served to heighten demand as well as to create new markets for the Japanese — that of trucks and luxury vehicles. Trucks were exempt from the restraints and the Japanese certainly knew how to build them — they had cut their teeth making them. The luxury market was a different story — it seemed to many that the American automakers were safe here at least — but that was until Honda released its Acura line in the United States and Toyota and Nissan followed with Lexus and Infiniti respectively. American consumers seemed quite willing to give Japanese luxury cars a try and the Japanese, knowing they would meet resistance, made the cars as near to perfect as they could. While at one time the Japanese had indicated their intentions to stay out of the larger car market, the restraints changed all of that. Any balance the Americans were striving for was quickly eliminated. But then the story of Japanese cars in America is not a story of equality or of balance.

The sequence of events is outlined in this text much as it played out in real life. I made no attempt to favor either nation's industry, but rather tried to let the facts— sales records, trade reviews— speak for themselves. And the facts are simply that Japan has succeeded where America has failed. Yet it was not always so.

For fifty years the American industry had a good portion of the world's automobile market cornered, including Japan's from the 1920s to the 1950s. And while the overall quality of Japanese vehicles is not in question, as good as they are, they cannot replace the nostalgia that anyone over forty feels when they see a 1964 Mustang, a 1966 Pontiac Bonneville, or a 1967 Chrysler Imperial. Going further back, what automobile collector or restorer wouldn't like to own a Packard, Auburn, Cadillac, or early Lincoln Continental? And there's always the romantic comedy of the "Tin Lizzie" Model T Ford.

All of these cars are part of America's proud heritage as an automobile manufacturer. The romance is not entirely gone — there are still die-hard loyal American car lovers out there. And I suspect there are those who cannot imagine a wedding procession of Datsuns, a head of state arriving in a Subaru, or movie stars pulling up to the red carpet at the Academy Awards in Toyotas. This is not to disparage the average American car, which has satisfactorily conveyed Americans for over one hundred years.

Those one hundred years of the American auto industry have not always been accurately documented, but the history of Japan's has been far less so. One of the greatest difficulties in compiling this text lay in trying to uncover sufficient material, or at the very least, accurate material. Toyota representatives informed me that very little archival material from the late 1950s and early 1960s has survived. Nissan reported much the same.

In addition to the lack of archival material, there were difficulties locating the early dealerships — many claimed to be the first but were not. Others weren't certain of their history, as their original owners had retired or passed away.

Equally confusing was the amount of conflicting information, particularly in regard to sales and production statistics, engine sizes, dates released, and even model names. Obviously I could not deal with each and every American or Japanese model, nor could I include all of the models made in Japan and not sold in America. And as this is a book on passenger cars, trucks and sport-utility vehicles have only been mentioned when they assumed a particular importance in the line in lieu of cars. I have endeavored to provide as complete and accurate a picture as possible and all information is annotated. As I am my own researcher, any errors are mine and mine alone.

Conversely, there certainly has been no shortage of material vilifying the American auto industry. The trends of Japanese cars were interestingly revealed in the pages of automotive trade magazines, going from condescension to near reverence, with a faint smattering of resentment thrown in. Some had nothing but harsh words for Detroit, while others took pains to defend it. What has been even more fascinating is the multitude of clubs and collectors now focusing on early Japanese cars. Pride of ownership is just as evident in the owner of a 1971 Celica as it is in the owner of a 1964 Mustang. As far as car culture goes, Americans have proved themselves to be amenable to change and willing to try new things. There are some, however, who remain steadfastly loyal to the "buy American" philosophy, except that the definition of what is American has in recent years been altered. Japanese cars are now built in America, Canada, Mexico, the Philippines, Australia and elsewhere. So are American cars. The lines are blurred and the balance has shifted.

The impact of Japanese cars on America has been dramatic in both positive and negative respects. Among them Japanese automakers they have invested billions of dollars in the U.S., both in industry and within American communities. They provide a prodigious source of revenue for America — in terms of employment, satellite industries, taxes, insurance, licensing fees, and a myriad of other assorted expenses. They are also now American exporters in their own right.

On the other hand, they have dealt a blow to the American auto industry that has been immeasurable in its scope. There have been heavy losses and many are asking who is to blame, if "blame" is even an appropriate word. How much has been as a result of Japan's actions and how much has been self-inflicted? It is difficult to determine. Each side has been well argued, but the bottom line is that American automakers have taken the wisest option available by forming alliances with the Japanese, among others. This is not to say these alliances have eliminated competition — they have not. Yet the situation has evolved into one whereby companies may actually be competing against themselves in a manner of speaking. It is certain that with the tough market ahead and the glut of vehicles on hand now, only the strongest will survive, and mergers will probably continue. Korea has entered the playing field and even they have already seen the wisdom of alliances, as is demonstrated by the Hyundai and Kia alliance.

The development of fuel cell technology and alternative fuel vehicles (AFVs) have presented new challenges and placed automobile manufacturers back on even footing in a sense, as each strives to be the first to produce the cleanest and most efficient vehicle.

All of the major players are deeply immersed in research and development and in the manner of the late nineteenth century, the race is on. Will a German or European company take the lead? Or will it be an American company or a Japanese company? Whatever the case, the story of Japanese cars in America will soon be more accurately described as the story of automobiles and the world market.

# 1

## America Builds an Industry

"It may even be that the twenty-first century will think of Henry Ford as the inventor of the automobile," wrote automotive pioneer Charles Duryea in 1931.[1] But if Duryea felt that Ford did not deserve that distinction, neither did he feel it belonged to a European, adding somewhat pompously: "I should like to read into the record the fact that most of the fundamentals of the motorcar were American — not European...."[2]

While Duryea's invention certainly did precede Ford's by about three years, his assertions only add to the considerable confusion surrounding the invention of the automobile. Incomplete research, inaccurate reporting, and patents never properly filed have left the history of the automobile in partial darkness.

It is commonly written that France's Nicolas Joseph Cugnot was the inventor of the first steam-propelled vehicle in 1770, and that Germany's Nikolaus Otto and Gottlieb Daimler were responsible for the first internal combustion engine circa 1885. But more thorough research reveals that a "steam-chariot" was produced by missionary Father Ferdinand Verbiest, who built the monstrosity as a gift for Chinese Emporer Khangi-hi in 1672.[3] As for the internal combustion engine, Isaac de Rivaz of Switzerland had built a crude one in 1805, decades before Otto and Daimler produced their more successful version of it.[4]

But no matter where or when the automobile had its origins, it has been irrefutably established that America was the automotive capital of the world by the end of the nineteenth century. Perhaps less established is the fact that Henry Ford did not invent mass production, but rather improved upon it by borrowing a system of interchangeable parts and moving assembly lines. His success has earned him Horatio Alger status, but as author Robert Lacey pointed out in *Ford: The Men and the Machine,* Ford did not rate it: "Henry Ford has conventionally been depicted as forsaking his farm in September 1891 ... intent on devising a horseless carriage in Detroit, but this squares neither with his four years of dabbling once he got there, nor with his own testimony."[5]

It was true, however, that the sixteen-year-old Ford walked from the family farm in Dearborn to fill positions in Detroit that would ultimately lead to his obsession with the automobile. It was while he was working at the Edison Illuminating Company that he began the tinkering that would produce his first automobile, the Quadricycle, in 1896. He scrambled to complete the car, realizing that others had preceded him. Henry's wife watched with some concern as her husband worked frantically. As Lacey recorded: "Clara later remembered that, at the end, Henry worked almost twice around the clock to get it finished."[6]

Ford, in fact, stood well behind in the race to produce the first successful automobile. John W. Lambert of Ohio had already been driving his three-wheeled, gas-powered car back in 1891; Charles and Frank Duryea built their first car in 1893 and had won America's first automobile race in Chicago in 1895; Elwood Haynes drove his vehicle in 1894, and Charles B. King of Detroit was seen driving his in 1896, six months before Henry's car was ready. As legend has it, an eager Henry rode alongside King on his bicycle. By the time Henry Ford wheeled his little Quadricycle onto the streets of Detroit in June of 1896, much of his thunder had already been stolen.

But Ford meant to be a contender. In 1899, the same year John Brisben founded the Locomobile Company of America, he built an improved version of the Quadricycle. Henry took potential investor William Murphy out for a spin. Murphy was impressed enough to help Ford establish the Detroit Automobile Company.

The enterprise was to become Ford's first failure in the industry. Frequently wandering off the job and showing little commitment to the company, Henry soon left to devote himself to his new obsession — race cars. Ford built his famous 2-cylinder, 26-horsepower 999 model and, with Barney Oldfield driving, won against Alexander Winton in October of 1902. This early example of "win on Sunday, sell on Monday" seduced a new group of potential investors and a few months later the Henry Ford Company was formed. When the business started to deteriorate, experienced engineer Henry Leland was brought in to revive it. Unfortunately, Ford's concepts differed from Leland's, and despite the fact the company bore his name, Ford was unceremoniously shown the door. Leland promptly took the third Quadricycle shell Ford left behind and dropped his own one-cylinder engine into it. He named the car and the new company Cadillac.[7]

Inevitably the determined Ford found a new partner, businessman Alexander Malcolmson. Ford and Malcolmson were joined by the astute James Couzens and engineering genius C. Harold Wills. It was at Ford and Malcolmson Ltd. that the Ford team developed a revolutionary vertical cylinder engine and built the first version of the Model A around it. Up until then all cylinders had been placed horizontally in engine blocks.

Realizing the importance of a recognized "name" in the industry — Henry by now had a reputation for racing — the team decided to drop the Malcolmson name and thus the Ford Motor Company was incorporated on June 16, 1903. The first plant was located on Piquette Avenue in Detroit and employed some three hundred men. While a portion of these employees were laborers, many of them were skilled craftsmen in an era where craftsmanship was paramount.

Until the advent of mass production all vehicles were craft-produced, i.e., hand-made — an extremely costly and labor-intensive way to build. The cost narrowed the potential market considerably. The automobile was widely regarded as a rich man's toy, which — as it cost more than an average annual salary — it was. Pioneer inventors like John W. Lambert were disgusted with the headaches and expenses involved, feeling there was no market for the automobile. Only the persistent, daring, and financially stable could establish a position in the increasingly volatile industry. Because of the enormous costs involved, the question was not how to produce a better automobile, but how to produce it the most cost-efficiently.

As early as 1903 there were approximately sixty companies involved in the automotive industry, all of them wrestling with the eternal craft-production dilemma of inefficiency and inaccuracy. Following a blueprint did not guarantee that two vehicles could be made exactly alike. There was a lack of standardized gauging, combined with the fact that tooling machines weren't capable of cutting hardened steel. Tempering the steel usually warped it, causing further misfits. The considerable filing and adjusting necessary to ensure a fit became known as "dimensional creep," which varied from car to car. In addition, workers moved from car to car, wasting much time and energy.

Ford and his team believed there was a more efficient way to work than having men lug tools from car to car, forcing together ill-fitting parts. They envisioned a system whereby parts were precisely the same size so that one could be used as easily as another on the same vehicle. This concept of interchangeable parts was not new — in fact it dated as far back as 1798 when Eli Whitney assembled ten thousand muskets to fill a U.S. government order. As far as automobile production went, Ford's old nemesis Henry Leland had been the first to use the system as early as 1902 in his Cadillac factory.

As for speeding up the assembly process, the use of a conveyor belt in factories was not new either. Oliver Evans, America's first steam-carriage builder, had used one in his grain mills back in 1783. Belts were also widely used in meat-packing plants and within the textile industry. Ford, with his keen eye on the ultimate production system, enlisted the aid of efficiency analyst Frederick Winslow Taylor who began conducting time and motion studies at the Ford factory.

By 1913, Ford's Highland Park plant was reaching optimal production by utilizing the interchangeable parts system while insulated magnetos ran down the plant's first assembly line. A network of such lines soon spread throughout the factory as the unquenchable demand for the new Model T literally catapulted the company onto the world stage.

The main impetus of mass production had been economy. Proof of its efficiency lay in the numbers. Upon its unveiling on October 1, 1908, before the advent of mass production, the car sold for $825. After Ford implemented his new system, the price had dropped to an economical $345. Offering the world's first "economy" car set a precedent for the price-slashing that would prove to be an integral part of Henry Ford's life-long business strategy.

But it wasn't just economy that put Ford at the top of the automotive world. It was an automobile that combined simplicity with innovation. The Model T had a revolutionary vanadium steel engine, transverse springs, a planetary transmission, and an insulated magneto. It may have had a modest four-cylinder engine, but it took off like a rocket. In 1909–1910 sales totaled an already impressive 18,664, but by the beginning of the 1920s they had soared to an astounding 933,720.[8]

Unfortunately for Ford, by the mid-twenties it was obvious to the consumer that there were other choices which surpassed the Model T in performance, style, and comfort. What had begun as a national love affair ended in derisive contempt as the "Tin Lizzie" became the target of ridicule. Among the jokes and riddles common to the time was this one:

> A salesman to a Ford owner: "Can I sell you a speedometer?" Customer: "I don't use one. When my Ford is running at five miles an hour, the fender rattles; twelve miles an hour, my teeth rattle; and fifteen miles an hour, the transmission drops out."[9]

It is doubtful that these jibes reached Henry's ears, for by then he was quite out of tune with and isolated from the multitudes he had so thoroughly mined. After the stellar success of the Model T he insisted the company, if not the entire industry, had reached a zenith. In 1918 he turned the presidency, but not the control of Ford, over to his son Edsel. But while the senior Ford kept an eagle eye on the company and its employees, those within it were warily eyeing the competition.

A man often lost in Ford's looming shadow was the real pioneer of automotive mass production, Ransom E. Olds. After encountering difficulty acquiring financing and establishing a location, Olds managed to build a few different prototypes at the Olds Motor Vehicle Company in 1897. Unfortunately that establishment burned to the ground, leaving him with only one small vehicle — the curved-dash Olds. He took this model and opened the Olds Motor Works in 1899, where he began his crude method of mass production. His assembly line basically consisted of a wooden platform on a set of rollers, which carried the vehicle along and allowed parts to be added to it from strategically placed bins.

The little two-passenger curved dash had a one-cylinder, seven-horsepower engine provided by Henry Leland, and a two-speed transmission supplied by the Dodge brothers. It retailed for $650 and was so popular it inspired Gus Edwards and Vincent Bryan to compose the song "In My Merry Oldsmobile" in 1905. But affairs within the company were far from merry as Ransom Olds clashed repeatedly with his partners when he learned they were interested in aiming at a luxury market. Firmly believing that the key to volume selling lay in the economy car, he departed the Olds Motor Works in 1904 and went on to form the less successful Reo Company which became defunct just before World War II. Olds proved to be correct in his early assessment of the market when the company that bore his name went into irretrievable debt in 1908.

Before Olds formed the Reo Company, Scottish immigrant David Dunbar Buick had organized his Buick Motor Company in 1902. Buick began his working life as a plumber whose claim to fame was bonding porcelain to iron, but like many of his contemporaries, Buick was soon caught up in the automotive craze. The car he created boasted an innovative valve-in-head engine, but although Buick was a talented engineer, he was less skilled as a businessman. In 1904 he lost the company and it eventually fell under the control of William Crapo Durant of the Durant-Dort Carriage Company.

Durant drove the Buick and was entranced with its speed and power. He quickly decided to take the company on, selling the cars alongside his carriages. By 1908 Buick's production of 8,820 vehicles was closing in on Ford's 10,202.[10] Although the Buick automobile went on to become one of the mainstays of the world's largest automobile conglomerate, its creator died poor and in obscurity in 1929 at the age of seventy-four.

In the early 1900s automobile manufacturers were springing up in substantial numbers, ensuring fierce competition for a market jealously guarded by some. American patent lawyer George B. Selden declared himself to be the inventor of the internal combustion automobile and insisted that other manufacturers were infringing on the patent he had taken out back in 1877. Setting out to monopolize what was proving to be a lucrative industry, Selden and his cohorts established the Association of Licensed Automobile Manufacturers (ALAM), and "persuaded" manufacturers to join it. Henry Ford not only refused to be coerced, but also called into question the validity of Selden's patent. The lengthy legal battle that ensued swayed first against Ford, but was appealed and ultimately judged in his favor.

Henry Ford had spent almost eight years and millions of dollars fighting the patent, but he fought alone. Even Billy Durant had paid over a million dollars in royalties to the ALAM before it was disbanded in 1911. By that time 199,319 cars and 10,681 trucks had been built in America.[11] Ford, whose company had made over half of them, became something of a folk hero in the industry after breaking Selden's patent. Offering his workers the unprecedented wage of five dollars a day in 1914 didn't hurt his image either. It soon became apparent, however, that Ford's benevolent image was just that — an image. The fantasy created by the five-dollar day was a world apart from the machiavellian reality. Over-worked employees quickly grew to resent the intrusion into their lives as Ford's "Sociological Department" inspectors trooped through their homes to search for signs of physical or moral decay. Ford believed a clean and morally upright employee was a productive employee. But many cynical workers believed that Ford's eye never left the "bottom line," and although he had always professed himself to be against "big business," Robert Lacey noted: "...when it came to the pursuit of his own interests, he demonstrated an opportunism to rival that of any robber baron."[12] Henry Ford, in fact, epitomized big business.

The years between 1913 and 1925 were the genesis years of the American automotive industry, and more specifically of the "Big Three" companies. Ford had firm control of the economy and mid-price market, with Buick and Oldsmobile dividing the remains, while Cadillac shared the luxury car market with the likes of Packard and Auburn. With Ford at the pinnacle it was inevitable that a challenger would soon appear on the scene.

Running one of America's largest carriage firms was not quite enough for William "Billy" Durant. It didn't take him long following the success of the Buick Company to determine that he wanted to become the world's largest automobile manufacturer and permanently diminish the Ford Motor Company.

A master salesman, Durant rubbed his hands together and put his skills to work. In the span of three years he acquired the Olds, Oakland, and Cadillac automobile companies. For good measure he added a few dozen automotive-related businesses, two of which were AC Spark Plug and Delco. The new conglomerate was christened the General Motors Company of New Jersey upon its incorporation on September 16, 1908.

It has often been written that GM began on a shoestring of two thousand dollars capital, but obviously the real number required to begin such a major enterprise was closer to two million. Working behind the scenes to gather cash in the hopes of a merger was automaker Benjamin Briscoe who had solicited the backing of J.P. Morgan's financial group. Morgan, however, pulled out of the deal when it became clear that Ransom Olds and Henry Ford were not interested in becoming part of the package. The deal might have died right then except that two wealthy Morgan partners were intrigued and agreed to invest independently in the new company. Within six days of incorporation, Durant had gathered together $1.5 million in stock for the General Motors. Briscoe had been shut out of the deal while Durant continued his acquisition spree. At one point he even tried to buy the Ford Motor Company but his bankers rejected Ford's firm price of eight million dollars.

Heavily engaged in an orgy of spending, Durant was too engrossed to see the wall that hit him. In less than two years, GM's finances were so hopelessly overextended that he was forced to surrender it to a group of eastern bankers lead by James J. Storrow. Durant stayed on as a financially powerless vice-president, enraged by the turn of events. But once he regained his equilibrium he continued to build his automotive pyramid behind the scenes. In 1915 he took over the floundering company named for race car driver Louis Chevrolet and by 1916, with a little help from financier Pierre du Pont, he was back at the wheel of GM. "It just so happens that I own General Motors,"[13] he haughtily informed the group of astonished bankers at their final board meeting. It soon became obvious, however, that he couldn't hold on to it. Before falling victim once more to his familiar cycle of destructive spending, he acquired the Fisher Body Company and set up the General Motors Acceptance Corporation (GMAC) which provided vehicle financing. But juggling over seventy factories combined with chronic over-spending exacted a toll. Durant left General Motors for the last time in 1920, and would have ended his days in poverty if not for the lifelong financial support surreptitiously arranged by Alfred P. Sloan. Pierre du Pont reluctantly stepped in as a temporary president until Sloan took over from him in 1923.

Alfred Sloan has been heralded as an industrial wizard, a corporate genius, and the ultimate "beancounter." In his personal dealings, he struck many as being cold and almost inhuman in his demeanor — the quintessential "company man." Summarizing Sloan's character in *Chrome Colossus*, the in-depth chronicle of General Motors, author Ed Cray recorded what seemed to be the general consensus: "The prissy boy became a prissy adult...."[14]

An academic through and through, Sloan was a stickler for detail and addicted to memoranda. Almost from the moment he came to GM as part of the Hyatt Roller Bearing parcel, Sloan began analyzing the many problems within GM's management. Correctly gauging the chaotic mess Durant had created, Sloan set about devising an organizational plan which he presented to his then boss. Durant's laconic response to his plan sent Sloan into a dither: "My anxiety about the management of the corporation and the direction it was taking became such that in the early summer of 1920 I asked for a thirty-day vacation to get away and decide what I should do."[15] Presumably Sloan was considering not only his own future, but the future of General Motors as well. His decision to stay gave him the opportunity to turn the hodgepodge of assorted concerns into a model of efficiency when he took over as president in 1923. Although Sloan's "people skills" may not have matched his business acumen, he did have friends in the industry, and Walter P. Chrysler was one of them.

Beginning his career as a master mechanic at the Chicago Great Western Railway in 1892, Walter Chrysler eventually moved to a managerial post at the American Locomobile Company in Pittsburgh in 1910. Chrysler, who was besotted with the automobile, ran up his first automotive-related debt when he purchased a $5,000 Locomobile which he proceeded to take apart and rebuild. In 1912 he joined General Motors" Buick division and his sound business sense soon earned him a reputation within the company. Billy Durant needed someone like Chrysler to head Buick, and with true Durant disregard for cost, he offered Walter $500,000 a year to run it. Chrysler was flabbergasted at Durant's offer even while he deplored the spending that, if uncurbed, would lead to ruination for General Motors. By 1920 he could take no more of Durant's profligate ways and he resigned from his position of manufacturing vice-president. The experience left such a bad taste that Chrysler was ready to retire completely from the industry, but his relative youth and love of the business led him to accept an invitation to assist the struggling Willys-Overland Company. It seemed Chrysler's parsimonious ways did not extend to his own salary, and just as he had readily accepted Durant's $500,000, neither did he turn his back on Willys-Overland's offer of $2 million.

By now in high demand within the industry, he was also enlisted to put the Maxwell-Chalmers company back on its feet. It was then that Chrysler realized what he really wanted was a company of his own. So it was that the Maxwell-Chrysler Company became the Chrysler Corporation on June 6, 1925. In 1928, Chrysler's clever strategies earned his company Big Three status when he introduced the Plymouth and DeSoto, and bought out the Dodge Brothers.

Even with the Big Three along with scores of smaller independents, the automobile industry was barely keeping pace with America's post-industrial boom, much of which was concentrated in the Midwest. Although popular belief holds that Detroit is the home of the automobile, it was in fact Indiana that held that distinction up until around 1904. By that time, inventors and manufacturers had migrated to Detroit, which went from being the tenth largest manufacturing center in 1899 to the third largest by the mid-twenties.[16]

The industrial boom naturally attracted immigrants who poured into the country from Europe, Great Britain, and Canada: 2 million Germans, 1.5 million Irish, 1.3 million British, 1 million Canadians, and eight hundred fifty thousand Scandinavians arrived in America between 1861 and 1890.[17] Most of them gravitated towards cities where work could be found. By 1910 approximately 30 percent of America's population lived in a city or suburb.[18]

One of the most significant manifestations of the industrial age came from the transportation sector. The building of the railroad system had fostered a new desire for personal travel. People were anxious to put the dirt and discomfort associated with horse and carriage conveyance behind them, a fact not lost on the new auto barons.

Their plans, however, were interrupted when in August of 1914 news came of a war in Europe. President Wilson was forced to abandon his "peace without victory" policy, having no choice but to break off diplomatic relations with Germany in February of 1917. Realizing that Germany would not hesitate to fire on neutral ships, Wilson mobilized the armed forces. He also called upon America's automobile manufacturers despite the fact that he had earlier "deplored the motorcar as likely to stimulate socialism in the United States by inciting the poor to envy the rich."[19]

Henry Ford, widely known as a confirmed pacifist, nonetheless converted his Highland Park plant into a military factory, creating everything from aircraft engines to gas masks. The Nash Motor Company was at the time the world's largest truck manufacturer and supplied the army with 11,494 four-wheel-drive utility vehicles.[20]

World War I proved to be the single largest spur to the auto industry to date. Neither did the boom end when armistice was declared on November 11, 1918. Vast numbers of former servicemen who had been impressed by the automobile during the war ordered them for their personal use, creating waiting lists numbering in the thousands. The wave peaked in 1919, and a year later a foretaste of the great stock market crash nearly annihilated the industry. Commenting on this crisis, Alfred Sloan wrote: "The automobile market had nearly vanished and with it our income. Most of our plants and those of the industry were shut down...."[21] Henry Ford not only laid off workers and closed plants, but also auctioned off office equipment in order to cut costs.

By the mid-twenties the industry recovered itself and rose to became the largest in the United States. By 1929 an estimated 3.7 million people were employed either directly or indirectly in it.[22]

While automobile production rose, so too did the need for highways, bridges, gas stations, repair garages, tourist resorts, and hospitality enterprises. Similarly spurred were the more direct satellites of the auto industry — steel, glass, rubber, iron, and lumber interests flourished. And of course, not least important were the oil and fuel industries.

There was no doubt that the industrial revolution drastically altered the face of America, and as both land and people reflected these changes, so did the products they produced. Automobiles were particularly illustrative of this evolution, the most notable change of the twenties being the introduction of the closed-body car by the Fisher Body Company.

The "roaring twenties" was the decade of the automobile as a pleasure-craft — "joy-riding" was all the rage. Cars now featured powerful engines, convenient electric starters (an invention scorned by Henry Ford as being "unmanly"), independent suspension, and cozy in-car heaters. Consumer vanity was tended to as well. Annual styling changes, also known as "planned obsolescence" and pioneered by the Cadillac division of GM, came into vogue. This concept too was firmly rejected by the

Spartan Ford who felt the changes were wasteful, a stance that would prove to be monumentally disastrous.

Defending those annual changes in his book *My Years with General Motors*, Alfred Sloan rejected the notion that models were changed solely for the sake of style, referring to them instead as a process of "constant improvements." Commenting on his rival's apparent stagnation, Sloan loftily summarized Ford's fall in the industry with a simple statement: "The fact is that he (Ford) left behind a car that no longer offered the best buy, even as raw, basic transportation."[23] Citing the fact that used cars now fed the ever-hungry economy market, Sloan added: "Mr. Ford failed to realize that it was not necessary for new cars to meet the need for basic transportation."[24]

The last of the Model Ts came off the line in May of 1927, by which time fifteen million had been sold worldwide. Ford was forced to shut down for almost a year to gear up for its new model. While the company was closed, the Chevrolet and Chrysler's new Plymouth and DeSoto filled the void. In 1927, Chevrolet had sold 1,001,820 cars over Ford's paltry 367,213, while the Plymouth proved to be instantly popular.[25] Mr. Chrysler could not resist showing Henry Ford his new creation, only to be warned: "Walter, you'll go broke trying to break into the low-price market."[26]

But it was Ford who was heading for bankruptcy, saved only by the release of the second version of the Model A. But GM struck back when William Knudsen unleashed the new Chevrolet "Six" onto the market, once again eclipsing Ford.

By 1930 all were suffering. Industry production fell sharply from 5,337,087 to 3,510,178 units as the effects of the stock market crash sank in.[27] By all accounts, 1932 was the worst year of the Depression. There were signs of recovery by 1935, but two years later the bottom again dropped out of the market.

Widespread lay-offs and a massive decline in production were the hallmarks of the decade, but there were other problems as well. Charges of antitrust and monopoly were filed and proved against the monolithic General Motors.

Survival, rather than monopoly, was the major concern at the Ford Motor Company. The thirties represented a further humiliating fall from grace as it became obvious to all but Henry Ford that the introduction of the Model A had come too late. Desperation drove management to increase wages to an unheard of seven dollars a day in 1931 in an attempt to hold workers. But the high wages could not be sustained as Ford dipped into the red by over $37 million that same year. The wage deflated first to six dollars, and finally settled at four. To further exacerbate the already dismal situation, ugly labor disputes and strikes broke out throughout the middle to late thirties, proving in some cases to be deadly.

The newly formed United Auto Workers union had evolved from the American Federation of Labor in 1936. It made its debut at the General Motors Corporation when on December 28, 1936, "...the most important strike in American labor history had begun."[28] Production at the Fisher Body plant came to a standstill as workers settled in for the duration. The National Guard was called in, but short of shooting the workers, their hands were tied. News of the strike reached President Roosevelt, who tried to shame Alfred Sloan into conceding to union demands. Sloan huffily refused. Matters deteriorated when the protest moved to GM's largest Chevrolet plant, halting the company's most vital production. Only when GM realized they were losing market share did they finally capitulate. They did not go gracefully. "Alfred Sloan complained, his outrage still clear more than a quarter of a century later," wrote Ed Cray.[29]

But if Sloan was outraged, Henry Ford was obdurate. He had no intention of giving in as easily as Chrysler had before him. In order to ward off future strike action, he armed the company with a squad of thugs led by Harry Bennett.

The first incident took place in 1932 when a group of Communists organized a Hunger March against Ford. As the marchers moved toward the River Rouge plant, panicked policemen fired on them. Four union organizers were killed and twenty more were wounded. But the episode only made the union more determined to organize Ford workers. In 1937, UAW leader Walter Reuther and three others were badly beaten by Ford's hired guns in what was later named the "Battle of the Overpass." Violence continued to plague the company until Henry Ford finally conceded in 1941, some say shamed into it by his wife Clara.

Chrysler, wisely diverting such labor difficulties, was instead beset by lackluster performance during the Depression. Sales were down by 40 percent from 1928 to 1929. Its rapid expansion within a relatively short time kept the company toiling under a heavy burden of debt. It was also saddled with bloated product lines. Poor sales for 1930 forced Chrysler to trim its lines. Plymouth, DeSoto, and Dodge, as well as the innovative "floating power" design, kept the company solvent through the ten-million-dollar loss it suffered in 1932. Yet compared to Ford's $70 million loss in the same year, affairs at Chrysler could even be considered stable.

By 1934 the industrial picture was brighter, if not for Ford, then for GM and Chrysler. GM now had the Cadillac V-16 and the Chevrolet Suburban, as well as an expanded Buick line. Synchromesh transmissions, the "no-draft" ventilation system, "knee-action" or independent front suspension, and hydraulic brakes all appeared within the decade, pioneered by General Motors engineers.

Chrysler's dubious contribution to the era was the radical aerodynamic Airflow design. Said Walter Chrysler of the new DeSoto Airflow: "I sincerely believe it will bring about a whole new trend in personal transportation."[30] But an advertising blitz which included cliff-hanging stunts and celebrity endorsements failed to endear the car to the skeptical public. Despite the fact that it was a brilliant feat in futuristic design, sales failed to materialize and the Airflow, born before its time, was scrapped. The failure hit Chrysler hard, forcing it to fall back on the reliable sales of the economical Plymouth. New president K. T. Keller immediately slashed costs, staff, and production, and within a year of his taking over, Chrysler was debt-free and ahead of Ford by 1936.

Despite Ford's new V-8, along with the introduction of the Lincoln and Mercury divisions, sales figures for 1936 translated to only 22 percent of the U.S. market. Chrysler topped them with 25 percent, while GM was far out in front with 43 percent.

Tough economic times were taking their toll on the consumer. In accordance, GM began some preliminary work on a small car near the end of the thirties, but it came to nothing. The task was instead taken up by the British-based Austin Motors firm. Opening under the name of American Austin, the company began production in Pennsylvania in 1930.

The diminutive Austin model had a wheelbase of only 75 inches and retailed for an equally humble $465. But despite the undisputed economy of the little car, Americans perceived it as cheap and therefore poorly made. Thus Austin was forced out of the American market in 1935.

The next mini-car came from refrigeration/air-conditioning magnate Powel Crosley, Jr., in 1939. The Crosley had an 80-inch wheelbase with an air-cooled, two-cylinder engine and was even cheaper than the Austin at only $325. Even though the company managed to survive into the 1950s, sales were modest to say the least. It seemed that while Americans wanted their cars to be economical, they didn't want them to look that way. They continued to turn to the "tried and true" offerings from the Big Three whose versions of the economy car accounted for 50 percent of all U.S. sales. The resulting drop in luxury car sales was merely a harbinger of what lay ahead. But if the Depression slowed the automobile industry, the onslaught of World War II temporarily halted it.

In 1942 passenger car production was suspended, with a total of 280,000 produced before the order took effect. Manufacturers once again produced military-related equipment. In 1944, the War Production Board authorized Detroit to build one million trucks for military and civilian use.

When the war ended in 1945, so eventually did gas rationing and other wartime restrictions. A seller's market dawned as people rushed to replace their pre-war automobiles. Americans felt a sense of cautious optimism, albeit tainted by troubles with Russia, labor unrest, and escalating inflation. Automobile manufacturers struggled to resume production but were hampered yet again by strikes in the steel, coal, and railway industries. Consumers, impatient with restrictions and rationing, wanted to luxuriate in comfort and power. Tentative plans for economical cars were tossed aside and automobile manufacturers embarked upon the "land-yacht" phase that would ultimately result in their near-demise. But while compression ratios rose and longer, lower, and wider cruisers floated along America's newly paved highways, a tiny bug made its way through immigration and onto an American car lot. The Germans called it the Volkswagen Beetle.

# 2

## America's Wide-Open Market

"What's Volkswagen's secret? What is there about this small, ugly, low-powered import that excites people all over the world and makes every owner talk like a salesman?"[1] *Popular Mechanics* editors posed these questions in the October 1956 edition of the magazine. But while they clearly doubted the appeal of the homely little VW Beetle, growing numbers of American consumers had no such qualms. "This is the first major love affair of my life," enthused a Florida businesswoman.[2] Floyd Clymer, automotive sage of the day, added his praise: "This German car has amazing performance and roadability ... I abused the Volkswagen in every way ... punishment seems to have little effect."[3]

According to the magazine's survey of hundreds of VW owners, 96.2 percent rated the car as excellent. None rated it as poor.[4] Sales, although at first weak, rapidly escalated, and by 1958 there was a waiting list for the German-made import.

But was Detroit paying attention? According to executives at the Ford Motor Company, they had their own people conducting surveys—which concluded that "Detroit had nothing to worry about."[5] Alfred Sloan apparently felt the VW didn't even rate a mention in his autobiographical book *My Years with General Motors*, devoting only a brief passage to "foreign cars." Years later, automotive analyst Maryann Keller was not quite as circumspect in her assessment of GM's attitude: "GM's arrogant we're-number-one posture, buttressed by a corporate culture that could not stand to hear the bad news about itself, set the company up for a fall as foreign competition began to make inroads ... GM hadn't understood the appeal of the dumpy little Volkswagen 'Bug'...," Keller wrote in *Rude Awakening: The Rise, Fall and Struggle for Recovery at General Motors*.[6]

Considering Detroit's record-breaking sales during the mid- to late fifties it's little wonder no feathers were ruffled by the VW. As far as the Big Three were concerned, the rather unimpressive impact of Britain's Austin and America's own Crosley cars in the thirties and forties confirmed the fact that Americans wanted big cars. For the few "eccentrics" who didn't there was always the Nash Metropolitan, introduced in 1954 as America's smallest car. Many were unaware that the car was American in design only. It was actually based on the Austin A-40, built by the very company Americans had rejected in the 1930s. Financially strapped Nash couldn't afford the retooling costs required to build the car themselves, but they did plan to build it in the United States if it proved to be successful. Its prospects for success were questionable given the dubious reception from both consumer and media alike. One review of the Metropolitan read: "Except for several faults, the car is highly satisfactory for its purpose."[7] That purpose was economy, but economy was the furthest thing from the auto executives' minds as the decade opened.

The outbreak of the Korean War in June of 1950 required that manufacturers turn for the third time in their history to war-related production. Shortages of raw materials severely limited passenger car production, automatically driving up demand. When the war ended in July of 1953, manufacturers were still scrambling to catch up on backed-up orders. Hasty efforts were made to revamp the utilitarian, heavy-duty appearance of pre-war and war-time vehicles, though the results were rather frumpy especially in contrast to the models that superseded them.

It wasn't until around 1953 that what became known as "the era of the designer" had officially arrived. Emphasis moved from bare-bones functional to aggressive and powerful. Cues were taken from the jetliner industry, and palettes moved from drab green and blue to colors with exotic names like Aquamarine, Tahitian Coral, Torch Red, and Persian Sand. Two-tone and even tri-colored paint schemes reached their apex during this decade.

Just as prominent was the new fascination with "technology" which found an epicenter in the automotive industry. By the end of the decade it was not unusual for a buyer to order "power everything." First available were power steering and brakes, followed by all manner of gadgetry meant to make driving easier and more pleasurable. Seats, windows, door locks, antennas, convertible and even hard-tops, operated with the touch of a switch. Radios, both stationary and removable, were popular options, and Chrysler's DeSoto even offered a portable "Hi-Fi" set in 1956. Sofa-like seats of real or imitation leather stretched across interiors that became increasingly "hi-tech." It was an era where a vehicle's style alone could easily make or break a model as consumers came to expect luxury, change, and variety. In fact, GM promoted this concept of the American "dream car" at their annual Motorama Show in 1953. The wrap-around windshield, quad headlights and plastic car bodies all made their debut in the fifties; and while the basic style and color of the automobile was changing, so were its dimensions.

In 1950 an average wheelbase measured around 200 inches, the height 62 inches, the width 75 inches, and the weight 3,200 pounds. By 1959, the wheelbase had stretched to approximately 220 inches, height shrunk to 54 inches, width expanded to 81 inches and weight increased to 4,100 pounds. In terms of cost, a 1950 Chevrolet retailed for about $1,400. Nine years later, a Chevrolet sold in the $2,800 range.

Some of the most significant alterations were concealed beneath the hood. Compression ratios had been a modest 6 or 7:1 at the start of the decade, but by 1955 they had crept toward 10:1. Four-barrel carburetors astride big-block V-8s producing horsepower in excess of 300 were not unusual vehicle features. By 1956, four-fifths

of American cars were powered by V-8 engines. The race to create the most powerful, stylish car in America was underway, but the automakers did not commence on
equal footing.

   Of the Big Three, Chrysler was on the bottom rung, not surprising considering
that K.T. Keller dismissed the new styling trends as "fads." The company was also hit
with a three-month strike at the beginning of the decade that put it well behind Ford
and GM. However, the over one billion dollars garnered from government war contracts helped soften the blow. As Richard Langworth and Jan Norbye wrote in *The
Complete History of the Chrysler Corporation*: "If there were problems, Chrysler simply threw money at them."[8] In fact it threw $100 million when designer Virgil Exner,
with the blessing of new leader Lester "Tex" Colbert, created the "Million Dollar
Look" in 1955 followed by the "Forward Look" in 1957. But innovative body-shells
could not disguise the fact that quality had been compromised for the sake of appearance. Even the introduction of the Torqueflite transmission, hydraulic shock
absorbers, the hemispherical combustion chamber, and four-wheel disc brakes could
not bolster the company's sagging production which stood at 1.27 million units in
1950 but dropped to 750,000 by 1959.[9] Chrysler faced 1960 with swollen inventories
of 383-cubic inch V-8s at a time when the consumer was searching for something a
little less thirsty. It would be up to new president Lynn Townsend to provide a plan
that would keep the company viable.

   The roller coaster ride that had begun at the Ford Motor Company in the twenties finally evened out somewhat in the fifties. Henry Ford II and his "whiz-kids" led
by Ernest Breech and Robert McNamara scored with the 1949 V-8 Ford and its robust
sales helped carry the company through the decade. It maintained second place
behind GM and actually outsold rival Chevrolet by a small margin in 1951. The Ford
team struck a major chord with the introduction of the Crestline Skyliner and Cus-
tomline Tudor models, but the Mercury and Lincoln divisions floundered. Nineteen
fifty-five, considered one of the peak years of American automobile production, was
also a banner year for Ford when it unveiled the immediately popular Thunderbird.
In the first year, 16,155 Thunderbirds were sold; together with the introduction of
the classics Fairlane and Victoria, they kept Ford ahead of Chrysler.[10] The Thunderbird, competing directly with the Chevrolet Corvette, had no problem outselling it;
the Corvette was a more exclusive plastic-body design and only limited numbers
were produced during its first years.

   Ford's other highlights for the fifties included the retractable hardtop, the "jet-
age" Mercury Monterey with lever controls mounted beside the steering wheel, the
"bubble-top" Mercury, and the Y-block V-8. The company's successes allowed it to
invest heavily in what industry buzz hinted would be the "car of the decade." Unfortunately, the Edsel turned out to be the "flop of the century'—a fact that was evident soon after its release in 1957. Long in planning but short in production, the
Edsel revealed itself to be a universal symbol of failure, not least because of its ugly
design features. But the startling appearance of the car was not at first perceived as
negative, according to Robert Lacey. "When the car was finally unveiled, auto writers joined in the chorus of praise, and it was only later that people started making
unkind jokes….," he wrote in *Ford: The Men and the Machines.*[11] As to the car's

chances on the market, Lacey added: "But the speed with which the Edsel went from concept in the spring of 1955 to sales in the summer of 1957 created problems of quality from which the vehicle never recovered."[12] The Edsel was optimistically marketed under four nameplates: the Citation, Pacer, Corsair, and Ranger. None were successful and by 1959, despite some hasty re-designing, the car was dropped from the line-up. Ford not only lost approximately $250 million in the Edsel fiasco, but much of its hard-won reputation for quality as well. Its efforts to overtake GM seemed more futile than ever going into the sixties.

The General Motors of the fifties was a corporation engaged in a fierce battle to retain supremacy in the industry. Management changes included the arrival of Harlow Curtice as CEO in 1953, and one year later renowned designer Harley J. Earl handed his division over to William Mitchell after creating some of automobile history's most memorable designs.

GM's best-selling Chevrolet continued to provide the company's bread and butter. They began the decade with the introduction of the stylish new "pillarless hardtop" featured on the DeLuxe Styleline Bel Air. They sold 76,662 in 1950, retailing at $1,741.[13] But Chevy's *pièce de résistance* came in 1953 with the unveiling of the Corvette sports car. Sales were at first disappointing but they picked up when new bodywork and a more substantial V-8 boosted both horsepower and image.

Olds with its Rocket V-8 passed struggling Buick by the end of the decade. Buick sales fell so drastically in 1957 that the Special, Limited, Roadmaster, and Century were replaced with the Electra, Invicta, and LeSabre in a desperate attempt to revamp the line.

Pontiac sales also slumped throughout the fifties despite the introduction of four new models of the Chieftain Catalina as well as a new Star Chief and a Safari station wagon. In 1959, GM leader Semon "Bunkie" Knudsen brought in Elliot "Pete" Estes and John Z. DeLorean who came up with a fresh look for Pontiac which included a wide-track stance and a split grille. The intended market age dropped by about 20 years as a result of the fresh designs. To solidify this aggressive move to a younger market, the first sightings of the Pontiac Firebird concept car provided a taste of where the division was headed.

Cadillac continued to hold down the luxury market and was considered the epitome of the American car as well as a hallmark of success. It entered the decade with the hint of fins and left it looking like a shark on wheels. The bullet-style bumpers added in 1951 earned the tag "Dagmars" after a curvaceous television character. Cadillac production was 103,857 in 1950 and rose to 142,272 by the end of the decade.[14] But Cadillac had made Chrysler's mistake of sizing themselves out of the market and they too were left with a glut of out-dated "batmobiles" on hand for the more size-conscious sixties.

Size was an issue in other areas as well. In an echo of days past, GM managers appeared before the Supreme Court, which ruled that du Pont's 23 percent interest in the company violated the Clayton Antitrust Act. In addition, hearings before the Senate Subcommittee on Antitrust and Monopoly were also held to determine the relationship between inflation and the automotive industry, with GM as a focal point.

Antitrust was a valid issue in an era where the Big Three were the titans surrounded by minnows trying to eke out a portion of the market for themselves. Companies like Packard, Studebaker, Hudson, Nash, Kaiser, and Willys offered competitive quality cars, but the only way they could gain a purchase on the market was to tie-in together.

In 1954 George Mason added Hudson to Nash to form the American Motors Corporation, thereby creating the new Big Four. Unfortunately, Mason died shortly after the birth of AMC, which was taken over by visionary George Romney. In 1957 Romney was forced to restructure the company, and decided to scrap the Nash and Hudson names. From then on, AMC's main model was the Rambler which came in four different configurations—the Rebel, American, Ambassador, and the compact Metropolitan.

Another noteworthy merger of 1954 was the joining of Packard and Studebaker. The Packard Motor Car Company had an illustrious history of creating fine quality automobiles aimed at the upscale market. Famous for its style and grace, the car was voted "the most beautiful car of the year" in 1951 by the Society of Motion Picture Art Directors.[15] But it failed to sustain sales against the more popular Cadillac which had the might of GM behind it. In 1950, Packard produced only 42,627 cars compared with Cadillac's 103,857.[16] Packard sales had slipped to an all-time low of a little over 2,000 in 1958, its last year of production. Anyone left owning a Packard Patrician, Clipper, Caribbean or Constellation had a future rare collector car in their driveway.

Studebaker, another marque that dated back to before the turn of the century, stayed in the American market only slightly longer than Packard, departing to Canada in 1963. Regardless of its ultimate demise, the Studebaker name left an indelible mark with a wide range of models which included the daring "bullet-nose" Champion Regal DeLuxe with optional propeller, the stylish President, the Commander, the "Loewy coupes," the Hawk, the Lark and finally the sporty Avanti.

Another independent that couldn't compete in the brutal market was Kaiser-Frazer. Founded in the late forties, the company enjoyed a modest success which peaked in the mid-fifties. From this company came the small economy car the Henry J., named for company founder Henry J. Kaiser. It appeared in 1951 and disappeared in 1954. Talented designer Howard "Dutch" Darrin was the creative force behind the company, designing some unusual and interesting cars that failed to appeal to American tastes. Kaiser-Frazer ceased production in the U.S. in 1955 and moved its operations to South America.

The Willys Company had been making automobiles since 1903, but its attempts to compete were also unsuccessful. But while the car division was taken over and relocated by Kaiser-Frazer, the company continued to produce the Jeepster—a larger and more comfortable version of the vehicle that had become a symbol of the American military.

Incredibly the smallest of the small independents was still producing in the early fifties. In 1947 the Crosley was available in a four-cylinder sedan, convertible, and station wagon with a sports model, the Hotshot, added in 1949. Crosley made an admirable effort with its odd-looking little cars but it was forced to shut down in 1952.

A few fly-by-night minicars including the King Midget and the Imp came and went during the fifties but none stayed the course. Imports, however, were steadily gaining in recognition, claiming around 8 percent of the American market by 1958.

"We fell out of love with American cars in the late fifties," remarked veteran automotive insider David E. Davis, Jr., in a commentary for the television program *World of Collector Cars.*[17]

But this observation, while universal in 2001, escaped those most vitally concerned at the time. Post-war patriotism, suburban sprawl, and the booming population hardly seemed indicative of a nation considering being "unfaithful" to American automotive manufacturers. The opening of Disneyland and McDonalds drive-in restaurants in 1955 seemed to confirm America's love affair with the American way. Families sat down to dinner together and later gathered around to watch *I Love Lucy* and *Perry Mason* on television. Dad washed the family car on Saturday, Mom cleaned the house, and the kids played with hula-hoops and rode their bikes down tree-lined streets.

Packing the family in the car to go on summer vacation became the thing to do. The Federal-Aid ("Interstate Highway") Highway Act of 1956 would soon open up 41,000 miles of virgin pavement before the newly affluent, newly mobile population. "See the USA in Your Chevrolet" ran the television jingle, and families did just that. Lengthy car trips were much more pleasant in "loaded" air-conditioned cars, and accommodations more economical with motels plentiful along the route. Camping was also in vogue, spawning an entire industry of recreational vehicles ranging from the humble truck-camper to the sophisticated Airstream trailer. Traveling was within the reach of most Americans in an age where a car cost around $2,800, a home $30,000, a loaf of bread 19 cents, and a Coke 7 cents. Neither was gasoline a concern at 30 cents a gallon.

In retrospect it seemed an idyllic life, especially when viewed through the romantic haze reserved for childhood memories. Words like down-size, information highway, and burn-out didn't even exist. A split-level home in the suburbs, preferably with a swimming pool, a large yard, and a two-car garage was one of the ultimate goals of the average American.

A counter-culture, however, was blossoming, fed by publications such as Jack Kerouac's *On the Road* which christened young rebels like James Dean as the "beat" generation. Critics of the book slammed Kerouac and the character he had created, the "hipster." Said reviewer Herbert Gold writing in a 1957 edition of the *Nation*: "The hipster is past caring. He is a criminal with no motivation in hunger, the delinquent with no zest, the gang follower with no love of the gang...."[18]

But if parents were mildly concerned about their kids becoming hipsters, they were much more unsettled at the thought of them behind the wheel. In order to instill a sense of healthy respect for the dangers of the automobile, high school students were forced to view "crash-and-burn" films like *The Terrible Truth, The Last Prom, What Made Sammy Speed,* and *Wheels of Tragedy.*[19]

But teenagers—being teenagers—still wanted to emulate James Dean racing his '49 Mercury. Even his death at the wheel of a Porsche in 1959 was, and still is, romanticized. This "need for speed" exhibited in young drivers was not surprising since the cars they learned to drive in were so obviously designed for just that.

As for those responsible for the designs, the average American automaker existed in happy oblivion to such concerns, and were quite willing to increase horsepower while perpetuating the idealistic view of the car and the American family. Automotive journalist Brock Yates, writing in *The Decline and Fall of the American Automobile Industry*, left little doubt as to his opinion of what he perceived as the American automaker's characteristic tunnel vision: "As the auto prince stands beside his lakeside home, he is not aware of his isolation from a rapidly moving world."[20]

The winds of change were indeed blowing even though the automakers may have failed to gauge them correctly, especially the trend that seemed to come out of nowhere and broadside the industry. Ironically, it sprang from the very hearth and home they were so anxious to idealize. Between 1950 and 1960 13 million new houses were built in America. The average income of a suburbanite was $6,500 per annum, 70 percent higher than the average salary of the rest of the nation.[21] But while there may have been money in the suburbs it didn't necessarily equate with happiness, and certainly not with freedom.

Beneath the "Plasticville USA" exteriors and ruffled drapes, a quiet revolution was building. Women, supposedly content raising the children and keeping house on an allowance, were finding the familial bonds somewhat restricting. While men drove off to work, women stayed at home and took care of an average of four "baby-boom" children. If they were lucky the family had two cars which allowed them to shop, run errands, and chauffeur the kids around when they weren't cooking, cleaning, and washing diapers. Her car was usually chosen by her husband and was generally a smaller version of his. In fact a large degree of the smaller Rambler's success was due to men purchasing something the "little woman" would find easy to drive and park. Apparently some women concurred about the size, if not the marque. It seemed that the Volkswagen held quite an appeal for female drivers. As an Ohio housewife gushed: "I could write pages about the VW. I'm scared to death to drive our full-size car, but I'll try anything in the 'bug.' It lets me feel I'm the boss when I'm behind the wheel and not as though I'm driving by remote control."[22] A California salesman obviously offered an opinion on behalf of his wife, saying the VW is: "The answer to the second-car problem. Small, easily parked, it is ideal for shopping."[23]

The traditional male in charge of the automobile industry failed to notice this potential segment of the market, never mind plumb its depths. Producing pink and salmon-colored versions of their cars was as far as they were prepared to go in that direction. Their focal point continued to be the production of the most ostentatious, powerful vehicle they could possibly create, and it was clear that being in tune with emerging social trends was not their forte. But there was one pressure they were forced to succumb to but only because it was mandated by the government. The issue was automobile speed and safety. Mounting fatality statistics brought an outraged public to their feet. They laid the blame squarely on the shoulders of the automaker.

In 1958 the Automotive Manufacturers' Association made the first move by disallowing the advertisement of a vehicle's speed and horsepower. Realizing the potential repercussions of non-compliance, the automakers went one up and pulled out of race car sponsorships when it was publicized that 36,981 people were killed in automobile accidents that year alone.[24]

Some manufacturers began to move towards padded interiors and dashes, seat belts, side mirrors, signal and reverse lights, recessed instrument panel knobs and "deep dish" steering wheels. Projectiles were hammered off bumpers and fins were flattened. These added expenses to building a car came at a time when the industry was already reeling from a sharp economic downturn in 1957. Car production dropped over 30 percent, and with nearly 5.5 million people unemployed, the consumer was looking to cut costs wherever possible.

The new word in the American lexicon was credit. The cash-strapped nation had its first real taste of plastic money when the Bank of America introduced the credit card that would later become VISA, and American Express offered its first card in order to compete with the popular Diners Club card already in existence. The "never-never" installment plan became a part of the American way of life.

In addition to becoming more economical and selective, consumer's tastes were more sophisticated in an age of nuclear power, satellites, and increased international travel. Americans had been exposed to European car designs and many liked what they saw. Even as far back as 1953 Studebaker wisely appealed to this burgeoning taste in their advertisement campaign. "The New American Car with the European Look!" ran one magazine ad. In what amounted to a back-handed compliment, the ad copy ran: "The dramatic 1953 Studebaker sparkles with the verve and flair of Europe's most distinguished cars ... but it's thoroughly American in comfort and handling ease."[25]

To sum up, the trends that would lead to the tremendous upheaval within the automotive industry in the seventies were taking root in the mid- to late fifties. Responding to the stinging criticisms that Big Three leaders were oblivious to all but Big Three profits, thereby missing the move toward smaller cars, Lee Iacocca wrote in his autobiography *Iacocca*: "In some industries, being ahead of your time is a great advantage. But not in Detroit. Just as the car industry can't afford to lag too far behind the customer, it also can't afford to be too far ahead of him. Coming out with a new product too early is just as bad as being too late."[26]

Denying the fact that the American industry had even missed the trend in the first place, Alfred Sloan wrote in *My Years with General Motors*: "In 1957 it still appeared far from certain that the demand for smaller cars would continue to grow, but the possibility had been recognized by General Motors for some time, and the designs for such cars had already been initiated. As early as 1952, Chevrolet had, with the approval of central management, set up a research and development group charged with the task of developing such a car, which would be ready if and when demand rose sufficiently to justify volume production."[27]

Sloan was referring to the Chevrolet Corvair, a model that was heralded as the car that would put Volkswagen in its place and keep the exploring Japanese at bay. Ford's contribution was the mournful-looking but still successful Ford Falcon, and Chrysler brought up the rear with the more vivacious Valiant. But once satisfied with the sales of the so-called "compacts" — all three of which weighed almost 1,000 pounds more than the VW and were approximately 21 inches longer — the Big Three turned their attention back to plans for the new big cars of the future. The economy market was now considered filled. No one noticed that the back door to that market had swung wide open, and through it came a little something from Japan.

# 3

# The Rise of Japan

In the heart of Tokyo stands 180 acres of wooded beauty, unspoiled by high-rises or automobile traffic. Devout pilgrims visit the spot regularly to pray to ancestral gods. This "inner garden forest" stands as a shrine to the Emperor Meiji and his Empress Shoken. That such an oasis exists in a city of more than eight million people, where land is valued at over $1,200 a square foot, is an amazing tribute to the era that created a world power.

Until 1868, Japan stagnated under oppressive shogunate rule whose feudal system divided the population into samurai, artisan, peasant, and merchant classes. Each was strictly regimented — samurai and peasants were forbidden to engage in trade, and merchants and artisans were equally restricted. But the inevitable unrest that had been brewing erupted after Japan's long period of isolation was broken by foreigners intent on opening her ports. Commodore Matthew Perry was the first of these to return to America in 1854 with a treaty that allowed U.S. ships to dock at two Japanese ports. Although privately incensed by the effrontery of the bold American, the shoguns were nonetheless intimidated by the strength of his fleet, which they darkly referred to as the "Black Ships" because of the clouds of coal smoke that emanated from them. On the other hand, they were intrigued by Perry's demonstration of a model locomotive running along a track, and by his explanation of the principle of the telegraph. This glimpse into modern progress led the shoguns to conclude that perhaps Japan was not as advanced as they thought it was. The blow to their collective ego, combined with a real fear of attack, convinced them it would be prudent to sign Perry's treaty. Their signatures immediately cleared a path for other countries waiting in the wings. First came Russia, followed closely by Britain and France. All departed with similar "mutually-agreed-upon" treaties. The intimidation inherent in the presentation of these documents left little choice but for the shoguns to sign away many of Japan's rights. In doing so, they lost their right to set their own tariffs, as well as the right to try and convict foreigners under Japanese law in Japanese courts. Thus the treaties became known in Japan as the "Unequal Treaties," triggering further sedition among an already disgruntled populace. The resulting revolution placed a new young Emperor on the throne and opened the era that was named for him — the Meiji Restoration period.

One of the Emperor's first actions was to move the capital city from Kyoto to Edo, which was later named Tokyo. The feudal system and rigid class structure were obliterated, a constitution was drawn up, and in 1889 the Japanese Diet, or parliament, was formed. Under the new rule, citizens were entitled to pursue any occupation they wished and a new banking system facilitated freedom in commerce and trade. Furthermore, an individual could hold a property title, whereas before only a family unit was permitted such a privilege. Personal travel restrictions were also lifted, but perhaps the most important new sanction was that "Knowledge shall be sought throughout the world so as to strengthen the foundations of imperial rule."[1]

The nation's new goal therefore was complete modernization. Only by advancing in this way could the Japanese achieve power and status, the two keys to opening the door to "equal treaties." This push for modernization, however, came at a tremendous human cost. As author John W. Dower wrote in *Embracing Defeat: Japan in the Wake of World War II,*

> Workers were housed in hovels on factory grounds and were little more than serfs. Often these laborers weren't permitted to leave for months. And to make sure no one tried to escape, guards were employed to patrol the grounds. It was common for workers, a majority of whom were women, to work fifteen- to sixteen-hour days. In 1897 a survey by the Cotton Spinners Association showed that 87 percent of the women working in that industry were sick or suffering from injuries.[2]

Former Tokyo University president Nanbara Shigeru summed up with one sentence the negative aspect of the Meiji Restoration in a speech delivered in Washington, D.C.: "Humanistic values had been subordinated to the goals of modernization."[3]

But Meiji leaders were not contemplating human values when they began their quest toward modernization by taking cues from the Western world. The opening of her ports for the first time since the Dutch and Chinese landed in the sixteenth century exposed foreign ways to curious Japanese eyes. Even fashion was not immune to Japanese scrutiny and soon many men sported western-style dress, particularly on formal occasions. The women, however, still adhered to traditional apparel. But while it may have outwardly appeared that the Japanese had altered their lifestyles to accommodate western influence, they held fast to their culture and retained their custom of reserved dignity. Still, there was no question that now that the country had opened up, it could never again close itself off from outside influence.

While the new rulers were engaged in establishing everything from a first-class educational system to the composing of a national anthem, much focus was placed on military development. Japan, growing fast but sorely lacking in natural resources, had long kept a possessive eye on territories in China. When in 1894 she moved to bring about that expansion, the first Sino-Japanese war broke out. From it Japan came away with its first colony, the island of Formosa, but it was not enough for the resource- and power-hungry nation. Ten years later, in a further effort to expand, Japan engaged in war with Russia, humiliating the proud and powerful nation. Despite the loss of 58,000 Japanese and Russia's formation of the "Triple Intervention" — an alliance with Germany and France — Japan's victory earned it control of Korea. The tiny nation of islands had been disastrously underestimated by Russia. As one Russian sailor later wrote: "We were outclassed by the Japanese in respect of speed and accuracy, in the quality of shells, and in the concentration of power."[4]

Russia wasn't the only nation caught off guard by the strength of tiny but mighty Japan — this conflict, combined with her efforts in World War I, earned the country world-power status.

The much-sought-after modernization and industrialization now came at a rapid rate. It soon became apparent that Japan's two main strengths lay in the shipbuilding and steel industries. Although denigrated by many as mere "copy-cats," the shrewd Japanese did not believe it necessary to re-invent the wheel, but rather sought always to improve upon it. Education was an essential part of this philosophy and they pursued it relentlessly. Representatives were sent to Europe and America to learn about modern industry. Because of this open and unabashed desire to learn, Westerners tended to believe that the Japanese were more backward than they actually were. Author and engineer Fukuzawa Yukichi illustrated this misconception in his book *Conditions in the West*, written in 1867 after he visited a manufacturing plant in America:

> I am sure that our hosts thought that they were showing us something entirely new, naturally looking for our surprise at each new devise of modern engineering. But on the contrary, there was really nothing new, at least to me. I knew the principle of telegraphy even if I had not seen the actual machine before; I had been studying nothing else but such scientific principles ever since I entered Ogata's School.[5]

The Japanese continued this process of acquiring knowledge from other nations until they themselves became purveyors of it, a practice that would later become a bone of contention between the American and Japanese automobile industries.

Because the nation was developing so quickly, there were ample opportunities in almost every sector. The government discouraged foreign investment, making it easier for groups like Mitsubishi and Mitsui to take financial and industrial control. These privileged few were known as the *zaibatsu*, which roughly translates into "financial clique." They were to hold much of the country's wealth and power until they were disbanded in 1945 by U.S. occupying forces. But the powerful corporations reincarnated themselves into what is known in Japan as the *keiretsu* — a group with interlocking directorates and common equity interests, a practice illegal in the United States.

With industry spurred on largely by the war efforts, Japan's exports more than paid for its many imports. But while the nation had ships, railroads, steel, textiles, and an effective communication system, it still lacked something Europe and America had in the late nineteenth century — automobiles.

While the Duryea brothers were making American history with their gas-powered prototypes, Japan was dependent on imported steam-powered vehicles from Europe and America. In fact Japan's main supplier of vehicles was the Locomobile Company of America. In 1901 the company set up a showroom in Tokyo, and although there was much curiosity surrounding the strange contraptions, there was little or no demand since most people relied on railroads, bicycles, and rickshaws. Aside from the fact that the country's roads were not much more than muddy trails, priorities centered around the military, agriculture, and heavy industry. But businessman Shintaro Yoshida and bicycle technician Komanosuke Uchiyama saw an opening and were determined to produce an all-Japanese automobile. In 1902 the team took an American engine and mounted it to a homemade chassis. The vehicle was one step closer to their goal of a made-in-Japan automobile, but was still not quite roadworthy.

Two years later Torao Yamaba had more success with his ten-passenger steam car which became the first all-Japanese vehicle on record.[6] Uchiyama and Yoshida nevertheless continued on with their plan to build a functional internal combustion automobile, and in 1907 they succeeded with the Takuri Type 3. The car was powered by a two-cylinder, 12-horsepower, water-cooled engine that was horizontally mounted beneath the seats. It strongly resembled most European models contemporary to the times, with a high, narrow body and short front end. Just over a dozen Takuris were made, but a deeply skeptical public considered that to be a dozen too many. After the unveiling of the car, Uchiyama and Yoshida formed the Tokyo Motor Car Works of which Yoshida assumed the presidency. But lack of public interest in a passenger car combined with military pressure led the company to begin producing trucks. Their competition took up the thread they had dropped, and in 1910 the Kunisue Automobile Works produced its first Kunisue automobile. A year later the company became the Tokyo Motor Vehicle Works, developing the comparatively luxurious "Tokyo car," powered by a four-cylinder, 1.3-liter, L-head engine with a magneto ignition.

Although automobile production progressed exceedingly slowly, with less than 50 units produced by 1911, it was nevertheless beginning to play an integral role in Japan's industrial development.

In 1912, Emperor Meiji died and was succeeded by his son who became Emperor Taisho. Emperors, though much idealized, were in reality mainly figureheads. The Diet continued to maintain a tenuous leadership against the military's growing balance of power — a power that was to eventually lead the nation to near-destruction. Ironically, it also served as a catalyst to the automobile industry with an increasing number of small enterprises gradually emerging. The company that would one day become Nissan was one of them.

Starting life in 1911 as the Kwaishinsha Motor Works of Tokyo headed by Masujiro Hashimoto, the company began manufacturing a ten-horsepower, two-cylinder car called the DAT. It was named for Hashimoto's three main financial backers, Kenjiro Den, Rokuro Aoyama, and Meitaro Takeuchi. While subsisting on the sales of imported British cars, Kwaishinsha managed to produce a small quantity of DATs between 1911 and 1917. The first model, a DAT 31, had a four-cylinder, 2.0-liter engine but was upgraded in 1916 to a five-passenger, 2.3-liter, 15-horsepower DAT 41. One year later, they produced the DAT 51, changing its name first to "Datson" (son of

DAT), then to Datsun, a name with more positive Japanese connotations. The Datsun was available in both sedan and roadster styles.

By this time the eyes of the powerful *zaibatsu* were on the industry and they were determined not to be upstaged by these "insignificants." In 1917 shipping giant Mitsubishi offered its Mitsubishi Model A. With 22 units manufactured in its first year, the car was considered by many to be Japan's first mass produced automobile.

But while passenger car production was still scant by 1917, World War I had induced a great need for trucks. No longer being able to import vehicles from Germany and France for political reasons, the military declared that truck production was to commence immediately at the Osaka Artillery factory. In order to reinforce the urgency of the need, the Military Vehicle Subsidy Law was passed in 1918 and was Japan's first automobile-related industry law.[7] In essence the law required among other things that any personal-use vehicles must be turned over to the military upon demand.

The years after World War I saw Japan resume its quest for modernization until yet another disaster struck. Containing approximately one-tenth of the world's active volcanoes in addition to record-breaking seismic activity, it is hardly surprising that the country is particularly vulnerable to earthquakes. In September of 1923 a massive one occurred, devastating the cities of Tokyo and Yokohama in the Kanto region. Over 100,000 were killed and many more injured. Homes, businesses, schools, and indeed entire infrastructures were obliterated. Emergency measures of an unprecedented nature were required, and in particular there was a pressing need for vehicles to help transport the casualties to outside facilities. The Japanese auto industry was too new and too undeveloped to fill that need, therefore a decision was made to import eight hundred Ford Model T trucks which could be converted to buses. These hybrid vehicles became known as the Entaro buses. Henry Ford shrewdly perceived his company's advantage and quickly moved to establish the Ford Motor Company of Japan in 1925. Ford set up a plant in the ravaged city of Yokohama.

Ford's arrival effectively wiped out the struggling Japanese auto industry, with names like the Ohta OS and the Ales M, models which had been introduced in 1921 and 1924 respectively, becoming extinct. The Hakuyosha Company which had produced the successful Otomo also collapsed under U.S. competition. But Ford was soon forced to make room for its own home-grown rival. Seeing a sizeable window of opportunity, General Motors arrived in 1927, setting up operations in Osaka. Japanese automobile manufacturers noted with discouragement that America now dominated their auto industry. But the government and military still favored the care and feeding of its own and they demonstrated this by stepping up the implementation of protectionist policies.

By 1926, Kwaishinsha Motor Works had become the DAT Motor Car Company when it merged with the Jitsuyo Automobile Company, and the Jitsuyo Lila became part of the new Datsun lineup. But if the new company believed they would be allowed to continue to build cars, they were mistaken. Military subsidies meant military rules, and the military demanded utility vehicles. Therefore the DAT Motor Car Company promptly ceased production of cars and turned its attention to building its one-and-one-half-ton DAT Model 61 truck.

Nineteen twenty-six also ushered in Japan's Showa era when Emperor Hirohito succeeded Emperor Taisho. It was around this time that Japan adopted the Asian continental policy which resulted in the ultimate rise of militarism in Japan. Prime Minister Tanaka Giichi's chief goal was conquering China by taking Manchuria and Mongolia. Tanaka fanatically believed this plan had been sanctioned by the Emperor Meiji himself. The fact that the country was facing severe economic and population-growth problems was seen as justification for military aggression. Therefore what began as a basically democratic multi-party system was eventually overturned by a corrupt, one-party militaristic government. The volatile conditions in the country were only exacerbated by the global recession experienced after the 1929 U.S. stock market crash, made worse still by a massive crop failure in 1931. While the military gathered force, the Japanese people were reduced to begging and eating plant roots. That same year Inukai Tsuyoshi was elected prime minister. Tsuyoshi took Japan off the gold standard and an immediate export boom followed, but his influence ended there when he was assassinated in 1932 for trying to restrict the army in Manchuria.

Mindful of the military's displeasure with using the larger foreign vehicles, the newly formed Ministry of Commerce and Industry decreed that "protective policies to assist in the wholesome development of the automobile industry"[8] were to be put into place. Thus the Committee for the Establishment of a Domestic Automobile Industry came about in 1931. In 1932, Ishikawajima Automobile Manufacturing Company, the Tokyo Gas & Electric Engineering Company, and the DAT Automobile Manufacturing Company banded together to create the Domestic Automobile Association, which later became the Tokyo Motor Co. Ltd. One of their first efforts was the production of the Isuzu truck prototype.

All manufacturers were encouraged to join forces to limit the number of small struggling companies, and to promote strength in the industry. To further strengthen it as the nation was on the verge of yet another military conflict, the Automobile Manufacturing Industries Act was passed in 1936.[9] One year later the second Sino-Japanese war broke out. Nineteen thirty-seven was also the year a new automobile manufacturer declared itself, led by the prosperous Toyoda clan.

With sixteen companies manufacturing automobiles in Japan, it was the American manufacturers' turn to feel the pressure. Japan's new protectionist policies drove up foreign exchange rates, rendering American products unaffordable. By 1939, Ford and GM had departed for America, but while in Japan, they had triumphed with combined sales of 208,967 units, dwarfing Japan's 12,127.[10]

The Nissan Motor Company was without a doubt the strongest of all the Japanese automobile manufacturers. Opened under the Nissan name in June of 1934 after Nihon Sangyo and Tobata Imono bought out Jidosha Seizo, the company had a variety of four-cylinder, 495-cc models with an average top speed of 35 miles per hour. It took one year for Nissan to reach production of 1,000 larger 722-cc Datsuns, forty-four of which were exported to India, Spain, and South America. Nissan was the first Japanese company to utilize assembly lines and mass production technology. In 1936 the company purchased the rights to America's Graham-Paige passenger car and based their new model 70 on it. It was Nissan's first real full-size car, carrying a six-cylinder, 80-horsepower engine. By 1939 Nissan had produced a total of 17,781 vehicles, 75 percent of which were trucks.[11] While the trucks wore the Nissan badge, the cars continued to be marketed under the Datsun name. In those early days Nissan had few worries over the recently opened Toyota Motor Company.

The Toyoda family business originated in the textile industry when Sakichi Toyoda started the Toyoda Loom Works in 1907. In 1918 the company became Toyoda Spinning and Weaving and in 1926 it had expanded into Toyoda Automatic Loom Works Ltd. During a trip to America in 1910, Sakichi had witnessed first-hand the success of the automobile and he immediately realized its enormous potential. Upon returning to Japan he urged his son Kiichiro to consider investigating the industry. Kiichiro, who was studying engineering at Tokyo University at the time, agreed to his father's wishes. By the time he graduated, Ford and GM were dominating Japan's auto industry, and although he complained that trying to compete with the two was "nonsense," he nonetheless established an automobile department in a corner of Toyoda Automatic Loom Works in 1933.

Kiichiro Toyoda, founder of the Toyota Motor Company. A smiling pose was rare in those days of strife during the late 1930s and early 1940s (courtesy Toyota Motor Sales Archives).

Kiichiro began by dismantling and rebuilding a Smith Motors 60 cc motorcycle engine, which he mounted to a bicycle frame. He then assembled his team, a collection of fellow engineers which included his cousin Eiji. The group's first task was the study of a German DKW front-wheel-drive model which they copied into a 2-cycle, 2-cylinder, charcoal-driven prototype. But the vehicle was nowhere close to the technically-advanced American models Kiichiro was trying to emulate, and thus the next project became the tear-down of a 1933 Chevrolet. In September of 1934 the group had their first successful engine. By May of 1935, they had built a chassis and the car became known as the Model A1. It was based on a Chevrolet engine, a Ford driveline and steering system, and Chrysler's Airflow body.

Unfortunately, Sakichi did not live to see his son's success, dying in 1930. An emotional Kiichiro's first action after the car was ready was to drive it to the cemetery where his father was buried.

After successfully producing the model A1, the team built the G1 truck which was unveiled in August of 1935. In April of 1936 improvements to the A1 led to the production of the model AA. Feeling as though they now had an established line of functional vehicles, Kiichiro and his colleagues opened the Toyota Motor Company on August 28, 1937. Kiichiro's brother-in-law Risaburo Toyoda was appointed president. Risaburo was in fact Sakichi's son-in-law, but the older man had adopted him

Eiji Toyoda, Kiichiro's cousin and one-time president of the company, circa 1936 (courtesy Toyota Motor Sales Archives).

as his own son and gave him the Toyoda name. While Kiichiro had been creating the automotive department, Risaburo had been running Toyoda Automatic Loom Works, keeping a tight rein on the company's finances. The relationship between the two men was acrimonious as Risaburo was not convinced that Toyoda had a future in automobiles and only grudgingly agreed to finance Kiichiro. On a more positive note, it was Risaburo who was behind the move to change the Toyoda name to Toyota. While Toyoda took ten brush strokes to write in Japanese, Toyota took only eight and since eight was considered a lucky number, the business was registered as the Toyota Motor Company.

Kiichiro realized that if Toyota wanted to compete seriously in the industry they would need larger facilities, and a new plant was constructed "in the middle of nowhere" at Koromo. There Toyota engineers continued work on the six-cylinder, 3.4-liter, 62-horsepower AA sedan. Just as the car was modeled on American technology, so were most of its parts imported from the United States. Citing unreliable and costly Japanese-made parts, Eiji Toyoda later wrote in his book *Toyota: Fifty Years in Motion*: "…we depended on imports for all our electrical components, carburetors, speedometers, and even spark plugs. Putting this in a modern perspective, I wonder what the local content was for those early Toyotas."[12]

But components weren't the only thing Toyota imported. Shortly after Eiji paid a visit to General Motors at Osaka, a young Shotaro Kamiya and two other GM employees came to work at Toyota, accepting a drastically reduced salary for the opportunity to develop Japan's auto industry. But plant equipment and tools were still needed from the United States and Europe, and the government facilitated this by waiving import duties as part of their "protectionist" plan. While glad of the assistance, Eiji later complained: "...the price of that support was having the government constantly breathing down our necks, pressuring us to increase production capacity."[13] This capacity was aimed at the production of 1,500 vehicles a month, which necessitated a mass hiring. Toyota, as was the custom in the country, offered life-long job security. There seemed no reason to doubt that promise while production rose to such a degree that further expansion was necessary.

In 1938 Toyota opened a new factory at Honsha and it was there that Kiichiro began his new production system, known in Japanese as *kanban*, or "just-in-time." Under this system no extra inventory was allowed, saving on expensive storage space. Parts and supplies were delivered on an as-needed basis only. No superfluous labor was allowed to weigh down the payroll. Each employee was cross-trained in all jobs in the event it became necessary to fill in for someone else. The other Toyota requirement was the pursuit of quality at all stages of the production process. Eiji later airily dismissed the notion that this was a revolutionary concept, remarking that it "would have occurred to anyone."[14]

After the model AA came models AB, AC, AE, and BA. The G1 truck was succeeded by the model GA. Despite its car production Toyota was known for its trucks, a fact which infuriated Kiichiro for the rest of his life. It wouldn't have been so difficult to accept had that reputation been a favorable one. Instead the defect-ridden trucks were often publicly ridiculed, as in one newspaper cartoon which showed a broken-down vehicle with the caption "Toyota truck in Zen meditation."[15]

Toyota and Nissan's race to supply the country with passenger cars was again aborted in 1939 at the outbreak of World War II, as was a potential tie-in with Ford. A tentative agreement had been drawn up between Nissan, Toyota, and Ford, but when Eiji visited the U.S. to close the deal, Ford backed out. He assumed there were military reasons behind the decision, and he was probably correct in this assumption. It was a mere two years later that Japan attacked Pearl Harbor.

The auto industry had all but ground to a halt during the war with production for the entire year of 1945 matching only one day of American output. What little that was being produced was a world away from the quality automobiles Kiichiro had envisioned. As Marco Ruiz wrote in *The Complete History of Japanese Cars 1907 to Present*: "Trucks came off the assembly line without radiator grilles, with parts of the bodywork and seats made out of wood, brakes for the rear wheels only, and a single front headlight..."[16]

In 1941, Kiichiro Toyoda assumed the presidency of the Toyota Motor Company, but due to widespread shortages and military control of supplies one of his first duties was to abandon his beloved *kanban* system and turn his abilities to military production. Toyota paired up with Kawasaki to produce aircraft, becoming the Tokai Company, which eventually fell under sole Toyota ownership. In addition to military trucks and aircraft, the company also produced amphibious vehicles, the most unusual of which could be "disassembled and backpacked across the mountains."[17]

The nation was fully engaged in the war when in December of 1944 it was hit again with a series of earthquakes. Between the war and the earthquakes Toyota lost seven thousand of its ten thousand employees. Military ranks were also depleted. Of those desperate times, Eiji, who himself served in the army, wrote: "…practically any man who could carry a rifle and shoot was rounded up and sent to the front."[18]

The nation was near collapse when the bombing of Hiroshima and Nagasaki brought it to its knees. After the formal surrender in August of 1945, Eiji noted that what had become known as "Toyota City" in Aichi Prefecture had been targeted for destruction only a week after the surrender. While most other industries sustained far more extensive physical damage, the automobile industry suffered more indirectly as manpower dwindled and automobiles fell to an all-time low on consumer priority lists. Production dropped over 50 percent from before the war, forcing manufacturers to produce anything they could sell, including tools, kitchenware, farm equipment, and food. Fortunately for Toyota they were already established in the textile business, and began producing clothing in addition to chinaware and even fish paste.

The procurement of food was everyone's number-one goal, and companies even allowed "food holidays" so that their employees might feed themselves and their families. Starvation was so rampant that stealing produce from fields became a common practice, and when that failed, "…the Emperor's loyal subjects were encouraged to supplement their starch intake by introducing such items as acorns, grain husks, peanut shells, and sawdust to their household larder," wrote John W. Dower. "For minerals, people were encouraged to introduce used tea leaves and the seeds, blossoms, and leaves of roses to their diet. Protein deficiencies could be remedied by eating silkworm cocoons, worms, grasshoppers, mice, rats, moles, snails, snakes, or a powder made by drying the blood of cows, horses, and pigs."[19]

Food and supplies began to pour into the country from America as General Douglas MacArthur took command of the nation. MacArthur, whose first task was to neutralize Japan's military, also took charge of its industry, believing that the military and the *zaibatsu* had wielded too much power over the common people. After the military was subdued and aid was arranged for the starving nation, he ordered Japanese auto manufacturers to commence with the repair of damaged American military vehicles. This gave them the opportunity to work with foreign vehicles, gaining a knowledge that they would later apply to their own industry.

In order to see to it that workers would be treated fairly under the new regime, MacArthur introduced organized labor unions. As the Japanese had long perceived unions as the product of communist agitators this was a bitter pill indeed for them to swallow; and as the automobile manufacturers struggled to resume production amidst a post-war recession, their deepest fears were realized when a desperate workforce rebelled.

The first such disruption took place in 1950 at chronically cash-strapped Toyota, where lack of incoming income forced an embattled Kiichiro to rescind his "permanent job security" offer. Over twenty-one hundred workers were "encouraged to resign,"[20] and those remaining had their wages drastically cut. Kiichiro was so dispirited by this turn of events that he left the company in shame and disgust, leaving Taizo Ishida to take over as president. Shotaro Kamiya was in charge of sales and

Eiji Toyoda was managing director. Although Kiichiro made a brief comeback after the strike was settled, he died shortly thereafter on March 27, 1952. Probably a factor that weighed on his mind was the Chairman of the Bank of Japan's pessimistic dismissal of Japan's auto industry in 1950 as "...meaningless," in light of "...the present international division of labor."[21] But perhaps he would have been heartened by the government's response had he lived to see it.

The Ministry of International Trade and Industry (MITI) acted swiftly, putting together a new Industry Rationalization Promotion Law which took effect the same month and year Kiichiro died. Under this law, the automobile, steel, machinist, automobile parts, and communication industries were designated as essential, and given tax advantages as well as low-interest loans. In addition, legislation for the promotion of exports was put in place after war restrictions had been lifted in 1949. It was measures such as these, together with the spur to industry brought about by the Korean War, that boosted the struggling nation. Toyota's post-war production leapt by 40 percent.[22]

The company now had its own dealership and distributor network, known as Toyota Motor Sales. It was one of nine companies under the Toyota umbrella, attracting the attention of an antitrust-wary government which promptly forced the company to separate itself from each concern. It was a move Eiji called "...tantamount to throwing Toyota Motor Sales naked out into the freezing cold."[23]

In order to remedy Toyota's problems with labor relations, below-standard quality, and general disorganization, the management enlisted the services of U.S. scientist W. Edwards Deming, who had come to Japan in 1947 as part of MacArthur's team. Deming's task was to assess the state of Japan's industry and identify its immediate needs. His approach was, according to many, gentle and understanding. As Andrea Gabor wrote in her book, *The Man Who Discovered Quality: How W. Edwards Deming Brought the Quality Revolution to America — The Stories of Ford, Xerox, and GM*: "When he stood before the recently vanquished enemy of the United States, Deming spoke not as a conqueror but as a man who had grown up poor, the son of Wyoming pioneers, and who understood the hardships involved in building something from nothing."[24] Both he and his wife came to be highly regarded in Japan, honored for their generous practice of bringing gifts of food, clothing, and sweets wherever they were invited.

The Deming philosophy was broken down into a fourteen-point system, the most essential of those being the ongoing training and education of employees; a system of performance ratings; statistical process control; understanding variation, and incisive market research. "Quality," said Deming, "has no meaning except as defined by the desires and needs of customers."[25]

The Japanese filled university halls to attend his seminars, even compiling a book from them. When Deming was offered the royalties from the sale of this book, he declined the money. The Japanese Union of Scientists and Engineers took those funds and created the Deming Prize in 1951. In 1960, the same year Nissan won its first Deming Prize, the man was honored with Japan's Second Class Sacred Treasure medal, awarded to him personally by the Emperor Hirohito.

Gabor wrote: "The new management movement Deming helped create and the new cadre of managers, as well as the way democracy in both government and the workplace was championed by MacArthur, were all instrumental in reinventing the Japanese corporation."[26]

In addition to applying Deming's theories, Eiji traveled to America in 1951 to study U.S. production and to explore potential tie-in relationships. He spent over a month at Ford, where he was told he "wanted to know too much."[27] From Ford he went on to visit the Chrysler Corporation. Upon leaving Detroit he concluded to himself that the United States was not doing anything Toyota couldn't do. But Toyota's biggest concern was not what the United States was doing, it was what was happening in their own backyard.

While it had always been "Toyota for trucks," Nissan had cornered Japan's passenger car market and more importantly it enjoyed almost complete monopoly of its lucrative taxi market. Derided for taking an unfair advantage when it bought licenses for both British and American cars, Nissan, with much more wealth and power behind it, had a distinct advantage over Toyota. A new plant strictly for car production had been opened at Yoshiwara while truck production stayed at the Yokohoma factory.

In 1951 the company released the first of the new "Thrift" series, an 860-cc car closely resembling the American Crosley automobile. A year later the company entered what it referred to as "a technological cooperation with Austin Motor Company, Ltd. of the United Kingdom."[28] From it came the model 110, based on the Austin A-40. It seemed as though Nissan would retain its hefty lead over Toyota until it experienced its first major strike in 1953 which lasted into 1954 and nearly dragged the company into bankruptcy. The strike set Nissan back badly and Toyota closed in with its Toyopet Crown, introduced in 1955.

Less expensive but more powerful than Nissan's 830-cc Type 110, the 1,453-cc, 48-horsepower Crown became extremely popular. A proud, formally-dressed Eiji Toyoda personally drove the first model off the line, ushering in the beginning of the company's rise in the industry. A short time later the upgraded Crown Deluxe was fittingly unveiled in the presence of Crown Prince Akihito. But while Toyota was finally becoming known for its cars, and luxurious ones at that, the government decreed that what Japan needed was a "people's car" similar to Germany's VW Beetle.

The criteria for this car were strict. It had to have a top speed of 60 miles per hour, fuel economy of 70 miles per gallon, travel 60,000 miles without major repair, carry at least four people, and weigh under 880 pounds with an engine not to exceed 500 cc. The manufacturers protested, believing it was an impossible order. Although the plan was later discarded, the companies did strive to meet the challenge in some approximation, bringing about a whole new era of the Japanese automobile. Toyota began its work on the "people's car" far behind other automakers, probably due to the fact it was preoccupied with quite another concern.

In 1956, Toyota Motor Sales president Shotaro Kamiya had sent an advance team to the United States to "assess the situation there." When they returned, Kamiya firmly declared to upper management that the Toyopet Crown was ready for the American market. But it was another matter entirely to convince them that the American market was ready for the Toyopet Crown.

# 4

# Toyota — First on Shore

In the late summer of 1957 the docks at Long Beach, California, hummed with activity as usual. Freighters from around the world laden with everything from steel to salt arrived daily at this vital American port. On this particular day a small crowd had gathered in front of the *Toyota Maru* freighter that had just arrived from Japan. Photographers and reporters stood to one side of a dignified contingent of tuxedo-clad Japanese businessmen engaged in conversation with their less-formally-dressed American counterparts. Another tiny coterie was headed by a radiantly smiling Miss Japan, Kyoko Otani, who held a large bouquet of flowers.[1]

All had been anxiously awaiting the arrival from Japan, but none were more eager than Toyota Motor Sales president Shotaro Kamiya whose vision of bringing Toyota's first export to the United States was finally being realized. Years later he described the occasion in his autobiography: "...I will never forget the feeling I had when the first two sample cars sailed from Yokohama on August 25, 1957. I felt almost like I was seeing my children off on a long journey."[2]

When the two small Toyota Toyopet Crown cars, one white and one black, finally sat on the docks, flashbulbs popped and reporters hastily scribbled in their notebooks. The Toyota representatives spoke a few words and there was applause as the audience moved closer to the shining cars. Miss Japan stepped forward and laid a bouquet on the first car, eliciting more applause. The Americans made complimentary remarks to the beaming Toyota team who fielded questions and conversed with reporters.

When Shotaro Kamiya first approached his superiors in 1956 with the proposal of exporting cars to the United States, he was faced with a hard sell. Management consensus of the time was that Toyota was not ready — that the export should be delayed for at least five years. But Kamiya was persistent. Armed with information from the three-man advance team he had sent to the United States in 1956 to survey the market, he pleaded his case. He had, he reminded them, traveled there himself in 1955 and was convinced that after the phenomenal success of Volkswagen America

**Getting ready to take America by storm ... but not quite yet. A Toyopet Crown at the docks (courtesy Toyota Motor Sales Archives).**

would soon close ranks against imported automobiles. Kamiya insisted that it was essential that Toyota move quickly to enter the market, reporting to his bosses that "...it was now or never."[3] Another green light shone when Toyota president Taizo Ishida visited Washington and was encouraged by a diplomat to try exporting to the United States. This encouragement together with the pride the team felt in their new Toyopet Crown clinched the decision to export. California was chosen as a base chiefly due to its proximity to Japan in terms of shipping, but also because of its large Japanese community and seemingly more welcoming attitude toward imports.

Unfortunately Kamiya soon had cause to doubt the wisdom of his decision after the Toyopets were taken to a motor vehicle inspection station in the Little Tokyo district of Los Angeles to receive their state certification. After a thorough inspection, authorities declared the car unfit for licensing. Among the defects were inadequate rearview mirrors and a defective lighting system, including weak head and taillights, and turn signals that did not flash.

While the car was undergoing its lengthy inspection, the crew from Toyota were enthusiastically accepting dealership applications from their Los Angeles hotel room. The media had reported favorably on this new arrival from Japan and Americans seemed eager to carry the Toyota product which they referred to as a "baby Cadillac."[4] Before knowing the results of the inspection, Kamiya was so exuberant that he wired home to say that he could probably sell 100,000 cars a year in the U.S. market.[5]

The only problem was that the Toyopet failed to pass its litmus test — a drive on a Los Angeles freeway, an attempt that could only be classified as disastrous. The little car strained to reach and maintain the speed necessary to stay in the traffic flow, and when pushed the engine roared and vibrated alarmingly due in part to the fact that the crankshaft had only three main bearings. On even the slightest elevations it began to overheat as it struggled to gain ground. At times it even slid backwards and the brakes were not strong enough to hold it.[6]

Anxious Toyota executives were only too aware that not only did their future in the country ride on the car's performance, but also that the Americans were watching closely. There was a growing sense of unease among both camps. The Toyota team was dismayed by the performance of their product, and the formerly eager potential dealers began to get cold feet when they realized the car was nowhere near ready for the U.S. market. In fact it wasn't until July of 1958 that the Toyota was considered minimally road-worthy.

Sadly, no news travels faster than bad news and word of the Toyota's failure spread, considerably dimming the company's future American prospects. As Eiji Toyoda later remembered of that discouraging occasion: "...the reception was horrible...." But he could not say the same about the company's timing, adding: "...that first initiative of ours was very poorly thought out indeed, but our timing was definitely not off. In fact, having this bitter experience behind us helped us work that much harder afterwards to build cars that were right for the U.S. market ... it was do or die."[7]

It was a tough way to learn a lesson. Despite the hard knocks the car was receiving, Kamiya pushed ahead with his sales plans, traveling door-to-door as was the custom in Japan. He wound his way from Los Angeles to San Francisco to try to entice dealers into accepting the Toyota. Meeting with little success, he dejectedly wired home again telling the production team to cancel his previous order. As his colleague and future CEO of Toyota Motor Company, Seisi Kato, put it upon hearing of the failure: "...our dreams sank out of sight like a ship with a giant hole in the bottom..."[8] Nevertheless, he and his fellow managers were not convinced it was yet time to give up. His superiors agreed, and the order came down from above that now that Toyota had gotten its foot in the door it would not close that door on itself. Thus it was with a good deal of trepidation that Toyota Motor Sales U.S.A., which had been established at 6850 Hollywood Boulevard on October 31, 1957, was allowed to live.

Operations began in a building leased from owner Ben Alexander, formerly of the television show *Dragnet*. Among other dealerships, Alexander owned Hollywood Ford which butted up against the new Toyota premises. Upon closing the deal with Toyota he also owned the first Toyota dealership in America, Hollywood Toyota Motor Incorporated. The dealership was originally managed by Sully Sullivan whose son Mike now owns and operates Toyota of Hollywood. Unfortunately very little information survives from the early days of this pioneer dealership, and as Mike Sullivan informed this author, "most of the people concerned are gone now, and no one really remembers anything about the business back then."[9] Neither did Ben Alexander's son Nicholas have any memories of his father's Toyota business when contacted.

Surprisingly, only sketchy information exists in Toyota's own archives regard-

ing their early days in America, but what can be reported was that Toyota Motor Sales U.S.A. was capitalized at one million dollars. Shotaro Kamiya was president, Toku-taro Kobayashi vice-president and together they headed thirteen or so employees, a small parts department, and a modest inventory of vehicles. Kobayashi brought over a few Japanese mechanics to train their American counterparts to repair the cars. This action, although a step in the right direction, proved to be woefully inadequate as one of the reasons later cited for the company's initial failure in the United States was its lack of service facilities.

Back in Japan, Toyota executives were poring over various strategies that would boost its poor U.S. showing. Executive vice-president of Toyota Motor Sales in Japan, Jun Nakayama was dispatched to the United States to assist in the reorganization of its division there. There were countless hurdles large and small to overcome. One was America's tax laws concerning import sales that Toyota circumvented by establishing Toyota Motor Distributors in February of 1958. That distributorship served the West Coast, while other distributorships were in the planning stages.

One of the first of these was the Hawaii division, established in March of 1958. Toyota entered into an agreement with the Service Motor Company to act as their distributor on the island. But despite their Herculean efforts, by the end of their first year in America only 288 vehicles had sold. Of those sales 287 were Toyopet Crowns and the remaining one was a Land Cruiser.[10]

As the Crown continued to fail, temporary respite came from a surprising quarter in the form of the rugged Land Cruiser which had arrived in time for the 1958 market. Toyota had developed the Land Cruiser prototype in 1950 with a sturdy 85-horsepower diesel engine based on a design that had been inspired by the Willys Jeepster. Although many were skeptical about its durability and quality, the Land Cruiser had no trouble proving itself by climbing to the sixth station of Mount Fuji, a feat no other vehicle had managed. In 1954, rising demand necessitated its mass production as it was proving to be valuable both domestically and as an export. In 1955 the Land Cruiser received an upgraded 125-horsepower, 3.8-liter gasoline engine, and was marketed as the model FJ25.

In 1957 Toyota decided that the Land Cruiser was ready for the American market. It was a wise move on the part of the company to appeal to the American love of rugged adventure. They also shrewdly perceived that many of its citizens lived in rougher rural areas and would appreciate the qualities of a four-wheel-drive vehicle. In fact it was the Land Cruiser that established Toyota in America and convinced the first five American dealers to sell the Toyota line. One of the first of those dealers was John A. Rose of San Diego.

Rose, predominantly a European import dealer, signed an agreement in 1957 to sell Toyotas despite the fact that fellow dealers laughed and told him the company would not survive in America.[11] While Rose himself was a little skeptical about the prospects of the Crown, he was quite impressed with the Land Cruiser, which turned

*Opposite, top:* Toyota's first headquarters in Hollywood, California (courtesy Toyota Motor Sales Archives). *Bottom:* One of the first showrooms in America to feature the Toyota product (courtesy Toyota Motor Sales Archives).

out to be the first Toyota he sold. But as Rose later testified, it was an uphill battle convincing American consumers of the virtues of the Toyota: "It was tough getting the public to accept Japanese products back then," he commented in an interview years later. In some ways he could understand the reluctance to buy displayed by many of his customers, as he himself admitted: "…the features and performance of the Toyopet didn't help much. It was heavy and slow, and not very comfortable."[12]

But Rose had confidence in Toyota if others did not. He was impressed with the way Toyota executives met with dealers and asked them directly what they wanted from the company. Rose said he knew that when Toyota "told us they'd retool and re-engineer to give us a car we could sell it wasn't just an empty promise."[13] True to their word, when the Corona came along sales began to take off. Obviously Rose's faith in the product paid off. Rose Toyota went on to flourish and to earn *Time* magazine's Quality Dealer Award in 1992.[14]

Another pioneer Toyota dealer was George Krause of Pennsylvania. Krause, who had already been selling Plymouth and Dodge, thought the Toyota product was well made, and was impressed with the "overall fit and finish of the car."[15] In those days, dealers of imports had scant support systems behind them, and little in the way of dealer incentives. Toyota was no different. The company could not even afford to transport directly to the dealer lots. Instead the cars were shipped to the nearest major

Krause Toyota of Schnecksville, Pennsylvania, was one of the few dealerships willing to take on the unknown Toyota product. The Toyopet was such a novelty that early owners and dealers photographed them (courtesy Krause Toyota).

The 1957 Toyopet Crown seen here was marketed to appeal to the "American family" (courtesy Toyota Motor Sales Archives).

city and it was up to the dealer to find a way to bring them to his establishment. George Krause later told of one such pick-up expedition he undertook in the fall of 1959. Krause and a friend boarded a bus to Newark, New Jersey, to take delivery of two Toyopet Crowns which they then drove back to the Krause dealership on Main Street in Schnecksville, Pennsylvania. "There were no car carriers in those days," explained great-grandson Robert Krause, the fourth generation in the business.[16] Apparently customers were almost as scarce. George Krause soon found he had the same problem as John Rose — no market for his product. Customers complained that "there wasn't enough horsepower in the cars," and, like Rose, Krause found the Land Cruiser was the only model he could sell.[17]

One problem was that there was absolutely no exposure for the product. Toyota could not afford any significant advertising, and it was usually left to the dealer to provide his own. When questioned about the lack of advertising, Robert Krause confirmed that his great-grandfather took care of that himself: "We had a newspaper ad we purchased on our own in the *Allentown Morning Call*—but even then, sales were very slow."[18]

Sales were so hard to come by that the dealership still proudly retains a fifty-year-old copy of a check in the amount of $7,600 representing the sale of its first four

Strong faith, as illustrated by the sign, was needed in the days before Toyota sales took off in the States. Advertising helped, but the budget was small (courtesy Krause Toyota).

Toyotas.[19] Despite this disappointing showing, George Krause didn't give up. "It took three to five years for sales to pick up," said Robert Krause of those lean times.[20] But Krause, like Rose, went on to create a very successful Toyota operation, having, as he put it, "our best year ever in 2001."[21]

Toyota was doing everything in its power to facilitate sales, and one of those moves included hiring ex–Ford man James F. McGraw as a sales administrator in 1959. McGraw joined regional manager Frank Mullen, general manager Eric Hansen and executive assistant Joe McCord as part of Toyota's "American team." McGraw, however, was less than impressed with the Toyopet which he was given as a company car. "You've got to be kidding," he said in his direct American fashion. "You're going to try to sell this?" He was incredulous, pointing out that: "This thing is underpowered, overpriced and it won't sell. And the name's all wrong. Toyopet. 'Toy' sounds like a toy and toys break. And 'pet' sounds like your dog. Send it back home until the product's right."[22]

But that had already been done and the Toyopet McGraw drove was the version Toyota intended to sell. Now the company was focusing on other problems, namely how to set up a parts and service department. This was accomplished in 1958 when Toyota's first U.S. parts warehouse in Long Beach, with a staff of seven and an inventory of 2,800 parts, was opened headed by Tatsuo Hashiguchi.[23] That same year the company moved its headquarters to 6023 Hollywood Boulevard; by that time almost 2,000 Crowns had been shipped to a total of 45 American dealers, but sadly most of them were "gathering dust on the dealer's lots."[24]

Dealerships were decorated to herald the arrival of the new Japanese car (courtesy Toyota Motor Sales Archives).

Although Toyota sales representatives had traveled across the country establishing field operations in private homes, interest in the cars failed to materialize as their poor reputation slowly spread. The product was becoming an object of derision, even in its home territory of California. A story has since been told that in the early sixties when the Los Angeles fire department ordered what were then known as Crown fire engines, they proved to be so weak that they were nicknamed "Toyopet Crowns" after the "pieces of junk that were sold in California at the time."[25] At $2,300 — more than 40 percent higher than the price of a VW Beetle — that was quite an expensive "piece of junk."

But not all reviews were entirely negative. *Motor Trend* magazine wrote: "While it may never win any stoplight Grand Prix (it wasn't intended to), neither will it come unglued at the seams on the first washboard road. The strength factor is a necessity in Japan where roads are notoriously rugged. Any automobile which is not several degrees more rugged than its road way is going to fall apart — (we personally know of a popular American make which has a life expectancy of less than six months on Japan's back roads)."[26] Another testament to the car's durability came in 1957 when it was driven from London to Tokyo, a 50,000-kilometer trip taken by two journalists.[27]

**Trying for that American look ... the Toyopet's first brochure (courtesy Toyota Motor Sales Archives).**

American dealers had agreed to sell the Toyotas hoping to scratch an as-yet-to-be-identified customer itch, but it seemed the Toyota was not the product to do it. Sales of the Crown peaked in 1959 at 1,028 sold through a dealer network of 97. A year later they had fallen to only 821.[28]

Still, they refused to give up and in the first month of 1959 Toyota pushed on, establishing another distributorship in New Jersey.

By 1960, the number of dealers carrying the Toyopets and Land Cruisers throughout America had dropped to 70.[29] Many of them were Big Three dealers who had small foreign car sections that included an assortment of imports. Those that had sold Volkswagens found a startling contrast when compared with Toyota sales.

When the far-below-anticipated sales records began to arrive at Toyota's head office, management decided it was time to concede defeat. In December of 1960 the exporting of passenger cars to the United States was halted. Aside from the considerable flaws in the vehicles, one major problem sprang from a deep-seated lack of trust in the product spawned by the ingrained "Made-in-Japan" low-quality image many Americans still harbored. And those that did take a chance and invest in a Toyota product were stymied by the fact that there were inadequate service facilities. Another major issue was the introduction of compact cars by Ford, Chrysler and General Motors.

Tough times required tough actions, and Eiji Toyoda traveled to the United States to personally handle the laying off of half of the 65 Toyota Motor Sales staff.

Toyota builds a good old-fashioned station wagon. The car featured such items as an outlet for an electric razor and optional windshield washers. This 1962 brochure is from Hollywood Toyota Motor, Inc.

Jim McGraw remembers a "bloody" day in the spring of 1961 when he "fired people on the phone all around the country."[30] The company was forced to leave its new Beverly Hills office and move back to its original location in Hollywood, with only the Land Cruiser left to represent it in the American market.

But while Toyota was floundering in the United States, it was on its way to becoming the number one automaker in Japan, opening a new plant at Motomachi in 1959 with a capacity to produce 10,000 vehicles a month.

With the Japanese market well in hand, work began to redesign a car for the American market. The next model to be exported was the Tiara (named Corona in Japan), shipped to the United States in 1961. Unfortunately it failed as well and was taken off the American market in 1964.

Advertising man Tom Loewy was hired to manage Toyota's marketing. He was asked to put together a five-year plan for sales and distribution at a time when the company had only one model to sell. The decision was also made to totally revamp the U.S. operations.

In February of 1962 fresh TMS staff were brought in from the Toyota Motor Company. Shiro Ohnishi was appointed as president of the Export Headquarters, which had been created with five divisions: North America; Latin America and the Caribbean; the Far East; the Middle East, and Africa. Each department's duty was to

**Convention, Vegas-style. This is probably one of the first Toyota dealership conventions to take place in America, in the early 1960s (courtesy Krause Toyota).**

appraise the market it was assigned to. This began in earnest for the U.S. market in particular, where it found that Toyota sales for 1962 were a dismal 711 through 90 dealerships.[31]

Desperate to find clues that would lead to success in the tough U.S. market, Toyota once again approached Ford to discuss a possible tie-in venture. The deal they proposed would see Ford market the Toyota Publica in the United States, while Toyota would sell it in Japan. The proposed ownership split of the new venture would be 60 percent for Toyota and 40 percent for Ford. Ford considered the offer and even sent engineers to Japan to inspect Toyota operations. Although admittedly impressed with what they saw, they ultimately rejected the proposal for reasons that were to remain unclear to Toyota management. That they should pull so suddenly out of the deal with no word of explanation incensed the Toyota team and struck Eiji Toyoda as a move that "...smacked of blatant disrespect."[32]

Toyota was once more left to their own devices to produce an acceptable automobile for the U.S. market. In McGraw's opinion what they needed was "a Chevrolet that's been miniaturized to the size of a Volkswagen."[33] The problem was the American market was changing faster than Toyota could draw up designs. Safety regulations were becoming an issue for automobile manufacturers, and importers now faced new challenges in their designs. In 1963 seatbelts became standard equipment, as did padded interiors. But safety standards were not the only challenge facing the Japanese automaker. The average American stature necessitated more head and leg room than was necessary for their Japanese counterparts. Ride was also a concern. Vast stretches of American highway required a smoother, quieter, "floating" ride. But the softer suspension used in America-bound cars resulted in Japanese head injuries as the cars bounced over less-developed Japanese roads.

While Toyota engineers were working on implementing all of the above design features into their new model, they offered one of their ubiquitous trucks to the American market. In 1964 Toyota began importing its Stout truck to the United States. But the Stout suffered the same fate as the Tiara and lasted only three years in America, being withdrawn in 1967.

It seemed that the only Toyota Americans wanted was the steadfast Land Cruiser, whose sales continued to rise slowly but surely. But giving up was not an option with still another, more promising, product in the works that same year.

The Toyota Corona had begun life in Japan in 1957 as the 995-cc, 35-horsepower ST10 model. Two years later it was upgraded to a slightly stronger PT10 model, which was further improved to the PT20 in 1960. In 1961, a 1453-cc, 60-horsepower engine was added and the car became known as the RT20. The third generation Corona of 1964 had an even stronger 1500-cc, 70-horsepower engine and was by then a best-seller in Japan. Toyota officials believed they finally had a vehicle that would crack the American market. Toyota Motor Sales U.S.A. representatives, including Jim McGraw, visited Japan to inspect the car and approve it for sale in the United States. The American reps were impressed but insisted that the engine be upgraded to at least 1900 cc's to stand up to long-distance driving conditions. They also requested that the armrests and seats be repositioned and that the rubber floor mats be replaced with carpets.

The final result was a 1900-cc, 90-horsepower model that made its debut in the American market in June of 1965, retailing for $1,860.[34] It had a wheelbase of 95.3 inches, weighed 2,140 pounds, and had a compression ratio of 8.0:1, providing a zero-to-sixty time of 14 seconds.[35] But as the Toyota archives reveal, not a single Corona was present at its own debut. The cars had been held up when they were shipped to Portland instead of Los Angeles.[36]

Toyota officials were determined to make this model a success and they pulled out all the stops to ensure that it would be. Former General Motors employee Seisi Kato spent $5,000 to develop the company's first-ever television commercial starring the Corona. The series of short ads focused on the durability of the vehicle as it was pushed off ramps and cliffs, only to be driven away at the bottom. These ads were supplemented by a sales campaign that mainly encompassed the American West Coast. Print advertisements were taken out in *Saturday Evening Post, Life, Look, Time,* and *Newsweek* magazines. The ads boasted the Corona's wall-to-wall carpeting, padded dash, two-speed wipers, courtesy lights, and lever-operated bucket seats. Air-conditioning and automatic transmission were available options.

*Consumer Reports* magazine reviewed the Corona in 1966, saying in particular that the car had "special virtues for long-distance driving."[37] *Popular Mechanics* magazine also had praise for the car in its test published in the January 1967 edition, saying: "The Corona is a civilized-looking car. Styling is modern and functional, with more than a passing Italian influence. Workmanship puts many luxury cars to shame."[38] The author of the piece, Alexander Markovich, called it an "Eastern import with Western values."[39] Although impressed with the car, Markovich could not resist just a touch of condescension: "An unadvertised Corona bonus is its owner's manual. Some of the translations from Japanese alone are worth the price of admission."

The car that saved Toyota in America: the 1965 Corona (courtesy Toyota Motor Sales Archives).

But in spite of the amusing manual, Toyota is firmly entrenched among the top 10 foreign makes in this country, thanks to a nationwide network of nearly 600 dealers."[40] More precisely there were 606 dealers at the time selling a grand total of 20,908 vehicles.[41]

In 1968, *Car Life* magazine editors were so taken with the Corona that they featured it twice. Explaining why the Corona was being mentioned in their "All-Japan Auto Show" edition after already having been reviewed, the editors explained that: "The Corona really didn't need to be in the All-Japan Auto Show. *Car Life* tested it just five issues ago. It's included in the survey mainly for an excuse to say more nice things about it."[42] They concluded their review with an unqualified compliment: "Many imports are cheap to buy and operate, and some imports have engines and suspensions suited to American driving conditions. The Corona combines the two, and that's rare."[43]

*Road Test* magazine also threw in its praise a year later when it voted the Corona the Import of the Year for 1969, devoting a special inside-cover editorial to Toyota which said in part: "We believe then, that the time is right for us to publicly recognize the outstanding automotive achievement of the Toyota Motor Company."[44]

But if automotive journalists were generous, the most valuable testimonial of all came from a private citizen who decided to film his own impressions of the car and send it to the company as a tribute. In the film, the enamored customer was quoted as saying about the Toyota: "Once you get your hands on one, you never want to let it go."[45] Toyota officials were so impressed by this endorsement that they edited it down to: "Get Your Hands on a Toyota and You'll Never Let Go!" and used it as their first U.S. slogan.

One year after the Corona was introduced, company sales had soared from 6,404 to 20,908.[46] As dealer John Rose put it: "Our whole world changed with the arrival of the Corona. There was no longer any doubt that the company would continue and be successful."[47]

By now Toyota had established 384 dealers across the United States, and were ready to move out of their humble headquarters in Hollywood. Construction on the new headquarters began on May 5, 1966, at 190th Street, Torrance, California. In 1965, the first exclusively Toyota dealership had been opened in San Fernando, California.

Hamer Motor had its origins in 1939 when Lee Hamer took on a Hudson franchise which he operated until 1958. In 1955, Hamer had also sold British Austins, MGs, and Sunbeams. His next import was the Volvo which he began selling in 1957. In April of 1965, Hamer decided to drop all of the other imports and deal exclusively with Toyota. He put all his effort into promoting the cars, taking out newspapers ads, putting up billboards, and placing signs on bus-stop benches. The efforts paid off for Hamer who is currently ranked as one of the top ten Toyota dealerships in America with sales approaching 700 vehicles per month.[48]

The year the Corona came to America was a banner year for the Toyota Motor Company in many respects. Not only had they finally gained a hard-won spot in the American market, they also captured the coveted Deming Prize in Japan. It was to be the first of many awards in their illustrious history. But resting on their laurels did not appeal to the go-getting Toyota leaders. Having acquired a certain knowledge of the American lifestyle and love of speed and racing, Toyota was ready to launch its next missile.

The company's first sports car, the low-slung, 2-seater 2000 GT arrived in California in 1967. Import manager Mitsuo Yamada, San Francisco manager Wes Haymond, and northern California regional manager Ottar Dahl were on hand as the car was unloaded from the Japan Air Line freighter at the San Francisco airport. It was officially unveiled to the American public at the eighth annual San Francisco Imported Automobile Show.

Retailing at a hefty $7,000, the GT was well above the buying range of the average consumer. The car was equipped with a double-overhead-cam, 2000-cc engine which produced 150 horsepower at 6,600 rpm. This engine was mated to a five-speed, all-synchromesh transmission. With three carburetors blasting fuel and air into the aluminum head, the 2000 GT was able to reach zero to sixty in 9.8 seconds with a top speed of 132 mph.

The car was a surprising departure for Toyota Motors and it was not widely known that it was actually originally intended for Nissan, who in 1963 had sub-contracted Yamaha to build it for them based on a design by German Albrecht Goertz. But by the time the prototype had been completed Nissan had lost interest. Yamaha then approached Toyota to partner in the development of the production car, which, although not ready for sale, was subsequently introduced at the 1965 Tokyo Motor Show.[49]

Toyota's first missile, the 1967 2000GT "Bond" car. Although it was featured in the movie *You Only Live Twice*, Sean Connery did not get to drive the 150-horsepower Toyota sports car, which turned out to be a limited edition. Production ended in 1968 (courtesy Toyota Motor Sales Archives).

The styling of the 2000GT clearly reflected the influence of the typical European race car of the period, epitomized by the Jaguar E-type. To maintain uniform stiffness, Toyota used an all-steel frame and body configuration. Suspension consisted of double wishbones and coil springs on front and rear. The steering system was rack-and-pinion and disc brakes were outfitted on all four wheels. The engine was based on the Crown's 2-liter six cylinder that featured seven main bearings as opposed to the usual five in the smaller Toyotas. An overall lighter version was produced for the racing circuit.

Those aspiring to racing heights were certainly taken with the car, among those *Car Life* editors, who after testing it took pains to set the scene for the reader:

> So. We are in Nevada, in a Toyota 2000GT. The Toyota is in full song, in fourth gear, an indicated 120 mph. The driver, a man who prides himself on keeping his cool at all times, nods at the speedometer and asks, "Shall we see how fast it'll go in fifth?" The passenger has blown his professional cool. "Geez" he says weakly, "maybe the rest of the world better start copying the Japanese."[50]

Apparently the driver concurred, putting it succinctly: "Toyota has progressed beyond the copying stage." In an era where speed was becoming taboo in America, he added: "Toyota has built a fine car, for doing things the American driver isn't supposed to do."[51]

But sales of the GT did not merit its return for 1968, and the company took it off the market in order to redesign it. In an interview with *Road Test* magazine in 1969, Shotaro Kamiya promised that the 2000GT would be available in the near future but only after complying with federal safety and smog requirements. Much research, he explained, was going into not only meeting but exceeding the smog standards. While he was at it, he also firmly pointed out that Toyota would be staying out of the mid- and full-size range so as not to infringe on traditional American territory. As for the Corona and Corolla, his feeling was that they were not in direct competition with the Ford Maverick (as was so frequently suggested in the automotive media) because the Ford was considerably larger.[52]

Whether or not Detroit took these comments at face value is uncertain. But if they felt no threat to their "traditional" market range, they were about to be shaken to the core by a return to Henry Ford's era of a "car for the masses"—only this time it did not come from one of their own.

# 5

## "A Legend in Its Time"—
## Toyota's Rise to the Top

First produced in Japan in November of 1966, the Toyota Corolla was smaller and lighter than the Corona, weighing only 1,640 pounds with a wheelbase of 90 inches. The version exported to the United States in the summer of 1968 was powered by an 1100-cc, (65.8-cubic inch) 60-horsepower engine joined to an all-synchronized four-speed transmission.

The Corolla's suspension was somewhat unorthodox with the front consisting of lower control arms, struts, shocks and transversely-mounted (from strut to strut) semi-elliptical springs. These springs were added to help reduce the strain and friction on the struts. At the rear was a live axle mounted on semi-elliptical springs and telescoping shocks. Steering was through an old-fashioned worm-and-roller type system.

Naturally the appearance of the Corolla invited comparison to the already established Corona. Surveys indicated that customers had been impressed with the Corona's superior gas mileage, economical maintenance, roominess, overall quality, and pep.[1] The Corolla managed to satisfy on all accounts except for the latter.

Whereas the 2000GT had tantalized a select few with its speed and the Corona catered to more conservative tastes, the Corolla's sharp drop of 30 horsepower provoked one editor to comment wryly: "Only the patient and non-competitive should cruise the turnpikes in a Corolla."[2] With only 60 horses, 61.5 ft-lb of torque at 3,800 rpm, a rear axle ratio of 4.22:1 and diminutive 12-inch wheels, any expectations of performance were bound to be dashed. Getting from zero to sixty took a sluggish 17 seconds, while the car needed 20.5 seconds to complete the standing quarter-mile with a top speed of 64 mph.[3]

There were other complaints as well. The small (7.87" × 1.38") drum brakes on all four wheels proved dismally inadequate, with *Car Life* testers rating the Corolla's stopping power as poor with "…quite a bit of control lost."[4] Handling, too, proved

America's favorite Toyota, and one Eiji Toyoda later called "A legend in its time"—the 1968 Corolla (courtesy Toyota Motor Sales Archives).

to be disappointing. The Corolla tended towards wheel-lift during high-speed cornering, as well as being vulnerable to buffeting by strong crosswinds.

On the plus side, one significant improvement over the Corona was a more streamlined design, accomplished by slightly tilting the engine so as to allow for a lower hood line. Accordingly the grille was lengthened and narrowed to achieve a sleeker appearance. Inside were reclining bucket seats, carpets, long floor shifter, and big round gauges. Seating easily accommodated four persons, windows were large and combined with the high seats allowed excellent visibility.

Summing up their test of the prototype Toyota had provided them with, *Car Life* concluded that: "The Corolla is a well-made car, at a very low price."[5] That "very low price" was $1,660—certainly a key factor in the car's instant popularity. By 1971 a steady and seemingly insatiable demand instigated production of five versions of the Corolla—the 1200 two-door sedan and coupe which now had a larger 1166-cc (71.1-cubic inch) engine; the 1600 two- or four-door sedan and four-door station wagon bearing an 88-horsepower 1588-cc engine (96.9-cubic inch).

That year *Car and Driver* magazine had positioned the Corolla 1200 in third place when compared with the Gremlin, Vega, Simca, Pinto, and Super Beetle. Failure to top the list was largely due to the Corolla's weak engine and lackluster performance. But with the enormously popular Datsun 510 on the scene, Toyota needed a model that would be able to compete in the same league. While matching and even exceeding the 510's capabilities, the 1600 easily eclipsed the 1200 in both power and consumer appeal.

Having pulled no punches in its review of the Corolla 1200, in September of 1971 *Car and Driver* was able to change its tune: "…Now enter the Toyota 1600 Corolla, and exit much of our criticism."[6] The most exciting thing, according to the reviewer, was that the 1600 was not just a re-hashed version of the 1200. "In fact, the 1600 engine is *not* the bored and stroked 1200 that many people seem to imagine; it's a new engine, with design features and operating characteristics different from any preceding Toyota…. It feels, from the driver's seat, like there might be a couple of dozen camshafts in its cylinder head," the testers raved.[7]

The engine was new — a hemi-head design in fact — which made 102 horsepower at 6,000 rpm, 101 ft-lb of torque at 3,800 rpm, and had a compression ratio of 8.5:1. The iron-block, aluminum-head engine with a 3.35-inch bore and 2.76-inch stroke was matched with an all-synchro four-speed manual transmission, or an optional two-speed automatic. The Corolla could now go from to zero to sixty in 11.4 seconds and the quarter-mile in 18.2 seconds at 75 mph.

Despite the other upgrades to the 1600, stopping still posed a problem. In fact, *Car and Driver* deemed it "unacceptable," lamenting: "The Corolla was introduced with substandard brakes and Toyota obviously intends to leave it that way."[8]

Even so, consumers couldn't seem to get enough of the product. And it wasn't just Toyota claiming fame. Japanese cars in general now had America's attention. *Car Life* magazine's August 1968 edition cover blared: "Move Over World, Here Come the Japanese." Leading with an assessment of the American automobile market and where the Japanese stood in it, the editors declared: "The Japanese are not building cars for the American market. There *is* no American market, no neat category into which the American car and the American car buyer can be stuffed. Instead, there are many American markets; for big cars, small cars, family cars, Ponycars, Super-cars, shopping cars, sports cars, station wagons, luxury cars, even off-road cars. The Japanese don't have a car for every market. Not yet, anyway."[9]

Perhaps not, but Toyota certainly seemed to have a market for every car, a fact that was all the more obvious after the 1973 oil crisis. In April of 1974, *Science and Mechanics* magazine voted the Corolla 1200 as one of the twelve best cars to own in a fuel shortage, estimating its mileage at between 26 and 31 mpg. Even the 1600 was given a nod, although it was acknowledged as "slightly less economical."[10]

It seemed that when a small imported car came to American minds, its name was Toyota Corolla. Eiji Toyoda himself later called the Corolla "a legend in its time."[11] Toyota Motor Sales president Shotaro Kamiya also paid tribute to the Corolla in his autobiographical *My Life with Toyota*: "During my forty years with Toyota, I have introduced many new types of automobiles to the market. Each one was special, and each brought me mixed feelings of pleasure and disappointment. Of all those cars, however, I became especially fond of the Corolla. It was the Corolla that most successfully fulfilled our expectations for boosting sales at home and building an export market."[12]

There was no question that Toyota was now producing an excellent product. But according to John Jardine, owner of a New York Toyota dealership established in 1968, it was not only the cars that put Toyota in the top spot — it was also superior management and efficiency coupled with an above-average dealer relationship.

Jardine praised Toyota's treatment of dealers, commenting: "They did everything they could to make us comfortable with their organization." Acknowledging that Toyota was also acutely aware of its public image, he added: "They were always concerned about what the public was thinking about the Toyota name."[13]

Toyota's fixation on customer satisfaction combined with their astute marketing strategies soon came to the attention of a young J.D. Power, a statistical analyst who immediately realized that Toyota was serious about gaining U.S. market-share—an undertaking he felt he could assist in.

Power, determined to gain his first automotive client, visited the Toyota Motor Sales U.S.A. office in person. Perhaps not trusting his motives, the American staff he encountered in the front office turned him away, but he was not daunted. Casually strolling around the building, he spied a back-door entrance where a few Japanese workers were handling forklifts. His conversation with these workers earned him an invitation to meet with Toyota executive Tatsuro Toyoda to discuss his propositions. As Power later remembered, he was then operating from his kitchen table and didn't have much experience behind him.[14] Nevertheless, Toyoda was impressed with Power and decided to take a chance on him. The result of their meeting led to the precursor of the first-ever J.D. Power Customer Satisfaction Index (CSI). Toyota owners were surveyed to discover what they thought about their Toyotas, as well as how they were treated by Toyota dealers.

Toyota managers pored over the survey results, using them as a guideline for changes to future products and services. Using surveys and following suggestions was to be an important part of Toyota's management style. As far back as 1953 the company slogan had been: "Toyota: Good Thinking, Good Products." This slogan had evolved from their famous "Good Ideas" suggestion system, which encouraged all Toyota workers to contribute ideas as to how to improve Toyota products and services. The company took enormous pride in this system and the practice became something of a ritual with each year's suggestions tallied and published for all to see. J.D. Power's auspicious visit provided the company with a new strategy that fit perfectly with their scheme to become the number one automobile manufacturer.

By 1970, other Japanese auto manufacturers had caught on to J.D. Power and began to follow Toyota's lead, paying thousands of dollars for CSIs of their own. Detroit, on the other hand, disdained Power's survey. As Doron P. Levin wrote in *Behind the Wheel at Chrysler: The Lee Iacocca Legacy*: "Detroit executives were coldly unimpressed: they believed their own research to be the finest in the world."[15]

By the time they belatedly realized the import companies' tactics were working, Toyota had the wherewithal in 1969 to invest $18.5 million in an advertising campaign. Accordingly, sales had risen to 130,000, creating a need to increase both staff and distributors.

The southeastern United States had yet to be developed, and for this project they researched the most successful dealers in the region. Naturally, they came across the name of James Moran, at the time a semi-retired Ford dealer.

Moran had been in the automotive industry since he was a very young man when he purchased a gas station in Chicago during the Depression. After serving in World War II, he returned home to buy his first used-car dealership and had soon acquired a few new-car dealerships as well. Moran turned his most successful operation, Courtesy Ford, into the world's largest Ford dealership, personally selling an impressive 1,800 cars a year. Moran retired to Florida in the late 1960s where he battled and won against cancer. He continued to build his empire of sales, leasing, financing and insurance businesses, and in 1966, he was offered one of his most lucrative yet.

At first he politely declined Toyota's offer of a franchise, but after being persuaded to drive one of their cars, he changed his mind. Moran was extremely impressed with the Toyota after it passed one of his ultimate durability tests: He threw the little car into reverse while cruising at 55 mph. "Nothing broke!" he exclaimed incredulously.[16] He enthusiastically endorsed the product to a group of potential dealers, promising they would become multi-millionaires selling Toyota. With equal confidence he assured Toyota officials that he could easily sell 10,000 vehicles. He admitted that it wasn't easy getting dealers to sign on, but reported that it was even more difficult for the dealers to get customers to drive the cars. But once they did, he said, they almost always bought them.[17]

Moran immediately turned to the most effective promotional tool he could find — television. He proceeded to buy 90 made-for-television movies so he could use Toyota ads in the commercial time-slots. He also took the unprecedented step of appearing in the ads himself. His tactics were effective. Before long, Moran had established the world's largest privately owned Toyota distributorship, Southeast Toyota Distributors, Incorporated. It served 162 dealers in five states: Florida, Georgia, Alabama, South Carolina, and North Carolina. Widely known for his philanthropy as well as his business acumen, Moran was inducted into the Entrepreneur Hall of Fame in 1995. The fact that Toyota sales had risen to 200,000 by 1970 was due in no small part to Moran's efforts. The sales were about to be boosted yet again by two new cars in the Toyota stable.

The 1969 Corona Mark II was intended to replace the Crown as Toyota's luxury model. The Mark II sedan was six inches longer than the base Corona and weighed 2,280 pounds. A two-door hardtop, four-door sedan, or four-door wagon were offered. Originally the Mark II carried an 1859-cc (113.4-cubic inch), 108-horsepower engine with a five-speed manual or three-speed automatic transmission. A new 1967-cc engine replaced the 1859-cc for 1972, after which the Corona Mark II became the Mark II MX with a 2254-cc, six-cylinder engine, which grew again to 2563 cubic centimeters by 1977.

After the Mark II came the sporty Celica ST coupe, introduced in 1971 and obviously geared toward both the young and young at heart. A journalist for Petersen Publishing remarked that the Celica's sporty look would "…do wonders for the playboy on a budget."[18]

The Celica was characterized by a Mustang-like long hood and short rear deck, with factory rally stripes, non-functional air louvers, and an interior designed to appeal to the would-be racer. The imitation wood-grain dash housed large round gauges that included a tachometer. Reclining bucket seats bracketed a console that traveled from the five-speed gearshift up into the dash in true sports-car fashion. To enhance the race-car image, an automatic transmission was not available. Under the

**"For the playboy on a budget"** said *Petersen's* of this 1971 Celica ST, but many others loved the car as well (courtesy Toyota Motor Sales Archives).

rear-opening hood was a cross-flow 1968-cc (120-cubic inch) in-line four which produced 97 horsepower and 106 ft-lb of torque at 3,600 rpm. Despite its looks, in actuality the Celica wasn't that fast — zero to sixty took 12.7 seconds and the quarter-mile 19 seconds, peaking at 74.5 mph. Top speed was estimated at 104 mph. The car rated an average of 24 mpg, and was priced at $2,598. Fast or not, it was a smash hit.[19]

Reviews were generally favorable. Wally Wyss reported on the car for *Motor Trend*'s August 1971 edition. Evoking images of Americana, Wyss wound up with this tongue-in-cheek observation: "Somewhere, somehow, a Japanese auto maker went and pulled a real sneakie — designing a car that is so apple-pie American — and amazingly like the first Mustang — that it could fit in just about anyplace — not just California where those nutballs will drive *anything* to be different."[20]

The Celica, although extremely popular, was unfortunately saddled with Toyota's reputation for below-par handling and braking. Regardless of its faults, people saw the Celica as "fun" and more economical than the 240Z.

In 1973 a fastback GT version was added to further emphasize the sports-car image Toyota was trying to cultivate. Although the GT came equipped with wider tires, a more sophisticated suspension, and five-speed transmission, *Car and Driver* gave the car a lukewarm review, calling its engine "an enigma … smooth at low speeds … but growing rough and exciting various unpleasant resonances…" at higher speeds.[21] Nevertheless, the Celica continued to sell well, eventually going on to win *Motor Trend*'s Import of the Year for 1978. *Car and Driver* reviewers, however, remained unimpressed, commenting on the Celica's lack of "sporting impulses," and concluding that: "Toyota has delivered the appearance of a GT, but not the spirit."[22] The Celica they tested was powered by a 2189-cc (134-cubic-inch), 95-horsepower engine with 122 ft-lb of torque at 2400 rpm.

In 1981 the Celica's engine was boosted to a 2.4 liter (144-cubic-inch). Also appearing that year was a convertible version called the Sunchaser. The following year the Celica was treated to a new angular design which sported pop-up headlights and an available two-tone black-and-silver paint scheme.

Before Toyota reached their first major milestone in 1975 (surpassing VW as the number-one import), the focus was very much on quality and economy, both of which were heavily emphasized in advertising campaigns of the time. A typical one in a series of "endurance" ads prominent in the late sixties and early seventies featured a 1966 Corona owned by Vic Tennison of Yucca Valley, California. The text boasted that the car had traveled 234,000 miles and was still going strong. "Oh sure, I've put it in the shop a couple of times," reported Tennison. "For instance, I needed new brake shoes at around 100,000 miles. And I think we put in new rings at 139,000 and another rear end at 175,000." He concluded: "You buy a good car. You take good care of it. It takes good care of you." Toyota joined in with their vow: "We promise you a car that's put together with care." At the bottom of the page the Toyota name was underlined with: "We're Quality Oriented."[23]

But sometimes even quality wasn't enough. At least it wasn't for the short-lived Carina which was introduced in 1972 and gone by 1973. While it used the same 1588-cc engine as the Corolla and had virtually the same body as the Corona, it would never reach the popularity of either. The Carina was thoroughly overshadowed by its older siblings, the Celica and Mark II. Toyota executives didn't believe in flogging a dead horse. Even when the beloved Mark II wore out its welcome in 1978, Toyota didn't hesitate to replace it with an even more luxurious model — the stylishly refined Cressida.

The Cressida came equipped with extensive power equipment, deluxe interior, superior sound system, air conditioning and power moonroof. The first generation Cressida contained a six-cylinder, 2.6-liter (168-cubic-inch) engine. Only two short years later the Cressida was completely restyled with a new 2.8-liter, 116-horsepower engine. The car had a 104.1 inch wheelbase from an overall length of 184.8 inches (sedan), weighed 2,851 pounds and retailed for $11,599 for the four-door sedan and $12,049 for the four-door wagon.[24]

During the 1980s the Cressida received a number of changes while it maintained Toyota's standard for luxury, but for all its attractions it failed to sell as well as Toyota's other flagship models. This was especially apparent during the aftermath of the second oil crisis when the car's particular brand of luxury seemed ill at ease in a company that emphasized economy. Even a decade later when Lexus took over from Cressida in 1990 buyers were still skeptical of Toyota as a high-end marque.

At the time of the Cressida's introduction in 1978, Toyota was selling nearly half a million cars a year.[25] Only six years earlier the company had sold their one-millionth vehicle (cumulative sales) in America. On September 1, 1972, a couple from Boston took purchase of the landmark vehicle from North Shore Toyota in Salem, Massachusetts.[26]

Toyota's journey to luxury was epitomized in this 1978 Cressida, which was loaded with standard equipment including four-wheel disc brakes and a power moonroof (courtesy Toyota Motor Sales Archives).

By 1975 Toyota was not only the largest automaker in Japan, but also the leading importer in the United States, surpassing the ever-popular Volkswagen as the number-one importer with sales of 328,918.[27]

The first fly in the ointment came from an unexpected quarter when the Honda Civic arrived on the fuel-starved scene in 1973, immediately dampening Toyota sales. Following that, the "in-between-fuel-crises" years (1974 to 1978) marked a downturn for all Japanese automakers and even Toyota was not quite immune. Fuel efficiency, emission controls and ongoing safety demands were juggled as Toyota strove for excellence. Through it all the company's philosophy remained steadfast — to continue to produce quality automobiles and fill every consumer need. To that end Toyota unveiled the Celica Supra in 1979, a high-end version of the Celica and one more capable of competing head-to-head with Datsun's latest Z, the 280.

The Celica gets serious — and a six-cylinder engine. This 1979 Celica Supra was the first of the line. It became known simply as the Supra in 1986 (courtesy Toyota Motor Sales Archives).

The Celica Supra's original in-line six-cylinder, 2560-cc (156-cubic-inch), single-overhead-cam carbureted engine was mated to a five-speed manual or four-speed automatic with overdrive. It was 103.5 inches long and weighed 2,866 pounds. In 1981 the car received an electronically fuel injected 2759-cc engine that produced 116 horsepower at 4,800 rpm and 145 ft-lb of torque at 3,600 rpm. Bore and stroke was 3.27" × 3.35" and compression measured at 8.0:1. Brakes were four-wheel discs and suspension consisted of McPherson struts in the front and a solid axle in the rear.

In 1979 *Motor Trend* pitted the Supra against the 280Z in an extensive comparison test. They timed the Supra in the zero-to-sixty in 11.5 seconds with the quarter-mile in 18.4 seconds at 74.6 mph. The 280Z's zero-to-sixty was 11.3 seconds.[28] In the final analysis, the pricier 280ZX (at $11,599 to the Supra's $9,500) came out with a slight advantage according to the editors. "The Supra is today, but the 280ZX is tomorrow," they prophesied.[29]

In 1982 a twin-cam, 145-horsepower 2.8-liter engine and new independent rear suspension improved the car's performance and ride.

In 1986 the Celica and the Celica Supra parted ways, with the Celica going front-wheel-drive with a turbo version offered in 1988 and the convertible coming back after a year's absence. After the split the Supra was allowed to come into its own with a 3.0-liter (180-cubic-inch), 200-horsepower engine. Anxious to prove that the car was more than just a luxury sports coupe, Toyota added an intercooled turbo for 1987 boosting the car to 230 horsepower. The Supra became the perfect car for the "showroom stock" racing circuit and quickly grew in status both on the track and as a collector's sports car.

The 1980s also ushered in the smallest Toyotas sold in America — the tiny Tercel introduced in 1980, and the Starlet, introduced in 1981.

The Corolla Tercel (as it was originally named) was Toyota's first front-wheel-drive model to go on sale in the United States, lagging well behind Japanese counterparts Subaru and Honda.

Available in a two-door coupe or three-door hatchback, the Corolla Tercel had a single-overhead-cam, 1.5-liter (89-cubic-inch) engine that produced a modest 60 horsepower. There was a choice of a four- or five-speed manual transmission or an optional three-speed automatic. The car was 161.4 inches long, weighed 1,900 pounds and retailed for $4,748 (base two-door coupe).

In 1983 it became known simply as the Tercel and a new four-wheel-drive "shift-on-the-fly" wagon with a six-speed (extra low gear) manual transmission was added to the popular line. Toyota built a huge advertising campaign around its first four-wheel-drive and front-wheel-drive vehicles, correctly assessing future market trends, if not the timing of those trends.

The Tercel became Toyota's ultimate utility car, a perfect blend of functionality and economy. As the 1980s progressed, the car became increasingly luxurious for its size and class, being totally redesigned in 1987 with a larger 78-horsepower engine and more refined interior. The wagon had disappeared in 1985, but the four-wheel-drive system was carried on in other models.

The Tercel entered the 1990s looking much like a 1980s Corolla, while the Corolla grew to 1980s Camry proportions.

In fact the Corolla's progress is probably one of the most interesting of all the Toyota models. Having been produced at the Toyota–GM facility, New United Motor Manufacturing International (NUMMI) in California since 1983, by 1986 the Corolla had a new model in the line — the FX16 — a front-drive, 16-valve, 1.6-liter hatchback. The FX16's twin-cam, fuel-injected engine produced 108 horsepower and was connected to a close-ratio five-speed transmission. Zero-to-sixty took 9.4 seconds with a top speed of 115 mph. The car had four-wheel disc brakes, a fuel rating of between 25 and 35 mpg, and retailed for approximately $9,850.[30]

Unfortunately there seemed to be little market for what appeared to be a sports car in an econo-box body. Disappointing sales figures forced the FX16 out of the Toyota lineup in 1988. A four-door sedan went into production at NUMMI in its stead — a new more aerodynamic Corolla.

With most of its angles gone in 1988, the Corolla finally joined the front-wheel-drive ranks. It was a larger and more mature-looking vehicle with four-wheel independent suspension and a 1.6-liter, 74-horsepower engine. Four-wheel drive was offered as an option on the Corolla sedan and wagon. The SR5 rear-wheel drive GT-S sports coupe and liftback, both of which featured a 16-valve, fuel-injected 112-horsepower engine, completed the line.

By 1993 there were seven versions of the Corolla, which no longer included the four-wheel drive wagon or the SR5 GT-S. Models with the DX trim package received a 1.8-liter engine good for 115 horsepower and 115 ft-lb of torque at 4800 rpm.

Not destined to share the prominence of either the Corolla or the Tercel was the short-lived rear-wheel-drive Starlet, Toyota's American "minicar" for 1981. *Car and Driver* called it a "…diminutive Scrooge-box."[31]

The Starlet was available only as a 58-horsepower, 1.3-liter three-door hatchback. The car was a disappointment to Toyota fans who expected something more than a rather lightweight (in all respects) minicar and their rejection of it was evident when it was unceremoniously dropped in 1984.

By 1981 five million Toyotas had been sold in the United States and new plants were going up in quick succession all over the world. While the Corolla, Tercel, and Celica were setting sales records, the company's next flagship — the Toyota Camry — made its debut in 1982. The Camry was produced to replace the aging Corona and to compete with the Honda Accord, which had a three-year head start on the market. To regain some of that share, the Camry was designed to "one-up" the Accord with a longer wheelbase of 102.4 inches (almost 6 inches longer than the Accord), as well as a more powerful 2.0-liter, 92-horsepower engine to pass Accord's 86-horsepower, 1.8-liter engine. John DiPietro, writing online for edmunds.com, labeled the first-generation Camry as being from the "…utilitarian school of design."[32] That didn't stop the multitudes of consumers who felt the attractive if square little car was perfect for their needs. Unlike the Accord, the Camry came as only a four-door sedan or four-door hatchback. Two trimlines were available — the DX basic level or the LE luxury level.

The appearance of the Camry sparked a "Pepsi-vs-Coke" war between the marques such as hadn't been seen since Chevrolet challenged Ford early in the twentieth century. As each generation of Camry appeared bringing with it more power and luxury, so did a new Accord arrive to challenge it. In 1988, in response to a totally redesigned Accord, the Camry received a thorough going-over, from the 2.0-liter 115-horsepower, 16-valve, twin-cam engine, to an upgraded interior with a quieter and smoother ride.

*Motor Trend* expressed delight with the new model: "Clearly, what we loved best about the Camry was the quality feel. Solid and well engineered. Plenty of storage space. Well-placed controls, outstanding climate control system and the road feel of a product costing several times more."[33]

A year later an even more impressive V-6, 2.5-liter, 153-horsepower model became available as did an all-wheel-drive, also known as the "All-Trac," model.

As Americans took the Camry to their hearts, Toyota decided it would be appropriate to build the car on American soil, and production commenced at Toyota's Kentucky plant. Being American-made boosted the car's popularity and by 1989 it was the fifth-best-selling car in America. It had also outgrown the compact category boundaries and Toyota accordingly referred to it as a mid-sized car.

By 1993 *Automobile* magazine was calling the Camry "the best car built in America."[34] The base engine was a 2.2-liter, 130-horsepower in-line four, with a 3.0-liter, 185-horsepower, twin-cam, four-valves-per-cylinder V-6 available on all 12 models

**The 1984 Camry LE was Toyota's family sedan benchmark. It is still their number-one seller (courtesy Toyota Motor Sales Archives).**

except the DX wagon. Other amenities included anti-lock brakes and driver's side airbag.

*Consumer Guide* reviewed the Camry and after raving over its power and features, asked "What's not to like? A hard, overly raked rearseat back, restricted vision directly aft—and cost. Toyota has let Camry prices drift upwards so that LE and LXE models now list near or above $20,000, even without options. That's a lot for a compact, even one this good, though high resale values somewhat offset the sticker shock." Nonetheless, they concluded that "…if you're shopping for a family car, don't decide until you drive this one."[35]

Also falling into the higher-cost category was perhaps the most interesting car Toyota ever released in the United States—apart from the 1967 2000GT—the MR2 sports car. The MR2 (standing for mid-engined runabout two-seater) had the distinction of being the first Japanese mid-engine sports car. Landing in America in February of 1985, the MR2 sparked an immediate debate over its merits. James M. Flammang remarked that "People tended to either love it or hate it."[36]

The MR2 was something of a novelty, but beneath the sharp-featured exterior was a borrowed engine—the same 1587-cc (97-cubic-inch) double-overhead-cam 16-valve powerplant that drove the Corolla SR5, producing 112 horsepower and 97 ft-lb of torque which in the MR2 could make zero to sixty in 8.73 seconds. Top speed was calculated at 116 mph. Compression was 9.4:1 with a maximum engine speed of 7500 rpm and a drag coefficient of 0.35.

**Japan's first mid-engined sports car on the American market, the daring MR2, introduced for the 1985 model year. Journalists said "You either love it or you hate it." It certainly gave the Pontiac Fiero a run for its money.**

The first generation MR2 was wedge-shaped in the fashion of the 1980 Triumph TR8 with sharply angled rooflines and a rear spoiler. The car was 154.5 inches long, 65.6 inches wide, 49.2 inches high and weighed 2,600 pounds. The wheelbase was 91.3 inches, and ground clearance was a mere five inches.

Driving the rear wheels was either a five-speed manual or optional four-speed automatic transmission. The final drive ratio was 3.53:1. Front suspension consisted of McPherson struts, coil springs and an anti-roll bar, while in the rear there were struts and trailing arms. There were disc brakes all around, and leather trim and power windows were optional equipment.

*Motor Trend* reviewed the MR2 in January of 1985 and had plenty of good things to say about the car. Comparisons were inevitably drawn to the Pontiac Fiero (to the detriment of the Pontiac) and the MR2 was allocated an eight-page spread. Reviewers seemed not to be bothered by the lack of power-assisted steering, the noticeable wind and exhaust noise, nor were they concerned with rear-end breakaway, which they referred to as "gradual." As they enthusiastically concluded: "By far the biggest problem with the MR2, however, is that there won't be enough to go around. Due to production limitations, we'll only get 3000 per month in the U.S. and the suggested retail will be around $11,000 or $12,000. Unless you were born in a pumpkin, you know this thing has got to be the biggest plum Toyota dealers ever got."[37]

In 1987 the car was dressed up with a removable-panel T-bar roof, and a year later the engine was boosted to 115 horsepower and 100 ft-lb of torque, with a supercharged 145-horsepower model on offer.

The next edition of the MR2 came in 1991 when the car was completely restyled and available in two versions—a 130-horsepower, 2.2-liter base model, or a 2.0-liter, 200-horsepower turbocharged edition that could move from zero to sixty in 6.9 seconds. The turbo replaced the troublesome and expensive supercharger.

Many loved the MR2's speed and style, but others complained of cramped quarters, restricted engine access, too much noise and a tendency to fish-tail on high-speed cornering. To correct at least one of these problems, the suspension received a thoroughly new treatment for 1993 to reduce rear-end breakaway. To accomplish this, the MR2 was lowered and equipped with stiffer shocks, springs, and bushings, while the rear toe-control arms were lengthened. The tires were upgraded from 195/60HR14s on the front and 205/60HR14s on the rear to 195/55VR15s and 225/50VR15s respectively. A driver's airbag was now standard, but anti-lock brakes were still optional. The new MR2 was longer at 164.2 inches with a 94.5 inch wheelbase. It retailed between $18,368 and $23,998.[38]

*Consumer Guide* writers referred to the car's cost, commenting that the "...solid Toyota workmanship" came at a price: "(The) MR2 isn't cheap ... but it's the most affordable mid-engine car this side of an Acura NSX, and good enough to earn our "Recommended" rating in the sports/GT class."[39]

Much less exotic than the MR2 was the Paseo, introduced in 1992 to replace the Corolla GTS. Based on the Tercel chassis, the four-cylinder, port-injected, double-overhead-cam, 1.5-liter Paseo generated 100 horsepower at 6400 rpm and 94 ft-lb of torque at 3,200 rpm. The engine was linked to either a five-speed manual or four-speed automatic transmission. It was 163.2 inches long with a 93.7-inch wheelbase, and quite light at 2,070 pounds. Fuel economy was rated at between 28 and 34 miles per gallon (five-speed).

Despite the fact that a convertible version was introduced in 1997, the Paseo failed to stimulate interest and production ceased in 1998. Toyota, however, could well afford a few missteps, with the Corolla and Camry continuing to receive top honors and generating millions of dollars in sales. The Camry was rated as the best-selling car in America for 1997.

At the end of the 1980s it seemed that Toyota had all segments of the market well tied up with a "car for every taste" (Alfred P. Sloan's philosophy that there is a market for all types of cars, and automakers should cater to every sector of the market)—but it had not yet completed its mission. Toyota's intention to conquer all became apparent at the 1989 Los Angeles Auto Show when it proudly spotlighted its new Lexus luxury car division.

Piqued that Honda had beaten them to it with the Acura introduced three years earlier, the first Lexus introduced was built with dominance in mind. Tagged the ES 250, the 1990 entry-level flagship carried a 2.5-liter, double-overhead-cam, 156-horsepower V-6. The ES 250 paved the way for its larger sibling, the LS 400, powered by a mighty 250-horsepower, 4.0-liter V-8 with 260 ft-lb of torque at 4,400 rpm. Both sedans were rear-wheel drive.[40]

In 1992 the ES 250 moved over for the ES 300, now a 3.0-liter V-6 four-door front-wheel-drive sedan with 185 horsepower and 195 ft-lb of torque. The 24-valve V-6 was capable of zero to sixty in a silent 8.1 seconds. The ES 300 was 187.8 inches

Toyota's upscale division, Lexus, was established in 1989. The cars pictured here are the LS400 and the ES250, both for 1990. With these cars Toyota proved it could do luxury very well indeed (courtesy Toyota Motor Sales Archives).

long with a 103.1-inch wheelbase and a weight of 3,362 pounds. Mileage for the five-speed came in at between 18 and 24 mpg and the car could be had for $27,500, base price. A driver's side airbag and antilock brakes were standard equipment, as were remote keyless entry, alarm system, power package, tilt steering, multi-adjustable power seats and cruise control. Options included a power moonroof, leather interior, heated seats and remote 6-CD auto changer. Toyota strove to dispel the notion that the ES was merely a high-end Camry by producing a more refined, pillar-less bodyshell and an upgraded interior, but even as late as November 2001, *Motor Trend* reviewers commented that "It's (the ES 300) still built off the Camry platform, but those roots— themselves more refined than ever — seem less apparent than before."[41]

The new LS 400, on the other hand, kept its rear-wheel-drive layout but added wider tires, 16-inch alloy wheels, and larger brake discs. For a base price of $46,600, a battery of techno-gadgetry could be had — everything from outside temperature display, brake wear warning light, seven-way power seats, and volume-adjustable keyless entry warning, to air filters and deodorizers for the automatic climate control system. A high-end Nakamichi audio system, traction control and electronic air suspension with memory were options on an already loaded vehicle.[42]

Also new were the Lexus SC 300 and SC 400 sport coupes, rear-wheel-drive models based on a shorter LS 400 platform. The SC 300 contained a 225-horsepower 3.0-liter in-line six, while the SC 400 shared the LS 400's 250-horsepower V-8 and four-speed automatic transmission. The 400 made zero to sixty in 7.3 seconds, while the 300 took a bit longer at 8.1 seconds.[43]

By the millennium, the Lexus was available in six versions—the ES 300, GS 300 and GS 430, IS 300, LS 430, and SC 430. New for 2002 was a SportCross wagon along the lines of the IS 300. Toyota also added a race-bred L-Tuned version of the IS 300 in 2002, conceived by Toyota Racing Development. For an extra $10,000 or so (including special suspension and wheel package), the IS 300 could run with 223 horsepower at 5,800 rpm and 218 ft-lb of torque at 3800 rpm. Zero to sixty would take 6.56 seconds and the quarter-mile 15.02 seconds at 93.19 mph.[44]

The Lexus name has become synonymous with luxury in America, putting Cadillac and Lincoln in the shade, and giving its compatriots Acura and Infiniti stiff competition. Mercedes-Benz and BMW have not gone unaffected either by Toyota's onslaught of luxury models.

While Lexus spun in its own direction, Toyota carefully nurtured its staple models, the Corolla, Camry, Celica, and MR2 (now called the MR2 Spyder), with additions at suitable intervals. The replacement for the Cressida, which was dropped in 1991, arrived in 1995 as the Avalon, a large five-passenger sedan with an all-aluminum, 3.0-liter, 24-valve, 192-horsepower engine.

Next came the sport versions of the Camry, the Solara coupe and convertible that arrived in 1999, sharing the Camry's basic 3.0-liter engine. These attractive cars were much larger and less controversial than the economy-level model that made its debut at the 1999 North American International Auto Show.

Wearing the name Echo, the Toyota that replaced the perennially popular Tercel elicited both praise and criticism for its unconventional "high-box" style. No one could question the efficiency that came from its 1.5-liter, 108-horsepower, twin-cam four cylinder with variable valve timing which allowed 45 mpg, but there were many questions concerning its design and safety. Long-time automotive critic Edmunds feature writer Chris Wardlaw panned the Echo under the heading "*Brand-New Cheap Toyota.*" After criticizing the styling, lack of power equipment, seat adjustments, lack of side air-bags, price, resale value and safety in crash tests, Wardlaw concluded: "…Toyota has missed the mark. (The) Echo is too expensive, and is not designed to meet the needs of North American consumers."[45]

Toyota took exception to the safety accusations and took pains to point out the Echo did indeed satisfy the standards for crash tests in its category. Aside from such criticism, and mixed opinion, the Echo continues to sell well as Toyota's base model.

If the accolades were lacking for the Echo, there was no such deficit for Toyota's very first road-ready hybrid vehicle. Introduced in 2000 as the Prius, the gas-electric hybrid ran with a 1.5-liter 70-horsepower engine fortified by a 44-horsepower electric motor. Mileage was rated at 52 city and 45 highway. Originally intending to release only 12,000 of the cars per year, Toyota sold 15,556 in 2001, and upgraded production to 17,000 for 2002.[46]

Taking a different market approach for the Prius, Toyota launched an internet

Toyota's response to the Environmental Protection Agency's continued pleas to reduce emissions was the 1998 Toyota Prius gas-electric hybrid (courtesy Toyota Motor Sales Archives).

campaign with an exclusive ordering system that allowed the customer to communicate directly with the company. With oil prices skyrocketing with each round of unrest in the Middle East, demand for the Prius and other hybrids is on the increase. Toyota planned a market launch for its first fuel-cell vehicle for the end of 2003, after road tests in California and Japan.

The Toyota Matrix, a 1.8-liter, 130- or 180-horsepower cross-over utility vehicle (CUV) with optional all-wheel drive, arrived in February 2002. Made in Canada, the Matrix was jointly developed with the Pontiac Vibe and is available in three versions—standard, XR and XRS. The XRS carries the 180-horsepower engine and 16-inch alloy wheels, while the standard and XR models have the more sedate 130-horsepower engine.

Success seems to beget success for the Toyota Motor Company and it not only dominates the home market in the Japan, but is poised to take over the American one as well. Sales that were strong in the 1970s have grown ever more robust and the potential seems limitless. Toyota has made no secret of the fact that it wishes to capture over 10 percent of the global market.

While there are many who admire that kind of raw ambition and drive, there are those who find it distasteful. Automotive analyst Maryann Keller noted that even in the 1990s Toyota was being seen as "too big and too successful," violating the long-held Japanese tradition of *kyosei*, or "symbiotic competition."[47] Obviously not everyone agreed, a fact that became evident when *Fortune* magazine rated Toyota the "Most Admired American Company" in the Motor Vehicle and Parts category.[48]

Toyota Motor Company has come a long way from an incident in 1948 when it responded to an American's request for information with a request of its own: "In this war-devastated Japan, we are having a hard time keeping up our production. It is very difficult to get information on the latest developments in the automotive industry around the world. We are deeply interested in the manufacture of American automobiles and trucks. Kindly send us automobile and truck catalogues."[49]

Some have criticized Toyota and Japanese automakers in general for copying the American automakers, a charge Japanese pioneer automakers have not entirely refuted—at least not in the early years. But when Toyota executives suffered the rejection of their first "copy" in America, they swallowed their pride and did their homework. Ironically, by the time the American manufacturers were scrambling to repair their rushed-into-production compacts and sub-compacts in the early 1970s, Toyota was more concerned about the progress in America of its long-time rival, the Nissan Motor Company.

# 6

## Datsun's Debut — Los Angeles, 1958

There is a rare photograph in circulation showing five Datsuns sitting in a semi-circle under the bright lights of the Los Angeles Auto Show. The group consists of a PLG220 pick-up truck, two PL310 sedans, a WPL310 wagon, and the SP213 sports car. This photograph has been identified as being taken at the 1958 show, captioned "the first Datsuns most Americans had ever seen."[1]

This photo has most likely been improperly dated, for two of the vehicles shown from the PL310 series weren't introduced in the United States until late 1959. Furthermore, David Halberstam's well-documented book *The Reckoning* states that the very first Datsuns introduced to America (there were three of them) were shown at the 1957 Los Angeles Auto Show. These models would have been the 1958 PL210, the PLG220 pickup truck, and possibly the SP211 or SP212 sports car.

Halberstam gives a finely detailed account of the steps that lead Nissan to export to the United States, which he claims began with the company's victory at the 1958 Australian Mobil Gas Trial. "So it was, after the triumph in Australia, that the people at Nissan began to think seriously about exporting cars. They had always known that they would have to export…. Still they were nervous about exporting to America … it was one thing to sell buses or trucks to the Thais and another to sell cars to Americans."[2]

Nissan, according to Halberstam's research, was not willing to export and had to be persuaded by people like young executive Yutaka Katayama and Nobe Wakatsuki, manager of Marubeni Trading Company's Los Angeles division.

Nissan officials later dismissed the notion that they needed to be prodded into exporting or that the Australian success had anything to do with it. If they were indeed hesitant it was understandable. Producing just about eight hundred cars in 1950 was hardly indicative of a company ready to conquer the world market, or at any rate the American market, within eight years' time.

Fortunately for Nissan, Wakatsuki had a great deal to offer. For one thing he lived in Los Angeles and had gotten to know Americans and how important automobiles were to them. For another, he could speak passable English and was able to field questions from potential customers and distributors. Wakatsuki didn't approach Nissan without doing his homework. He informed them that the market was open for automobiles and that exporting them from Japan was really quite simple, especially when compared to Japan's strict import regulations and procedures. The window of opportunity was there. "In the fall of 1957 there was to be an auto show in Los Angeles and Wakatsuki exhorted Nissan to send some cars."[3]

Sadly, the cars they sent seemed unlikely to impress Americans who not only had the pick of American luxury, speed, and style, but also an array of other imports. How would he ever sell these cars, wondered Wakatsuki, whose heart sank as he watched the vehicles being unloaded. In his view the Datsun "…was the ugliest thing he had ever seen."[4]

Nissan archival information indicates these first vehicles made a good impression, but press reports of the time seemed to support Wakatsuki's pessimistic outlook. The *Detroit News*, perhaps at a loss for words, summed up Datsun's presence by stating the obvious: "The Datsun is in the small car field."[5]

Other journalists weren't much more enthusiastic, with some hinting that the import market had already been filled. But while the *Detroit News* concluded that "Company officials did not disclose if there are any plans for the sale of the car in this country,"[6] plans were already underway for export.

Halberstam concludes his story of the Nissan's American debut thus: "With a feeling that bordered on terror, Nissan had decided to export to the United States. The Japanese were going to try to sell their strong but sad little car in the land of Gorham."[7] (An American mechanical engineer, William Gorham, had moved to Japan and gained legendary status among Japanese automobile manufacturers for his prowess.)

By August of 1958 distributorships on both the West and East Coast were operating. Since Marubeni could not handle both coasts, Nissan hired the Mitsubishi Trading Company to negotiate in the East. Subsequently Marubeni entered into an agreement with Woolverton Motors of North Hollywood while Mitsubishi negotiated with Luby Chevrolet of New York. Woolverton became the Western Datsun Distributorship while Luby became the Luby Datsun Distributorship. Shortly afterwards, Nissan also had distributorships in Honolulu, Hawaii, managed by the Von Hamm-Young Company, as well as one in Dallas, Texas under the direction of the Clarence Talley Automobile Company.

Initial demand for franchises was satisfactory and by the end of 1960 there were close to 50 dealerships in the United States. Thus established, Nissan Motor Corporation U.S.A. opened its doors in September of 1960 in Gardena, California, capitalized at one million dollars. Initially it was managed by a staff of about 20 people.

The task ahead was to convince Americans of the quality of the product. But if the American consumer had not yet caught on to the Datsun, a man named Deming had. In June of 1960 Nissan won the tenth annual Deming Prize for excellence in engineering, the first Japanese automobile company to win the prestigious award.

*1958*

**DATSUN – Combines Rugged Dependability with Comfort and Economy !!**

**DATSUN 1000 SEDAN**

DATSUN

**A little Japan in America. Calling this 1958 Datsun 1000 "The Little Giant from Japan," Nissan offered the car in "a wide range of beautiful shades" including red and white.**

Nissan's American managers were Soichi Kawazoe and Yutaka Katayama. Kawazoe was put in charge of the East Coast while Katayama (who soon become known simply as "Mr. K."), headed up the West Coast division. While Kawazoe was strictly a company man trying to work his way up by paying his dues, Katayama was not. His differences and rebelliousness earned him his ticket to America, at that time considered something of a demotion. Once there he remained virtually unsupported due to his volatile relationship with president Katsuji Kawamata, which extended into the later reign of Nissan U.S.A. president Takashi Ishihara.

Unperturbed by his position as Nissan's black sheep, Katayama doggedly proceeded to enlist dealers in the traditional Japanese manner — door-to-door soliciting. His battle was arduous considering the first Datsuns were no more suitable to American driving conditions than the Toyopet Crown was. Nissan's own salesmen called them "mobile coffins" because they trapped the heat and lacked air conditioning.[8]

The car they were attempting to sell was the PL210, based on the Austin A50. It had a four-cylinder, 988-cc (60.2-cubic-inch), 37-horsepower engine with 49.2 ft-lb of torque at 2,400 rpm, and a compression ratio of 7.5:1. The engine had solid valve lifters and only three main bearings on the crank. Current was supplied by a 12-volt electrical system and fuel delivery was through a single-barrel Hitachi carburetor. The three-speed transmission was synchronized except for first gear, and the steer-

The first Datsun to set wheels on American soil, the 1958 PL210. "PL" stood for passenger, left-hand drive. This car was based on the British Austin A-50. Sales numbered under a hundred in its first year.

ing was of the worm-and-roller type. Suspension on both ends consisted of semi-elliptic springs and solid axles, with a stabilizer bar added to the rear.

James M. Flammang described this car in his *Standard Catalog of Imported Cars 1946–1990*: "Squarish in appearance, with its door hinges exposed, the little Datsun four-door sedan had front-hinged doors, front and rear vent windows, and rode an 87.4-inch wheelbase.... The grille was made up of thick horizontal bars, with 'DAT-SUN' nameplate on the top bar. Round parking lights stood directly below the single headlamps."[9] He also made note of the little extras that would come to be a hallmark of Japanese cars—things like a tool kit, under-hood worklight, glovebox, and passenger handgrips.

Unfortunately a Japanese Austin held little appeal for American buyers in search of something new and exciting, not to mention functional. As the editors of *Petersen's Complete Book of Datsun* recalled: "Datsun first tried the U.S. market in the late '50s with a rather miserable little sedan that was frankly a Japanese copy of an equally miserable English car. It didn't sell too well, for the same reasons that small English sedans have never sold well in the U.S.—lack of power and indifferent engineering."[10]

Yet Datsun advertisements of the period displayed a certain pathetic bravado. One full-page ad headlined: "Datsun — The Foreign Car CLASSIC," concluding: "The *only* fine car combining weight plus economy. $1616 poe. The Outstanding Import Value."[11]

Classic or not, the consumers didn't seem to be interested. A four-man team was promptly dispatched from Nissan to study the market and make the necessary improvements to the Datsuns. This team found themselves faced with many of the same problems as their counterparts at Toyota — excessive engine vibration, lack of

**LUBY DATSUN DISTRIBUTORS, LTD.**
*107-36 Queens Boulevard, Forest Hills 75, New York City • BOulevard 3-7555*

Dear Sir:

     We are pleased to have this opportunity to introduce you to the Datsun, the newest and most important car to arrive on the American Market.

     The Datsun is manufactured in Japan by Nissan Motor Co., Japan's outstanding manufacturer of quality motor vehicles for over twenty years.

     Here, for the first time is a car specifically engineered for the American Motorist. Embodying the fine quality and workmanship economically possible in Japan, the 4 door Datsun Sedan combines 40 mile per gallon economy with over 2000 pound comfort and safety.

     Combining a 37 H.P. water cooled engine under the hood with a four speed forward synchromesh transmission, with American style gear shift on steering column, the performance of the Datsun is so outstanding it must be driven to be appreciated.

     Standard features of the Datsun are numerous. They include: complete vinyl interior, full front and rear seats, front and rear bumper guards, dual electric windshield wipers, directional lights, underhood lamp, front and rear ashtrays, undercoating, arm rests, safety door locks, interior light, glove compartment and map pockets on doors, hydraulic brakes and 12 volt electric system, to mention a few.

     With a retail price of $1,799. P.O.E., the Datsun is the one car of superior value in America today.

     For further information regarding the Datsun do not hesitate to call or write us.

                    Very truly yours,

                    LUBY DATSUN DISTRIBUTORS, LTD.

                    William Lane
                    Sales Promotion

*The Datsun Motor Car / Designed in Japan For Superior Value*

A letter from Luby Datsun Distributors, first East Coast distributor, enlisting dealers. "We are pleased to have this opportunity to introduce you to the Datsun, the newest and most important car to arrive on the American market." Signed William Lane, Sales Promotion. June 16, 1958.

Datsun's 1958 1000 truck. Japanese gardeners and "crazy Californians" loved the little pickup. Its strong sales allowed Nissan to maintain a presence in the United States (courtesy Nissan Motor Corporation USA).

performance, sub-standard brakes, poor heating and ventilation, and difficult cold-starting. When they filed their report (following some terrifying but amusing incidents on the Los Angeles freeway), to Nissan president Kawamata, they were told to sell the pickup truck and fix what they could on the car.

Katayama had mined a wide and varied market for the durable Datsun truck, ranging from young business executives and students, to farmers and the multitudes of Japanese gardeners in Southern California. With the same engine as the PL210 and a one-quarter-ton payload it was easy to operate and park; it was also economical and needed little maintenance.

Realizing the potential market for the pick-up was even larger than they could imagine, Katayama urged his superiors to expand exports but was firmly told to concentrate his efforts on passenger cars. He responded by demanding that the cars be improved to at least meet American standards. That the PL210 had failed was evident not only in the poor sales records but also in automotive trade magazine reviews. *Road and Track* was generous in calling it "...a sturdy, if uninspired, performer,"[12] but such reviews were hardly the stuff of legends. And although a smattering of journalists tried to find something positive to say about the Datsun, the depth of their aversion was not fully appreciated until the company released its first popular car, which naturally invited comparisons.

Halberstam was blunt in his assessment of the situation: "...the first Datsun in America was a disaster. It sold for $1616, and both Katayama and Kawazoe often wondered why anyone bothered to buy it."[13] He also noted that "Katayama's attempt to get Tokyo to upgrade and Americanize the car was a constant struggle."[14]

But the abysmal sales records could not be disputed and Nissan poured all its efforts into the building of its next car, the PL310, which arrived in America in late 1959 and went on the market in 1960. The PL310 is historically important by virtue of the fact that it was the first of Japan's renowned Bluebird line. Considered a lucky symbol in Japan, Nissan sincerely hoped this Bluebird would live up to its name in the American market as well as it had in Japan, where it ran neck-and-neck with Toyota's Corona in what was known as the "BC war."

It is worth taking the time here to explain the origins of Datsun's vehicle designations, which have caused a great deal of confusion over the years. All vehicles were assigned a factory code number, e.g. 210, along with a type and drive classification, e.g., "PL" (passenger, left-hand drive), PLG (pick-up), or "SP" (sport). They were also given numerical identifiers especially for the American market. The PL210 was sold in the United States as the Datsun 1000; the PL310 was the 1200, the PL410 and PL411 were the 1300, and the RL411 was more commonly known as the 1600sss (super sport sedan). The SPL311 sold as the Sports 1600.

In addition to these numbers, Nissan also tried to market the cars in the United States under their names— Bluebird for the PL310 and Fairlady for the SPL211-212. While the names remain to this day in the Japanese market, Americans soon rejected them in favor of their numbers.

Even more confusing was Nissan's practice of adding a single digit to each number as it changed years— hence the PL310 became the PL311 and then the PL312 before it rolled over into the four-hundred series.

In the interest of consistency, the original factory codes are used in this text, which is how most Japanese-car aficionados refer to them. With the advent of the PL510, the cars became known simply by their numbers— 510, 610, 710, etc.

The PL310 was Nissan's first all-Japanese design and came in either a sedan or station wagon version. It was powered by a cast-iron in-line four-cylinder, 1189-cc (72.5-cubic-inch) engine with overhead valves and a lateral camshaft that generated 48 horsepower at 4,800 rpm. The PL310 carried the same transmission as the PL210. The chassis was flat and front suspension was made up of coil springs, wishbones and shock absorbers, while the rear featured a rigid axle with leaf springs. There were drum brakes for both front and rear.[15]

Nissan also introduced a sports car in 1959, the SPL211, the first of the Fairlady series. It was replaced in 1960 by the SPL212, and then again in 1961 by the SPL213 which was introduced at the 1962 New York Auto Show.

This car was fitted with an 1189-cc, 60-horsepower engine and a four-speed stick-shift transmission with a final drive ratio of 4.63:1. Its body was made of fiberglass-reinforced plastic, and side curtains stood in for windows while a snap-on tonneau cover made a roof. Top speed was clocked at 81 mph.[16]

The attractive little four-seater roadster looked much like an earlier Austin Healey with a curving arch up the sides, a rounded trunk, oval grille and whitewall tires. A special red-and-white two-tone paint scheme was available. But the car was not a success. As write Mike Lawrence noted in his *A to Z of Sports Cars*: "...only a brave, or foolish man would have predicted the line's success on the strength of this car."[17]

Despite the attraction of a roadster and the improved power and appearance of the PL310, sales remained flat. This most likely could be attributed to the relatively old-fashioned styling of the PL310, as well as its below-par performance — zero to sixty took 27.5 seconds with a top speed of between 75 and 85 mph. Minimally revised versions of the PL310, numbered the PL311 and PL312, were introduced in 1960 and 1961 and also failed to perk up sales. With expenses mounting and tensions peaking it was more crucial than ever that Nissan produce a viable car since there were now almost 150 dealers in the field. These first Datsun dealers were typically less affluent and usually couldn't afford a domestic car dealership, although some of these actually sold a few imports on the side. Said Halberstam: "They were, in truth, a most unlikely group, with a high incidence of eccentricity."[18]

The records are not clear regarding exactly who was the very first Datsun dealer in the United States, but certainly Universal City Nissan of Los Angeles was among the pioneers, as was Ray Lemke, a former auto mechanic turned dealer. Lemke is described in *The Reckoning* as "...the perfect new Datsun dealer; he was hungry and he knew cars."[19]

Other pioneer dealers included Bedford Nissan, operated in Ohio by Phillip Greenberg; Stang Motor Sales and Tri-City Motors, both of which were based in Ohio as well. A large percentage of these dealers reported that the parent company treated them as partners.

Katayama certainly placed great importance on dealer relations and made it a point to deliver as many vehicles in person as he was able to. Even though his English was sketchy at best, he managed to convey his belief in clear and open communication between all parties. Katayama had closely observed Volkswagen's success in the United States and gleaned from it the magic ingredients—good service and availability of parts. He was against having large and impersonal trading companies distributing the Datsuns, believing that they were interested purely in profits. Customers came first, quality was all, according to Katayama. He once alluded to this philosophy in an interview long after he had retired: "(A) car itself is not a kind of porcelain ... we are not selling the body. We are selling the efficiency of the car."[20]

Although at that early stage the dealerships were something of a rag-tag group, Katayama and Kawazoe found they had less trouble with them than they did with the company itself. It was little wonder then that between the unpopularity of the product and the difficult management, vehicle sales for 1962 totaled a mere 2,629.[21]

It wasn't until 1963–64 that things began to turn around for Nissan with the arrival of a new sports car, the SPL310, and the first of the 400 series, the PL410.

The SPL310 originally housed a small jump seat in the back, but became a two-seater shortly thereafter. There were single-barrel and double-barrel carbureted versions of the 1488-cc (90.8-cubic-inch) engine, with the double-barrel putting out 85 horsepower with a compression ratio of 9.0:1 and 92 ft-lb of torque at 4,400 rpm. The now lower and much trimmer car had roll-up windows and a radio. It retailed for $1,996.[22]

More significant to the line was the newest Datsun passenger car, the PL410, available in a sedan or station wagon, with the all-steel uni-body designed by Pininfarina. The car featured quad headlights, a narrower "eggcrate" grille and streamlined trim with none of the chubby stodginess of the PL310. Comparisons have since been drawn between the PL410 and the BMW 1600.

The PL410 was powered by an in-line four-cylinder 1299-cc (72.5-cubic-inch) engine that produced 60 horsepower and 67 ft-lb of torque at 3,600 rpm. The car was 157.5 inches long, weighed 1,980 pounds (sedan) and retailed for between $1,600 and $1,800. Available transmissions were a three-speed or four-speed manual with a 4.11:1 final gear ratio. There were wishbones and coil springs on the front and a solid axle with semi-elliptic springs on the back.

Without seeing much change for 1965 other than a modified grille, the PL410 turned into the PL411 in 1966. Even then it kept the same body but with a double-barrel carburetor, seven more horsepower (67) and 77 ft-lb of torque at 2,800 rpm. It also was fractionally shorter than its predecessor and a few pounds heavier, which Nissan equated with greater durability. A stabilizer bar was added to the front suspension, and front discs replaced the old drums.

In 1964, *Car and Driver* reviewed the 410 under the heading: "Japan's cars are getting better and better all the time." Their impressions were as follows: "We like it. If its ride was up to modern standards we'd love it. Ride, however, is an extremely subjective area of automotive performance, and there are people who think that 'Early English Rigid' is exactly what a modern car should be. Stiffness not withstanding, this little car does everything an economy car is supposed to do, and we like its spirit. One thing's for sure, any design that can withstand the rigors of Japanese road and traffic conditions has to be pretty doggone durable, and that's a highly laudable thing in itself."[23]

Floyd Clymer looked at the car a year later in the November edition of *Auto Topics* magazine, and raved over its new and more powerful engine, "rugged all-steel unitized body," "rich vinyl upholstery … 33 mpg and road hugging big car ride."[24]

In 1967 the RL411 was added to the 400 series (which ended that year) and was the first "sss" model — a "racing/rally" version of the basic PL411. As such it was equipped with a more muscular 1595-cc (97.3-cubic-inch) in-line four producing 96 horsepower, 103 ft-lb of torque at 4,000 rpm and a 9.0:1 compression ratio. This engine was a very significant one for Nissan, marking the company's move to five main bearings, dual Hitachi SU carburetors and an all-synchronized four-speed gearbox. A three-speed Borg Warner automatic was available as an exotic option.

Robert Schilling reviewed the RL411 for *Motor Trend*'s March 1967 edition under the heading "Detroit's Economy Car Gap." Considered the best features of the car were its "quick-starting, peppy engine … along with the excellent gearbox."

Worst features were "the harshness of the ride" and that the "headlight dimmer switch is incorporated into the fore-and-aft motion of the turn signal control." Handling was evaluated as "precise and predictable if not sporty," and room and comfort were found to be "adequate" with "very comfortable" seats.[25]

Datsuns were finally catching on. In 1963 there had been just over 250 dealers selling around 4,000 vehicles.[26] Only three short years later sales had jumped to 29,239.[27]

Nissan's advertising before the success of the 400 series consisted of low-budget black-and-white brochures and small print ads. A typical ad was represented by

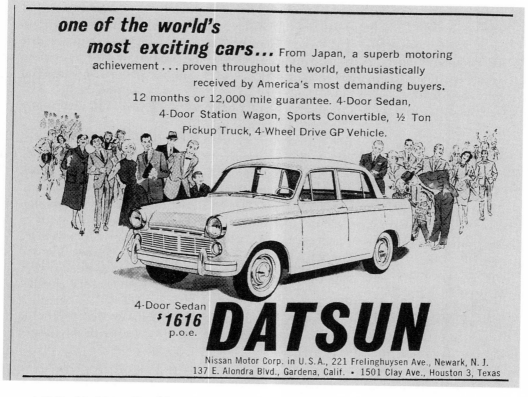

**one of the world's most exciting cars...** From Japan, a superb motoring achievement . . . proven throughout the world, enthusiastically received by America's most demanding buyers. 12 months or 12,000 mile guarantee. 4-Door Sedan, 4-Door Station Wagon, Sports Convertible, ½ Ton Pickup Truck, 4-Wheel Drive GP Vehicle.

4-Door Sedan
**$1616**
p.o.e.
# DATSUN

Nissan Motor Corp. in U.S.A., 221 Frelinghuysen Ave., Newark, N. J.
137 E. Alondra Blvd., Gardena, Calif. • 1501 Clay Ave., Houston 3, Texas

A 1962 ad in *Motor Trend* for the Datsun 310, or Bluebird — a name Americans rejected.

the quarter-page, black-and-white illustrated layout in the September 1962 edition of *Motor Trend* magazine. An ink rendering of the PL310, looking much like a miniature Checker cab and surrounded by crowds of admirers, was described in the headline as "One of the world's most exciting cars."[28]

With cash beginning to flow these ads evolved into full-page color spreads which began to appear in the popular press and trade magazines. Money was set aside to produce a sixty-second television clip featuring the four-wheel-drive Patrol which had been introduced to the market in 1964. Famed American cowboy Roy Rogers was enlisted to appear in these television ads which boosted the image of the rugged Jeep-like Patrol. The Patrol was much more successful than the Cedric, the larger and more luxurious sedan that came to America in 1960 and limped along in the market for five years before it was withdrawn.

Nissan finally turned its first modest profit in America the year the Patrol appeared. Sales had exceeded five hundred per month out of some 367 dealers. One of those was Bob Dailey who sold Datsuns out of his Chula Vista, California, location which had opened in 1965, eventually becoming Mossy Nissan.

Bob and Charles Melloy of Albuquerque, New Mexico, also took on the franchise, adding it to an assortment of British cars, DKWs, and Studebakers. The Melloys were impressed enough with the Datsun to "order seven or eight truckloads over the phone." They did, however, feel some improvements were necessary, as they recalled "...the floormats and upholstery were cheap," which were quickly replaced with better ones. The Melloys were pleased to deal with Nissan, finding that the company "...treated us like family." Customer response was varied but on the whole favorable. There were the inevitable naysayers and racially biased who asked why the Melloys were selling "slant-eyed cars," but these were few. Melloy Nissan, now managed by Bob Hayes, has been in business for 45 years and is currently thriving.[29]

Sales for Nissan had first materialized on the West Coast for the same reasons they had done so for the Toyota Motor Corporation. The East Coast was traditionally a more difficult environment, both geographically and demographically. Brock Yates related a telling incident concerning location as well as American attitudes: "During the early 1960s a New York State Datsun dealer folded, a not uncommon occurrence in those days, and a large auto finance firm was left with a stock of unwanted, presumably unsalable cars. The firm decided to let their salesmen drive the leftovers. Accustomed to plush Impalas and Bonnevilles, the salesmen despised the narrow midget "Jap" cars and did everything they could to destroy them. They refused to lubricate the bearings, they rode the clutches, over-revved the engines, jammed the gears and left them to rust in the bleak winters. But the ugly duckling Datsuns refused to die. They plugged ahead under the awesome abuses, generating a grudging, if confused, respect among men who had grown up with the idea of "tinny" Jap goods embedded in their brains."[30]

But if sales were slow to pick up in America, Nissan Japan was booming. The company's first overseas production plant had opened in Taiwan in 1959, followed by one in Mexico in 1961. Domestically, the Oppama plant began business in 1962, and Nissan's most famous plant of all at Zama opened in 1965. The Zama factory featured the latest in cutting-edge technology. As James Higgins wrote in the *Detroit News*: "In the late 1970s, every manufacturing engineer in the auto industry made a pilgrimage to Nissan's Zama assembly plant. There, the company had pioneered the use of robots in painting, welding and assembly; it was a wonderland of automation. High-tech assembly came to define the company."[31]

Further overseas expansion took place in 1965 when Nissan Canada Incorporated was launched in Toronto, Ontario, followed by the opening of an Australian base in 1966.

By the mid–1960s Nissan had become a leading Japanese automobile manufacturer with exports exceeding 200,000. Film footage exists of the company's first transoceanic car carrier, the *Oppama Maru* with "Datsun" printed on its side, making its maiden voyage to the United States.

In 1965 Yutaka Katayama became president of Nissan U.S.A. One of the major irritants to deal with was trying to sell the product under names the eccentric Kawamata had chosen. Legend has it that Kawamata named the Fairlady after attending the Broadway musical *My Fair Lady* on a trip to the United States in 1958. Equally legendary is the fact that when the cars arrived in America, Katayama pried off the nameplates and replaced them with the numerical codes.[32]

Katayama felt he was fully justified in making these changes for he was in tune with Americans—closely observing their tastes and habits. He held a genuine affection for both the country and its people, adapting easily to the lack of formality and immersing himself in all things American — sports, races, picnics, and flying kites. He was once quoted as saying: "I think I understand American people... I can plainly talk to American people."[33]

Katayama's "love life" philosophy was reflected in the cars he helped design — most especially the dazzling 240Z. Long after he had retired he joked that he would still like to own a 240Z.[34]

David Halberstam devotes an extensive passage in *The Reckoning* to Katayama's struggles to get Nissan to produce suitable cars, but most particularly he wanted a 1600-cc engine which he considered an absolute necessity to compete with major rival Toyota. "On this Tokyo remained surprisingly resistant; if 1400-cc was good enough for Japan, it was good enough for America. Katayama pleaded. His cars, he said, were underpowered, and there was no way Nissan would ever have the right car for America unless it went to 1600-cc. He tried shock tactics, pointing out that Toyota, with a 1900-cc model, was making sizable inroads where Datsun had once been strong. Even this failed."[35] However, when a man named Keiichi Matsumura entered the picture, Katayama had an important ally — an ally who helped persuade Nissan to build a 1600-cc engine. Halberstam continued: "in 1968 the engine was ready for the new Datsun called the 510."[36] In this manner Halberstam introduces the reader to the 510, calling its arrival "the beginning of the end of the small car in America as a clumsy, flimsy econo-box."[37]

And yet we have seen that the 1600-cc engine had already been in existence since 1966 when it powered the SPL311, and in 1967 when it was shared by the RL411 sport sedan. Of course, neither of these would reach the heights of the 510, with the RL411 particularly being lost in the shuffle.

The model that succeeded it so effectively came as either a handsome four-door sedan or a wagon, driven by a 1595-cc (97.3-cubic-inch) cast-iron-block, aluminum-head engine that produced 96 horsepower at 5,600 rpm and 99.8 ft-lb of torque at 3,600 rpm. It was bored to 3.27" and stroked to 2.90" with a compression ratio of 8.5: 1. Zero to sixty took between 12.7 and 14.6 seconds, the quarter-mile 19.7 at 67.5 mph, and top speed was rated somewhere around 98 to 100 mph.

Produced especially for the American market, the 510 had front disc brakes and fully-independent suspension — MacPherson struts and coil springs on the front and independent semi-trailing arms and coils at the rear. It measured 162.2 inches long, 55.1 inches high and 61.4 inches wide. The wheelbase was 95.3 inches while the scale read approximately 2,000 pounds. Standard on the 510 was a four-speed manual transmission with a final drive ratio of 3.70:1. An automatic transmission and air conditioning were offered as options. Steering was of the recirculating ball type. A customer could drive a 510 sedan away for $1,996 and a wagon for $2,196.[38]

The 510 was quite powerful for its class— by comparison Chrysler's Simca and GM's Opel Kadett had only 55 horsepower, while Ford's Cortina produced 71. More importantly, the newest Datsun gave Toyota cause for concern because the heavier and less-well-equipped Corona could not match the 510's efficiency and the lightweight Corolla could not match its power. When fuel consumption was tallied, the

**Best of the Bluebirds — the first generation (1972) Datsun 510. This car brought Datsun's image up to par with Toyota's — some said beyond it (courtesy Nissan Motor Corporation USA).**

510 ranked second only to the Renault with a rating of 26 mpg. Toyota fell behind with 24.4 mpg.[39]

Although not designed by Pininfarina, the 510 fell under the influence of engineers from the Prince Automobile Company, which had merged with Nissan in 1966. A select few of these had aeronautical engineering expertise and were experienced in lightweight construction techniques. Designers working on the car included Kazumi Yotsumoto and Teruo Uchino.

*Road Test* magazine took a look at the new Datsun and gave it an "A" grade. They also praised Nissan's progress: "…the Datsun isn't just another cookie cutter made with the same old cutter, but the American tendency to go for more and more power is being adhered to."[40] And in reference to Nissan's past faults: "Datsun has gone all out to rectify certain shortcomings of the earlier models."[41]

*Motor Trend* called the 510 "…reliable, comfortable, maneuverable and economical to run — a true fun car."[42] *Car Life* said: "The Datsun 510 is a remarkable piece of engineering at a low price."[43]

Mr. Katayama was extremely proud of the car, as Halberstam recorded: "He was for the first few months like a kid with a new toy. He made everyone drive it, first his colleagues at the office, then journalists, then anyone who walked near the showroom. He loved the car…."[44]

In 1969 there were approximately 650 dealers selling over 85,000 vehicles per year. Over 300,000 510s alone were sold between 1967 and 1973.[45]

The 510 went on to distinguish itself as both a race and rally car. It began with rallies, claiming victories in America and East Africa. A modified BRE version won both the 1971 and 1972 SCCA 2.5-liter Trans-Am Championships. The 510 seemed to be the ideal small car, a perfect blend of performance, comfort, and economy. In recognition of the car's stellar qualities, *Road & Track* magazine named it number 71 of the "Top 100 Cars of the Century."[46]

Of less note but still producing a ripple was the 1968 arrival of the newest Fairlady — the SRL311, also known as the 2000 roadster. Looking like a cross between an MG and a Sunbeam, the 2000 two-seater convertible was powered by an aluminum-head, 1982-cc (120.9-cubic-inch) engine which produced 135 horsepower at 6,000 rpm and 132 ft-lb of torque at 4,400 rpm. Its compression ratio came in at 9.5:1. A sports car stance was emphasized by the 2000's 50.2-inch front tread and 47.2-inch rear tread. Wheelbase was 89.8 inches with an overall length of 155.7 inches. Transmission was a five-speed manual with a final drive ratio of 3.70:1. Top speed was rated between 108 and 118 mph with zero to sixty accomplished in 8.4 to 10.3 seconds. The car reached 80.5 mph at the end of a 17.6-second quarter-mile. The 2000 cost about a dollar and a half a pound, weighing in at 2,006 pounds and priced at $2,998.[47]

Although very attractive and quite impressive for its class, the 2000 was only a harbinger of what was to come from Nissan. When the 2000's successor was unveiled in 1969 it revealed a breathtaking new design which quite literally took the world by storm.

# 7

## Lost and Found — From Datsun to Nissan

By 1969 Nissan was at the top of its game. A multiple-arm robot was being put to work in the Oppama plant and brand recognition throughout the world was on the increase. The ascension was about to receive a major boost upon the arrival of the latest model on its way to America. Yutaka Katayama knew Nissan had a winner on its hands, but not with an old-fashioned name like Fairlady. As was by now his habit, he immediately set to work replacing the Fairlady badge with the car's factory numerical code — 240Z.

The 240Z was the Datsun that won over the American consumer who wanted something more than a square sedan or a sedate roadster. This car *looked* powerful, with deeply-recessed Jaguar-type headlights, swept-back lines, muscular haunches, and lower ground clearance. Car buffs and automotive journalists lined up to try it and then floated away singing its praises. Entering the market for 1970, Nissan introduced the 240Z as a "personalized two passenger fastback."[1]

As Mike Lawrence wrote in *A to Z of Sports Cars, 1945–1990*, the 240Z was the car that "…showed that Nissan had learned how to make a car with an up-to-date specification and lavish equipment at very reasonable prices, although its styling was not admired. To that end, the company engaged Count Albrecht Goertz (who had styled the BMW 503 and 507) and this proved to be an inspired decision."[2]

The German count's design perfectly complemented the 2.4-liter, single-over-head-cam, six-cylinder engine that featured seven main bearings and produced 151 horsepower at 5,600 rpm and 148 ft-lb of torque at 3,500 rpm. Dual Hitachi SU car-buretors, a 9.0:1 compression ratio and a final drive ratio of 3.36:1 helped the 2,350-pound, 162-inch-long vehicle get from zero to sixty in approximately 8 seconds. Nissan claimed, some said optimistically, a top speed of 125 mph.

The steering arrangement was rack-and-pinion and suspension was fully independent with McPherson struts and coil springs with an A-type transverse stabilizer

Another winner both on the track and in the showroom: the 1970 240Z, a car that has inspired a legend (courtesy Nissan Motor Corporation USA).

bar on the front, and Chapman struts, coils, and lower wishbones on the rear. Tires were 14-inch, 175 series with wider ones offered as an option. With this combination the Z handled and cornered very well. Shifting was also smooth from an all-synchronized four-speed manual, but a three-speed automatic was on offer for the few who wanted it. Stopping power was provided by front discs and rear drums. Air conditioning was optional.

Gas mileage, hardly the car's primary drawing card, was rated at about 20 mpg for this two-seater "poor man's Ferrari." Reviewers gushed over the car's interior, which managed to balance sport and luxury in equal portions. The straightforward dash contained a comprehensive set of gauges which included tachometer, oil pressure, ammeter, water temperature, and fuel level indicators. The steering wheel and shifter knob were of real wood, the bucket seats well-cushioned yet supportive, and arm- and footrests aided in driver comfort. Other equipment included a locking glovebox, AM/FM radio, clock, and coat hangers. For safety's sake, the steering wheel was designed to collapse if the three-point seatbelts did not sufficiently restrain the driver in a collision. There were also bumper guards and a full complement of body reflectors. All in all, the 240Z was quite an impressive package, especially when the cost — a mere $3,500 — was figured in. Nissan's American passenger car sales climbed from just over 60,872 in 1969 to 188,030 in 1971.[3]

The 240Z won *Car and Driver*'s 1971 Reader's Choice Award for best in its category of Sports/GT models. The editors commented: "For a brand new car to unseat one of the old favorites in one of the Sports/GT categories is almost unheard of, but Datsun's sleek entry did so and the results weren't even close — an astounding 30 percentage points separated the Datsun from its closest competitor."[4] Its closest competitor was GM's Opel GT, a car the company billed as "The only thing it's designed to win is people."[5] The 240Z also beat out the Porsche 914/4, the Lotus Elan S4, and the Fiat 124 Spider.

*Car and Driver* voted the 240Z Import of the Year in 1971 and offered an editorial on its market impact: "...there have been reports that at least Camaro and Firebird will be phased out by 1973. If correct, they will probably be replaced in 1974 with smaller models sized somewhere between the present sporty cars and the subcompact group. With nearly 25 percent of U.S. car sales already being of sub-compacts, the era of the domestic super coupe may be arriving."[6]

In 1972 Petersen's observed that "The 240Z has been on the American scene for about three years now and its popularity is unquestioned; it sells so quickly you'll still have a difficult time finding a new one in some areas of the country."[7]

*Motor Trend* even pitted the 240Z against the revered American Z car, the Camaro Z28, to the detriment of the Camaro. "The real annoyance comes with knowing that Chevrolet can do better; they've proven the fact abundantly in the Corvette and the Nova.... Mix in the bumps, squeaks, jolts and rattles with which our test car came factory-equipped and what could and should be one of the better offerings *chez* Chevrolet, (or even Detroit), in this age, becomes one of their greater disappointments.... In this case it's just damnfool carelessness, not greed."[8]

As for the 240Z, *Motor Trend* was impressed with the snappy little car, writing: "In the case of the Datsun the hardware is first rate, as is the application."[9]

The original 240Z was in such great demand that it was given a new treatment in 1974, emerging as the 2.6-liter 260Z with a 2 +2 body style and a minimal increase in horsepower (156), due to emission controls. The new Z was about an inch longer, and featured a new transistor-type ignition system as well as an electromagnetically-driven fuel pump. Externally, a spoiler and more aggressive 5-mph bumpers were added, which many complained spoiled the look of the car. Purists were also uneasy about the addition of jump seats, which somehow defiled the original sports car premise.

In 1975 the Z was revised yet again into the 2.8-liter 280Z and by 1977 horsepower had climbed back up to 170, driving sales to a feverish pitch. But beginning with the 1979 model year the car seemed to reach its peak on the market. From then on it steadily gained weight and bulk, evolving from a lean, mean fighting machine to a languid luxury coupe. The four-seater now had standard features such as air conditioning, power package, remote controls, and deep pile carpeting. Further to that, an optional "Grand Luxury" package was available. Even the name was longer — 280ZX.

In 1984 the car grew again, this time into the 300ZX, with a 3.0-liter, 160-horsepower engine. But during the late eighties and early nineties the Z finally lost its market altogether and the car was discontinued in 1996.

The Z-car fan clubs that have since developed throughout the world devote themselves to keeping the spirit of the original Z alive, many claiming that the rigid speed restrictions and gas rationing in the wake of the oil shortage killed the car. *Petersen's Complete Book of Datsun* offered a tongue-in-cheek comment about the speed limits and the Z's power to exceed them: "...we assume the 280Z's cruising speed is somewhere above 70 mph."[10]

Although Nissan did very well with the Z, the bulk of sales continued to come from the humble 1200 (60 percent) and the 510 (32 percent). The Lil' Hustler pickup truck comprised the rest in 1972.[11] At this point Nissan ranked in ninth spot with 8.5 percent of the import market,[12] reaching a major milestone in 1973 when the one-millionth Datsun was sold in the United States.[13]

Like all other automotive manufacturers, Nissan found themselves hard-pressed during this difficult decade. Emission controls, fuel shortages, and safety issues propelled research and development to new levels. Diesel engines, being more fuel-efficient, were constantly under development but this was nothing new for Nissan who had been building them since the 1940s. A newer alternative was a liquefied petroleum gas (LPG) engine. Developing this engine, together with creating a series of experimental safety vehicles (ESVs), kept Nissan engineers and technicians fully occupied. Yet despite these obligatory pressures, Nissan still managed to produce high-quality vehicles at a reasonable cost, and certainly economy had become a top priority for the consumer. To cater to this market, Nissan concentrated a larger portion of its efforts into fortifying its low-end line, beginning with the B110, or the 1200 as it was more popularly known.

Introduced in 1970, the presence of the 1200 was aptly summarized in *Petersen's Complete Book of Datsun*: "The bread and butter model from the Nissan stable is the unassuming little Datsun 1200.... The cars are touted as filling a solid niche in this country; a very low-priced four-seater with adequate roominess, crisp styling, great economy and sporty performance."[14]

Available in a two-door sedan or two-door coupe, the 1200 featured an 1171-cc (1.2-liter) cam-in-block, overhead-valve engine which produced 69 horsepower at 6,000 rpm. A 90.6 inch wheelbase and 150.4-inch overall length combined with a slight weight of 1,600 pounds allowed the car to reach a top speed of 90 mph. It came to a stop via front disc and rear drum brakes and shifted through an all-synchronized four-speed, with a two-speed automatic coming along in 1972. More importantly, gas mileage was rated at an economical 32 mpg. Photos of the car show a cleanly designed, well-proportioned little car with large single round headlights and three simple horizontal bars across the grille. The sedan had only one slight curve from rear window down to the trunk lid to break its squareness.

The coupe was actually more of a liftback with a long, sloping trunk line and non-functional stacked miniature louvers on its rear quarter-panels. As attractive as these little cars were, the 1200 was the kind of bargain-basement car that people generally didn't brag about owning even while loving it.

Commanding more respect and attention was the 1973 610, arriving as a replacement for the 510, which disappeared from the market that year. The 610 was available in three styles; a two-door hardtop, a four-door sedan, and a four-door wagon. All were powered by an in-line four, overhead-cam 1770-cc (108-cubic-inch) engine which produced 105 horsepower and 108 ft-lb of torque at 3,600 rpm. Although the 610 was seven inches longer and two inches wider than the 510 and more luxurious with power disc brakes and a rear window defogger, it was not as appealing. Much of the innocent-but-roguish look of the 510 was gone, replaced by heavier, longer lines and panels combined with fussier details.

Even an over-the-top advertising campaign which featured the work of artists like Peter Hurd and Salvador Dali could not earn the 610 the cult status of the 510. The series of ads was the brainchild of none other than Katayama who, as an amateur artist himself, was thrilled to be associated with such celebrated talent. He was particularly fascinated by Dali and enchanted with his painting of a melting clock falling from a tree with the hands stuck on 6:10. Nissan added a small picture of the 610 at the vortex of the piece and printed its clever slogan — "Datsun Originals" at the bottom.

Unfortunately the ads weren't allowed much time to impress before the full impact of the oil embargo hit later in the year. Once again Nissan executives and marketing people put their heads together and came up with the more pertinent "Datsun Saves."

Attention again swung back in full force to the economy factor which was reflected in the newest ten series, the scaled-down 710 for 1974. The 710 shared the same engine and transmission as the 610 but made even less of a stir on the market which was in the throes of the oil shock. Automakers were scrambling to produce the most efficient cars and get them into the showrooms as soon as possible. To that end, Nissan's next offering came in 1975 as the B-210, a better-equipped but still economical replacement for the 1200.

The first generation B-210 had an overhead-valve, 1397-cc engine that managed 80 horsepower and 83 ft-lb of torque at 3,600 rpm. It boasted excellent fuel economy with the automatic achieving 26 to 33 mpg (city and highway), and the manual getting 30 to 40 mpg.[15] The car was soon available in four versions: two- and four-door sedans, a hatchback, and a "Honeybee" edition. These were now the least expensive Datsuns, retailing for around $2,850.[16]

The fact that companies like Nissan and Toyota could market such low-priced, high-quality vehicles in a time of virtual crisis was a thorn the Big Three could no longer ignore. Their chagrin was perfectly illustrated in a piece from the December 1977 edition of *Motor Trend*. In response to customers flocking to cars like the B-210, a Detroit executive, who first stated that if he was quoted by name he would deny everything, huffed: "The Japanese don't know how to sell quality, features, durability, ease of service or razzmatazz... They build great cars for the money, but the only thing they know is to sell price. Actually, they could ask $200 to $300 more without losing a single sale."[17]

But the *Motor Trend* journalist begged to differ: "As Datsun's B-210 experience reveals, however, the Japanese know exactly what's going on and don't appear to be in a hurry to change things. After all, they seem to have a model for each pocketbook."[18]

That much was evident even two years earlier when Nissan had four models on the American market, with three versions of the 610, four of the 710, two of the 260Z and two of the 280Z, ranging in price from $2,979 to $7,084.[19] Total U.S. sales for passenger cars was then 289,842.[20]

But while these marketing strategies and successes may have irked the domestic automakers, they were not considered outstanding by Japanese standards. Assessing the market and the competition, Nissan was determined to do better. By comparison to other Japanese companies such as Honda, Mazda, and Subaru, which were all introducing new technologies, it seemed almost as though Nissan was stagnating. The hoopla surrounding the Z car had subsided and the 610 and 710 sedans had failed to create the hype associated with the 510. As a result, in an effort to catch up to the trends, Nissan finally released its first front-wheel-drive passenger car, the F-10, in 1976. Before it arrived in America, *Motor Trend* offered a sneak peak. Under the heading "Japanese Front-Wheel Drive Madness" was a small pen-and-ink rendering of the F-10. Seemingly more concerned with the car's given name, the author continued: "...the Datsun Cherry (that's its name in Japan, folks, and since it'll be coming here, you'd better get used to it), has a roof section which bears more than a passing resemblance to the late Citroen SM.... A number of these Civic-sized beasts were seen of late near Datsun's U.S. headquarters, so it might be very safe to assume that the Cherries will be blossoming on our shores sometime between January and April."[21]

Petersen's merely asked: "Front-wheel-drive Datsuns. What will they think of next?"[22]

Other than the fact it was the company's flagship front-wheel drive, there wasn't much else to comment on. The transversely mounted engine was by now a common layout in order to accommodate the transaxle. Aside from that, the axle ratio was higher (numerically lower at 3.47:1), with the transmission geared lower to allow for speedier acceleration without sacrificing mileage, but the engine was borrowed from the B-210. This combination was fitted into either a five-speed hatchback with overdrive or a four-speed wagon. Mileage was outstanding at 39.2 mpg, and for around $3,000 it was difficult to beat the F-10 as a good economical, if not inspiring, buy. Petersen's remarked: "When it comes to the F-10, the "Datsun Saves" slogan is telling the truth."[23]

Marking the grand finale of the ten series was the 810, which arrived in 1977, and was introduced as a top-of-the-line luxury Datsun. The 610 had been dropped from the line and the 710 overshadowed by its larger new sibling, which featured the same powerful engine that had been in the first 240Z, with the addition of electronic fuel injection. The 810 was accordingly billed as "...the touring car with the heart of a Z."[24] It came as a rear-drive, four-door sedan or five-door wagon and featured such luxuries as a six-way adjustable driver's seat, tilt steering wheel, AM/FM stereo, and rear defogger, with a rear washer/wiper for the wagon. Those concerned with the general trend toward "idiot lights" were no doubt happy to see that a complete set of gauges ran half-way across the dash.

Demand was so great for the 810 that Nissan U.S.A.'s sales vice-president Robert Link had to ask headquarters for an increase in production.[25] The only complaints about the sophisticated new Datsun seemed to stem from a rough-running engine, which Nissan attributed to the addition of new pollution control devices.

Also new for 1977 was the 200-SX, designed to fill the sport-economy gap left between the 810 and the 280Z. Powered by a 1952-cc (119-cubic-inch) overhead-cam four-cylinder engine, the rear-wheel-drive 200-SX sports coupe produced 107 horsepower and 112 ft-lb of torque. Transmissions were a four-speed or five-speed overdrive manual. Targeted at the Celica, the 200-SX didn't quite measure up. There were complaints about the cramped cabin, hard shifting, poor visibility, inadequate air conditioning and disappointing mileage (21.8 mpg). And in April of 1977, a *Motor Trend* reviewer added yet another negative response: "The 200-SX is regrettably not the performer it could be in the handling department...."[26]

The car's styling drew both praise and criticism, but it was nothing if not original. Most noticeable from the front were the large round single headlights and protruding grille. At the back end the wide quarter panels arched sharply up to the roof reducing the rear windows to a triangle and almost eliminating the pillar between them and the rear window. From there they drooped low over the rear wheels, creating an almost square wheel-well. The 200-SX did not get a major restyling until 1980 when it emerged as a longer and wider car with improved interior space and visibility. There were two models in the line as well — a hatchback and a notchback, both available in Deluxe or Sport Luxury trim. Although the transmissions— a five-speed and a three-speed automatic — remained the same and the car was still a rear-wheel-drive, a new 1952-cc overhead-cam engine boosted horsepower to 100 and torque to 112 ft-lb at 3,200 rpm.[27]

By the time 1978 rolled around and both the 200-SX and the 810 were in their second year, Nissan's U.S. sales totaled 339,364 passenger cars.[28] Also that year the revered 510 name was towed out of retirement and used on a new sedan (which looked suspiciously like the 810) that was in the running for *Motor Trend's* 1978 Import Car of the Year. Even *Motor Trend* acknowledged the resemblance of certain competitors to their predecessors: "Some people may argue that the Datsun 510, Subaru DL and Toyota Celica are just "old wines in a new bottle," but in each case the bottle has been considerably improved over its predecessor."[29]

Ironically, a few pages over was a two-page color spread for the car. "The New 510. Best All-Around Datsun Yet. A whole new class of economy car, in Wagon, 2- and 4-Door Sedans and a Hatchback that got 35 mpg highway, 25 mpg city," the ad boasted. Also present at the bottom of the page was the company's new slogan: "Datsun. We Are Driven."[30]

Nissan entered the 1980s on slightly less secure footing than they had in the 1970s. They now had six major product lines: the base 210 series (the "B" had been dropped); a new 310 introduced in 1979 to replace the F-10; the familiar 510; and the steadily evolving Z, 810, and 200-SX. (The company also offered their now-famous pick-up trucks which included the king-cab version).

Yutaka Katayama had retired in 1977 after serving his final two years as chairman. Some say he left without ever being recognized within the company for his invaluable contributions, yet today his name has reached legendary proportions. David Halberstam offered this tribute: "By dint of rare human vision, he [Katayama] had helped make a small, incompetent Japanese company an exciting one, pushing it relentlessly to produce its best."[31]

Nissan now had branches all over the world, including Australia, Belgium, Germany, Spain, Italy, and the United Kingdom. Worldwide sales exceeded two million vehicles per year, with 584,490 of those sold in the United States (including trucks).[32] Construction on a plant in Smyrna, Tennessee, where Nissan intended to produce their pick-up truck, followed by passenger cars at a later date, commenced in 1981.

With attention being diverted to the new plant, some automotive critics felt Nissan was neglecting its product. The new front-wheel-drive F-10 and the 310 drew harsh criticism, with *Car and Driver* calling the F-10 "...an unhappy little car," urging Datsun to "keep trying."[33] They also panned the 310 for being "totally devoid of personality."[34]

*Motor Trend*, however, was kinder, crediting the 310's "crisp, straightforward styling," as well as its "solid-feel road manners and larger interior space." As for the newest 510, it was "reliable and economical." The 200-SX was "competent," but the reviewer, joining a multitude of others, questioned the car's rather "bulbous styling, inconsistent with Nissan cars sold here."[35]

Still on safe ground by all accounts were the classics—the 810, 280ZX and the 200-SX. The first of these returned in 1981 as a larger but thinner car, powered by the same 2393-cc (146-cubic-inch) EFI (electronic fuel injection) V-6 engine as the 1980 model, but finally graduating to a five-speed transmission (with an optional automatic). A three-speed automatic as standard equipment was reserved for the new upscale-trim-level 810, called the Maxima. The Maxima edition featured all-wheel disc brakes, voice-warning system, power equipment package, deluxe interior, AM/FM cassette and power moonroof. While a base 810 sedan could be purchased for $7,979, the Maxima went for $10,379.[36]

The legendary "father of the Z car," Yutaka Katayama — or "Mr. K." as he was generally known. He loved America, fast cars, kites, picnics, and life — and we loved his cars.

In mid–1981 a diesel version of the 810 and Maxima came out, to little acclaim. Much more noticeable was the fact that by 1982 the Datsun 810 had evolved into the Nissan Maxima. The only significant changes were an upgraded interior and a more "high tech" instrument panel.

The 200SX was now powered by a 102-horsepower EFI 2.0-liter engine and a somewhat restyled, color-keyed body.

There were now four versions of the 280ZX — a two-seater, a 2 + 2, a turbo-

*Top:* In 1979, when Nissan decided to build in America, it chose Tennessee as its home state (courtesy Nissan Motor Corporation USA). *Bottom:* The 1981 810 Maxima — a Datsun or a Nissan? No one knew for sure. This car, as well as the Stanza, was sold as both (courtesy Nissan Motor Corporation USA).

charged two-seater and a turbo 2 + 2. The turbo version produced 180 horsepower at 5,600 rpm and 202 ft-lb of torque at 2,800 rpm.[37]

The 1981-82 season heralded the arrival of Nissan's new front-wheel drive models. First to appear in September 1981 for the 1982 year was the all-new Stanza. The Stanza bore the dubious distinction of being badged as both a Nissan and a Datsun. Intended as a replacement for the venerated 510, it was a 2.0-liter four-cylinder that produced 88 horsepower and 112 ft-lb of torque at 2,800 rpm. This engine was linked to either a five-speed manual gearbox or optional three-speed automatic. The car also featured a two-barrel, down-draft carburetor and transistorized ignition. Fuel mileage was a thrifty 31 mpg on average.[38]

The Stanza was originally available as a three-door or five-door hatchback in three trim levels—Standard, Deluxe or XE. The XE package included cruise control, power sunroof, two-tone paint, tilt steering wheel, variable speed wipers, cloth bucket seats and AM/FM cassette. The car could be purchased for approximately $8,000 and parts costs were rated as medium.[39]

In 1985, a four-door sedan replaced the three-door hatchback. Throughout the years the Stanza has been steadily acknowledged as a very good buy in its class, offering durability, quality, and economy with few complaints registered against it. As the car aged and put on weight (it went from 2,190 pounds to 2,788), it suffered not only in the area of fuel economy, but also in crash-test ratings, which fell between poor and very poor. Before the car was phased out in 1992 it had lost its popularity and very few were willing to spend $12,000 for it.[40]

Receiving wider acclaim than the Stanza was its smaller sister, which came on board in mid–1981 as the Sentra. This model had a long and proven track record in Japan, the United Kingdom and Australia, where it was marketed as the Sunny. When the Sentra arrived in America it came in a variety of shapes from a two-door hatchback to a five-door wagon with the same trim levels as the Stanza. A special high-efficiency model called the MPG was also available.

The first-generation Sentra was powered by a four-cylinder, overhead-cam 1,488-cc (1.5-liter) engine that manufactured 67 horsepower and 85 ft-lb of torque at 3,200 rpm. A three-speed automatic with lock-up torque converter was an option, while the ubiquitous five-speed was standard equipment. Fuel came through either a double-barrel carburetor or electronic fuel injection, while the spark was provided by the same electronic ignition as in the Stanza. Mileage came in at 32 mpg on average, not surprising in view of the 1,895-pound curb weight and spare packaging. The MPG edition provided an even more efficient 35-plus mpg.

*Car and Driver* called the Sentra a "Hi-tech, lightweight personnel carrier with no sporting pretensions."[41] Brock Yates was less kind in his assessment: "This is not a truly bad automobile, but it is simply outmatched by the Honda Civic, Mazda GLC, Toyota Tercel, and a host of other small front-wheel drive cars at the bottom of the market."[42]

There are, no doubt, legions of those who would disagree with Mr. Yates' assessment. Certainly the GLC, Tercel, and even Civic in those early years were nothing more than Spartan by any account.

Consumers, however, thought enough of the Sentra to raise it to top-seller status, with consistently favorable reviews from all corners. Naturally there were complaints against the car, most of which stemmed from its under-powered and noisy engine. Nissan responded in 1983 by boosting horsepower to 69 through a new 1.6-liter engine. A diesel-powered Sentra became available which also raised the car's overall efficiency ranking but did nothing to quell the noise factor.

The Sentra may have held what many considered a lowly position but it repeatedly acquitted itself by winning numerous awards for dependability and economy. And when it went into production in America from 1985 onwards, customers felt an additional pull toward the car. They were sold on its economy and easy driving, but what kept them coming back was the car's outstanding dependability.

In 1986 *Consumer Reports* rated the Sentra's predicted reliability as "better than average," based on past Sentra performance. It received only one black circle (much worse than average) for its fuel system in the 1984 and 1985 models.[43] Crash tests came in with mixed results. *The Used Car Book* by Jack Gillis rather confusingly rated the Sentra's crash-tests as "good," but later warned that consumers should stay away from Sentras built before 1987, as they experienced front-end collapse upon impact.[44]

*Road & Track* reviewed the 1987 Sentra SE Sport Coupe, taking Nissan to task for a "bland" interior and slow acceleration, but praising its "torquey engine," smooth shifter and good road handling. "Altogether," they concluded, "the Sentra is a more sporting car than it seems initially. It's much more *alive* than previous small Nissans: fun to drive without giving away everyday practicality. It's reasonably easy on fuel and should be extremely reliable over the years."[45]

The Sentra continued to receive "much better than average" ratings from consumer magazines despite criticisms of its boxy styling and lackluster performance. The 1987–88 models certainly epitomized square styling, but in 1989 the edges were rounded off to help soften the car's austere appearance.

By 1993 the Sentra was 170.3 inches long with a 95.7 inch wheelbase and a curb weight of 2,324 pounds. The 1.6-liter engine could generate 110 horsepower and 108 ft-lb of torque, while a 2.0-liter SE-R version produced 140 horsepower and 132 ft-lb of torque at 4,800 rpm. Fuel economy came in at 29 mpg (city) and 38 (highway) for the five-speed overdrive manual, and 27 and 35 respectively for the four-speed automatic with overdrive (1.6-liter engine).

A driver-side airbag was standard equipment on the top GXE four-door and optional on other models. Trim levels were now E, XE, GXE, SE and SE-R. Nonetheless, *Consumer Guide* demoted the Sentra to "recommended" from "best-buy" status, stating that the "Sentra stays mostly static while most competitors move forward...." They qualified this judgment by saying "Make no mistake: (the) Sentra is a modern, reasonably priced small car offering high mileage, top-notch assembly, and the newly added safety of an air bag."[46]

The problem of performance which plagued the Sentra was also an issue for the car that was released in 1983 as a replacement for the 310 series.

The Pulsar was basically a sport version of the Sentra, sharing many mechanical elements but housed in a sharply-angled coupe body with pop-up headlights. A four-door sedan version was offered for the first year only, because it was the NX Sport Coupe that brought in the sales. Its 1,907-pound weight allowed the car to be quicker than the 1.6-liter engine might have otherwise allowed, and more economical as well, with an average fuel rating of 35 mpg. A stiffer suspension and sport package was offered to create a sports-coupe environment, as was a 1.5-liter, 90-horsepower turbo model. Zero to sixty was accomplished in 12.8 seconds and the quarter-mile in 18.8 seconds for the base model, while the NX SE (1989) achieved the former in a much-improved 10.3 seconds and the latter in 17.8 seconds.

Despite its attributes, the Pulsar seemed to get off to a bad start in America. Even though a T-bar roof was available for 1987, the addition of an optional "Sportbak" trunk lid did nothing to alter the common consensus that the car was odd-looking. If nothing else, the Sportbak package established the Pulsar as one of the very first crossover vehicles, a look which was not popular in the late 1980s, although it later grew to be.

Yet the car had its merits. It was agile, dependable, and economical and in 1986 *Consumer Guide* gave it a "better than average" rating.[47] A year later it won Japan's Car of the Year award, an honor bestowed by a distinguished panel of 54 automotive journalists. But the car, while popular in Japan, failed to captivate American buyers and in 1991 it was replaced with the redesigned NX 1600 sports coupe.

The year the Pulsar won accolades in Japan Nissan posted its first operating loss since World War II.[48] Nissan's brand image began to suffer in the mid-eighties; critics were calling their cars "unimaginative" and "uninspired." The 300ZX was now a large luxury coupe, the Sentra, Stanza and Maxima were boxy, and the 200SX was not yet the attractive little coupe it would eventually become. But perhaps most damaging of all was Nissan's midstream name change, which disconcerted consumers and caused massive confusion in the market. Nissan's own Tom Orbe, vice-president of marketing at the time, was quoted by *Ward's AutoWorld* as saying: "From the consumer's point of view, Datsun went away and Nissan was a new company," adding that "It took five years for Nissan to get the same level of name recognition as Datsun."[49]

Nissan officials in Japan thought it best that the new name be introduced gradually, overlapping the Datsun and Nissan names during the changeover. This, however, only served to add to the confusion because many thought Nissan was simply a designation of some sort. Bob Thomas, a public relations representative from a firm representing Nissan, admitted that the manner of the change was perhaps mishandled: "That name change hurt the momentum of an exciting company. They threw away a lot of equity. And they let the change happen in a slow, cumbersome way." He also added: "They lost so much identity that they couldn't reclaim it ... it was very, very costly."[50]

There can be no more scathing indictment than that and the scores of critics that have flailed the company for its errors offer nothing more substantial. Suffice it to say it was a lesson well-paid-for.

With that painful episode behind it, Nissan made its next move. The introduction of its super-luxury Infiniti line came in 1989 and brought the company into a league it had been straining toward with the 300ZX and the Maxima sedan.

To create a frisson of anticipation during 1989, Nissan produced a series of "teaser" advertisements built around the debut of their new Infiniti line. The print ads showed only text and mystical background photography. Television ads displayed only scenery interspersed with the Infiniti name or logo. These advanced to cryptic narration and background shots. Finally shots of the cars themselves appeared.

A prime example of a typical print ad ran in the April 1989 edition of *Road & Track*. The left side of the two-page spread contained nothing but text on a plain white background. In part it read: "Japanese. Luxury. This experience isn't something you can pick up from the pages of a magazine — a picture with a list of specifications will contribute marginally to understanding what makes the Infiniti experience different.... If you can wait, we promise you won't be disappointed."[51]

But one of the two first cars out did prove to be disappointing. The entry level 3.0-liter V-6 M30 did not even survive into its second year and was quickly replaced by the G20. The G20 came only as a four-door front-wheel-drive sedan that was powered by a 2.0-liter twin-cam four, producing 140 horsepower and 132 ft-lb of torque at 4,800 rpm. The transmission was either a five-speed manual or four-speed automatic and brakes were anti-lock discs all around. The G20 was smallish, with an overall length of 175 inches, a 100.4-inch wheelbase, and a weight of 2,535 pounds. EPA ratings stood at 22 mpg city, 29 highway. Other options besides the automatic transmission were power sunroof and leather upholstery. *Consumer Guide's 1992 Auto Report* found the G20 was "a well-equipped compact sedan with good performance overall." But according to the reviewer, two major elements were lacking: "A quieter engine that works better with (the) automatic transmission and a standard driver-side air bag."[52]

More impressive was the larger rear-wheel-drive Infiniti also unveiled in 1990. The Q45's elegant stance spoke of both luxury and power, and it delivered on both counts. More able to compete against Lexus and Acura, the Q45 weighed in at nearly 4,000 pounds and its wheelbase took 113.2 inches from a total of 199.8. The Q45's bulk rested on standard 215/65VR15 tires which covered the four-wheel anti-lock disc brakes.

As a four-door luxury sedan that produced 278 horsepower and 292 ft-lb of torque at 4,000 rpm through its 4.5-liter V-8 powerplant, the Q45 was well able to compete with any luxury sedan on the road — domestic or import. In fact it tied for first place with Toyota's Lexus for the J.D. Power CSI award in 1991.

As automotive journalists succumbed to its charms, there weren't many who were left unimpressed by the finely built Infiniti. Loaded with every possible extra and luxury, there wasn't much Nissan could add as options to the car, apart from the Full Active Suspension system, traction control, and Nissan's HICAS four-wheel steering system. Cabin room was ample and there were no complaints about comfort or features — but there were some grumblings about fuel consumption, which at an average of 16.6 mpg (premium gas only) made the Q45 a costly preposition for most, especially when the gas-guzzler tax was applied. Yet its base price for the 1990 model (approximately $40,000) fell well below the cost of many European sedans of similar quality. In fact one reviewer dinged Toyota with his evaluation of the Q45: "The Japanese-built Q45 feels more like a European luxury sedan than the rival LS 400."[53]

Next to join the Infiniti group was the rear-wheel-drive J30 sedan, in 1993. Fit-

On its third generation — the Q45 proves Japanese automakers have no trouble building luxury cars of V-8s. This 2003 Infiniti has 340 horses beneath its svelte hood. "Stellar acceleration," said *Motor Trend* (courtesy Nissan Motor Corporation USA).

ting between the G20 and the Q45, the J30 featured a 3.0-liter V-6 which delivered 210 horsepower and 193 ft-lb of torque at 4,800 rpm and was joined to a four-speed automatic with overdrive. This car was smaller and lighter than the Q45, yet larger than the G20, with a wheelbase of 108.7 inches and a weight of 3,527 pounds. Driver- and passenger-side airbags were now standard equipment, and the same suspension, touring package and four-wheel steering options of the Q45 were also offered on the J30, in addition to alloy wheels, spoiler, and high-performance tires. A telephone antenna was built into the rear window. Zero to sixty was clocked at 8.9 seconds and some of the engine noise and harsh shifting present in earlier models were ironed out. Complaints registered concerned cabin and cargo space, with critics asking why people should spend $35,000 for this car when a Maxima SE was basically the same car for much less? A more comprehensive warranty was one answer. The Infiniti was covered by a four-year/60,000-mile warranty with six-year/70,000-mile powertrain coverage. Twenty-four-hour roadside assistance and a free loaner car also sweetened the aspect of a new Infiniti.[54]

But even the arrival of Infiniti could not support a company that was repeatedly being outdone by the likes of Honda and arch-rival Toyota. Products suffered more from yawning indifference than criticism as models arrived, only to be replaced by marginally improved versions. In 1989 the more powerful 240SX arrived to take over from the 200SX, with convertibles offered in 1992 and 1994, but three years later the

*Top:* Another "latest" from Infiniti — the 2003 M45 (courtesy Nissan Motor Corporation USA). *Bottom:* The 2003 G35, a 280-horsepower, rear-wheel-drive replacement for the G20 (courtesy Nissan Motor Corporation USA).

car had disappeared. The NX 1600 and 2000 stood in for the defunct Pulsar in 1991, but neither of these made a lasting impression and they were also withdrawn.

More successful was the 1993 Altima, which appeared as a front-wheel-drive, four-door replacement for the dated Stanza. The Altima was something of a "make it or break it" vehicle, as *Consumer Guide* acknowledged: "Nissan has a lot riding on the Altima in a mid-size family car field dominated by Taurus, Accord, and Camry. The company has spent $490 million to produce [the] Altima at its Tennessee plant, and hopes to sell up to 120,000 a year — more than triple the Stanza's average annual volume."[55]

Thanks to a brilliant marketing strategy combined with a well-made product, the Altima went on to fulfill Nissan's wishes for a best-seller. In some ways it was able to compensate for the 300ZX, whose personality was split between a sports car and Grand Touring coupe. In 1996 its spark finally died out, much to the distress of die-hard Z-car fans. The addition of a convertible model in 1992 had only served to further split its identity and emphasize its awkward position on the market. The 300ZX was generally acknowledged to be a fine automobile, but its lack of a decisive image hurt it more than any critic could have.

Steadfast was the Sentra, which slowly shed its ugly-duckling image and blossomed into an attractive, sporty, and efficient little machine. Unfortunately, before things could pick up for Nissan, they got much worse, plunging to new depths throughout the bleak late 1980s and mid–1990s. During this period both Nissan and Infiniti products fell behind Toyota and Honda in popularity, despite positive reviews. Nissan management seemed to come undone as the company slowly lost its direction and sense of brand identity. Debts continued to mount as models failed to overtake their competition and good money was frantically thrown after bad.

When interviewed in the late 1990s, the old chief Yutaka Katayama attributed many of the company's problems to poor leadership: "Nissan engineering, they excel [*sic*], but ... they don't have a leadership right now.... The lack of leadership and lack of love of the car ... that is the weakest point today."[56]

Public perception was also at an all-time low. Don Spetner, vice-president of Nissan's Corporate Communications, wrote in the 1996-1997 *Journal of Integrated Communications*: "For more than 20 years, the corporation communications function at Nissan Motor Corporation U.S.A. was essentially forgotten.... By the late 1980s, Nissan began to clean up and expand its public relations activities, but with no real strategic plan in place for the function. As a result, it grew haphazardly.... There were numerous redundancies in functional areas and glaring inefficiencies in spending that needed to be addressed."[57]

The solutions, as put forth by Spetner, involved improved productivity and teamwork, aligning departmental objectives with overall corporate objectives, and the establishment of and focus on clear goals. Unfortunately all the restructuring in the world was not enough to save Nissan. Cash, and massive doses of it, would also be required.

An article in a 1999 edition of *Asiaweek* magazine referred to Nissan's predicament and its possible saviors: "Nissan is being courted by two suitors, the recently-merged German-American giant DaimlerChrysler and France's Renault."[58]

Nissan needed a new image in the competitive 1990s, so it placed a 240-horsepower engine into what appeared to be a sedate sedan, the 2002 Altima (courtesy Nissan Motor Corporation USA).

It seemed impossible that a large and proud company like Nissan would consider such a bid, but President Hanawa Yoshikazu was quoted as saying: "We will consider anything, including a capital tie-up, if the prospective partner is a plus for Nissan."[59]

Preliminary results of Renault's tie-in with Nissan show a company on the upswing. The rather drastic alterations and strict cost-cutting measures enforced by new leader Carlos Ghosn seem to have paid off as is evident in the new and more powerful Altima, with an available 3.5-liter, V-6 240-horsepower engine that has raised the bar in its class. Also bearing little resemblance to their Plain-Jane ancestors are the Sentra and 260-horsepower V-6 Maxima, both refined and finely tuned for peak performance.

The Sentra now came in two new models—the CA, and the revisited SE-R. The 1.8-liter, 146-horsepower CA (Clean Air) model introduced in 2001 (sold only in California) was the first gasoline-powered vehicle ever to meet the super-ultra-low-emissions standards, earning the initials SULEV behind its name.

Speed fans were more interested in the two versions of the SE-R—the SE-R and the SE-R Spec V. Both were powered by a 2.5-liter four-cylinder engine, with 170 horsepower for the SE-R and 180 for the SE-R Spec V. An optional six-speed manual helped contribute to the sports car allure. The SE-R replaced the base SE which

*Top:* Fast-forward to the new generation: the 2002 Sentra GXE—"from humble beginnings…" (courtesy Nissan Motor Corporation USA). *Bottom:* Power to burn: the 2003 Sentra SE-R (courtesy Nissan Motor Corporation USA).

The 2004 Maxima: all grown up (courtesy Nissan Motor Corporation USA).

*Motor Trend* reviewed in 2001. Even the SE's less-powerful 140-horsepower, 2.0-liter engine burned the tarmac while getting from zero to sixty in only 7.9 seconds, and completing the quarter-mile in 16 seconds at 85.5 mph. Reviewer Chris Walton called the Sentra SE "a blast to drive," noting that it handily beat out both the Corolla and Civic.[60]

On the more deceptively sedate front, the Maxima continued to honor the Nissan name by evolving into a sleek and powerful sedan. *Consumer Reports* called it "...among the best in its class"[61] for 2002, and *Motor Trend* remarked that the new 3.5-liter 260-horsepower Maxima was "...an expression of Nissan's revived performance philosophy."[62]

A hint of that "performance philosophy" became even more evident at the 1999 Detroit Auto Show when Nissan showed its new concept Z-car, announcing a 2003 production date.

Ron Sessions reviewed the 350Z for *Motor Trend's* September 2002 edition in a piece that touched on the Z's features while exploring its illustrious ancestry. While working on the concept, the design team apparently "hauled out a '70 Z and parked it in the middle of the studio" for inspiration. The design involved Japanese, American and European studios, with the car's shell drawn up by Nissan Design America's Ajay Panchal. And if Panchal's design rated an "in-your-face" grade which Sessions counted as both a positive and a negative, the car came in for a final tribute: "The 350Z goes its own way, proudly and confidently — and is a bargain in the process."[63]

For approximately $34,000, the proud owner of a 350Z would receive a rear-wheel-drive two-seater with an all-cast-aluminum 3.5-liter V-6 engine that produced 287 horsepower at 6,200 rpm and 274 ft-lb of torque at 4,800. A six-speed manual transmission provided the gears with a final drive ratio of 2.81:1 and an axle ratio of 3.54:1. Front and rear suspension consisted of multilinks, coil springs and anti-roll bars. Brakes were anti-lock with 11.7-inch vented discs on the front and 11.5-inch vented discs on the rear.

The 350Z's wheelbase measured 104.3 out of a total length of 169.6 inches and it weighed in at 3,247 pounds. Weight distribution was configured to 53/47, front and back. The car's front track measured 60.4 inches while the rear spread to 60.8 inches. The 18-inch wheels were cast-aluminum alloy, 7.5 inches wide in the front and 8.0 inches wide in the rear. Rear tires were also larger, 235/45WR18 Bridgestone Potenza RE 040s on the back and 225/45WR18 on the front.

This package managed zero-to-sixty in 5.49 seconds and the quarter-mile in 13.95 seconds at 102.25 mph. Braking from 60 mph was accomplished in 115 feet. Safety was a consideration as well with standard driver- and passenger-side airbags, as well as optional side and head curtains. Fuel economy came in at 20 mpg city, 26 estimated on the highway.[64]

The 350Z has caused something of a sensation with plenty of hype generated and reports so far indicate strong sales as of 2003. As Sessions noted, "Nissan figures there's a significant pool of buyers out there."[65]

With such an array of successful vehicles bearing the Nissan name and a total of four Infinitis to choose from — the I35 and G35 recently replacing the I30 and J30 models of the mid–1990s— Nissan has now reclaimed a top spot in the industry.

The Z car is back and perhaps something of Mr. K's spirit came with it.

# 8

# Honda's American Dream

"You meet the nicest people on a Honda"[1] promised the American Honda Motor Company's slogan in 1962. By 1972 thousands of Americans agreed. Having conquered the motorcycle market at home in Japan, Honda intended to follow the same path to success in America. But what appeared to Americans in 1959 to be the company's first step was actually the midpoint of a journey that began in 1922, when 16-year-old Soichiro Honda left home to apprentice at Art Shokai's Tokyo Auto Service Station.

A quick study but not particularly academic, with only eight years' formal schooling, young Honda already had a knack with tools and machinery courtesy of Gihei, his blacksmith–bicycle repairman father. Honda biographer Tetsuo Sakiya documented Honda's early interest in things mechanical: "The family was poor and Soichiro, from the time he was a child, helped with his father's business. Even as a baby he seemed fascinated by machinery. Several miles from his house was a rice polishing mill with a gasoline-powered engine, which was quite an oddity in those days. His grandfather would carry him there on his back and watching the motor became one of young Honda's favorite pastimes."[2]

Automotive historians have drawn many parallels between Henry Ford's beginning in the industry and Soichiro Honda's. They both left rural life at the same age to seek a job in the automotive industry, and, like Ford, Honda also nurtured a dream to build motorized vehicles. Another similarity between the two was their great obsession with speed. Honda, however, had neither Ford's resources nor his experience and had to be content with driving vehicles built by someone else. This in no way deterred him as he achieved repeated success on the track where he was known as a daring and fearless driver. But in 1936 Honda's luck suddenly and painfully ran out.

Competing in the All-Japan Speed Rally, Honda drove a car with a Ford engine, albeit one he heavily modified, adding among other things a supercharger and an auxiliary radiator. He also tilted the engine to the left because races ran counter-clockwise in Japan and the tilted engine helped with cornering. Nothing could help

Soichiro, however, when just as he was approaching the finish line another car attempted to pass and cut him off. Both Honda and his car tumbled end-over-end, with Honda sustaining serious injuries that would take almost two years to heal. His only consolation was that during the race he had managed to set an all-time speed record of 75 mph.[3]

The accident, although it abruptly halted Honda's career as a driver, only served to fuel his resolve to become an automotive engineer. Never content to remain on the sidelines, Honda searched for ways and means to accomplish his goals. One of his first goals was fairly modest — to be able to service automobiles. To this end he persuaded his boss Art Shokai to let him open a branch garage at Hamamatsu.

By 1937 the enterprising Honda had amassed enough money and experience to launch his first independent business, which he named Tokai Seiki Heavy Industry. First to be produced were piston rings, which was a very shrewd move on Honda's part, as Sakiya attested: "In the late 1930s, a piston ring was worth more than solid silver of the same weight."[4]

From rings Honda turned to creating cast-iron spokes for wheels. As spokes had traditionally been made of wood, Honda was granted a patent for his new technology. Despite his laudable achievements, Honda was troubled by the feeling that his products were not as good as they could be. Painfully conscious of his lack of scientific knowledge, he embarked upon part-time studies at the Hamamatsu High School of Technology, where he approached professor Takashi Tashiro for help. He received the answer he needed to improve his products — the metals he produced did not contain enough silicon, the addition of which would both strengthen them and increase their resilience. Having gained this crucial knowledge, Honda was able to proceed with the confidence he was making a superior product.

His single-minded determination to succeed at all costs made him something of a hermit, and like Ford, he often had to be almost forcibly removed from his shop. If anyone, including his own wife, wanted to see him, they had to visit him at work: "his wife had to come to the factory to cut his long, straggling hair," wrote Sakiya.[5]

Despite the ravages of the Sino-Japanese war, Honda's improved piston rings caught the eye of an automaker named Toyoda, who was so impressed with the product that he acquired 40 percent of Honda's company in 1942. Honda was pleased to deal with Toyoda but because of extreme labor shortages, he was predominately occupied by devising automated equipment in his factory which was then actively engaged in military-related production. In 1944 his efforts came to grief when the plant was bombed and very nearly destroyed. Further damage was sustained in a massive 1945 earthquake. Once he had repaired and salvaged what he could, Honda sold the company to Toyoda.

In a very un–Ford-like maneuver, he decided to take a year off to relax, offering a glimpse of the youthful spirit he would later inculcate into his future company: "Perhaps to demonstrate a more exuberant approach to life," wrote Sakiya of Honda, "he spent 10,000 yen (over $17,000 today), on a large drum of medical alcohol. The drum was installed in his house, where he made his own whisky and he spent the next year partying with friends and playing the shakuhachi (a Japanese wind instrument)."[6]

Perhaps it was this rest that inspired Honda's next enterprise, the creation of the Honda Technical Research Institute, in October of 1946. As many were doing in post-war Japan, Honda became immersed in salvage operations, repairing damaged engines and mounting them on bicycle frames. When he ran out of salvage he built his own engines and continued to sell them. In this way Honda was able to turn a quick profit in a country frantic for cheap transportation. So rapidly did demand grow that Honda realized he needed further capital as well as a business plan in order to expand his enterprise. Although not too shy to acknowledge his own skills, he was wise enough to know that marketing was not one of them.

While mulling over his options the problem was solved quite serendipitously, when a mutual friend introduced him to the man whose business acumen perfectly complemented his own mechanical genius.

Takeo Fujisawa had been charting his own course to success from an equally early age, and by the time he met Honda he was 38 years old to Honda's 42. When asked about their propitious meeting years later, Honda was able to summarize their joint success succinctly: "...both Fujisawa and I had the same goal."[7]

During that period, their goals included the creation of a superior motorcycle. They were joined in this pursuit by Kiyoshi Kawashima, a young engineering graduate whose skills would one day take him to the presidency of Honda's American operations.

By 1949 the Honda team, which now numbered twenty-one, had completed their first prototype, appropriately named the Dream Type D. Fitted with a two-stroke, 98-cc engine that produced a modest three horsepower, this engine represented the company's first summit. Initially only the engine had been developed while the body was contracted out to another company, but Honda was working to remedy the situation by developing its own frame. Also in development was a much smaller 50-cc engine that they already had a frame for and could sell as a complete unit. This bike was dubbed the Type A.

Now that the products were in hand, what remained to be sorted out was marketing and distributing. Fujisawa effectively applied himself to these tasks, stubbornly insisting that anyone who offered to sell the Honda product must be an exclusive Honda distributor. His methods, although risky and irksome to a few, proved successful in the long run, particularly when the potential distributor perceived just how well the bikes were made.

By 1950 a Honda Motor Sales office was opened to act as a hub for the regional distributors. A year later Honda was producing its latest invention, the four-stroke, 146-cc, Dream Type E, the first motorcycle to use overhead valves. The Type E was able to produce 5.5 horsepower and reach a speed of 45 mph, which in those days was enormously fast. The Japanese gobbled up these sturdy bikes and Honda's production quickly soared to 900 units per month.[8]

Although the Type D and E were extremely successful, there was an even greater market waiting to be tapped. While a select few could manage the heavier Dream bikes, many could not. Honda left no problem without a solution, and this time the solution inspired an all-new motorcycle — the Honda Cub, a scooter-type bike with a light frame and a 50-cc, 1.2-horsepower engine. Sales for 1953–1954 hit 7,729.[9]

By 1954 Honda had become a publicly-owned corporation but was held in a certain amount of disdain by the established motor industry as well as the government. But Soichiro Honda was not a man to be intimidated or manipulated. As many have testified, he went his own way and was his own man in a country where conformity was prized above all. Biographical consensus proves the point. As Robert L. Shook wrote in *Honda: An American Success Story*: "Soichiro Honda himself seemed to shun the establishment.... He was a non-conformist ... (who) wore dirty cover-alls to meetings with bankers."[10]

Brock Yates also made reference to the legendary character: "Honda was not the silent, stoical Japanese who operated in an ethereal Buddhist state beyond the comprehension of the Western mind. He was a passionate man of almost Latin propensities who would rap uncomprehending young engineers over the head with a wrench — what he called his 'thundering method' of education."[11]

Honda's volatile style often terrorized his juniors. Any error, no matter how small and seemingly insignificant, would provoke yells of rage and derision, followed by a public humiliation for the unfortunate worker, who was forced to apologize to anyone even remotely concerned with the matter.[12]

The formation of a labor union in 1953 had virtually no effect on Honda's teaching methods — he had more pressing matters to be concerned with, for the latest Honda motorcycles were failing on the market. The Type J Benley and the Type K Juno were succumbing to repeated engine failure and the subsequent loss of sales drove Honda to the verge of bankruptcy. Ironically, it was the union that eventually came to Honda's aid by showing a united front and pitching in to improve the Honda product, the quality of which, as union members knew, reflected directly upon themselves. They worked day and night to make the necessary changes, feeling assured that their efforts would be rewarded. But when business once again resumed, it seemed management had forgotten their heroic efforts and, driven to frustration, the labor union threatened to strike. Honda quickly moved to appease them, and the only serious labor trouble in Honda's history was thus diverted.

During the late 1950s the Honda Motor Company was heavily occupied with building racing motorcycles. These were entered in famous races in São Paulo and the Isle of Man, where Honda was victorious with their RG 142 model, which could rev up to 14,000 rpm. But while racing was an exciting challenge, the money still lay in mass production. After having produced motorcycles for less than ten years, Honda created a major stir by announcing its intention to export its bikes to America.

It was a bold move, and was denounced as foolhardy throughout the industry, and even by Honda's own preliminary research team. Soichiro Honda quite typically made his own decision on the matter. After extensive market research, entailing numerous trips to the United States, the first Honda motorcycles arrived in America in the summer of 1959.

A tiny storefront office was opened on June 11, located on Pico Boulevard in Los Angeles. The sign at the top of the building read "American Honda Motor Company Inc." The new operation was headed up by the thirty-nine year-old Kawashima who was supported by a seven-member team. Among them were Koichiro Yoshizawa, Satoshi Okubo, and Tadashi Kume, all of whom would eventually fill top-ranking positions in the company.

The Ministry of International Trade and Industry (MITI), already irritated by Honda's bid for independence, which they were loath to approve, severely restricted the amount of money the company could take out of the country — $250,000 — half of which was to be in cash, and half in inventory.[13]

Thus hampered, the small team faced the enormously daunting task of converting a population accustomed to roaring Harleys, Indians, and BSAs, over to a tiny bike that sounded rather like a lawnmower. To accomplish this they placed small ads in motorcycle trade magazines and traveled door-to-door to enlist dealers, all the while subsisting on rapidly decreasing funds.

When only 200 motorcycles had been sold at the end of that first year, the Honda team realized their projections of 7,500 sales per month had been wildly optimistic. As Robert Shook noted: "Much of the first six months' failure resulted because Honda failed to realize that the American motorcycle business runs from April through August. The company had arrived in the United States in June, close to the end of the 1959 season."[14]

The failure was also due to the poor performance of the bikes, which, when opened up on long stretches of American highway, blew gaskets and burned clutches. They were hastily returned to Japan for redesign, but the damage had been done, and Honda's reputation, as wobbly as a new-born foal, was badly hurt.

In order to sell the new and improved bike, now called the Super Cub, Kawashima realized that an entirely new promotional direction was called for. Honda motorcycles were driven by the team and showed off whenever and wherever possible. Sample bikes were handed over without charge for dealers to try. The sales team attempted to sell to any remotely related retail outlets. Their efforts finally paid off. By 1961 there were 500 Honda dealers directed by three zone offices — in California, Wisconsin, and New Jersey. Honda now had a staff of over 150 associates, as Honda preferred they be called.

In addition to cold-selling, the services of the Grey Advertising agency were enlisted, with approximately five million dollars being invested in the creation of a corporate image. Ironically it was an advertising student who clinched Honda's American reputation, in 1962, with the simple but highly effective slogan "You meet the nicest people on a Honda."

The boost to Honda's image was almost instantaneous and by 1963 sales had exceeded 100,000.[15] By that year the company had 6,000 associates, including Shoichiro Irimajiri, a future American Honda leader. Honda single-handedly made Americans realize that one didn't have to have bulging biceps to ride a motorcycle. The Honda's push-button electric starter opened up motorcycling to great numbers of people who would have been unwilling — or simply unable — to kick-start an American or British motorcycle. The incredible savings at the pumps also helped convince ordinary citizens to become "bikers."

Soichiro was enormously pleased with the American success which had come about through Kawashima's dedication. This left Honda free to do battle with MITI on quite another front — that of automobile production. In essence MITI was ready to shut the door on new automakers and consolidate the existing ones into three groups by 1968. Honda wanted to get his foot in that door before it closed. It was a feat that forced him to produce the tiny and hastily built S-360, which was followed by a small sports car and light-duty truck. It was enough — only just — to prove he had serious intentions as an automaker and MITI was once again forced to concede to Honda.

That Honda was not easily daunted by what many perceived as the government's bullying was perfectly illustrated as early as 1961, when he was asked by an interviewer what his next objective after being the number-one motorcycle manufacturer was. The indomitable Honda replied: "I will make the best cars in Japan. To do that, I must make the best cars in the world."[16]

To some such a statement might have sounded arrogant, but to those who knew the man and the product, it sounded just about right. But even the best car in the world had to begin somewhere and the first Honda automobiles were no exception.

The 44-horsepower S-500 sports model wasn't much more than a motorcycle disguised as a car. If one looked beneath it, one would even spy a chain-driven rear axle rather than a traditional driveshaft. The small T-360 truck was no more advanced.

But the S-500 was soon followed by the 57-horsepower S-600, and the company's first sedan, the L-700 Estate car, both produced in 1965. These first models were more prototypes than serious contenders in the mass market. The car that came next was much more suitable for that purpose.

The front-wheel-drive N-360 had a four-stroke, two-cylinder, 354-cc air-cooled engine that produced approximately 30 horsepower. It was quite fast for its minicar category, achieving a top speed of over 70 mph. The little car sold extremely well in Japan, assuming a proud position among the numerous other "360" minicars of the 1960s. The Honda team continued to develop the car, and before long the larger and improved N-600 made its first appearance. Like the N-360, the N-600 rose to the top of Japan's minicar segment.

Ever the entrepreneur, Fujisawa saw an even wider market for the N-600. Having been exposed to America as motorcycle exporters, both Fujisawa and Honda firmly believed there was a virtually untapped segment for minicars in that country. Plans for exporting Honda automobiles immediately went into effect.

By 1968 the editors of *Car Life* magazine were able to confirm if not encourage Honda's intentions: "...Honda ... better known for motorcycles, ... have announced plans to create a mini-car market by convincing Americans tiny cars with tiny engines are suitable or tolerable for city driving."[17]

A short while later, *Car Life* was given a sneak preview of the N-600 that Honda intended to export, and described it rather discouragingly as "Half box and half motorcycle; a sobering thought."[18]

Ready or not, the N-600 coupe made its debut in America in May of 1970. A small quantity was shipped to the United States, arriving at established Honda motorcycle dealerships such as Richards' Cycle Center in Little Rock, Arkansas, the Norm Reeves dealership in Bellflower, California, and Carmichael Honda of Sacramento. Others went to Honda of Hollywood's one-car showroom, one of the first exclusively Honda car dealerships in America.

Customers who had been impressed by the bikes were curious about the little unitized steel-body N-600, which had a wheelbase of only 78.7 inches (three feet shorter than a Pinto), weighed a mere 1,355 pounds and sold for around $1,500. Although its very impressive 42 mpg fuel economy was a bonus, in those pre–oil crisis days it was not the car's primary attraction. Its size and agility made it the perfect run-about, the ideal second car or a teenager's first car. It was amazingly well-appointed, with unexpected options such as a tachometer, stereo tape player, roof and ski racks, wood or leather-trimmed steering wheel and a fold-down rear seat. Standard equipment included rack-and-pinion steering, strut, coil spring and lower wishbone suspension on the front and semi-elliptical springs and a rigid axle on the back, front disc brakes and an all-aluminum block and head.

*Car and Driver* featured the N-600 in April of 1972, marveling over its attributes, most prominent of which was its compact size: "You enter a scaled-down motoring world where sidewalks are as inviting as empty freeways and you can damn near make a U-turn in one lane." Going for a nautical analogy, the magazine summarized its feelings on the N-600: "...if you're the kind that goes to sea in a row boat you might find the Honda amusing between voyages."[19]

It was not exactly an endorsement designed to appeal to the business classes but it was definitely attractive to the youth market, which was precisely Honda's intention. The N-600's advertising clearly reflected this aim. A full-page ad featuring a bright-red N-600 surrounded by young women dressed in various sporting outfits did not attempt to portray the car as something it was not. The copy read: "Which would you rather have? Automatic transmission, air conditioning, and a 400-horsepower engine? Or Michelle and Tammy and Alison?"[20] It was the perfect appeal to the free-spirited love-and-peace generation whose members were pulled in by psychedelic colors and a down-to-earth approach.

Before long new Honda customers were requesting cars, rather than the motorcycles for which the company was best known. Their choice fell between an N-600 coupe or a sedan, although one could hardly tell the difference, as both looked exactly like miniature hatchbacks.

Even with such modest offerings, the cars and the company continued to attract notice in automotive trade magazines. Petersen Publishing, the editors of *The Complete Book of Japanese Import Cars*, was among those who documented Honda's arrival: "When it (Honda) first brought its little fun car to the U.S. a couple of years ago, it was marketed only on the West Coast and in limited quantities. But the 600 sedan touched a responsive chord with youthful car buyers in Southern California...."[21]

However, much in accordance with the Americans' condescending tone concerning most early Japanese imports, the review continued: "...the transversely mounted power plant puts out 36 hp (SAE) from its 36.5 cu.-in. displacement, and if you'll stop laughing long enough to read on, let us assure you that either Honda will do 75 mph on expressways without straining."[22]

Soon there were rumors of an even larger Honda appearing in America, a possibility that inspired *Motor Trend* to ask what had Honda owners "all turned on" in August of 1971. Honda's public relations department assured the editors that any model other than the 600 was "at least a year away."[23]

Perhaps acting on the belief they knew which car Honda would export next,

*Motor Trend* went ahead and printed a photograph of the 1300, a four-cylinder, 100-horsepower model already being offered in Japan. But a competitor magazine had scooped them long before.

*Road Test* published an exclusive review of the innovative 1300 in their August 1969 edition. Gushing over its two-way air cooling system and dry sump lubrication, *Road Test* expressed the opinion that "The overall engineering design of the 1300 is virtually flawless."[24] They also swept aside bias by concluding that the 1300 put Ford's new best-selling Maverick in the shade: "The Honda represents what an all new car should be, unlike the Maverick which is a conglomeration of existing engines etc. with a minimum of original engineering. With quality control at a very high standard it is, all in all, a most impressive car."[25]

If the sentiment was correct, the new model predicted to arrive by *Road Test* and *Motor Trend* was slightly off the mark.

In October of 1972 Brock Yates pontificated that "A majority of moss-backs remain in Detroit waiting for the present insanity to pass and the new renaissance to come when decent folk will again frolic in 'full-size' cars." According to Yates, there were "vast holes in the present market," which he accurately predicted would be filled by someone other than the Big Three: "...Detroit, in its lethargy, can hardly be expected to fill them. That duty will fall to a smaller, more mobile competitor — very likely the Japanese or the Germans."[26] The little car that managed to fill these "vast holes" arrived in the very month of Yates' soliloquy.

The Honda Civic was significantly larger than the N-600 and was selling so well in Japan that it was voted Japan's Car of the Year for 1972. Honda needed no convincing to export the car, which had in fact been designed specifically with the American market in mind.

Arriving in California just in time for the 1973 season, Honda couldn't have picked a more propitious time. With the first reverberations of the oil shocks being felt around the country, the fuel-efficient Civic filled the economy niche as neatly as it filled a parking spot. Its "homely-but-cute" looks won over the hearts of Americans who were tired of land yachts and escalating fuel costs.

Available as a two-door sedan or two-door hatchback, the front-wheel-drive Civic had the same steering system as the N-600 but a revised fully-independent suspension arrangement with McPherson struts, coil springs and single wishbones on the rear. A smooth four-speed manual transmission or an optional two-speed semi-automatic ("Hondamatic") provided the gears.

Unexpected creature comforts for such an inexpensive (under $2,100) small car included dual-speed wipers, reclining bucket seats, carpets, woodgrain dash, cloth interior, and whitewall tires. Radials, air-conditioning and an AM radio were options.

The Civic was still quite tiny by American standards, at 139.8 inches long with an 86.6-inch wheelbase and standing 53 inches tall. It was lighter than any American "subcompact" as well, weighing only 1,535 pounds. Making the car seem even smaller were its twelve-inch wheels, which covered power front disc brakes and rear drums.

The Civic's in-line four-cylinder engine, like the N-600's, was constructed of aluminum alloy for both block and head, which further helped to reduce the weight

The 1973 Civic got nearly 40 mpg and, appropriately, arrived in America the year of the first oil crisis in the Middle East. The American market did not get this four-door model (courtesy American Honda Motor Company).

and increase the efficiency. An overhead cam ran the solid-lifter valve-train, and the 1169-cc (71.3-cubic-inch) displacement produced 50 horsepower at 5,500 rpm and 59 ft-lb of torque at 3,000 rpm. The water-cooled, five-main-bearing engine had a compression ratio of 8.3:1 and was fed by a two-barrel Hitachi carburetor. The 2.76-inch bore and 2.99-inch stroke made for an almost perfectly "square" engine. Honda's well-made transmission with its final drive ratio of 4.13:1 perfectly complemented the engine's torque and horsepower.[27]

Honda's popular little car became an instant media darling. Brock Yates called it "…surely the most brilliant small car in automotive history."[28] *Car and Driver* voted it the Best Economy Sedan for 1974, by which time the car had increased slightly in size and was powered by a larger 1237-cc (75.5-cubic-inch) 52-horsepower engine.

*Science and Mechanics* gave the Civic a position on its "Twelve best cars to own in an energy crisis," adding, "Done in the best tradition of Honda's great motorcycles, the Civic goes and handles. The front-wheel-drive, again, is excellent in foul weather. Similar sedan and hatchback models are produced. This is not a funny toy. Unfortunately, availability is limited and some dealers are over-optioning their cars, some up to $3,500."[29]

So proud was Honda of their outstanding gas mileage that they based an entire advertisement campaign around it. A typical ad presented a full print-out of the EPA's test results for 1974 with the Civic, of course, listed in the number one spot.[30] It was certainly the right approach, as the soaring sales records proved. With the N-600 no longer in production, the Civic had been responsible for the bulk of Honda's sales total (43,119) in 1974. Only one year later they had jumped to 102,389, and were about to go even higher.[31]

In February of 1971, much to the chagrin of all other automakers—with the possible exception of Mazda—Honda's Japan headquarters released the statement that it would have no trouble meeting the new emission standards set for 1975. The same announcement was made in America in April of 1972. The CVCC (compound vortex controlled combustion) technology that enabled Honda to do so placed it far ahead of its competitors and earned it a place in automotive history. The company now not only produced the most fuel-efficient vehicle in the United States, but also one that produced the lowest emissions without the need for an expensive catalytic converter. A more detailed explanation of the CVCC engine is included in Chapter 13.

The Civic CVCC arrived in America on January 1, 1975. Its engine featured a cast-iron block and an aluminum alloy head, with a displacement of 1488 cc (90.8-cubic inches). The bore was now 2.91 inches and the stroke 3.41 inches. Horsepower was increased to 53 and torque to 69 ft-lb at 2,500 rpm, but compression remained the same at 8.1:1 A three-barrel Keihin carburetor replaced the previous two-barrel unit.

A CVCC Civic could beat the regular Civic's 15.1-second time for zero-to-sixty, reaching the same speed in 13.8 seconds. A quarter-mile driven in the CVCC took 19.6 seconds with a top speed of 69.2 mph. Not sports car standards by any means, but the CVCC's efficiency more than compensated with an average rating of 39 mpg.[32] Perhaps the most unfortunate aspect of the newest Civic was its limited choice of colors—a dull brownish-orange or mustard yellow were the only options available.

More positive changes for 1975 included the addition of a new five-speed transmission and a wooden steering wheel and gearshift knob. There were now five versions of the car to choose from — the Civic two-door sedan and two-door hatchback, and a Civic CVCC two-door sedan, two-door hatchback, and two-door wagon. With only one model being offered, Honda intended to reap sales in as many categories as it could.

While Toyota and Nissan's U.S. sales fell off in the aftermath of the first oil crisis, Honda's surged ahead. As Robert Shook wrote: "...Honda bucked the trend, with an increasingly high reputation for quality combined with a lower price. The Civic was one of the few successes of the time, an indication the company had not only established a strong base in the United States but was also well situated to increase both volume and market share."[33]

Between 1975 and 1978 very few modifications were made to the Civic and, apart from some minor body styling changes, none were needed. If anything, Honda fans wanted more Hondas. That Honda was enjoying worldwide success with both automobiles and motorcycles must have been a tremendous source of pride to company founders Honda and Fujisawa. Perhaps it's not surprising that both men decided to go out "in a blaze of glory" at the peak of their careers. Fujisawa was the first to make the decision to retire and when Honda heard about it, he knew that if Fujisawa left it was fitting that he should leave too. The pair chose 1973, Honda's twenty-fifth anniversary, to depart the company they had founded. Although only 62 and 67 years old respectively, Fujisawa and Honda felt strongly about allowing younger minds to

The larger Civic, called the Civic CVCC, arrived in 1975 and was the first car to beat emissions standards without using a catalytic converter. It could run on leaded or unleaded fuel (courtesy American Honda Motor Company).

keep the company sharply competitive. As Sakiya noted, "At Honda a great deal of authority is delegated to the lower ranks, reflecting the corporate confidence in the enthusiasm and abilities of the employees ... at most Japanese companies, the hiring of new college graduates is regarded as an important event, one that determines the future of the organization."[34]

But if younger managers were to lead the company, their names would not be Honda or Fujisawa. "Never once has Honda claimed ownership of the company he founded," Sakiya explained, adding that "It is also significant that Honda Motor's founders refused to let their sons run the company, and even barred them from entering as low-rank employees."[35]

When Fujisawa and Honda left the company (the latter to assume an honorary chair position), four senior managers acted as directors, one of whom was soon-to-be-president Kiyoshi Kawashima. Although Soichiro Honda was no longer head of the company, his legacy was still very much in evidence, and is to this day. Far too complex to be contained within these pages, it can nevertheless be summarized in a few simple words: quality, innovation, communication, and service. Honda, like Toyota and Nissan valued the importance of surveys, and was always striving to learn more about the needs of its customers and the complexities of dealer relations. Honda's relationship with its dealerships has, on the whole, been excellent but there were times when that relationship was strained. This was particularly evident in the early years when demand far outstripped supply and pressures were running high.

Brock Yates recorded one such example: "The small group of Honda dealers, operating with the bare-fanged avarice that has blighted the franchised system since its origins, responded to this booming market with price-gouging. Accords were suddenly loaded down with after-market gewgaws and bolt-ons to boost their base price despite angry threats from the Japanese parent company."[36]

Certainly the appearance of Honda's latest offering not only placed great strain on Honda management but also on the six hundred or so dealers as well. In the summer of 1976 both were faced with an unprecedented demand with the arrival of the Honda Accord.

# 9

## Honda's American Dream — Part Two

In December of 1975, *Motor Trend* magazine gave their readers a hint of what was about to come from Honda. Beneath a surprisingly accurate ink drawing, the text read in part: "The little car here is an as-yet-unnamed Honda which is very much in the mold of the Volkswagen Scirocco. Very little is known about this one, other than that it is slightly larger than a Civic, and that it will also have a CVCC engine…. No definite introduction date is known, but judging from the finish detail work of the prototypes which have been seen, it cannot be too far off."[1]

The Honda Accord's actual time of arrival was the summer of 1976. The attractive little hatchback (the first model available) proudly displayed the CVCC badge next to dual round headlights and the ubiquitous "H" on the grille. The front-wheel-drive Accord was 162.8 inches long with a 93.7-inch wheelbase and a weight of 1,993 pounds. Power came through a 1600-cc (97-cubic-inch), in-line four-cylinder engine that produced 68 horsepower, 85 ft-lb of torque, and a compression ratio of 8.0:1. Sharing much else with the Civic CVCC, the Accord also shared its Keihin carburetor as well as a zero-to-sixty time of 13.8 seconds. When pushed to its absolute limits the Accord could reach 90 mph but there were no attempts by Honda to portray it as fast — only comfortable and economical. Being larger than the Civic it was naturally not quite as efficient, but mileage was still a very respectable 32 mpg.[2]

Honda's smooth five-speed transmission came as standard equipment with the two-speed Hondamatic offered as an option. Transverse arms added extra stability to the suspension which was otherwise the same as that of the Civic. A customer could expect to pay around $3,995 for a 1976 Accord which was slightly higher than average for a Japanese import, and considerably higher than a domestic marque.

Despite the sticker-shock, the Accord caused an even greater sensation than the Civic and drove the automotive literati to new heights. *Motor Trend* promptly voted it Import Car of the Year, and the normally blasé Brock Yates devoted almost four

The car that made automotive journalists stop laughing at small imports — the 1976 Honda Accord (courtesy American Honda Motor Company).

running pages to it in his book *The Decline and Fall of the American Automobile Industry.*

He opened his tribute by calling the Accord "...the automobile that shook the secure base of the business from Michigan to Stuttgart," and proceeded to wax lyrical: "The Accord looked exquisite even to the most unpracticed eye. Its painted surface shimmered like a miniature Rolls-Royce. The minimal chrome bright work trim fit perfectly; the body panels appeared to have been aligned by a surgeon's scalpel. The interior upholstery and vinyl trim had the look of functional elegance normally associated with expensive European cars and executive jet aircraft."[3] And squaring off against those who criticized Honda buyers as being unpatriotic, Yates insisted: "Pecksniffs and bohemians be damned. Honda owners were real Americans, even super-Americans."[4]

In view of the overwhelmingly positive response the Accord received, it is incredible to learn that when future Honda president Takashi Kume presented his concept car to his superiors they scorned it for having no trunk. As Kume recounted to an interviewer years later: "My overwhelming recollection of the Accord is as a failure."[5]

The so-called trunk problem was rectified in 1978 with the arrival of the four-door Accord sedan which took its place beside the also-new "LX" luxury edition hatchback. The Accord was a sensation, but not an overnight one. From modest sales of 18,643 in its debut year, the car steadily gathered steam and went on to win 370,000 customers by 1981.[6]

Paying court to the acknowledged American weakness for luxury despite their hunger for economy, Honda engineers began the trend toward higher-end designs that would become more evident with each passing year. Among the first extras offered were power steering, velour upholstery, air conditioning, digital clocks, electronic warning bells, power windows and remote latches.

The new Accord was not only more luxurious than its predecessor, but almost nine inches longer with four more horsepower. A more substantial radiator replaced the old undersized unit, suspension was stiffened and the exhaust system was similarly fortified. It was clear that Honda intended that the Accord be their benchmark of quality, built to compete with the ever-more-luxurious Toyota Corona and Mazda's impressive new 626.

*Car and Driver* was unabashedly sold, calling the Accord LX, "A mini-Mercedes for mainstream America."[7] Obviously the car was granted such high praise because of its outstanding qualities, but perhaps the Mercedes analogy was an oblique reference to the Accord's price. David E. Davis, Jr., repeatedly slipped references about cost into his review with statements such as, "The Honda is a remarkably successful car in this country, in spite of the fact it costs the very earth to buy." And, feeling that some would be deterred by the fact, he added, "That culturally deprived segment of American society that still believes small cars are, by definition, cheap and chintzy will choke on the price and never come to know all the goodies that await on the other side of the sticker."[8]

But no matter the price, there was no denying the Accord's value — even in adverse conditions. When Davis and his crew found themselves testing the Accord over snow- and ice-covered roads, he remarked that the car "cruised along without even breathing hard ... as true as a die."[9]

The review's summary contained a stinging parting shot to the American industry: "Ironically, Detroit simply hasn't come up with anything to touch this most American of imported cars. The Chevette is a great little trouper in its way, but one could 'LX' the living hell out of a Chevette and still not have a Honda Accord."[10]

This was a fact that Detroit was understandably reluctant to accept, but that they tried to do so was illustrated by their eagerness to find out what made the Accord so popular. "A number of Accords had been purchased by General Motors and examined with the curiosity that might be devoted to an alien spaceship.... Across town in Dearborn, Ford engineers were doing likewise," reported Brock Yates.[11] Eventually the Chrysler Corporation also swallowed its pride and sent engineers over to Honda for the same purposes, albeit much later in the decade.

While Detroit was investigating the Honda, Honda was investigating the United States. Although some journalists have intimated that Honda decided to manufacture in America because of the threat of voluntary export restraints, the company's history reveals that plans to build in the United States had been in the works since 1974, about five years before the restraints were confirmed.

Therefore in 1979, despite skepticism and even outright hostility, the Honda Motor Company officially opened its new motorcycle plant in Marysville, Ohio. It took only three more years to tool up for automobile production. The first American-made Accord rolled off the line in 1982. Honda had once again proved itself an industry leader by being the first Japanese company to manufacture independently in the United States, although they were followed closely by Nissan.

Now that Honda was on American soil the process of learning American culture and getting to know the American people began in earnest. It was essential that the company understand its future customers, as well as its new dealers. As the dealership network spread across North America, Honda worked diligently to maintain its reputation not only for quality vehicles but outstanding service as well. Open communication remained a key issue. Robert Shook attributed a large portion of Honda's success to the fact that it was in touch with its buyers: "Honda listens to its customers and then builds the cars those customers want."[12]

What the customers seemed to want was a Honda to rival the sporty Toyota Celica. With the Accord filling the family car slot and the Civic that of economy, there was a noticeable vacancy in the sports coupe class. Believing in the philosophy of anticipating consumer needs before being told, Honda had already been working on a 2 + 2 sports coupe since late 1974.

As a result, the two-door Honda Prelude went on sale in the United States in the spring of 1979. Swept along on the wave of Hondas before it, the Prelude charmed customers by the thousands. Also fitted with a CVCC in-line single-overhead-cam four, the Prelude's displacement was higher than the Accord at 1751 cc (106.8 cubic inches). The car was not especially fast but it was extraordinarily nimble with snappy acceleration. Its modest 72 horsepower was put to efficient, if not thrilling, use.

A more detailed technical examination of the engine revealed a bore and stroke of 3.03 by 3.70 inches, a compression ratio of 8.0:1, and 94 ft-lb of torque at 3,000 rpm. The Prelude borrowed its siblings' three-barrel Keihnin carb, fully-independent suspension, rack-and-pinion steering, and available transmissions, but as the top Honda its list of options was more extensive. These included a power moonroof with sliding sunshade, a tachometer, tinted glass, wheel trim rings, interior light package and reclining bucket seats. The 2,100-pound, 161-inch-long sports coupe came in three colors—burgundy, blue, or silver.[13]

In March of 1979 *Car and Driver* displayed a photograph of the Prelude as it appeared on the Japanese market, with its mirrors clipped to the front fenders. "Play it again, Honda," punned the editors in reference to the car's musical name. "The new Prelude is a variation on the Accord theme, which should debut here in May," they informed their readers.[14]

In April the magazine sent representatives to Japan to road-test the newest Honda. After having absorbed the shock of Japanese traffic conditions and driving styles that would "make a New York cabbie need assertiveness training," Chuck Nerpel and his crew found much to like about the Prelude, in particular its "excellent all-around visibility, good acceleration, quick rack-and-pinion steering, brakes that give positive sure-footed stopping time after time, and a fuel-thrifty engine," that was "as much at home on the highway and winding mountain road as it is in the city."[15]

Most fascinating to the American team was the Prelude's combination speedometer/tachometer with two needles on the same axis, an arrangement Honda referred to as the "centralized target meter."

So impressive was the car that Nerpel guessed it would probably retail for close to $10,000 and was shocked to be informed by Honda that it would be sold in the same price range as the Accord. In fact, the Prelude hit American shores with a price tag of $6,445, while an Accord LX of the same vintage sold for $6,799.[16]

One of the first ads for the Prelude showed a full-length profile of the car in its burgundy coat beneath the heading: "The Honda Prelude: A sports car for grown-ups." In a phrase reminiscent of another popular Japanese company, Honda's tagline read: "Once you get in, you may never want to get out."[17]

Honda's official slogan of the time, "We Make It Simple," belied the brilliant and intricate engineering behind their products, and the Prelude was no exception. It was the perfect blend of simplicity and complexity, a balance it maintained until well into its later years. It was Honda's policy to release a new generation every four years, and true to form they introduced a new Prelude for 1983.

The car lost its endearing chubbiness and was lean and angular with a reduced drag coefficient and ground clearance. To complement the exterior design there was an extra 25 horsepower beneath the hood and an even longer list of standard and optional equipment which included AM/FM cassette, dual remote mirrors, rear spoiler, lumbar seats, and side and rear window defrosters. Also available were four-wheel disc brakes, variable-assist power steering, and a new four-speed automatic transmission.

The reviews poured in and they were consistently positive, along the lines of *Road & Track*'s May 1983 report. The Prelude, they declared, was "a benchmark car that will send competitors back to the drawing boards."[18] A year later the same magazine named it one of the "12 Best Enthusiast Cars, 1984."[19]

It seemed that few could resist the alluring new look of the Prelude and so popular was the design that Honda tried to adhere to it until past its due change in 1987. A new 2.0-liter Si edition had been added in 1986 that came with a "sport" interior and power equipment package. Honda's Si trim level, which was introduced on the Civic and Prelude in 1985/86 (and as the LXi on the Accord), indicated that the car used the company's own electronically controlled multi-point Programmed Fuel Injection system (PFI). On the whole, the fuel-injection system offered approximately 12 to 15 more horsepower than a carbureted engine of the same displacement, but it also raised the car's price.

While the base second-generation Prelude was selling for between $10,000 and $11,000, the Si retailed for approximately $13,500. This was quite a jump from the first generation's cost, but the car's powerful attraction still drew in thousands of customers.

When *Road & Track* revisited the Prelude in 1987 their accolades were plentiful and criticisms few, with minor complaints associated with lack of head room and inadequate air conditioning. The Prelude drew praise not only for its quality but also for its economy — 25 to 35 mpg, which came out to an estimated driving cost of only 15 cents per mile. Said the editors: "That to us, rates as a bargain price for all the entertainment and utilitarian value we've gotten from our 20 months of living with the Honda."[20] Another favorable point was the car's high resale value, an attribute shared by many other Japanese cars.

A more aerodynamic third-generation Prelude emerged in 1988, with both the base model and the Si being powered by the same 2.0-liter engine. The base model featured a single-overhead-cam, 12-valve configuration producing 104 horsepower and 111 ft-lb of torque at 4,500 rpm, while the Si 16-valve double-overhead-cam version produced 135 horsepower and 127 ft-lb of torque at 4,500 rpm. The Si's compression ratio was approaching sports car levels at 9.4:1. Most notable for this generation was Honda's mechanically-operated four-wheel steering system which was only available on the Si model.

In 1988 *Consumer Reports* featured this Prelude Si 4WS and drew attention to the fact that while Honda's unit was mechanical, Mazda had already produced a similar, albeit much more complex electronically driven version. But the overall advantages of four-wheel steering, according to *Consumer Reports*, were wasted on the already agile Prelude. A tighter turning radius certainly made the car easier to park, but it took some practicing to anticipate in which direction both front and rear wheels were going. A significant number of minor dents and scratches were recorded by Honda dealers and owners alike who were learning the ways of their new four-wheel-steering vehicles.

Unfortunately the system did make the Prelude more difficult and therefore more expensive to service, particularly during wheel alignments and accident repair. But as Honda sales were now over the half-million-units-per-year mark, with 640,747 vehicles sold in 1988,[21] higher servicing costs just seemed to be part and parcel of the product's overall higher price and the general trend that was sweeping the import industry.

In the final analysis *Consumer Reports* was impressed with the latest Prelude, but not unequivocally. In yet another reference to the steadily increasing price of Hondas, they opined that the $18,409 figure attached to their 4WS car was not worth it. "We'd rather have seen Honda offer antilock brakes, as more and more automakers are doing," they concluded. Nevertheless, the Prelude won high marks for its engine, transmission, ride and handling, climate controls, safety features, convenience, and reliability, all of which earned it the magazine's coveted "red doughnut" representing a "much higher than average" rating. The only black dot went beside the Prelude's singularly uncomfortable rear seat, a complaint that was to continue to plague Honda for years to come.[22]

But rear seat discomforts failed to discourage consumers determined to own an attractive sports coupe that could get from a standstill to sixty mph in 10.6 seconds and still sip gas at a rate of 21 mpg city, 34 highway.

In 1992 the Prelude was again redesigned with a higher and bulkier hind-quarters, elongated hood, protruding grille, and more aggressive stance. Although the overall length was shorter than the previous model at 174.8 inches, the Prelude was now two inches wider. It also weighed more and looked every ounce of its 2,866 pounds. Complaints about the car were becoming more audible, and whereas it was once only the rear seating that caused disapproval, that complaint had been extended to include trunk space which had been sacrificed to design principles.

The Prelude still came in three models—the base "S," which produced 135 horsepower from its 2.2-liter four cylinder; the 160-horsepower Si; and the now electronically controlled 4WS model with the same engine as the Si.

New for the Prelude were standard antilock brakes and a driver-side airbag with an optional one on the passenger side. While the Prelude's outward appearance had been strikingly altered, the car's interior contained its most startling and controversial design elements. A one-piece dash curved from window to window, with only a narrow slot allowed for the placement of the gauges. One reviewer complained these were nearly invisible in the daytime when the lights were on. *Consumer Guide* was of the opinion that the new dash fell "short of Honda's standards."[23] *The Used Car Book* published by Jack Gillis went much further by pronouncing the Prelude's new dash "an overstyled mess."[24]

Now retailing for over $20,000 (4WS Si), the newest Prelude bore little resemblance to its humble but noble ancestor. Fortunately the next change was not quite as drastic or noteworthy. It came in 1993 with the addition of a new 55-horsepower stronger VTEC engine. The VTEC also increased engine torque which now measured 158 ft-lb as compared to the earlier 142 ft-lb for the S, and 156 ft-lb for the Si.[25]

In 1996 the Prelude was still drawing fire for its interior design, cramped rear seat and reduced trunk space. Even while winning a place in *Car and Driver*'s annual Ten Best Cars list, the editors noted that its back seat "was more suited to groceries than to humans," and that it still retained its "peculiar dashboard." On a more positive note *Car and Driver* professed themselves "mesmerized by the Prelude's driver delights."[26]

By 2001 the venerable Prelude could no longer hold its own on the leaner sports car market. Taking its place was the new and much sleeker S2000 two-seater, more along Porsche lines than the Prelude ever hoped to be. With a 240-horsepower 2.0-liter VTEC twin-cam engine, the S2000 produced 240 horsepower and 153 ft-lb of torque. A heavy-footed driver had to rev the throttle to 9,300 rpm to reach the S2000's redline.

This car's heritage dated back to the days of the also-high-revving S500, S600, and S800 models, but that's where the similarity ended. The new rear-wheel-drive Honda, with its power fabric convertible top, 50/50 weight distribution, ultra-modern styling and $33,000 price tag bears little resemblance to the rough little Honda sports cars of the 1960s that found a fringe audience. And while one could cruise down the highway quite nicely if noisily in the S800, it certainly couldn't match the snarling zero-to-sixty time of 5.6 seconds or quarter-mile record of 14.4 seconds at 97 mph of the S2000.[27] *Consumer Reports* declared the S2000 was simply a "pure uncompromising sports car," with excellent reliability.[28]

"Compromising" is not a word Honda engineers seem to be familiar with. They have consistently produced award-winning designs, if at times controversial ones. The CRX, an older cousin of the S2000 introduced in 1984, was a prime example of Honda's earlier engineering excellence.

The CRX was only 144.6 inches long with an 86.6-inch wheelbase, which made it approximately six inches shorter than the regular Civic. It was also two inches lower and trimmer in width by an inch or so. Its short stature was emphasized by its abruptly-sawed-off tail and high hatchback lift-over tailgate.

Produced in two versions, the base model was known as the Civic CRX 1300, while the other was called the CRX 1.5. The base CRX was powered by an all-aluminum

1342-cc single-overhead-cam four cylinder that produced 60 horsepower at 5,500 rpm and 73 ft-lb of torque at 3,500 rpm. Compression was 10.0:1.

The CRX 1.5 version had a 12-valve, 1488-cc engine with 76 horsepower at 6,000 rpm and 84 ft-lb of torque. Its compression ratio was 9.2:1. Bore and stroke were 2.91 inches by 3.41 inches. Mileage for the CRX 1300 was an astounding 51 mpg (city) and 67 (highway), and only slightly less for the more powerful 1.5. They both shared the same three-barrel carburetor as their larger Honda siblings.

Much of the CRX's body was made of special-density high-impact plastic and suspension was the typical McPherson strut/coil spring arrangement supplemented by an anti-roll bar in front and a beam axle at the rear. The CRX was designed for sport with a tachometer, front air dam, rear spoiler, tinted windows, and sport-package steering wheel and seats. Its colors were Greek White, Baltic Blue, or Victoria Red.

In 1985 two new CRXs appeared, the CRX-HF (high fuel economy) and the CRX Si. Horsepower dropped to 58 in the HF in an effort to squeeze out even more miles per gallon. But CRX fans displayed an aversion to this model—they wanted the car for its looks and speed and felt it was already economical enough. As a result they were much more interested in the Si 1.5-liter engine that produced 91 horsepower, making it the fastest Civic in the group. Zero-to-sixty was accomplished in under 9 seconds, and the CRX Si was probably the least expensive sports coupe that could go that fast yet be so economical. A retail price of around $6,500 placed it at least $3,000 below the Prelude and well below other similarly equipped Japanese sports rivals.

The CRX might have been a blast to drive but it fared poorly in crash tests, with especially weak bumpers; and at the speeds it usually traveled, combined with its diminutive size, safety was perhaps more of an issue than it ordinarily would have been. Although it was rated as an overall high-quality vehicle and it survived to grow by four inches and receive a more powerful engine in 1988, the CRX eventually lost its place in the line, and by 1991 it was gone.

The CRX was replaced in 1993 by the two-seater del Sol, Honda's first attempt at an open-air design, using a removable targa roof and a power retractable rear window to simulate the effect of a convertible. Shorter than the Civic but longer than the CRX, the del Sol came as a base S with a 102-horsepower 1.5-liter, or a 125-horsepower 1.6-liter, VTEC engine. But despite its attributes and colorful shells (one of which was brilliant grass-green) the del Sol could not override its reputation as Honda's novelty car, and since it was taken off the market only a few years after it appeared, it has retained its status as such.

Of less interest to the younger set was the Civic wagon or "Tallboy," as Honda called it, which had been released in 1985. The wagon was the first Honda in America to feature four-wheel drive, although it didn't go to full-time (real-time) four-wheel drive until 1987. Like the Toyota wagon, the Tallboy had a six-speed manual transmission with an extra low gear. It was powered by the standard 1.5-liter common to all Civics, and when the rear seat was folded, an extensive 60.3 cubic feet of cargo space became available, a fact the company was proud to include in the car's advertising.

Although the wagon found select and discerning buyers among shoppers and even rock-hounds, it fell victim to the onset of the trend toward "real" four-by-fours that was being sparked by the Cherokee, Jimmy, Blazer, and Bronco. Thus the Tallboy also made its exit in 1991 beside the CRX.

By 1993 there was certainly no shortage of Civics to choose from. There were three new models—a three-door hatchback, four-door sedan, and a new high-efficiency VX model. The base Civics created 102 horsepower, the Si 125, and the VX only 96 in order to increase efficiency. All models had a 1.6-liter engine.

The new more aerodynamic Civics had grown both in stature and price. As *Consumer Guide* reported, "the new Civic sedans have about as much useful interior room as the 1986–1989 Accord sedans."[29] Of course that expansion came at a price. Honda was now well aware that people were willing to dig deep in order to own their products, which had been elevated to the highest firmament by journalists. In 1993 a base Civic could be purchased in the neighborhood of $10,500, while a high-end Civic EX could exceed $14,000. To put it into market perspective, a similar domestic car such as the Neon or Ford Escort topped out at $12,500.

The Civic had eleven different faces by 1996, at which time the cars had standard driver-side airbags and antilock brakes. Mileage was still an economical 34 mpg (average), and reviews continued to be exceptional. Anyone turning to a consumer magazine to help guide them in their choice could rely on a steadfast recommendation for any Honda product. Even though the price range now fell between $12,000 and $17,500, *Car and Driver* considered that for the quality, the Civic's price was well worth it.[30] *Consumer Reports* signed off on the car by saying: "We expect the newly designed Civic to prove exceptional reliability, like its predecessors."[31]

As Honda's first flagship vehicle, the Civic has been chosen throughout the years to showcase some of the company's finest innovations. It was the first Honda to receive the catalytic-converter-free CVCC engine, although when even stricter emissions standards were issued in 1979 the Civic had to concede to the use of a three-way catalytic converter. It was by then larger and more luxurious although still highly efficient.

In the eighties the Civic was the first Honda to use both four-wheel drive as well as the CVT (Continuously Variable Transmission), although Subaru was the first Japanese auto company to feature it. It also won praise for being the first vehicle to meet California's lower emission standards with its Civic LEV edition (low-emission vehicle) in 1996.

The Civic therefore entered the new millennium with a long and proud history behind it. Still in its familiar DX, LX, and EX trim levels, it was now powered by a 1.7-liter 115- or 127-horsepower engine. The latest high-efficiency Civic is the 117-horsepower HX edition. Returning after an extended absence is the Civic Si which came back as a hatchback with a 160-horsepower, twin-cam, 16-valve 2.0-liter powerplant. Although still quick, it has lost some of its former edge and both the Golf GTI and BMW's new Mini Cooper came in under its zero-to-sixty time of 8.4 seconds.[32]

If the Civic saw a proliferation of changes and styles throughout the years, the Accord was the recipient of even more, at one point offered in 18 different configurations. By 1986 the Accord was three inches longer and 500 pounds heavier than its predecessor and was available in DX, LX, and LXi versions. The DX and LX versions received the carbureted 2.0-liter engine while the LXi was powered by the fuel-injected version.

The Accord shed its boxy image in 1986, assuming a similar body-style to that of the Prelude. By 1988 the Accord was the fourth-best-selling car in America but went on to take top honors away from the Ford Taurus by the first of the new decade.[33]

Trade magazines "Letters to the editors" departments began to include examples such as the one from Bill Cheek of Ann Arbor, Michigan, who wrote to *Motor Trend* in 1987: "But as good as it is, our Accord has one frightening problem: I have tried and tried, but I can't find anything wrong with it."[34]

It was true that there weren't many complaints registered against the Accord, particularly against the new-for-1988 SEi coupe with its leather upholstery and Bose sound system. There were, however, some dissatisfied customers—particularly those who ended up with Accords that stalled or hesitated upon acceleration. Between 1986 and 1989 the Accord experienced difficulties with both of its fuel delivery systems. These problems were related to improper idle speed or a sticking throttle wire and usually only required a cleaning and minor adjustment to set them right.

Another fault common to both the Accord and Prelude during this time was a tendency towards premature wear on the control arm bushings which when worn squeaked annoyingly. Aside from these minor hitches, the Accord provided excellent value for the money, although there were continued grumbles about how much of that it took to own one.

Further dramatic restyling came in 1990 when the Accord emerged as a rounded version of its former self. Its wheelbase was now 107.1 inches, up from its previous 96.5 inches, and it now weighed in at 2,733 pounds.

The new design was seen as a positive change, a style that announced the Accord had grown up. It certainly looked stately with its clean, simple lines and perfectly balanced allocation of glass versus steel which allowed excellent visibility. The interior was more sophisticated (if more difficult to repair) and more firmly lush. The car was also more powerful with an aluminum 16-valve 2.2-liter engine that produced a smooth and snappy 125 horsepower and 137 ft-lb of torque. A more refined multi-port injection system regulated the fuel delivery which finally put an end to its history of related troubles. An Accord wagon was introduced in 1991 but was not successful on the market, fading out after 1995.

The Accord of 1992 improved its already very good safety record with the addition of a driver-side airbag and antilock brakes as standard equipment. A passenger-side airbag was offered as an option in 1993 for the Special Edition model only. This model had a throatier 140-horsepower 2.2-liter engine in addition to its upscale interior and sound system, alloy wheels, and rear spoiler.

In 1994 the Accord changed again — some thought for the worse. It received the same high rear-quarter panels and trunk that threw the Prelude off balance but it did not receive the V-6 engine many were clamoring for. That came in 1996 when the Accord was officially upgraded to a "mid-sized" vehicle from its former compact status. Yet some of the sheen had worn off the Accord's luster. *Car and Driver* left it off their Ten Best Cars list for 1996, leaving a noticeable gap between the chosen Civic and Prelude. *Consumer Reports* rapped the Accord for failing to respond as well as the Camry or Taurus and for having less rear seat room than both. Although giving the Accord a nod for above-average predicted reliability, the magazine doused cold water on the new V-6 by remarking that "the old fours [cylinder] provide better value." Considering the car was now retailing for between $15,000 and $25,500 this was of major concern to consumers.[35]

The Accord's long and well-documented rivalry with the Camry has provided limitless fodder for automotive journalists who have indulged in a virtual symphony of comparison tests throughout the decades. Interestingly enough, both cars have been awarded "the best-selling car in America" status, which in itself is not notable apart from the fact they were so acclaimed simultaneously and by the same magazine. On page 76 of the October 2001 edition of *Motor Trend*, the editors pointedly asked if the Toyota Camry was good enough to remain America's best-selling car. Then on page 94 their description of the Accord read in part that "the midsized Accord remains Honda's—and currently America's—best-selling passenger car."[36]

So which car *is* the best-selling car in America? Honda and Toyota offer conflicting reports. But according to *Motor Trend*'s Kevin Smith, it *should* be the Accord: "Get a Camry and you're a smart consumer who picked a really good car. Choosing an Accord says you prefer a car to be light on its feet, crisper in its responses, and more efficient in its use of space and natural resources."[37] By the time Smith's report saw print in 2002, the Accord had boosted its V-6 up to 240 horsepower.

It seems that automakers have once again returned to the horsepower-happy days of the 1960s, only this time the Japanese are leading the pack. Sports cars of the 1980s and 1990s may have been more coupe than racer, but they have ever so slowly crept back into favor as powerful cars not afraid to look the part. It has been a movement that Honda could claim pioneer status in as early as 1986 when they introduced their second division to the United States. The appearance of Acura not only made Honda the first Japanese automaker to have two divisions in the United States, but it also gave them an excuse to show just how diverse they could be.

In an effort to retain a certain aura of mystery, Honda did not lend its name to the Acura, nor was any sign of the familiar Honda "H" visible anywhere on the car or in the sales literature. Instead, what could be construed as a modified "H" bent into an "A" became the "new" company's logo. In the earliest advertisements of 1986, Honda had written "A division of the American Honda Company" under the Acura name by way of introduction, but thereafter the reference was removed.

The first Acura to appear on the scene was the refined and luxurious Legend, a 2.5-liter V-6 four-door sedan. Jointly designed with Britain's Austin-Rover, the Legend was the twin of that company's Sterling model and was intended to compete with the likes of Audi, BMW, and Volvo.

The svelte Legend looked like the parent of the Prelude and Accord with the best attributes of both. It measured 189.4 inches overall with a 108.6-inch wheelbase and a weight of 3,000 pounds. The 24-valve V-6 could create 151 horsepower and 154 ft-lb of torque at 4,500 rpm and had a 9.0:1 compression ratio. Suspension was the traditional McPherson strut, coils and anti-roll bar arrangement, and brakes were discs

Honda was the first Japanese automaker to have two divisions in the United States once they introduced their new Acura product. This stately 1986 Legend sedan was the first to represent the division (courtesy American Honda Motor Company).

and drums. A five-speed manual or four-speed automatic with overdrive were the transmissions on offer. Steering for the front-wheel-drive Legend was rack-and-pinion, so there were no surprises there either.

*Auto Guide* magazine thought the new Acura was a study of elegance, remarking that: "The Legend immediately impresses you with its compliant ride and super-smooth engine."[38]

It didn't take *Motor Trend* long to discover the virtues of Acura's personal luxury car either. Soon after its arrival in the United States, the magazine bestowed its Import Car of the Year award upon it. They were also delighted to find there was another Legend to "ooh and aah" over only a year later.

The Legend coupe arrived in 1987 and, like the sedan, was available in three trim levels—base, L, and LS. But while the sedan made do with the 2.5-liter engine, the new coupe benefited from a 2.7-liter, single-cam, 24-valve version which produced 161 horsepower and 162 ft-lb of torque at 4,500 rpm. The coupe was marginally shorter than the sedan at 188.0 inches with a 106.5-inch wheelbase and was designed from a completely separate platform.

A Legend coupe could scoot from zero to sixty in 8.12 seconds and perform the quarter-mile at 16.4 seconds by which time it reached 87.5 mph. The L and LS versions included antilock brakes, leather interior, power equipment, and Bose stereo. The Legend was the first Honda product to offer a driver-side airbag and antilock brakes (LS). Sold for between $22,000 and $24,500, the car was a definite winner. *Motor Trend* spoke for Acura when it said: "The intended objective is to blend performance with enhanced driving pleasure. The result is nothing short of a resounding success."[39]

*Consumer Reports* said the Legend "started and ran flawlessly," and gave it an overall excellent rating.[40] *Road & Track* called it a "nice substitute for a Jaguar," although they did find a few minor faults such as difficult shifting into reverse and some cold-starting problems.[41] The Acura also won J.D. Power's CSI award for 1988 and 1989.

In 1991 the Legend underwent a complete overhaul, receiving a new 200-horse-power 3.2-liter V-6 which broke with front-wheel-drive tradition by being longitudinally mounted rather than transversely. The car had stretched to 194.9 inches long with a 114.6-inch wheelbase and tipped the scales at 3,486 pounds. A driver-side airbag was standard equipment, but remained optional for the passenger side. Heated seats added to the overall sense of luxury which was immediately apparent upon entry.

But as elegant as the Legend appeared despite its growth spurt, it blotted its copybook by giving way to sudden acceleration, producing excessive road noise and allowing passengers less head-room than other large cars of its class. The automatic transmission also drew complaints for its tendency toward harsh shifting. *The Used Car Book* for 1994 rated the Legend's complaint index between average and very poor.[42] The Legend sold for between $31,850 and $36,500 (four-door sedan), but in 1996 it was replaced by the Acura RL, an even larger car with a 3.5-liter V-6 as well as a larger price of over $40,000.

Bearing little resemblance to its larger sibling, the Acura Integra pulled alongside the Legend in late 1986. Built to fill the sporty side of luxury, the Integra was substantially smaller with a wheelbase of only 99.2 inches (sedan) and a weight of 2,400 pounds. It was driven by a more Honda-like twin-cam, 16-valve 1.6-liter aluminum engine that generated 113 horsepower and 99 ft-lb of torque at 5,500 rpm. Its compression ratio was measured at 9.3:1 and bore and stroke were 2.95 by 3.54 inches. As the car looked sporty even in its sedan dress, many preferred the five-speed transmission over the four-speed overdrive automatic. A base-model, five-speed Integra RS coupe sold for $9,859, while a five-speed LS sedan sold for around $12,159. Between the Legend and the Integra, Acura managed to sell 52,869 units in the United States in 1986, followed by 109,470 in 1987.[43]

In 1988 an SE limited edition coupe joined the base Integra for that year only. One new feature was an increased compression ratio of 9.5:1 that allowed five more horsepower. Probably in an effort to emphasize its exclusivity, the SE Coupe was offered only in black or white.

Not much about the Integra changed until 1992 when a growling GS-R sports coupe was added to the profusion of RS, LS, and GS coupes and sedans. *Popular Mechanics* viewed the GS-R almost as though it were a scientific experiment, which in many ways it was. Their remarks offer as good an overview as any of the car as it first appeared on the market: "Remarkably, Honda has quickened this Integra's paces by reducing the displacement of its dohc 16-valve alloy 4-cylinder engine, from 1834 cc to 1678. Bore remains the same at 81mm (3.19 in.), but stroke is reduced from 89mm to 81.4 (3.2 in.). Compression is up from 9.2:1 to 9.7:1. The power secret lies

The Legend's sporty sibling came along a little later in 1986. Some referred to the Integra as a "fast Accord" (courtesy American Honda Motor Company).

in the GS-R's VTEC system. Adapted from the NSX sports car, this system raises both the engine's redline and power peak, from 140 hp at 6300 rpm for the standard Integra 1.8L to 160 hp at 7600 for the GS-R." The Integra GS-R, the editors wrote, has the "...highest hp/displacement ratio available in production cars sold in the U.S."[44]

The Integra emerged in 1994 with a new body and refinements such as standard antilock brakes, dual airbags and a stronger 142-horsepower, 1.8-liter engine with a 170-horsepower version for the GS-R.

In 1996 the Integra once again made *Car and Driver*'s Ten Best list while the editors promised that "any Integra will provide one of the most satisfying small-car rides on the planet — all the more remarkable considering the sticker prices begin below $17,000. If gas weren't cheaper than bottled water, this might be one of the best-selling cars in the country."[45]

The Integra line had by then grown to an astounding 19 different combinations and was truly a car for every taste, despite the fact that the car's appearance was beginning to elicit mixed reviews. Four tiny dots represented the headlights which sat unadorned in the fascia like drilled holes while the high rear end, most attractive to street-racers, was a bit over the top for a trip-to-the-store sedan. Other complaints that didn't ruffle speed fans one bit included excessive engine and road noise, harsh ride, and insufficient interior space. But some journalists hinted that one could find just as much satisfaction with a top-of-the-line Accord and save a few dollars while they were at it.

While both the Legend and Integra names are no longer in Acura's lexicon, the

**The Legend as it appeared in 1990, the year Lexus and Infiniti stole some of its thunder (courtesy American Honda Motor Company).**

Integra has found lasting fame as a street racer and makes regular appearances in sports car and street-legal racing magazines. But if the Integra GS-R was impressive, more well-heeled sports car fans had given their hearts to Honda's NSX supercar which had arrived in 1990.

When the NSX literally burst onto the scene at the February of 1989 Chicago Auto Show it caused a major sensation. No other Japanese car could match its Ferrari-like low-slung body and bulging wheel-well muscles. The car's lines flowed so smoothly and in the right places that it didn't take much of a stretch of the imagination to picture it on the Formula One circuit. But the tempting package didn't come cheaply.

When *Road & Track* previewed the NSX in 1989, they noted that the latest Acura would have a 3.0-liter, normally aspirated 270-horsepower VTEC engine with Honda's Programmed Fuel Injection and double overhead cams. This powerplant would be transversely-mounted amidships. The NSX, they reported, was to sell for between $50,000 and $60,000, making it the most expensive Japanese car on the market.[46]

Fully equipped with four-wheel disc antilock brakes, traction control, driver-side airbag, automatic climate control, leather power seats, cruise control and power equipment, the NSX had forged alloy wheels which wore 205/50ZR15 tires on the front and 222/50ZR16s on the back. A five-speed manual or less-popular four-speed automatic were the first transmissions to appear on the NSX. The four-speed, however, dropped the available horsepower to 252. The five-speed NSX attained zero-to-sixty in a quick 5.6 seconds with the quarter-mile coming in at 13.9 seconds. Even with such speed the NSX was surprisingly fuel-efficient, traveling an average 18 miles on a gallon of gas.

*Sport Compact Car* magazine referred to the NSX as "…the halo-car of the entire Acura/Honda line."[47]

Honda's racing heritage was clearly evident in this exciting mid-engine NSX prototype that dazzled in 1989 (courtesy American Honda Motor Company).

High demand meant that dealers attached above-cost stickers which, at that price, seemed to make little difference to the select few who could afford one. *Motor Trend* paid the NSX the ultimate compliment, calling it "the best sports car ever built," while *Road & Track* found that "Technically, it's brilliant, dynamically, it's outstanding." *Car and Driver* heralded the NSX as "a breakthrough sports car."[48]

There were no major changes to the NSX until 1995 when the NSX-T appeared beside it with a targa roof and new "drive-by-wire" throttle system, reinforced side panels and the SportShift feature for the four-speed automatic.

In 1997 a 3.2-liter engine gave it 290 horsepower and 222 ft-lb of torque while the addition of a new six-speed manual transmission helped the car achieve smoother shifts at higher revs. To accommodate the extra power, larger brakes and tires were added.

By 2002 the NSX was lower and meaner with a new front fascia and ground effects in addition to fixed Xenon headlights which replaced the tired pop-up units. Other improvements included larger exhaust ports, 17-inch wheels, still-wider tires, reinforced roof pillars and a more refined suspension. The NSX could now scream to sixty mph in only 4.6 seconds.

The NSX has received overall favorable reviews, particularly for its exclusive class, with the typical expected complaints about limited cargo space (it couldn't hold much more than a large briefcase), noise, and harsh ride. In recent years NSX sales have dropped off, with 238 sold in 1999, 221 in 2000, and only 182 in 2001.[49]

As an exotic, it was to be expected that the car would not sell on a large scale, although Honda must be disappointed with its showing over the past four years. But with an alternator costing nearly $600 and a radiator $1,000, it is definitely not a car for the masses. Some looked instead toward a Porsche 911 Carrera which could be had for about $6,000 less than the high-end $88,500 NSX. Others sought out Chrysler's stronger-by-150-horsepower Dodge Viper for $10,000 less.

Honda and Acura have received regular criticism about costs since the advent of the Accord and David E. Davis' shock over its price. Yet Honda seems to know what its market will bear and is prepared to get the most out of it. In return for the price, the company offers ongoing quality and reliability, in addition to the prestige now associated with the Honda and Acura nameplates. When compared to European imports, Honda has stayed on the conservative end of the spectrum with the notable exception of the NSX. But when matched with domestics Honda appears overpriced. It is a criticism the company continues to do battle with, as does Toyota whose sharp increases have also raised eyebrows.

By 2002 the Acura line included the CL, RL, TL, NSX and new RSX, a front-wheel-drive hatchback coupe with a 2.0-liter i-VTEC four-cylinder producing 160 horsepower (base) or the Type S, which produced 200 horsepower. The "L" series evolved from the RL introduced in 1996. The CL was a smaller car based on the Honda Accord coupe with the Accord's 2.2-liter VTEC four-cylinder. The other new Acura was the TL, first introduced in 1996 as the 2.5 TL, a model *Consumer Reports* called "vanilla — although a premium grade vanilla, to be sure."[50]

The TL eventually gained in popularity when it turned into the 3.0-liter TL. While the "L" series has been predominantly successful, Acura produced a car in 1992 that represented its most significant failure on the market. Jack Gillis' *Used Car Book* described the Vigor as looking "as though marketing people rather than engineers controlled its design."[51]

This view was shared by many and the car received a high number of complaints in consumer indexes. It also bowed to lukewarm reviews. Aside from featuring a unique five-cylinder 2.5-liter engine, there was little else to be said about the car. It was attractive enough, but seemed redundant in light of the already present Legend and similarly equipped Honda Prelude.

Failures present unfamiliar territory to the perennially popular Honda Motor Company and it seemed unlikely to change its record during the creation of its latest innovative technology, although it came close with the Civic Insight. The two-seater gas-electric hybrid was introduced in the late 1990s and was powered by Honda's Integrated Motor Assist (IMA) system. This engine was basically an in-line three cylinder that produced 67 horsepower and 66 ft-lb of torque. An electric motor boosted the power to a total of 73 horsepower — not a rocket by any means, but with its ultra-efficient engine and CVT transmission the car could go 57 miles on a gallon of gas.

Buyers were put off by three major factors— the car's cost (around $3,000 more than a regular Civic); the car's untried status, and finally its rather strange appearance with swooping side panels reminiscent of an amusement-park bumper-car. After testing the Insight among others, *Motor Trend* commented dryly that: "We had an uneasy feeling that we were participating in a science experiment when driving the production hybrid-drive cars." That opinion held true "at least until this latest Civic hybrid."[52]

The four-passenger, four-door Civic GX was introduced in 2002 for the 2003 year and is an infinitely more refined automobile than the Insight. It has a more powerful 1.3-liter, 84-horsepower in-line four which is paired with a direct-current electric motor that allows an additional 13.4 horsepower, helping the GX get to sixty in a very respectable 12 seconds. For the present all hybrid vehicles are still about $2,000 to $3,000 more than the regular models because of the extra production costs but Honda, like the other automakers, is working to devise a way to make them more cost-attractive. As it is, most companies selling these vehicles have experienced losses, particularly in the first year or so.

The man who started it all—Soichiro Honda. His ambition was to "make the greatest car in the world." Many believe he has succeeded (courtesy American Honda Motor Company).

Soichiro Honda did not live to see these new and exciting innovations but it is certain he would have been proud that the company he founded is breaking new trails as he always wished it would. He must have realized by the late 1980s the direction Honda was going, but he passed away in 1990, a year after becoming the first Asian to be inducted into the American Automotive Hall of Fame.

The Honda Motor Company continues to set standards through its research on solar-power, gas-electric hybrids and now fuel-cell vehicles which are covered in more detail in a later chapter. It easily entered the sport utility field with its CR-V and then the traditionally American domain of minivans with its Odyssey, but it is fuel-cell technology that provides the company's latest and greatest challenge.

It seems almost as though Honda can do no wrong and find no boundaries. Its success can largely be attributed to the quality of its products, but also to outstanding leadership as well. Leaders like Nobohiko Kawamoto and Hiroyuki Yoshino have carried on the traditions begun by Fujisawa, Kawashima, and Honda himself. Honda is one of the few Japanese automakers consistently operating in the black, even throughout Japan's recent severe recession.

How the little company went from selling a few hundred motorcycles in 1959 with a staff of 64 employees to a multi-billion-dollar global corporation almost defies belief, but Honda officials modestly attribute their success to a good product, effective marketing, and strong customer relations. They are proud to boast that Honda is now an American company, with more than 70 percent of its operating profits coming from the U.S. market.[53] And while the trend seems to be moving toward bigger automobiles, Honda continues to maintain that "small is smart."[54]

As Mr. Yoshino expressed it: "The most important thing ... is to supply the products which customers like to buy."[55]

Sounds deceptively simple, but it hasn't been. Honda has earned its place in the industry through sheer hard work and determination. Perhaps its practically inviolable reputation has also allowed it a degree of immunity from issues that would have seriously injured a lesser company. David Gelsanliter aptly summarized Honda's status in the industry in 1991 and his words still hold true today: "Honda won for itself a halo effect ... despite problems with the UAW, unsafe all-terrain vehicles and the Equal Employment Opportunity Commission."[56]

No one, not even perfectionist Soichiro Honda, could have asked for more than the astounding success of the company that has come so far.

# 10

## Mazda Makes Its Mark

The man who would one day lead one of the world's largest automobile companies was born in Hiroshima Prefecture in August of 1875, the twelfth son of a fisherman. Jujiro Matsuda was an apprentice by the age of 13 and at 20 he was operating his own small pump shop. Although he lost that business, he regrouped in 1912 and formed the Matsuda Works with 4,000 employees. In 1920 this company was acquired by a larger one and Matsuda turned instead to cork production, naming his new venture the Toyo (Orient) Cork Kogyo (industry) company.

Toyo Cork Kogyo produced cork for the Japanese market which had been cut off from European supplies as a result of World War I. But it wasn't exactly where Matsuda wanted to be and before long he pursued his interest in mechanics. Two other major factors influenced Matsuda's decision to switch from cork to industrial production. One was the Kanto earthquake which necessitated widescale rebuilding, and the other was that imported European cork was again available in Japan. Due to the tremendous need for industry, Toyo Cork Kogyo's bankers supported machinery factories, and so it was that in 1927 Toyo Cork Kogyo became known simply as the Toyo Kogyo Company.

Toyo Kogyo primarily produced tools, but these were followed by around 30 crude motorized bicycles with one winning a local race in 1930.[1] From these early motorcycles came small three-wheeled vehicles in 1931— a type of 500-cc motorcycle-truck hybrid called the Mazda DA. The name Mazda was chosen by Matsuda because it was derived from the Zoroastrian god of light, Ahura Mazda, and because it shared a certain harmony with his own name.

That Toyo Kogyo was serious about vehicle production is evident in the fact that they were exporting their three-wheelers to China by 1932. Matsuda obviously harbored a desire to compete in Japan's extremely restricted passenger car industry, for by 1940 he had produced a prototype car. Unfortunately, like his compatriots, his production was limited by the advent of World War II which had him producing tools, rock drills, gauge blocks, and even small firearms.

In light of the fact that Toyo Kogyo was only five kilometers from the center of the Hiroshima bombing, it's not surprising that the plant was severely damaged by the atomic bombing in 1945. Miraculously, production was able to resume by the end of the year. Toyo Kogyo joined other companies scrounging for precious supplies and materials. Many even purchased used tanks to harvest their damaged metals.

The new decade saw Toyo Kogyo sufficiently recovered to begin producing the Type C1, an 1157-cc, 32-horsepower, three-wheeled truck. This was followed by the CA four-wheeled truck and the CF small fire engine. By this time young engineer Kenichi Yamamoto had come on board and became instrumental in developing Toyo Kogyo's product line. As a former aircraft engineer he was able to apply his expertise to the development of a new overhead-valve engine, giving Toyo Kogyo an edge over their competition who were still using side-valve engines. But Jujiro Matsuda did not live to witness the full range of Yamamoto's talents or the direction his company was now taking. His son Tsuneji had assumed the presidency of Toyo Kogyo in 1951 and a year later Jujiro was dead.

Tsuneji oversaw the production of Toyo Kogyo's first marketable passenger car, the R360 coupe, introduced in May of 1960. The R360 had a rear-mounted 356-cc, two-cylinder, air-cooled engine. By the time the R360 was released, Toyo Kogyo was exploring the possibility of developing their own version of Felix Wankel's rotary engine, the rights to which were held by Germany's NSU automobile company. Since Japanese passenger car production was on the rise during the late fifties, Toyo Kogyo anxiously sought any advantage over their larger rivals, Toyota and Nissan. Improving on Wankel technology seemed an ideal way to achieve this lead. Matsuda also shared the apprehension among the smaller automobile companies due to MITI's heavy-handed attempts to force consolidation of the industry into two or three major companies.

Toyo Kogyo had no desire to be swallowed whole by their competitors and fought to stay independent. Manufacturing a radically different and superior vehicle would be one way to ensure this independence. But when Matsuda approached his staff about developing rotary technology, Kenichi Yamamoto's first response was an unequivocal "no way."[2] He though it foolhardy to take a risk whereby failure would bring the company down.

In an interview years later, Yamamoto commented: "…when I was first told to head up the Rotary Engine Research Department, I just felt that I couldn't go along with the president's whim."[3] But when the unique features of the Wankel were demonstrated to him and he was able to explore its potential himself, he was converted. Work then began in earnest after Toyo Kogyo received the first portion of the licensing rights in 1961. By 1963 two rotary-powered Cosmo sports cars were proudly displayed under the Toyo Kogyo banner at the Tokyo Motor Show.

But if Yamamoto had been lukewarm about the engine, Matsuda was passionate — so passionate that it seemed he was quite willing to swallow his not inconsiderable pride. In fact Yamamoto and his colleagues were quite shocked at the lengths their boss was prepared to go to in order to produce the engine: "…we were surprised to see the President, who we thought to be quite an autocrat, visit the Industrial Bank of Japan and Nomura Securities to kow-tow in order to get funding to develop the engine."[4]

It wasn't that Toyo Kogyo didn't have traditionally powered vehicles of their own, for they had released the Carol 360 and 600 in 1962, followed by the 800 Estate in 1963, with the F2000 and 800 sedan coming a year later. But these were not enough to remain competitive in the stiff minicar market.

Toyo Kogyo therefore invested heavily in the development and marketing of the rotary engine. Initially there were some serious problems with its performance, or to be more precise, its durability. The rotors were prone to premature wear and often "chattered" as they rotated. It wasn't that the engine was particularly difficult or expensive to repair, but rather that so few were familiar with its complexities. Regardless, Toyo Kogyo engineers were finally successful in their improvements to NSU's design — something no other company before or after it had been able to do. The thrust of the improvements quite naturally involved the rotors. While the original Wankel had one main rotor with cast-iron rotor seals, Toyo Kogyo had two, outfitted with carbon aluminum seals. Two spark plugs per chamber also performed better than NSU's single-plug configuration. In addition, Toyo Kogyo refined the combustion process by using side intake ports thus reducing intake and exhaust overlap.

In January of 1965 the Mazda Cosmo was market-ready, but only on a trial basis. However the trial proved so successful that after some final tweaking the Cosmo went into production in May of 1967 at the sparse rate of 20 units per month. The sporty car contained a 982-cc, 108-horsepower engine with a four-barrel Hitachi carburetor. It was a sleek and silent car with a low hood profile concealing the compact "pancake" engine. But being virtually hand-made, the car was far too expensive for the average consumer. With such a limited market, the first-generation Cosmo's life spanned only five years with production totaling slightly over 1,500 units.[5]

The development of the Cosmo had not been Toyo Kogyo's only endeavor. The company had also produced the Luce (1500) in 1964, the Familia 1000 in 1967 and the Familia Rotary SS in 1969. The Familia Rotary SS was the first rotary-powered vehicle shown at the Tokyo Motor Show. This model is important to our story for one major reason — it was the first Mazda to arrive in America, badged for sale here as the R100.

In 1970 Toyo Kogyo exported around 380 vehicles to the Seattle area without benefit of a developed sales organization. The first vehicles shipped were the R100 and its internal-combustion twin, the Mazda 1200; the RX-2 whose mate was the 616; and the larger 1800 sedan and wagon, not available in rotary form.

The 1200, the first non-rotary Mazda to arrive, was powered by a modest 1169 cc (71.3-cubic-inch) in-line four-cylinder engine that produced 64 horsepower and 67 ft-lb of torque at 3,500 rpm. The block was of cast iron with five main bearings and the aluminum head's valve train operated with solid lifters. The 1200's rotary version, the R100, produced a more substantial 100 horsepower from its twin-rotor Wankel.

Commanding the lion's share of the spotlight was the RX-2 which came as a coupe or sedan. The RX-2 proved to be a great attention-grabber. Although quite small, with a 97-inch wheelbase and an overall length of 163 inches, the car's sturdy sheetmetal gave it a solid weight of 2,270 pounds (coupe). Steering was through a recirculating ball unit and the only available transmission was a four-speed manual.

Mazda arrived in America in the spring of 1970. Although an R100 was offered as well as the twin piston-engine 1200, this RX-2 came along a year later and stole the show with its 120-horse-power rotary engine. Its more conventional twin was the 616 (courtesy Mazda Canada).

Suspension consisted of McPherson struts and coils on the front and a rigid axle with parallel links and coils at the back. Brakes were front discs and rear drums.

But most exciting was the car's engine, not only a novelty of great proportions, but a power-pack at that. Generating a healthy 120 horsepower and 98 ft-lb of torque, the 1146-cc (70-cubic-inch) engine catapulted the car ahead of most of its competition — Japanese imports included. The RX-2's twin, the 616, was powered by a traditional 1587-cc engine that managed a milder 88 horsepower.

Much less attention was given to the larger 1800 sedan and wagon, powered by a 1796-cc, 98-horsepower piston engine.

These early Mazdas retailed for between $1,798 (base 1200) and $2,750 (RX-2 sedan). They found just over 2,000 owners through approximately 38 Mazda dealerships like University Mazda of Seattle which opened in March of 1970 as part of the dealership body known collectively as Mazda Motors of America.[6]

This network of dealerships soon spread from Washington down the Pacific coast to California, and from there across to Texas and Florida. The American branch reported back to Japan that the cars were selling so well they were having a hard time meeting the demand. By 1972 there were Mazdas in the Midwest and the presence was steadily growing alongside the product's good reputation. This was fed by consistently positive automotive magazine reviews, the majority of which expressed fascination with rotary technology.

The April 1971 edition of *Motor Trend* magazine covered Toyo Kogyo's initial progress in America for their "Import Report" column: "Mazdas, those funny little cars from Hiroshima that glide along silently, propelled by Wankel rotary engines, are now being sold in California, the make-it-or-break-it market for importers on the West Coast. Heretofore, Mazdas had only been sold in Canada, the Pacific Northwest and Florida."[7]

Only one month after this dubious introduction, the magazine featured a comparison test between RX-2 and the Mercury Comet. Remarking that the Mazda was "innocuously styled" and the interior was a little more crowded than the Comet's, the reviewers were nonetheless impressed with the RX-2's speed and agility: "Even though the Comet had more than four times the displacement of the Mazda, the cars proved to be amazingly well matched out on the dragstrip."[8] Probably as a direct result, the editors found that the Mazda was "more fun to drive," disparaging the Comet as "the automotive equivalent of a $69 suit."[9] In fact the only problem *Motor Trend* could find with the Mazda was not with the car itself but with the lack of service facilities for it: "…you've probably got more chance of finding a Ferrari mechanic for your GTB than of finding a guy who knows Wankels."[10]

*Car and Driver* magazine basically concurred with *Motor Trend* when it published its review of the RX-2 the same month. Here impressions were couched in somewhat stronger terms, with very little editorial reserve. The RX-2, said the editors, "…will just about suck the doors off any other small sedan and give all but the bigger and more exotic sports cars a purple fit in a contest of straight-line speed."[11]

All in all, the RX-2 passed muster as a well-built, peppy and economical little car: "…the Mazda RX-2 doesn't exactly look like $3000, but it feels like it from the driver's seat and that is what really counts," enthused *Car and Driver*'s reviewers.[12]

One year later when the RX-2 had been supplanted by the RX-3, *Motor Trend* reviewed the new Mazda and called it "a fine achievement."[13]

Automotive publisher Petersen also found Toyo Kogyo's products praiseworthy, writing, "The Mazdas— all of them — are good, quality cars, economical to buy and operate, and if present sales indications are healthy signs, they'll soon be giving their counterparts from Japan a good run for the money."[14]

By 1972 the 1587-cc, 70-horsepower 808 sedan and coupe had arrived to replace the 1200 model, and the 616 evolved into the basically unchanged 618 which was available in three versions. But the most anticipation centered around the arrival of the latest "R" which appeared that year when the RX-3 joined its RX-2 predecessor rather than replacing it. Toyo Kogyo also offered a rotary-powered truck, the B-1600.

The RX-3 was basically the 808's rotary version and its wagon version earned the distinction of the being the world's first rotary-powered wagon. Some controversy surrounded the RX-3 in regards to its horsepower which was rated as 102. Many thought this was a typographical error, refusing to believe it could plummet so far in such a short time. The lower horsepower reading was in actuality attributed to the car's much-smaller dimensions and also to the battle Toyo Kogyo was beginning to fight with the rotary's excessive fuel consumption. Nevertheless, Mazda seemed to be getting off to a good start with 104,960 vehicles sold by 1973, approximately 92 percent of them rotary-powered.[15]

As business increased, so did media and public attention. Executives at Toyo Kogyo were jubilant over their Wankel advantage, with major players like Ford, GM, Toyota and Nissan unable to divine the secrets of a successful rotary engine. But the euphoria was short-lived. The fuel-efficiency question would not die and the failure to resolve it meant Toyo Kogyo would not pass unscathed through the 1973 oil crisis. When measured against Toyota, Datsun, and Honda, the paltry average of 14 mpg achieved by the Mazda effectively eliminated it from the competitive economy car market. In the span of only one year sales fell to only 61,192 vehicles.[16]

Toyo Kogyo officials acted quickly to control the damage, embarking on what they code-named "Project P" (for Phoenix). Despite the fact that they were able to reduce fuel consumption by 40 percent between 1973 and 1974, sales remained flat. By the end of 1974 the company was on the verge of bankruptcy. Now being led by Tsuneji's son Kohei Matsuda, Toyo Kogyo was stuck with massive inventories stockpiled — over 80,000 on the U.S. market alone, some of which included the larger new 110-horsepower RX-4.

By 1975 the RX-2 had disappeared to be replaced in 1976 with the Cosmo, a rotary-powered coupe intended as the top-of-the-line Mazda with a five-speed transmission, spoilers, velour upholstery, and a full complement of small luxuries and courtesies.

An advertisement for the Cosmo appeared in the December 1975 issue of *Motor Trend*, which was headlined with "Your year to come out of the ordinary ... and into the 1976 Mazda Cosmo." Beside a cross-section view of the rotary engine, the text rhymed off the car's attributes which included steel-belted radials, independent suspension, all disc brakes, electric fuel pump, oil- and gas-filled shocks, and rear window defroster. Also shown was a small photo of the car's simulated woodgrain dash and wooden steering wheel and gearshift knob. The Cosmo pictured had quad headlights and a "radiator" style grille, but most strangely, the rear windows were sectioned-off into two triangles—one of which represented an opera window. "Test drive your kind of Mazda today. If you think it's just an ordinary car, you haven't driven it around," promised Toyo Kogyo.[17]

But even the addition of a new high-efficiency series appropriately tagged the "Mizer" could not bring the company onto more stable ground. Mizer 808 and 1300 editions were powered, or rather under-powered, by a four-cylinder 1272-cc engine which produced a meager 49 horsepower, a travesty at a time when Honda and Datsun were breaking fuel-rating records without sacrificing that much power. Obviously this weakness was responsible for the Mizer's miserly survival rate — it lasted only two years on the American market, despite its 42 mpg rating.[18]

It was already appalling apparent by 1975 that no one wanted a Mazda and offering underpowered editions or overdone coupes could not alter the fact. That year Toyo Kogyo admitted to a deficit of approximately 17 billion yen and would have collapsed if a member of its *keiretsu*, the Sumitomo Bank, hadn't rescued it. Both the bank and Toyo Kogyo's upper management called for a total and sweeping restructuring plan. A new leader, Yoshiki Yamasaki, took over in 1977, ending three generations of Matsuda control. Yamasaki had the unenviable task of bringing what appeared to be a deceased company back to life.

Aside from the Sumitomo Bank's appointing some of its own members to Toyo Kogyo's board, Toyo Kogyo was also aided by its return to the manufacture of traditional internal-combustion engines. Of even greater assistance was the introduction of the piston-engined GLC replacement for the 808.

Jokingly referred to as the "Great Little Car" (although Toyo Kogyo claimed there was no real significance behind the initials), the GLC began life in 1977 as a 1272-cc, overhead-cam four-cylinder, four-speed Standard or Deluxe two-door hatchback. Both versions produced 52 horsepower and 64 ft-lb of torque at 3,000 rpm, but a special 49-horsepower engine was fitted to cars sold in California or in high-altitude regions. Fuel came through a two-barrel carburetor.

The GLC was 153.4 inches long with a 91.1-inch wheelbase and a weight of 1,965 pounds. Its rear tread was half an inch wider than the front at 51.6 inches. The rear-wheel-drive GLC's suspension was nothing new, with McPherson struts and coils on the front and a rigid axle with coils at the rear. Steering was recirculating-ball type, a unit fast losing ground in favor of rack-and-pinion systems. The Standard GLC featured a four-speed manual transmission while the Deluxe version got a five-speed with an optional three-speed automatic. Luxuries like the optional AM radio and air conditioning were few on this Spartan little model, but much was sacrificed to gain its EPA rating of 35 mpg city, 45 highway.[19]

*Car and Driver* tested the GLC in the winter of 1977 and had this to say: "Our driving impression was based on a brief fling in pre-production models at Mazda's Miyoshi proving ground in Japan. In that session the GLC was a real charmer. It's roomy, the ride is comfortable and the car's behavior is so predictable you get the feeling you've driven it before. The five-speed is crisp, and the pedals are perfect for heel-and-toeing. Mazda plans to bring the base GLC into the U.S. for less than $3000. At that price, it really is a great little car."[20]

*Motor Trend* also featured the Sport trim level which came with a few extras like rally stripes, wider tires, wooden steering wheel and shift knob, color-keyed mirror, electric clock, and black velour upholstery. Reviewer Bob Hall concluded that, "All in all, the GLC Sport is one of the better subcompacts on the market. Aside from the questionable stripes, the GLC Sport package seems good value for the money"— which at $4,339 the author of the piece felt was "a tad steep."[21]

But despite this generally positive feedback and the addition of a new racing model called the RX-3SP that same year, Mazda's sales dropped to new low of 50,608, an alarming development for the over 500 dealers trying to sell them.[22]

It took some time for consumers to catch on to the quality of the new GLC but when they did sales began to ascend, reaching 75,309 by 1978.[23] Providing a rocket-blaster boost was the arrival of what would become one of the world's most popular sports cars, the Savanna RX-7, known in the United States simply as the RX-7.

Unveiled in April of 1978, the RX-7 instantaneously zeroed in on its market. Any fears that it would not sell due to its more expensive rotary-powered engine were immediately dispelled when the car soared into the record books.

Rotary power! The venerable RX-7 as it first appeared in 1979 — the best thing since the 240Z. Some called it simply *the* best (courtesy Mazda Canada).

Sales echoed those of the first Datsun Z, with customers prepared to pay more than its asking price — some as much as $2,500 over — just to ensure their orders.[24] The base price of $7,195 for the S and $7,995 for the GS luxury edition didn't faze power-hungry customers in the least. For that amount they received a dramatically styled rear-wheel-drive two-seater coupe with an all-glass hatch, pop-up headlights, reclining bucket seats, tinted glass, AM/FM stereo, a complete set of gauges, steel-belted radials, leather-wrapped steering wheel and a digital clock. All of this came even with the S model, and for the GS there were extra "goodies" including larger alloy wheels, intermittent wipers, rear anti-roll bar, and an electric remote hatch release.

Best of all was the RX-7's engine which propelled the car to sixty mph in approximately 9.2 seconds, with a top speed that exceeded 120 mph. The quarter-mile test was clocked at around 17 seconds and 83 mph.

Dual-coaxial, three-lobe cast-iron rotors were contained in an aluminum alloy trochoid housing and a cast-iron side housing. This arrangement gave a displacement of 1146-cc (70-cubic-inches), a horsepower rating of 100 at 6,000 rpm, a compression ratio of 9.4:1 and 105 ft-lb of torque at 4,000 rpm. A four-barrel carburetor served as the fuel delivery system.

The RX-7 was a trim 169 inches long with a 95.3-inch wheelbase and a weight of 2,350 pounds (S) and 2,420 (GS). For sports-car handling, the car received McPherson struts with lower lateral links, compliance struts, coils, and an anti-roll bar for the front, and a rigid axle with lower trailing links, torque rods, Watts linkage and coil springs on the rear. Brakes were front discs and rear drums. Steering was surprisingly of the recirculating-ball type and available transmissions were four- or five-speed manuals, with the GS having an optional three-speed automatic.[25]

That the car was built to race was evident in the fact that it took first and second place in its class at LeMans in its debut year, becoming the first Japanese sports car to do so.[26]

Toyo Kogyo advertised the RX-7 by declaring "It's the real thing — A sports car with all the traditional virtues and then some."[27] Another magazine advertisement said "A truly great value in sports cars doesn't come along very often. Mazda. The more you look, the more you like."[28]

Automotive journalist Tony Swan later wrote that "If the GLC had stabilized Mazda's deteriorating foothold in the U.S. marketplace, the RX-7 turned the company's image around completely, and Toyo Kogyo couldn't build them quickly enough."[29]

By the end of 1979, sales had shot up to an astounding 156,535.[30] But the question of fuel economy continued to be a monkey on the rotary's back with estimates of the new RX-7's mileage ratings falling between 20 and 22 mpg. In March of 1979 *Car and Driver* reported that "Mazda is working hard to boost the fuel economy of the RX-7 and other rotary-equipped cars. We should see a combined mpg figure of 25 mpg — up from the current 21 — by 1980, says Kenichi Yamamoto, managing director of Mazda. The eventual goal is 27.5 mpg, and turbocharging may be one way of getting there."[31]

By 1981 the RX-7S received a new optional sunroof as well as a new sibling called the GSL, fully equipped with alloy wheels, cruise control, all-disc brakes, leather interior, sport power package and a new limited-slip differential. It also carried a bigger price of just over $11,000.

A year later *Motor Trend* pitted the car against the 280ZX and the Supra under the heading "Showdown of the Sudden Samurai." Although the RX-7's zero-to-sixty time of 9.97 seconds fell short of the Z's 8.77 and the Supra's supreme 8.4, reviewers concluded that the RX-7's engine was "the most interesting and the smoothest."[32]

While the first RX-7 was winning critical acclaim, a more humble but steadfast model made its debut in the same year. Beginning life in Japan as the Capella, the 626 appeared in the March 1979 edition of *Car and Driver*, which opened with "Now that waiting lines are block-long outside Mazda's showrooms, the Japanese have responded. To help satisfy America's newfound lust for Mazdas, parent company Toyo Kogyo has sent us a pair of all-new sedans — a sport coupe and a four-door — both rather lamely labeled "Mazda 626".... The 626s are both piston-powered, now that the rotary engine is reserved for sport duty only."[33]

Although the review found fault with the 626's engine as being "truck-like," Toyo Kogyo was finally making a name for itself on the economy market, as the review indicated: "Where this car sparkles is in fuel economy. With an EPA city rating of 25 mpg both in five-speed and in automatic trim, the 626 matches the VW Rabbit for efficiency, and beats most of its direct competition by a wide margin. The Toyota Celica, for example, has an EPA rating of only 18 mpg this year. Superior fuel economy is part of Mazda's "high value engineering" philosophy.[34]

Mazda's first serious entry against the likes of Accord and Camry, the 1979 626 (courtesy Mazda Canada).

After looking over the car's impressive interior with its "corduroy-like uphol-stery" and nice finishing touches, the reviewers gave the little car good marks for han-dling and shifting, as well as for its unique 60/40 split folding rear seat. Remaining noncommittal about the appearance of the 626, the magazine instead quoted a proud Mazda official: "Mr. Tsutomu Murai, executive vice-president of Toyo Kogyo, has proclaimed: 'The 626 is a strikingly beautiful car. In fact, we think that the 626 is the best-looking sedan ever manufactured in Japan.'" *Car and Driver* concluded, "The crowds milling through Mazda showrooms will have their chance to agree when the 626 goes on sale March 1."[35]

The rear-wheel-drive 626 had an in-line four-cylinder engine that produced 80 horsepower through a 1970-cc (120.4-cubic-inch) displacement. The car was 173.8 inches long with a 98.8-inch wheelbase and a weight of 2,550 pounds. Front sus-pension and steering were borrowed from the RX-7, a fact Toyo Kogyo was anxious to draw attention to. Advertisements displayed this tendency as well, with repeated reference to sports cars running through the text: "The Mazda RX-7 set a new stan-dard of value in sports cars. And now, the Mazda 626 sets a new standard of value in sport coupes: $5795."[36]

Although the 626 got off to a somewhat shaky start on the market, refinements put in place for 1983 helped it become a strong performer in the Mazda line. That year it became a front-wheel-drive vehicle, and received a wide assortment of accou-trements. The car was now available in five versions, including a new four-door "Touring" hatchback. *Car and Driver* judged that the 626 was now "up to world-class competitiveness ... and heavily laced with convenience features."[37]

The company did seem to find its equilibrium with sales for 1983 hitting 173,388.[38] Commenting on those precarious years of failure and recovery in the United States, Kenichi Yamamoto said: "I think the U.S. is an interesting country: even if you fail once, if you can stand up again, people respect and support you. Thanks to them, the rotary engine was saved from dying out. If the engine could not have survived, I would have left Mazda."[39]

During this period Japanese imports had reached record numbers in the United States Mazda alone had 17 versions of its three main models, while Nissan, Toyota, and Honda had substantially more. The Voluntary Export Restraint system had taken effect in 1981 which naturally impacted the Japanese automakers, but not as severely as some might have thought. Toyo Kogyo had luckily already established ties with the Ford Motor Company a decade before and thought it wise to sell 25 percent of its shares to Ford in 1979. In addition to the deal with Ford which offered some protection, Toyo Kogyo also relied on the export of its B-series pickup trucks which were exempt from the restraints. The pickup enjoyed enormous popularity, particularly as it undersold its competition at only $6,000.

Despite these positive factors, the trade friction between Japan and America had many Japanese automakers very nervous about the possibility of a closed U.S. market. The only way to circumvent that potential occurrence, they reasoned, was to *become* an American automaker — geographically speaking, that is.

As then-company-president Kenichi Yamamoto confirmed in 1984: "If we didn't go for production in the U.S., we would suffer a very heavy blow. It might even mean that would could no longer survive."[40] The construction of Mazda Manufacturing USA in Michigan, covered in more detail in a later chapter, therefore ensured Toyo Kogyo's place in the American market.

Yamamoto personally visited the new U.S. plant where he was told that "top level management giving encouragement in the workplace was unthinkable in America."[41] Yamamoto was pleased to see that although his beloved rotary engine did not quite create the automotive revolution he had hoped for, Toyo Kogyo was irrevocably established in the North American market.

Along with the new American facilities Toyo Kogyo assumed a new name in 1984. Realizing that Americans knew the product only as Mazda, the company officially became known as the Mazda Motor Corporation.

By 1984 the beloved RX-7 had a new SE sibling, with a six-port, three-stage variable fuel induction system with electronic fuel injection and a 14 percent greater displacement. Horsepower now measured 135 at 6,000 rpm and torque 133 ft-lb at 2,750 rpm. Standard features included Pirelli P6VR tires on 14-inch alloys, all-wheel disc brakes, performance suspension package, removable steel targa/sunroof, full power package, and a close-ratio five-speed manual transmission. "This is a serious car, folks," said Mazda.[42]

The GLC was proving to be a popular choice as well, with the wagon being dropped in 1984 allowing the front-wheel-drive sedans and hatchbacks to hold the market on their own. The 626 was gathering speed and yet the mid-eighties spelled further trouble for the company with sales dropping to 169,666 for the 1985 year.[43]

The arrival in 1986 of the 323 — the GLC's replacement — moderately helped

In 1986 the RX-7 celebrated its birthday with a new style (courtesy Mazda Canada).

revive sagging sales. A slightly larger overall size earned it a promotion from sub-compact to compact status. A peppier fuel-injected 1.6 liter engine now powered the two-door hatchback and four-door sedan, putting out 82 horsepower. Of the new 323 *Consumer Reports* said: "The 1.6-liter 4 started and ran flawlessly; spirited acceleration. The 5-speed manual transmission shifted crisply and precisely. This front-wheel drive model gave excellent routine handling, sloppy but safe emergency handling. The brakes were a little difficult to modulate." As to comfort and convenience, the review continued: "Very comfortable front seats; very good driving position. Uncomfortable rear seat. Moderate noise level. Typical small-car ride. Excellent climate control system. Excellent controls and displays … mpg with manual transmission: city 22; expressway 42." The car's listed price range was between $5,645 (base hatchback) and $8,095 (Luxury sedan).[44]

In August of 1986, *Road & Track* featured a story on four-wheel-drive Japanese imports. "4WD Craze," read the headline. "All nine manufacturers in Japan offer 4wd cars and light trucks of some sort, which have until recently lacked center differentials and were therefore part-time systems. Mazda introduced the first Japanese full-time 4wd last year in the 323 now followed by offerings from Nissan and Subaru."[45]

When *Auto Guide* magazine reviewed the 323 in 1988, its "Bottom Line" was that "The 323 is probably the best car Mazda makes. It's reasonably priced and well-designed. The car is cleanly styled, if a bit on the ordinary side, and does everything you'd expect of a small, but upscale economy car." Also noted under the "On the Horizon" section was the advent of the four-wheel-drive 323.[46]

In April of 1988, *Road & Track* carried an advertisement for the newly arrived GTX, calling it the "hot new 4WD, 16-valve, turbo 323," with a four-wheel-drive system that was "one of the most advanced full-time four-wheel-drive systems in the world." This special design consisted of a planetary center differential with an electric lock-up mechanism. Also worth noting were the car's four-wheel disc brakes, twin trapezoidal link rear suspension, intercooled turbo which allowed 132 horsepower out of the 1.6-liter plant, hydraulic valves, double overhead cams, and multi-adjustable contour seats.[47]

The GTX retailed for $12,999, while the slightly less lavish but also turbocharged GT sold for $11,799.[48] A new station wagon also made a brief appearance for 1988, but met the same fate as a multitude of other wagons of the era, both domestic and imported.

There weren't any further changes to the 323 until 1990 when the sedan series separated from the hatchbacks and became known as the 323 Protegé. This series was a completely different design despite some design-feature resemblance. The Protegé had a 103-horsepower, 1.8-liter engine and a wheelbase of 98.4 inches, while the 323 hatchback kept the 1.6-liter and had a 96.5-inch wheelbase. The Protegé also had a high-end 1.8-liter engine with twin cams and 125 horsepower. Although there were no more turbocharged versions, a four-wheel-drive Protegé came in mid–1990 but experienced such poor sales that it was withdrawn in 1991.

Throughout the 1990s, the 323-Protegé team received very little in the way of criticism, some of which was directed toward the car's rising price, as well as its crash-test safety factor.[49] In the mid-nineties a more-fuel-efficient 1.5-liter engine was offered on the DX and LX models but it didn't last long on the market, yielding once again to the basic 1.6-liter.

By 2001 a new youth-oriented MP3 edition of the Protegé was released with a 2.0-liter, 130-horsepower engine and loaded with aftermarket equipment including a Kenwood stereo. The car, as *Motor Trend*'s Chris Walton reported, was named for the popular computer download music files, and although long on extras was a little short on horsepower.[50]

The most recent Protegé still comes with only that engine for all models. The car now retails for between $13,005 and $16,445. *Consumer Reports* said the Protegé was a "solid small-sedan choice," but noted that it had recently been "surpassed by the Ford Focus and the redesigned Honda Civic."[51]

Like the Protegé, the 626 gave many good years of service in several different guises. It received its second major re-working in 1986 when it was equipped with a port fuel injection system for its 2.0-liter engine that added nine horsepower to its previous 84. A new turbocharged GT model gave outlet to 120 horses and a redesigned Automatic Adjusting Suspension system. At that time there were two Deluxe versions, three Luxury versions, and three GT editions to choose from in a price range from $9,245 (two-door coupe Deluxe) to $13,195 (four-door GT).[52]

In September of 1986 *Road & Track* looked at the 626 GT and although it beat both Honda LXi Accord and Chrysler's LeBaron GTS to sixty mph in an impressive 7.8 seconds, *Motor Trend* gave the car a mixed review, concluding that "despite the improved interior and powerful engine, this latest 626 fails to convince the way the

626 did when it was a fresh design. Mazda updated it to keep pace with a fast-moving market, but it appears that the market has moved a little too fast."[53]

Something a little splashier was on its way. Making its debut in 1988 was the MX-6, Mazda's answer to the Celica and Prelude. The MX-6 had a shorter wheelbase than the 626 at 99 inches and came in 2.2-liter, 110-horsepower DX and LX coupes as well as a turbocharged GT that generated 145 horsepower and 190 ft-lb of torque. This model also featured four-wheel disc brakes with antilock brakes as an option, while its sister 626 turbo sedan received Mazda's new electronically controlled four-wheel-steering system which proved to be a slow seller and was given to the MX-6 in 1989. But like Honda's four-wheel-steering system, Mazda's also became defunct.

The 626 series was superficially restyled in 1990 but not much else changed until 1993 when the car benefited from a larger 118-horsepower 2.0-liter engine for the DX and LX models, with a new 164-horsepower 2.5-liter V-6 for the 626 ES and MX-6 LS. Also new was a standard driver-side airbag to complement the antilock brakes which had become optional in 1991. The other major distinction shared by the 626 and MX-6 was that they were the first Japanese cars to qualify as domestics, being built in Mazda's Flat Rock plant with over 75 percent North American content.[54]

In 1996 the 626 LX with four-speed automatic transmission and every available option sold for around $22,795. Although *Consumer Reports* said "Mazda's 626 — with either a Four or V-6 — is a well-rounded and high-rated family sedan," they gave it only an average predicated reliability rating.[55]

By 2002 the 626 was 187 inches long with a 105-inch wheelbase. Curb weight measured in at a heavy 3,095 pounds and fuel economy estimates ranged between 20 and 26 mpg. There were now only two models to choose from — the LX with its smaller 125-horsepower four, or the ES with a 165-horsepower V-6 engine. A base LX could be had for $18,785, while the more luxurious ES cost $21,885, which *Motor Trend* counted as a "price advantage over other more costly Japanese imports of the class."[56]

While the 626 was finally replaced in 2002 by the more exciting Mazda 6, other models have not shared the 626's longevity. The one that comes to mind in particular is the MX-3.

Arriving in 1992 to compete with the Toyota Paseo and Nissan NX 2000, the MX-3 looked very much like both of those models. It came in two styles of three-door hatchbacks — the base 1.6-liter, 88-horsepower version, or the stronger 1.8-liter, 130-horsepower V-6, which made history as the world's smallest V-6 engine.[57]

Unfortunately the MX-3 suffered from the same disinterest as its Japanese compatriots and fell by the wayside by 1996. One model that was of similar size that has stayed the course has been the incredibly popular Mazda MX-5, also known as the Miata.

The Miata was introduced in 1989, and James M. Flammang accurately described the scene after the car's arrival: "Not many cars have earned such frenzied attention and consumer demand as Mazda's retro two-seat sports car. Patterned after the 1960s Lotus Elan, the Miata was conceived in the U.S., at Mazda's design headquarters in California, though developed and built in Japan." The Miata, Flammang continued, "was a curvaceous little rear-drive roadster ... and customers clamored to pay thousands of dollars above the car's $13,000 sticker price to be one of the first to own one. Comparatively small supply was part of the reason, as only 20,000 were expected to go on sale during 1989, and another 40,000 in 1990."[58]

The Miata had a 1.6-liter twin-cam engine beneath its hood that gave the car 116 horsepower and 100 ft-lb of torque at 5,500 rpm. Fuel came through a multi-port injection system, and the only transmission available was a five-speed, with an optional automatic coming later. The front-wheel-drive car was listed as a convertible with a manually-operated top, but there was also a removable-hardtop edition available. Standard equipment included all-disc brakes and a driver-side airbag, while options listed were air-conditioning, CD player, power steering, antilock brakes, and a limited-slip differential. Suspension was the conventional arrangement common to all Mazdas except the RX-7, and steering was the now-standard rack-and-pinion unit. It was quite an impressive compact package at 155.4 inches long, 48.2 inches high, with a wheelbase of only 89.2 inches, making it the smallest Mazda available. The car could scamper to sixty in 8.6 seconds, thanks in part to its slight weight of just over 2,000 pounds.

It seemed that everyone fell in love with the appealing little roadster. *The Used Car Book* for 1990 referred to it as "a phenomenon ... with all the fun of a traditional English sports car along with improved comfort and a minimum of reliability problems."[59]

*Consumer Guide* said "The Miata is our favorite sports car because it's reasonably priced, economical to operate, and, unlike old British roadsters, reliable."[60] EPA ratings of the first generation Miata averaged out at 24 to 30 mpg.

In 1991 the Miata came in British racing green with tan interior to further cement its British roadster connection. A year later it sported a "Brilliant Black" coat with Crystal White or Classic Red interior as well as an optional 130-watt "Sensory Sound System."

The 1994 Miata's power was lifted by a new 1.8-liter twin-cam engine that created 128 horsepower. Two years later the little Mazda commanded prices from $18,000 up to $23,500 which now included dual airbags and an average fuel rating of 29 mpg. Complaints continued to center around noise, cargo space, and harsh ride.

The Miata has now passed its twelfth birthday and resembles the mid–1990s RX-7 with more pronounced curves, arching hood lines, and gaping front air dam. It's slightly heavier at over 2,300 pounds and much stronger with a 142-horsepower engine that goes nicely with the newly optional six-speed shifter. *Motor Trend* remarked that "The Miata is Mazda's image centerpiece, and one of the world's finest small-displacement cars."[61]

But Mazda also needed something larger. When Honda unveiled its Acura division in 1986 and rumors circulated about Toyota and Nissan following suit by the end of the decade, Mazda's only possible rebuttal was to offer its most luxurious model to date, the premium 929 edition, introduced in 1988. It was a car well designed to meet the Acura Legend on equal ground even where costs were concerned, with both cars retailing for around $22,500.

The stately 929 was much larger than the 626, and as such carried a more powerful 3.0-liter, V-6 engine that produced 158 horsepower and 170 ft-lb of torque. A multi-port fuel injection system and an electronically controlled four-speed automatic transmission came as standard equipment in 1989. A power moonroof and power seats helped accentuate the feeling of luxury within the car's velour or optional leather interior. A premium sound system and comprehensive climate controls rounded-out the features. The only throwback, in some eyes, was the car's rear-wheel-drive configuration.

Peter Albrecht reviewed the 929 for *Road & Track* in 1988 and summarized that the car "cut through big-car conservatism with typical Mazda sportiness."[62]

In 1990 a 190-horsepower, twin-cam version of the car appeared as the 929 S model but failed to draw a large crowd. The car was restyled for a much softer look in 1992 which helped its appeal but *Consumer Reports* summed up what seemed to be the general consensus that "the 929's overall performance fails to excite us the way the new styling does…"[63]

In 1995 the 929 gave way to Mazda's new luxury Millenia. Mazda had its image as a luxury-car producer riding on the supercharged 2.3 liter V-6 car, which ranged in price from $27,525 to $35,595.

*Road & Track* put the Millenia S through a long-term test and the results, apart from a few minor glitches involving the CD system and an air-conditioning odor, came up positive: "Despite the mildly frustrating experience, the car itself has been performing magnificently." The average mileage, said *Road & Track*, was 25.0 mpg.[64] *Consumer Reports* called it "spunky and refined," and gave it an "Excellent Reliability" rating in 1996.[65]

The front-wheel drive Millenia survived the millennium — just — by filling the vacancy left by the 626; but as *Consumer Reports* warned in 2002, "the end is nigh for the aging Millenia, which will effectively be replaced by the V-6-powered version of the new Mazda 6 sedan early next year."[66] The Millenia unfortunately drew a negative response from both that magazine as well as *Motor Trend*, which after praising it as an "elegant passenger sedan with sporting ability," called it a "John Doe car."[67]

Comments such as these had plagued Mazda from the very beginning and though while not sounding the company's death knell, did little to help it reach the prominence of its Japanese competitors. But when the RX-7 started to fail on the market after its drastic restyling in 1986 when it gained a rear seat as well as approximately 240 pounds, Mazda had the Miata to substantially boost sales.

Still, the loss of the RX-7 was acutely felt. Even a 10th anniversary edition in 1988 which included a convertible could not win back those early RX-7 fans. When the car was restyled back to a rounder version of its former self *sans* the convertible and 2 + 2 in 1993, its popularity again rose, though not quickly or high enough. Cost may have been a factor for it now hovered around $30,000, and some felt there was more fun to be had in a Miata for much less money.

Still rear-wheel-drive, the RX-7 of 1993–94 was powered by a seemingly modest 1.3-liter engine — at least before taking into account the twin turbochargers which blasted out 255 horsepower and 217 ft-lb of torque at 5,000 rpm. Shorter, wider, and lower than its predecessor, the new RX-7 could reach 60 mph in a dazzling 5.6 seconds

The third-generation RX-7 — a little heavier but still sexy after all these years. Unfortunately it was on its way out by then (courtesy Mazda Canada).

but its fuel economy left something to be desired with even the five-speed manual only getting 17 mpg city, 25 highway.[68]

Tony Swan wrote a short piece on the newest RX-7 for *Popular Mechanics* magazine in 1992. While acknowledging that while the old RX-7 "didn't have the suds to run with the likes of Chevrolet Corvette, Nissan 300ZX Turbo, Dodge Stealth or Acura," but Swan immediately affirmed that "the new one does." His view of the higher price-tag was philosophical: "You could think of it as a lot of money for an RX-7. Or you could think of it as we do: a sports car that will match the superb Acura NSX stride for stride, at half the price."[69]

Only three years later *Road & Track* was asking "Is this the next RX-7?" in its "Ampersand" feature, referring to Mazda's new concept they were calling the RX-01. "I hope the powers that be, at Hiroshima and Dearborn, will approve the project," said Jack Yamaguchi.[70]

This was the car that was far in Mazda's future, for the RX-7 died in 1995. As *Car and Driver* mourned, "There is no 1996 Mazda RX-7 ... and if (it) does return, it may be without a rotary engine." As the author continued somewhat irreverently, "In the 90s, sales of Japanese sports cars have plunged neatly into the vehicular toilet. In calendar year 1994, Mazda sold 2212 RX-7's in the U.S., versus 56,203 in 1986."[71]

Strong demand and sales as of the time of writing indicate that the RX-8 is a leader in the sports car revival, just as so many automotive journalists predicted it

The 2003 replacement for the tired 626 has arrived. Mazda's new 6 is impressive but will face stiff competition from Honda, Toyota, and Nissan (courtesy Mazda of North America).

would be. The 2,933-pound 2 + 2 RX-8 comes with two different engines—a base 210-horsepower for the automatic transmission edition, and a 250-horsepower for the six-speed manual. Mazda calls its new engine "Renesis." *Motor Trend*'s preliminary test found the RX-8 was "balanced, easy to drive, fast, comfortable and competent," although there was a "lack of torque, lack of edge."[72]

As for the new 6 sedan, Kevin Smith wrote for the same magazine that the car "corners flat, steers with a quality feel, and the ride is beautifully controlled without being too stiffly sprung..." but "Nissan's 240-horsepower Altima has raised the bar awfully high."[73] With the new six's top 3.0 liter 24-valve V-6 generating 219 hp that bar is high indeed, but so far the Mazda 6 is holding its own.

Mazda has also been developing a concept car called the Demio, a fuel-cell electric vehicle (FCEV) that uses hydrogen as its fuel. The company has been working on hydrogen vehicles since the 1980s with the production of the HR-X and HRX-2, as well as on turbine power and an experimental safety vehicle. That Mazda has run into trouble has not necessarily been due to lack of innovation—it did manage to be the only Japanese automaker with piston, rotary, and diesel engines in production simultaneously. More accurately, its problems could in large part be attributed to the rising yen, United States–Japan trade friction, and stiff competition from Toyota, Honda, and Nissan which kept Mazda in the red throughout much of the 1990s. Sales were weak and management disorganized. Accordingly, a new effort was made to consolidate its U.S. operations with the merging of East and West Coast sales forces and the creation of a unified dealer council. Mazda's only independent distributorship, Mazda Great Lakes, handled operations in the Midwest.

The wave of the future is fuel-cell technology. This Mazda Demio hybrid is Mazda's response (courtesy Mazda of North America).

From 1,420,000 vehicles produced in 1990, production fell to 770,000 in 1995.[74] Ford stepped in once again, this time assuming 33.4 percent of the Mazda Motor Corporation. But Ford's own troubles hindered it from being the protector it once might have been. Nonetheless Mazda's reputation for high-quality, attractive vehicles has stood it in good stead during the lean years, borrowing enough time to allow for ongoing restructuring and renewed brand identification. Although the restructuring expenses were high and, when combined with Japan's recession, dealt the company a severe blow, they are recovering nicely with an impressive new model line.

Mazda is now well established as a major player in the global automotive industry with operations all over the world. Its success continues to rely on a strong competitive presence necessary to compete with companies such as Toyota, Honda, and Nissan. New management would do well to remember Mr. Yamamoto's simple message to his successors: "I want them to pursue brand individuality, and go on making products of value."[75]

# 11

## Subaru and Suzuki
## Stake Their Claim

### *Subaru*

In 1968 a small, very un–American little car had Americans asking "what was that?" as the Subaru 360 puttered by. Inspiring everything from derision to fascination, Subaru's "so-homely-it's-kinda-cute" offering seemed distinctly out of place among the massive muscle cars prevalent to the decade. It looked perfect for the beach and possibly even the water, but the 360 frightened away many who would have wanted to drive it on a ferocious Los Angeles freeway.

Americans can be forgiven for thinking the Subaru was an entirely new entity on the planet, as they were most likely unaware of its long and illustrious history as a division of Japan's mammoth Fuji Heavy Industries (FHI). Founded in 1917 when Chikuhei Nakajima established an aircraft research laboratory in Ota, Gunma, FHI was reorganized in 1931 as the Nakajima Aircraft Company and later rose to become Japan's leading aircraft manufacturer with close to 250,000 employees.

Nakajima Aircraft ceased production at the end of World War II by which time it had re-created itself into the Fuji Sangyo Company. In accordance with Japan's new laws concerning large corporate groups, Fuji Sangyo was divided into 12 smaller companies in 1950. In July of 1953, Fuji Heavy Industries (FHI) was created from a merger of five of those small companies. Today FHI has five manufacturing divisions: aerospace; bus manufacturing and house prefabricating; transportation and ecology systems; industrial products; and, most relevant to this text, automobiles.

The name Subaru was chosen for the automobile division. It is a shortened form of the name Mutsurobushi. The word Subaru means "unite," and is also the Japanese nickname for the Pleiades, a cluster of six stars within the constellation Taurus. From these six stars came the company logo.

Subaru's very first vehicle was the Rabbit motor scooter built in 1956, but in

Malcolm Bricklin thought this little Subaru 360 would be perfect for America's new economy market when he brought it from Japan in 1968. Although the car could go forever on a tank of gas, its 23-horsepower output made it a hazard on the freeway. Sales failed to materialize (courtesy Subaru of America).

1958 the company produced its first serious four-wheeled vehicle, the tiny 360 introduced in March of that year. The 360 evolved from the P-1 1500 unibody prototype which, when shown, failed to appeal to the Japanese consumer. The rear-mounted two-stroke, two-cylinder, air-cooled 356-cc engine provided a scant 16 horsepower — quite underpowered even as a minicar, but by 1964 it had been upgraded to include a four-speed transmission, rack-and-pinion steering, and independent, torsion-bar suspension. By then the car had 22 horsepower with a top speed of around 60 mph — albeit with some straining.

The 360 was 118 inches long and at 800 pounds was as light as it was short which allowed it an extremely efficient 55 mpg fuel consumption. The car had such a comfortable ride that it earned the nickname "Subaru cushion," and was quite popular in Japan's minicar market. Six hundred were produced in 1958, 5,000 in 1959 and 22,319 in 1960.[1]

In 1966 Subaru introduced a new model, the FF-1, a front-wheel-drive 977-cc, four-cylinder sedan for the Japanese market. By 1968 the company was producing 100,000 vehicles annually with exports representing 73 percent of that.[2]

The tiny Subarus caught the eye of Malcolm Bricklin of the Bricklin Automobile Company while he was traveling in Japan in 1968. Legend has it that Bricklin, predicting that American fuel prices would rise in the very near future, struck a deal to become the exclusive distributor of Subaru in America. Together he and his partner Harvey Lamm created Subaru of America, headquartered in Pennsauken, New Jersey.

Interestingly, when *Car Life* magazine announced the arrival of the Subaru in the United States no mention of Bricklin was made, nor was there any attempt to disguise the skepticism evident in the brief introduction: "Maybe there is a market for a mini-car in America, German and Italian efforts to the contrary. If there is, the Japanese will find it."[3]

But the skepticism seemed to be justified when no market materialized for the frog-like little 360, and much to the new distributor's dismay, its poor reputation proved impossible to eradicate. When *Road Test* magazine featured a preview of the new Subaru R-2, speculating whether or not it would be imported from Japan, the editors reminded the reader of the failed 360. Calling the R-2 a "gigantic step forward ... in relation to the previous 360 cc," they nonetheless still found the product lacking: "If the R-2 is exported to the United States, it would do Subaru well to consider increasing the displacement of the engine."[4]

Petersen Publishing was even more blunt in their assessment of Subaru's first product sold in America, calling the 360 "easily the most useless car for American driving ever to be imported to our shores. It more than laid an egg, it bombed completely ... we remember seeing several brand new but dirt-covered versions priced down to $50.00. Still, they went unsold."[5]

When it became apparent that the 360s were not going to succeed on the American market, Bricklin turned them into dune buggies but even that didn't work. By 1970 sales totaled 600 and Subaru of America was on the verge of returning to Japan.

Fortunately the car that would revive the company's fortunes arrived in the United States in 1969 and was greeted with much more enthusiasm. *Road Test* called it a "groovy car to drive," saying "there are enough things right about the Subaru FF-1 to make up for a multitude of sins. Following fresh on the tail of the unsuccessful Subaru 360, the 1100cc FF-1 admittedly faces an uphill battle."[6]

*Motor Trend* praised the car as being "quick and nimble,"[7] while Subaru's own advertising bragged: "At 70 mph it doesn't even breathe hard."[8] Certainly not in comparison to the hapless 360 at any rate. At 155 inches long and around 1,420 pounds, the FF-1 (sometimes called the Star) was considerably larger with a more powerful 62-horsepower, 1088-cc (64-cubic-inch) engine. It came as a two- or four-door sedan as well as a four-door station wagon.

The FF-1 was unique in a number of ways—it incorporated Subaru's "flat-four" horizontally opposed engine and was a front-wheel-drive vehicle. It also featured a

Better luck this time. This much-more-powerful 1970 FF-1. *Popular Mechanics'* Tom "Mr. Cool" McCahill tried to temper his admiration by calling the FF-1 a "chipmunk chaser" (courtesy Subaru of America).

dual-radiator cooling system that used a small thermostatically controlled electric auxiliary fan. Steering was the advanced-for-the-time rack-and-pinion, and suspension consisted of wishbones with torsion bars on the front, and independent with trailing arms and torsion bars on the rear. Surprisingly, the old-fashioned arrangement of drum brakes on all four wheels was found on Subarus well into the 1970s. Automotive journalists seemed to pounce as a body upon the new Subaru innovations, perhaps trying to make up for the forced negative reviews of the past.

*Road Test* investigated the Subaru's cooling system with great interest, calling it "…just about impossible to overheat…." They also had praise for the car's performance, handling, interior, and fuel economy, which they rated at between 29 mpg and 32 mpg. As for its bargain price, they commented, "The FF-1 doesn't *look* like a $1600 car."[9] That comment could have been taken two ways, but in light of the overall positive review it is assumed it was meant as a compliment.

Strengthened by these much-needed accolades and by sales of 14,116 for 1971, Subaru came up with a further-improved product, released in 1972 as the 1300 series.[10] These consisted of the A15L sedans and the A44L wagon. These models were powered by a 1267-cc, 61-horsepower engine and a slightly revised body. Later in the year the GL coupe arrived to much acclaim. The GL had the same overhead-valve 1267-cc engine with a two-barrel carburetor, but was slightly larger and had a different grille design.

In September of 1972 the GL was joined by the DL (Leone). The DL had a longer wheelbase at 96.7 inches and acted as the sedan and wagon replacement for the 1300 series. What was new was the four-wheel-drive configuration on the station wagon — making Subaru the first Japanese company to offer four-wheel-drive passenger cars in America.

The DL was powered by a 1361-cc engine with 61 horsepower which fell to 58 after the oil crisis. A total of 37,793 Subarus were sold in the United States by the end of 1973, a number which dipped to 22,980 in 1974 but recovered to 48,928 by 1975.[11] The Subaru's mileage, rated at just over 30 mpg, became one of its strongest selling points after 1973. The company was also able to beat the emissions standards by adding various vacuum-operated valves as well as a catalytic converter. But it was the four-wheel-drive capability that drew the most interest.

*Motor Trend* appropriately examined the DL in its December issue, leading the piece with: "Winter Wondercar: Subaru scores with 4-wheel-drive and 29 mpg." David Carlton undertook a comprehensive review of the DL and found it met and exceeded all expectations. From its "unique city/country horn," to its "innovative" four-wheel-drive system, Carlton felt the car had "very impressive" fuel economy and efficient brakes, if a slightly underpowered engine. After a technically detailed explanation of the four-wheel-drive mechanicals (which is covered further in the "Advantage Japan" chapter), Carlton drew his conclusion: "All things considered, the Subaru would be ideal if you're looking for an economical 4WD for use in areas of poor road conditions... You're not going to win the 1000 or the Mint 400 in it, but for skiers or winter commuters it could be just the Baja ticket."[12]

The only major complaint aside from lack of power was the four-wheel-drive shift lever which when engaged tilted to the left and straight into the driver's leg. Carlton also cautioned that buyers should not expect a wagon of American proportions, or as he so eloquently put it, "a bus it ain't."[13]

Two years later the DL made it to *Motor Trend*'s nominee list for Import Car of the Year and was continuing to receive positive reaction. It certainly was a very attractive little car — well proportioned and gracefully styled, fully able to compete with anything from Nissan, Honda, or Toyota in both looks and innovation. Customers were a bit surprised to see the spare tire mounted in the engine compartment, but once they drove the car they usually lost their reservations about its unusual features.

In 1979, *Motor Trend* gave the DL yet another look, this time matching it against the revered Jeep Wagoneer. Fred Stafford tested the two vehicles and found that the $5,800 Subaru was a good investment for the budget-conscious who could not afford the $12,500 for the Jeep. As for the Subaru's performance in the mountains, Stafford said: "The little scrambler would just dig in and go in the snow. The responsive steer-

By 1975 there were few laughs at Subaru's expense. They were becoming famous for their four-wheel-drive system and their smooth horizontally opposed "flat" engines. Customers became used to seeing the spare tire in the engine compartment. Wagons were, and remain, the company's strong point. This early example is a DL four-wheel-drive wagon (courtesy Subaru of America).

ing and firm suspension allowed it to skip down slippery snow-covered roads like a jackrabbit." Complaints centered around a lack of interior space, under-powered engine, and bare-bones interior.[14]

By the time that article appeared there was a new Subaru on the scene. Now known as the 1600 series (for its 67-horsepower, 1.6-liter engines) the sporty Subaru GF appeared in 1977 as a five-speed hardtop coupe only—a twin of the DL pillared coupe. Front suspension on the four-wheel-drive wagons was height-adjustable, a feature that raised the car's road clearance by an inch. Brakes for all Subarus were now front discs and rear drums and there were four- or five-speed transmissions to choose from. An automatic had become available in 1975. The GL model acted as the top-of-the-line Subaru with luxuries like a woodgrain dash, full gauge package, reclining buckets, AM/FM radio, and clock.

Subaru sales by 1979 had reached 127,871,[15] a fact attributable to the new craze for four-wheel-drive vehicles. As Stafford said that year, "To this point the growth of the segment (market) has apparently been to the benefit of all concerned."[16]

A year earlier Subaru introduced the BRAT, a four-wheel-drive car/truck hybrid resembling a mini–El Camino or Ranchero whose acronym stood for "Bi-drive Recreational All-terrain Transporter."[17] This debut date of 1978 put Subaru in the running as an early SUV manufacturer, as well as a leader in four-wheel-drive production.

All Subarus received new styling for the new decade. In addition to the 1600 series

The evolution of a legend — the 1985 Subaru DL (Leone) (courtesy Subaru of America).

there was a new, stronger 1800 series with 1781-cc engines that produced 72 horse-power and 92 ft-lb of torque at 2,400 rpm. Four-wheel-drive units could now be found on the STD two-door hatchback, the DL two-door hatchback, the DL wagon and the GL wagon.

Subaru vehicles (except the BRAT) stayed remarkably confined to dimension, mechanicals, weight, and price throughout the early- to mid-eighties. Styles were slightly changed but there were no surprises, with the possible exception of the 95-horsepower turbo engine which first appeared between 1983 and 1984.

In 1985 the Subaru joined the overhead-cam crowd with a much longer body that created 25 percent more cargo space in the wagons.[18] Horsepower was now between 73 for the base four-cylinder engines and 111 for the new turbo editions. The sedan was now 172 inches long over the 164.4 inches of its earliest predecessor. There were two new models in the line — the turbocharged, four-wheel-drive RX four-door sedan with computer-controlled suspension, and the XT Sports Coupe with a conventional or turbocharged engine.

The XT was a drastic departure for Subaru, looking like a cross between a Honda Prelude and a Toyota GTS, yet with its own unique touches. Generating 111 horse-power and 134 ft-lb of torque at 2,800 rpm through its multi-point fuel-injected engine, the XT had all-disc brakes, was 175.2 inches long and retailed for around $10,000. The four-wheel-drive turbo XT could get from zero to sixty in 10.3 seconds and perform the quarter-mile in 17.7 seconds. Top speed was rated at around 120 mph and it managed an estimated 21 mpg.[19]

Advertisements for Subaru continued to focus on reasonable costs and rugged-

Subaru revealed the other side of its utilitarian personality with this 1985 XT Coupe, which came in conventional and turbocharged editions (courtesy Subaru of America).

ness. In a 1986 edition of *Motor Trend*, such an ad featured the heading "A car built to withstand mother nature. And human nature. Subaru. Inexpensive and built to stay that way."[20]

Also that year a *Consumer Reports* review of the profusion of Subaru GLs and DLs prompted the editors to grade the cars as follows: "The 1.8 liter 4 started easily but surged briefly during sharp acceleration. The engine knocked on regular unleaded gasoline. The 5-speed manual transmission shifted smoothly, though not as precisely as some. A "hill-holder" feature keeps the car from rolling back when starting uphill. This front-wheel-drive model was easy to control, but steering was a bit sluggish. Excellent brakes. Very comfortable front seats and driving position." Also noted was the Subarus' "much better than average predicted reliability, and inexpensive maintenance and repair costs."[21]

Those costs were about to go even lower with the introduction of the smallest Subaru on the market since the 360 — the Subaru Justy, a three-cylinder, 66–horsepower 1.2-liter hatchback. "History in the Making..." said *Motor Trend* of the new Justy, asking readers to "forget the fact it's a very ordinary-looking runabout — the Subaru Justy has become the first car in the world to be made available with continuously variable transmission."[22] But as James M. Flammang noted, CVT principles had been applied by the Dutch automaker DAF "three decades earlier."[23]

The Justy was only 139.1 inches long with a 90.0-inch wheelbase. It weighed a mere 1,655 pounds and retailed for approximately $5,695 (hatchback DL). Four versions were available — two DL hatchbacks, a four-wheel-drive GL, and a four-wheel-

**Subaru had something for the economy market as well. The little three-cylinder, front-wheel-drive Justy GL was introduced in 1987 (courtesy Subaru of America).**

drive RS. Initially all Justys were two-door, five-speed hatchbacks, but in 1989 the much-talked-about ECVT (electronically controlled CVT) became the car's new transmission and in 1990 a four-door hatchback joined the line while a fuel-injection system added seven horsepower to all but the base-model Justy, which remained carbureted.

"Think of it as a Range Rover that's more in your range,"[24] suggested an advertisement for the new Justy, while *Road & Track* writer Douglas Kott said "Transmission trickery from a known innovator" in his review of the Justy. "On balance," said Kott, "the Justy ECVT handled Orange County's traffic-snarled streets and the stop-and-go rigors of what we laughingly refer to as 'freeways' with aplomb. The sore spot is out-of-the-gate-acceleration.... Niggling criticisms aside, this is a very attractive alternative to the 3-speed automatic transmissions usually offered in cars of this class ... dare-to-be-different Subaru has bragging rights for being the first manufacturer to market one in the United States."[25]

Also making its debut beside the Justy was the newest and most upscale Subaru — the XT6 — Subaru's response to the call for more high-end Japanese imports. With speed-sensitive power steering and a 2.7-liter flat six producing 145 horsepower and 156 ft-lb of torque, the XT6 replaced the older XT four-cylinder model.

There were changes for the 1988 sedans, wagons, and coupes as well. Full-time four-wheel-drive now replaced the earlier part-time units and the DL and GL designations were eliminated with the cars now known collectively as the Subaru Loyale. Interestingly, Subaru held fast to its flat engines which ran very smoothly and allowed a much lower hoodline.

More innovations from Subaru. This 1989 Justy was the first Japanese import to use an electronically controlled continuously variable transmission, earning it the initials ECVT behind its name and a place in automotive history (courtesy Subaru of America).

The 1988 *Auto Guide* heaped a liberal helping of praise on the Subaru, writing: "All the Subaru owners we've ever talked to rave about the toughness and reliability of their cars. If this is your prime concern, you won't be disappointed in any Subaru. In addition, if you live in a part of the country that gets a lot of rain, snow, or other slippery stuff, a four-wheel-drive Subaru will serve you well." And the Subaru was still economical in an age of rising prices. Mileage then rated between 26 and 31 mpg, and the average price of a Subaru was approximately $9,000.[26]

The Subaru Legacy made its debut in 1990 as a 2.2-liter, four-door wagon and sedan with a 101.6-inch wheelbase, a stretch that moved the car from subcompact to compact status. The engine produced 130 horsepower and was connected to a five-speed manual or four-speed automatic transmission. Four-wheel disc brakes were standard equipment. Some of these models were now produced in the joint Subaru-Isuzu plant in Lafayette, Indiana, the rest in Japan.

New for 1992 was the XT6's replacement, the bizarrely styled SVX coupe that put out 230 horsepower from its 3.3-liter flat six. Four inches longer than the old XT, the SVX was advanced not only because it had a driver-side airbag and antilock brakes as standard equipment, but also because of its unique glass-work, or as it was known in the business, "a window within a window," whereby only a small portion of the side windows were operational while the surrounding glass stayed in place. The purpose of this design was to reduce drag coefficient when the windows were lowered,

The first of the Legacy line — the 1990 Legacy LS sedan. Function meets luxury (courtesy Subaru of America).

but it must have also acted as a protector from incoming rain. Thin roof pillars arched up through what appeared to be a glass roof and dropped gently down into the rear deck where an optional spoiler topped a thin band of side-to-side wrap-around tail-lights. This was Subaru's "permanent" four-wheel-drive vehicle, with the phrase "all-wheel-drive" now beginning to come into vogue. A luxurious touring package was available with speed-sensitive power steering, leather interior, power moonroof, CD stereo, and rear spoiler. The SVX certainly bore little resemblance to its Loyale sibling which was on its way out by 1993, or to the squarish Justy and recently introduced Legacy.

With the advent of the Legacy, Subaru abandoned its boxy look and went for the rounded softer look of the period. By 1993 the Legacy came in 12 different versions in L, LS, LSi and Sport Sedan trim levels. Eight of these were all-wheel-drive vehicles, and a turbocharged engine was still available as an option on certain models. The high-end Touring Wagon had all the accoutrements of the SVX (except its speed) but at a lower cost — $22,600 to the SVX's $26,500.

While the also-newly rounded Justy graduated to the 73-horsepower engine for all five of its models, the newest Subaru arrived in showrooms as the Impreza, introduced in 1993 as a replacement for the Loyale. Slightly longer than the Loyale but around two inches shorter than the Legacy, the subcompact Impreza was available as a four-door sedan or five-door wagon in L and LS trim levels. All were powered by a 110-horsepower, 1.8-liter, flat-four engine, and all-wheel-drive was an option to the regular front-wheel-drive outfit. A five-speed manual transmission was standard equipment on the L, while the LS received an electronically controlled four-speed automatic with overdrive. Prices ranged between $12,000 and $16,000 for the first-generation Impreza.

Subaru emphasized its rallying roots and contrasted them with its more refined spirit of adventure evident in this 1993 Touring Wagon (courtesy Subaru of America).

It was becoming apparent that Subaru was moving up in the world, in all respects. Its all-wheel-drive system experienced increasing demand during the 1990s as consumers discovered the cars' amazing practicality and versatility. One could go camping, off-roading, or rallying in a Subaru. Conversely, they were great for taking kids to practice, picking up sales at flea markets or carpooling. As demand rose, so did market price as the cars became more of a status symbol.

Although they complained about the Impreza's tendency to "stumble after a cold start" and the need to "dig" to get engine power, *Consumer Reports* gave the car an excellent reliability rating as well as a nod for its 29 mpg fuel economy in a 1996 report.

Of the largest Subaru, the Legacy, the editors commented: "There is much to recommend about the Legacy." Speed continued to be a problem with the 2.2-liter engine but the "all-wheel-drive option performs flawlessly." They were not quite as taken with the new Legacy Outback wagon, commenting rather tersely, "It's not as tough as it looks. Get the regular Legacy AWD instead." Faults were found with the Outback's fuel-economy (about 21 mpg of premium fuel for the optional 2.5-liter engine and 23 mpg on regular fuel for the 2.2-liter), as well as the car's 31-cubic-foot cargo space, which was not "all that large for a medium-size wagon." Handling was found to be less impressive than the Legacy's, but on the positive side, the Outback was loaded with safety equipment such as dual airbags, "dynamic side-impact protection," and adjustable shoulder-belt anchors. Reliability was also rated as excellent.[27]

The car that would entice a generation of racers had humble beginnings as this 1993 Impreza sedan (courtesy Subaru of America).

The last Subaru to be tested was the SVX, a model *Consumer Reports* called "an able but not spectacular performer." Zero-to-sixty came in at 8.8 seconds and fuel economy at only 19 mpg. According to the editors, the SVX was roomy and stable, but with noticeable body roll on corners and light steering. The odd window arrangement drew a warning for its power switch location which could be accidentally activated, "squeezing anything in its way as it tries to close." Subaru prices now ranged from $13,495 for an Impreza (the Justy was no longer in the line) to $35,500 for a top-of-the-line SVX.[28]

By the year 2000 the Impreza series included the 2.5 TS Sport Wagon, 2.5 RS sedan, Outback Sport Wagon, and the rally-inspired WRX sedan and Sport Wagon. Still using the horizontally opposed engines, the TS, RS, and Outback were powered by a 165-horsepower 2.5-liter, while the WRX used a 2.0-liter, 227-horsepower, twin-cam, turbocharged flat four.

The Legacy line kept the same 165-horsepower engine as in the base Impreza and was available in five trim levels. As *Motor Trend* put it in 2001, the Legacy's "rough-and-ready Outback cousin gets all the attention, but the Legacy is a solid-buy Japanese family sedan or wagon."[29]

At the top of the heap was the Outback, which was newly redesigned for 2000. A sedan version was added to the array of wagons which included a Limited wagon, H6-3.0 L.L. Bean edition, and H6-3.0 VDC wagon. The latter came with heavy duty differential, traction control, stability control and antilock brakes as standard equip-

**Definite racing tendencies and a precursor of things to come — the 1998 Impreza 2.5 RS (courtesy Subaru of America).**

ment. The Outback engine was the 2.5-liter, with an optional 212-horsepower single-overhead-cam 3.0-liter six-cylinder introduced in 2001. All Subarus were now all-wheel-drive vehicles, and all were top sellers.

The most exciting Subaru to come along in a long time was the WRX. Widely known for its rally/racing abilities, the wide-eyed little Subaru has a pugilist's stance and power behind its punch. Looking more like a sedan than a mini muscle car, the WRX drew high praise from *Motor Trend*'s Chris Walton in his review of 2001. "Imagine an innocuous four-door sedan about the size and stature of a Honda Civic, packing a 227-horsepower wallop from an engine whose specific output is rivaled only by the vaunted 911 Turbo — the Porsche churns out 115 horsepower per liter versus the Subaru's 114. Subaru's corporate all-wheel drive system manages this prodigious power and puts it to effective use, and the car's interior packaging would be at home in any true sports car."

What was there not to like? "Widely-spaced gear ratios and not enough low-end torque." Other than that, the WRX provided "great sport sedan value" according to Walton.[30]

With a five-speed or optional four-speed overdrive transmission, 16-inch wheels, all-disc brakes, intercooled turbo, and sport-tuned suspension, the WRX moved like a true sports car, zipping to sixty in a speedy 6.2 seconds with a quarter-mile timing of 14.9 seconds at 92 mph. Stopping from sixty was accomplished in 136 feet. Fuel economy was somewhat sacrificed for speed at an average 21 mpg, but still better than some cars with equal power. *Consumer Reports* said the WRX "brings a new

This car-based sport-utility Forester arrived in Subaru showrooms in 1998 and was an instant success among off-roaders and suburbanites alike (courtesy Subaru of America).

level of driving enjoyment to the Impreza line." A prospective buyer could experience some of that enjoyment for a very reasonable $21,000 in 2002.[31]

The team at *Sport Compact Car* magazine couldn't say enough about the car that epitomized the name of their publication. "When the WRX roared up to our offices, it was nirvana times 10," said Larry Saavedra.[32] His colleagues concurred.

A little less "wacky" and more in keeping with Subaru's image as an all-wheel-drive master was the addition of the Forester wagon, a car-based SUV powered by the ubiquitous 2.5-liter four-cylinder engine. With a 99-inch wheelbase, an overall length of 175 inches, and 5.5 inches of ground clearance, the Forester was small enough for tight spaces yet high enough to go into rough territory. Cargo space measured 36 cubic feet with the rear seat folded, which *Consumer Reports* called "generous," although they found the back seat provided insufficient passenger room. Fuel economy came in at an average of 20 mpg and the Forester retailed for between $21,000 and $23,000 (2002 price).[33]

Being known for all-wheel-drive vehicles is perhaps an apt metaphor for Subaru, whose road to success in America has not always been paved. After the struggles of the early years, the company rallied only to fall again by the mid- to late eighties. The effects of the 1987 "Black Monday" stock market crash and the consequent exchange-rate fluctuations had a particularly hard-hitting effect on the auto industry and those who were already struggling found it even more difficult to survive. Subaru was just as conscious as its competitors of the need to form alliances within the industry and to transplant itself onto American soil. Choosing a like-

**Subaru goes Australia, and Paul "Crocodile Dundee" Hogan was hired to demonstrate how the car won its Outback name. The 1996 Legacy Outback (courtesy Subaru of America).**

minded partner was the difficult part. They found one in the Isuzu Automobile Company. The announcement that Subaru would join Isuzu, forming Subaru-Isuzu America (SIA), came during the turbulent year of 1987 as currency values shifted dramatically and the future looked far from certain.

As part of a massive corporate restructuring plan, an entirely new management team was put in place led by Chief Operating Officer George Muller. The new team, as was reported in the American International Automobile Dealer Association's newsletter, *Showroom,* "faced the grim realities of six consecutive years of declining sales; a record annual financial loss of $250 million in 1992; a 300-day supply of unsold inventory; unpopular and ineffective advertising and marketing programs; a muddled brand image and declining dealer profits and morale."[34] Certainly there is not much more that could possibly go wrong inside a corporation, short of labor disputes.

Key among Subaru's turnaround strategies was reducing costs, re-invigorating the corporate culture, shifting to a niche market, and developing new brand and marketing strategies.[35] It was a tall order, but the plan soon proved effective. "By 1994, Subaru of America had recorded its first profits in eight years and increased revenues by $248 million."[36]

The rugged appeal of the Subaru vehicles was enhanced by the appearance of Paul "Crocodile Dundee" Hogan racing across the rough terrain of the Australian outback in television and print ads. With the addition of the sporty WRX, Subaru has competently covered another market segment and is now one of the world's fastest growing automobile companies. The days of the little 360 are long forgotten in a country where a Subaru that might once have been hidden in a garage is now left in the driveway as an object of pride.

## Suzuki

Another rapidly expanding Japanese company has recently emerged from the shadows as an automobile manufacturer. Suzuki, like Toyota, began life a century ago in the textile industry as a loom manufacturing company. Established by Michio Suzuki in Hamamatsu (Soichiro Honda's old territory) circa 1909, the loom business thrived for 30 years until a combination of factors persuaded Suzuki to turn to motorized vehicle production. By 1939 Suzuki had fitted a series of four-stroke, four-cylinder, liquid-cooled engines with aluminum crankcases, quite advanced for their time, into prototype automobiles.

But like all other automakers, established or otherwise, Suzuki found his plans to build cars thwarted by the onset of World War II and he returned to the more reliable loom industry. But when the cotton market all but collapsed in 1951, Suzuki was forced to change his tactics once again, and he began by producing a motorized bicycle. With a widespread shortage of fuel and materials, motorcycles were considered a wise and viable alternative to automobiles which were prohibitively expensive to produce.

Suzuki's first "motorcycle" was the Power Free, built around a two-stroke, 36-cc engine. It was uniquely designed to allow it to operate via manual pedaling or on engine power. It was this clever design that earned Suzuki much-needed financial assistance from the government. The Power Free was soon joined by the larger 60-cc Diamond Free.

In 1954 the Suzuki Motor Company was officially established with a production rate of 6,000 motorcycles a month.[36] The company's first automobile, the Suzulight minicar, appeared only a year later. The diminutive Suzuki was front-wheel-drive with an air-cooled, two-stroke, two-cylinder engine. Its innovations included independent suspension and rack-and-pinion steering.

The Suzulight was further refined and reintroduced in 1962 as the Suzulight 360, with only a very small number produced. The 360 was followed in 1964 by the Fronte, a three-cylinder, 785-cc model.

Motorcycles, however, remained Suzuki's forte and it was there that the company made its fortunes. It exported its first samples to the United States in 1963 after winning the European 50-cc Grand Prix World Championship in 1962. Yet Suzuki persisted in its automobile production and it enjoyed a substantial growth spurt during the 1960s, producing around 120,000 automobiles by 1969.[37]

The late seventies saw Suzuki branching into marine engines and in 1982 the company introduced its first four-wheel all-terrain-vehicle (ATV), the QuadRunner LT 125. Many believe that Suzuki actually pioneered the ATV, but an article in the September 1971 edition of *Mechanix Illustrated* tells us otherwise, pointing out in the opening paragraph that ATV's "burst upon the scene" as early as 1968.[38]

With minicar sales holding their own in Japan's bustling market of the late sixties, Suzuki began its move toward the production of small Jeep-like four-wheel-drive vehicles, now known as compact SUVs. The year 1970 saw the arrival of the LJ-10, sold in the United States as the Brute IV. This little off-road vehicle had a 75-inch wheelbase and was motivated by an air-cooled 359-cc, two-cylinder, two-stroke engine that produced 32 horsepower. American sales were handled in large part by race car driver Tim Sharp who directed Suzuki's American marketing in the early 1970s out of his California office. Distributorship for those first vehicles was limited to California, Nevada, and Arizona.[39]

*Petersen's Complete Book of Japanese Import Cars* gave the Brute IV a mixed review, appreciating some of its finer qualities while pointing out its rather obvious shortcomings, writing: "...with its present 360cc engine and 32 hp, it must be considered more of an amusing curiosity than a serious on-road or off-road vehicle."[40]

Suzuki did improve upon the LJ-10, following it up with more-powerful LJ-55 and LJ-80 models which it continued to export. However, of the 69,798 vehicles Suzuki produced in 1979, only 5.5 percent were exported. Only a year later that number had climbed to almost 25 percent.[41]

In 1981 General Motors purchased 5 percent of Suzuki in a move to further expand its Japanese import line. As GM also owned a large slice of Isuzu, Suzuki and Isuzu began a collaboration which resulted in the production of the 1.3-liter Cultus hatchback, marketed in the United States through GM as the Chevrolet Sprint. The car was the most basic of transportation, and as such received tepid reviews.

Suzuki, however, wanted to export under their own name and establish themselves as an independent Japanese manufacturer and exporter. To that end they opened an American division in 1985 and began sales of Suzuki-badged vehicles through it, although some confusion reigned when it was learned that vehicles with the Suzuki name had slipped through the net beforehand.

In 1985, *Motor Trend*'s "Trends" column featured an item they titled the "Gray Mini-Market." It seemed that some so-called Sprints had "shown up outside the nine-Western-state 'official' distribution area ... wearing Suzuki badges, no less." As the editors explained, "Seems an enterprising distributor in Puerto Rico has sent cars to American destinations as far east as Long Island, New York. Chevy's concern (in addition to the piece of action it's *not* getting) is that dealers outside the nine-state region aren't prepared to service the little import."[42]

The first "legitimate" Suzuki to arrive in the very limited number of showrooms was the four-wheel-drive Samurai, introduced for the 1986 model year. The Samurai immediately drew interest because of its unusually short body, a design that proved to be both a blessing and a curse. Young people were drawn to it like a magnet, but the Center for Auto Safety and Consumers Union weren't so convinced of the little SUV's virtues. They claimed the vehicle had an alarming tendency to roll over even at moderate speeds or directional changes and gave it black marks across the board.

Accordingly, buyers were frightened away by the allegations against the vehicle's safety and Suzuki's sales dropped sharply from a 1987 high of 81,349 units.

But as *Car and Driver* later reported, the Suzuki had been badly maligned: "...to Suzuki's everlasting regret, some character assassins, masquerading as the staffs of

Suzuki wanted its own brand-image in the United States. It started with this 1986 Samurai —
first of the compact SUVs (courtesy Suzuki of America).

*Consumer Reports* and the Center for Auto Safety, claimed the Samurai was easier to
flip than a toilet seat. Sales went down the tube. Though the National Highway Traffic
Safety Administration later vindicated the Samurai and slapped *Consumer Reports'*
wrist, the Samurai went on life support and never recovered."[43]

But safety concerns were not the only issues that scared customers away. Also
heavily criticized were the Samurai's power and handling. As *The Used Car Book*
reported, "The Samurai's 1.3-liter 4 provides minimal acceleration and requires a lot
of shifting of the 5-speed transmission. Automatic isn't offered. If it were, it would
sap what little power that engine develops.... Ride is truly wretched, and the Samurai is extremely noisy inside. Accommodations and comfort are sparse for two. Any
luggage or cargo might adversely affect handling and acceleration. Worth staying
away from."[44]

In 1988 Suzuki expanded its line and revived its sales somewhat with the addition of the Swift hatchback coupe. Although the Swift was basically the same car as
the Chevrolet Sprint, there was a base 70-horsepower 1.3-liter, three-cylinder engine
for the four-door hatchback GLX, as well as a 100-horsepower, twin-cam, multi-
point fuel-injected engine for the two-door hatchback GTi. This model also had a
few sporty features such as spoilers, "ground-effects" (widened rocker panels) and
all-wheel disc brakes. Transmissions were either a five-speed manual or an available
electronically-controlled three-speed automatic.

It is quite difficult to find information on the early Suzukis as magazines and journals seemed to have almost studiously avoided reviewing them, or gave them a passing glance at best. Even James Flammang's voluminous *Standard Catalog of Imported Cars 1946–1990* gives only a cursory report of the company's first years in America. Although out of the harsh spotlight, Suzuki was at work devising badly needed improvements to its product line.

One of these revisions included the upgraded version of the Samurai which arrived as the similarly styled Sidekick. An advertisement in 1989 referred to the Sidekick as "A diamond in the rough." Hoping to reinvent itself as a fast and smooth rider, Suzuki drew attention to its independent suspension which provided a "cushy ride," as well as its "energetic 1.6 liter, fuel-injected engine" and a "roomy interior that's plush from the dash to the rear door." Slightly optimistic thought some, who still viewed the Suzuki with great suspicion.[45]

Next to come was the new and improved Swift in 1990. The four-door hatchback was replaced by a four-door sedan, and the GTi was downgraded to simply the GT, as according to James Flammang, "Volkswagen hadn't been pleased with the use of Suzuki's GTi designation a year earlier."[46]

By 1993 *Consumer Guide* was reporting that "Suzuki is de-emphasizing the Samurai which remains a rather crude conveyance...." Their report on the Swift, which now came in GA and GT three-door hatchbacks, as well as GA and GS four-door sedans, was more positive. "(The) Swift's primary attractions are low prices and great fuel economy. In earlier tests, we averaged nearly 36 mpg with a 4-door and more than 31 mpg with the GT, a pint-sized performer with sports-car moves."[47]

It was a beginning, although points were still deducted for an excessively harsh ride, highway and engine noise, and sheet-metal weakness. Still, with a price range of $7,300 to $10,000, it was one of the least expensive modes of transport available.

By 1995 the Swift GT was holding its own as an economy car with sports car tendencies, including a zero-to-sixty time of 10.1 seconds, a quarter-mile in 17.4 seconds and a top speed of 105 mph, while still getting 30 miles to the gallon and retailing for $10,000.[48]

Suzuki's next vehicle came forth with attitude as the X-90, for which advertisements asked "What are you staring at?"[49]

*Car and Driver* asked essentially the same question when it tested the X-90 in 1996. "And now for something completely different," ran the headline. Billed as a "front-engine rear/4-wheel-drive, 2-passenger, 2-door coupe," the X-90 retailed for around $16,000, and was powered by a 1.6-liter four-cylinder aluminum engine that produced 95 horsepower and 98 ft-lb of torque. The only transmission available was a five-speed and the final drive ratio was 4.63:1. Extremely short at 146.1 inches with a 86.6-inch wheelbase, the X-90 weighed only 2,500 pounds and had a ground clearance of 6.5 inches. Mileage was recorded at an estimated 25 mpg city, 28 highway. A T-bar roof prompted *Car and Driver* to call the car "a mini off-roader morphed with a sporty car, a Jeep-meets-del Sol kind of two-passenger thing that's unlike anything else." Praise came for the X-90's "Camryesque" cabin and comfort and for its performance on bad roads, but complaints followed in quick succession. The shifter had long throws, the body and suspension were as "stiff as a frozen flounder," and there

Suzuki's first passenger cars enjoyed only modest success. The company hopes their new all-wheel-drive Aerio will turn things around. The Aerio comes in four-door hatchback or sporty coupe; the 2003 models are pictured here (courtesy Suzuki of America).

was a noticeable lack of long-range power. *Car and Driver*'s conclusion was that "People will either love or hate the X-90. Its appeal is emotional, and that isn't something that can be quantified in a road test."[50]

By the time that report had been printed there was a new Suzuki up for review. The Esteem joined the Swift as Suzuki's larger passenger car, but did so to mixed reviews. *Consumer Reports*, perhaps remembering that "slap on the wrist" it earned over the Samurai, took a dim view of the Esteem GLX in its 1996 guide book, calling it "functional and workmanlike — no more, no less." Finding fault in almost every category from shifting to seatbelts, the magazine allowed mild praise for the car's "respectable" mileage of 29 mpg, and for the "small front seats (which gave) good, firm, support."[51]

Almost 16 inches longer than the Swift, the Esteem was introduced in the spring of 1995 and featured Suzuki's multi-point-injected, single-overhead-cam, 16-valve 1.6-liter engine that produced 98 horsepower. There was a base GL, mid-range GLX, and a high-end GLX with AM/FM cassette, power equipment package, cruise control and antilock brakes. A four-speed automatic transmission was optional on all models except when it became standard equipment on the top GLX in 1997.

*Consumer Guide* was also unkind to the Esteem in its assessment of the latest Suzuki: "Unimpressive in most areas, except for fuel economy, the Esteem does not deliver acceptable value."[52]

Despite such negative reaction, there was a new Esteem station wagon for 1998 with roof racks and a cavernous 61 cubic feet of cargo space, as well as a new Sport sedan in 2000 which had a more powerful 122-horsepower twin-cam four-cylinder engine.

The Swift also continued to garner poor reviews even with its newly designed aerodynamic body. Much more successful were Suzuki's new SUVs, the Vitara and Grand Vitara. A further edition called the XL-7 was the object of a 2001 *Motor Trend* long-term road test, with the reviewers reaching the conclusion that "Our test truck certainly speaks well to any fears about this brand's reliability; its 7500-mile service cost just over 50 bucks, and there's been nary a mechanical issue to report on."[53]

Even after receiving a more powerful 122-horsepower 1.8-liter engine and a proliferation of standard equipment, the Suzuki Esteem was recently replaced by the new four-door sedan and four-door wagon Aerio. The newest Suzuki also takes the place of the now obsolete Swift. A 2.0-liter, 144-horsepower engine powers the Aerio which is also available in all-wheel-drive.

Suzuki is struggling to gain in the all-wheel-drive passenger car market segment, receiving only lukewarm reviews and sales for its newest passenger car model.

In the year 2000 Suzuki was rated as the fastest-growing Japanese automobile company in America.[54] A year later the company had products in more than 170 countries worldwide with sales topping 1,800,000 vehicles per year.[55]

The steady rise of Suzuki in America has been both helped and hindered by its affiliation with GM which now owns 20 percent of it. Many of the models Suzuki created for GM have also come under fire for being "cheap" and poorly made. Perhaps its interests have been too diversified, with some production not only going to GM, but also to Mazda and Nissan as well. Although it remains a number-one motorcycle manufacturer, Suzuki's position in the United States as an automaker seems less clearly defined and it is still vulnerable to threats from so many other high-quality Japanese-based products.

# 12

---

# Isuzu and Mitsubishi —
# Captive No More

### *Isuzu*

"Isuzu of America says it's here to stay," reported *Car and Driver* in 1982.[1] Although new to America only a year before, Isuzu's history as an automaker dates back to the turn of the 19th century. The company advertises itself as "The first car builders of Japan,"[2] but that honor rightly belongs to the Mitsubishi Motor Corporation.

Isuzu's roots were as deep as the Tokyo Ishikawajima Shipbuilding and Engineering Company which established an automotive division in 1917. That division became known as the Automotive Industries Company and it focused primarily on engines — diesel engines in particular.

Under the leadership of Tomonosuke Kano, a diesel research committee had been established in 1934, the result of which was the company's first air-cooled diesel engine in 1936. A year later the Automotive Industries Company became known simply as the Isuzu Corporation, but it wasn't until 1949 that its present name, Isuzu Motors Limited, was adopted.

During the war years Isuzu rose to become a top producer of diesel trucks and buses and was recognized as such by the Japanese government which gave it sole rights to produce diesel-powered vehicles.[3] The heavy demand for industrial vehicles solidified Isuzu's position, allowing it to invest in passenger car research and development. Realizing it would benefit from European input and know-how, Isuzu signed an agreement with Rootes Motors of Great Britain to produce the Hillman car.

In 1959 Isuzu also produced a light diesel-powered truck called the ELF. Gaining much from British technology, Isuzu was able to develop its first passenger car, the four-cylinder, 1471-cc, 2.0-liter diesel Bellel sedan. In 1963 came the Bellett, a model very similar to the Bellel.

Isuzu formed another alliance in 1966—this time with Fuji Heavy Industries, a deal that was followed by one with Mitsubishi in 1968. Both of these joint ventures were aborted after a short period. There was a similarly short-lived agreement with Nissan in 1968. Clearly Isuzu was seeking the long-term partner it would not find for another three years.

By this time Isuzu had produced another passenger car, the Florian, with body-work by Ghia. These cars were never exported to the United States, and in fact Isuzu's first exports to America came from its agreement with General Motors in 1971. GM, anxious to gain access to Isuzu's diesel technology, purchased 34.2 percent of Isuzu shares. In return Isuzu, eager to claim a share of the U.S. market, began exporting light-duty trucks in 1972. These were sold by GM under the LUV badge.

In 1974 Isuzu built the first-generation Gemini which was based on the Opel Kadett, GM's captive import sold through Buick dealerships beginning in 1976. But the relationship with GM was an uneasy one. Isuzu was straining for independence on the American market and they finally achieved it by establishing their own sales company in 1980, American Isuzu Motors Incorporated, located in Los Angeles.

The first vehicles to arrive under Isuzu's own name were the Trooper sport-utility vehicle and the I-Mark sedan and two-door hatchback. The rear-wheel-drive I-Mark was described by *Car and Driver* as "the Japanese adaptation of (the) American Chevette," which in many respects it was, but in others it was a more advanced car than the Chevette, particularly in its more sophisticated body style.[4]

The I-Mark had a choice of a gasoline-powered 78-horsepower, 1.8-liter four-cylinder with a cast-iron block and aluminum head, or a 51-horsepower diesel version of the 1.8-liter. A-arms and coil springs made up the front suspension, while a rigid axle with coils could be found at the rear. Steering was rack-and-pinion and available transmissions were a four- or five-speed manual. There were discs on the front and drum brakes on the rear. Automatic transmission, air-conditioning, rally package, power steering, and AM/FM radio were offered as options. An I-Mark sold for between $5,900 and $6,500, depending on model and options chosen.

Isuzu's sales for its first year in America reached 17,805 vehicles.[5] They picked up two years later with the introduction of the sporty Impulse with its 2.0-liter, fuel-injected four-cylinder engine and a full range of creature comforts. Its most unusual feature was its very narrow grille and "eyelid" headlight covers.

The Impulse made its debut as a sports coupe only, riding on a 96.1-inch wheelbase and weighing a substantial 2,714 pounds. Fuel economy was rated at an estimated 24 mpg. The car's shell was designed by Italy's Giorgetto Giugiaro and the engine was a single-overhead-cam four that produced 90 horsepower and 108 ft-lb of torque at 3,000 rpm. Everything from air-conditioning to a stop-watch was included as standard equipment, as were four-wheel disc brakes and raised-letter sport tires.

In 1986, Isuzu released a limited edition "White-on-White" version of its new RS Turbo model. Powered by an intercooled, turbocharged 2.0-liter engine, the RS was able to create 140 horsepower and get from zero to sixty in 8.5 seconds. There was also a limited-slip differential, heavy duty sway bars and high-performance tires. Isuzu declared competitors would be "green with envy" when they viewed the new white Impulse.[7]

The Impulse came along in 1984, designed by Italy's Giorgetto Giugiaro. This 1986 hatchback coupe was loaded with features, including a seven-way adjustable driver's seat and complete power package. A normally aspirated 90-horsepower engine was standard, and a 140-horsepower turbo version was available. A limited-edition Turbo RS with sport suspension, available in white only, arrived for 1988 (courtesy Isuzu of America).

American consumers weren't quite sure how to view the Isuzu — many were unaware that the cars were related to certain GM models because the distinct styling of the Isuzu was like nothing seen before in the country, particularly the Impulse.

The I-Mark remained the company's bread-and-butter model with a complete redesign for 1985, when it became a front-wheel-drive two-door hatchback or four-door sedan powered by a smaller 1.5-liter four-cylinder engine. In 1986 *Consumer Reports* did not even bother to review the car under its own name, instead referring readers to the Chevrolet Spectrum report. "Both models should perform similarly," the reviewers advised. If going by the Spectrum's report, this meant a "much better than average" reliability record, but a poor grade for comfort, engine performance, and ride.[8]

The Impulse, on the other hand, received its own column and a more flattering report card: "The 1.9-liter 4 started and ran well. The 5-speed manual transmission shifted very smoothly through the forward gears, but shifting into reverse required a hard downward push. This front-wheel-drive model handled precisely, but rough pavement made it step to the side. Excellent brakes. Very comfortable front seats …

The I-Mark was introduced in 1981 as a rear-wheel-drive fastback coupe or sedan. By the time this photograph was taken in 1986, the car was front-wheel-drive and produced 70 horsepower from a 1.5-liter engine. A 110-horsepower turbo version followed in 1987. This is a domestic model, with the steering wheel on the right (courtesy Isuzu of America).

firm but reasonably steady ride. Erratic climate-control system. Unusual control layout."[9]

Even more erratic was *Consumer Reports*' reporting. In 1986 they referred to the Impulse Turbo as a "front-wheel-drive" vehicle, but in 1988 they said of the same car that "The Impulse retains a rear-wheel-drive chassis, but its styling is very contemporary."[10] The car was actually a rear-wheel-drive vehicle until 1990.

By 1989 there were nine Isuzus on the list. Two were turbos—the Impulse Turbo Coupe and the I-Mark LS Turbo, and the remainder were hatchbacks, sedans, and coupes. Despite offering competitive features, the Isuzu failed to make a dent in the market. For a while it seemed as though sales would keep climbing, but they reached a peak in 1986 at 38,910 units sold, then dropped to only 16,296 by 1989.[11]

This was also the year the I-Mark was cut loose from the model range and the only car to hold its place was the now-modified front-wheel-drive Impulse XS 2+ 2 coupe for 1990. A much-tamer 1.6-liter engine gave the new coupe a respectable 130 horsepower, but it kept the same overall appearance with some refinements, including a driver-side airbag. Optional antilock brakes came along for the RS version in 1992.

Like the I-Mark before it, the Impulse also suffered a very high rate of consumer complaints, very poor crash-test reports, and increasing parts costs.[12]

While doing moderately well with its trucks and SUVs, Isuzu's passenger car division was floundering. In 1988 *Road & Track* featured an announcement concerning Isuzu in its "ASAP News, Views, & Hype" column. "Isuzu has been looking for a second (non-import-quota constrained) car line for its U.S. dealers to sell alongside its I-Marks and Impulses and increase showroom interest and volume. The new Steyr-Daimler-Puch-built Bitter car, based on the Opel Omega (which may itself be imported to the U.S. in 1989 or 1990 by GM), would have given Isuzu an exciting $30,000-plus GT. But the plummeting U.S. dollar would have raised the price of the Bitter car to more than $40,000 — too high to maintain the required 10,000-car volume."[13]

In order to repair the brand's failing image a new model called the Stylus was introduced in 1991 as a replacement for the I-Mark. The fact that it was the very first Japanese import to carry a driver-side airbag as standard equipment seemed indicative that Isuzu was determined to try harder to keep up with the competition.[14]

The Stylus was available as an S, XS or RS model, all powered by a 1.6-liter four-cylinder, with the XS and RS models receiving a twin-cam version. *The Used Car Book* for 1994–1995 reported that the Stylus' "Driving position and view take some getting used to … and the twin-cam is very noisy."[15]

Similar reviews put the Isuzu cars in a very precarious market position. By 1993, *Consumer Guide* was reporting that Isuzu's "passenger cars just aren't that competitive against established subcompacts. This explains their continuing meager sales, which has fueled rumors that Isuzu may quit selling cars in the U.S. altogether."[16]

*Consumer Guide*'s review was ominous. Although much had been made of the fact that the Impulse carried a suspension by Lotus (which GM owned), and approval was bestowed for the car's standard safety equipment, fuel economy, handling, acceleration, and traction on its four-wheel-drive version, it still didn't seem to be enough. Even though the cars rated a disappointment in the area of noise and cramped rear seat — which many higher-end marques were also guilty of — the Isuzu just couldn't seem to stabilize on the market.

By 1996 there were no entries in *Consumer Reports* for Isuzu passenger cars, although the Trooper, Rodeo, Hombre, and Oasis SUVs were listed. To date Isuzu has continued to focus on its strength — truck-building, for which it has become famous.

During the mid-eighties the company rose to become Japan's third-largest manufacturer of industrial vehicles as well as the third largest diesel engine producer in the world.

In 1991 it developed the world's first electric truck and also continued to refine its adiabatic ceramic engine which is extremely light and heat tolerant. With such a wide range of technologies, Isuzu's future successes will most likely continue to come from trucks and SUVs.

## Mitsubishi

The origins of today's Mitsubishi Motor Corporation can be traced back to the founding of the Tsukuma-Shokai Shipbuilding Company by Yataro Iwasaki in 1870. This company was diversified and restructured in 1875, becoming the Mitsubishi Corporation. This new enterprise produced approximately 20 hand-made Mitsubishi Model A passenger cars in 1917. Although it seemed a propitious beginning in automobile production there was virtually no market, and Mitsubishi soon turned to industrial vehicles which they sold under the Fuso name. In 1934 the company's shipbuilding operations were merged with the aircraft division to form Mitsubishi Heavy Industries.

When the war ended and Japan's government signaled the return to automobile production, Mitsubishi had only a tiny motor scooter to offer, the Silver Pigeon, built in 1946.

Following the scooter came a small truck and then for a brief time Mitsubishi dealt in the importation of Kaiser-Frazer automobiles. Its own first post-war passenger car didn't come into being until 1960. The A10 500 was a 493-cc, 21-horsepower, two-cylinder minicar, precursor of the Minica and the Colt, both introduced in 1962. In 1964 Mitsubishi produced a luxury sedan, the Debonair. A succession of improvements to the Colt followed during the 1960s as production steadily rose. In 1960 only 5,203 vehicles had been manufactured but by 1967 that number had risen to slightly over 105,000.[16]

The coming of the new decade brought major changes for Mitsubishi. One was its name change to the Mitsubishi Motor Corporation in 1970, another was its agreement with Chrysler that same year, shortly after which it commenced exporting to the United States, and yet another triumph was its production record of over 240,000 cars.[17]

The deal with Chrysler was launched under shaky conditions when it was discovered that the cash-strapped American corporation didn't have the promised funds to purchase the agreed-upon shares. A new deal was arranged whereby Chrysler bought a smaller percentage, agreeing to take the rest at a later date. When the deal was finally ratified, Chrysler had its new captive import, the Dodge Colt, and Mitsubishi had their foot in the door. But like Isuzu, they wanted to develop their own brand image in the United States.

In 1982 they succeeded with their plan when Mitsubishi Motor Sales of America was established, with initial dealerships first appearing along the coastal regions of the United States. The first Mitsubishi vehicles to be sold in America were the Cordia, Tredia, and Starion.

The Cordia was a coupe based on the Colt design and came in three trim levels—base, L, and LS. Displacement was 1.8 liters, with the overhead-cam four-cylinder "Silent Shaft" engine producing 82 horsepower and 93 ft-lb of torque. While the L and LS models had a "4 + 4" eight-speed manual or optional three-speed auto-

*Top:* When Mitsubishi entered the American market in 1982, the Tredia was one of its first offerings. The car came out in three versions — the L, LS, and Turbo. The model here is a 1988 front-wheel-drive LS (courtesy Mitsubishi Motor Corporation). *Bottom:* The Cordia was also introduced in 1982 as a sporty companion to the Tredia and built with some of the components of the Dodge Colt. It featured the "Silent Shaft" engine, as well as sport air dams, rear spoiler, and color-keyed trim. This 1988 Cordia showcased Mitsubishi's Turbo engine (courtesy Mitsubishi Motor Corporation).

matic transmission, the base model only came with a five-speed manual. Measuring 176 inches long with a 96.3-inch wheelbase, the Cordia weighed around 2,150 pounds and had rack-and-pinion steering, independent suspension, and front disc brakes with drums at the rear. The front-wheel-drive Cordia managed an economical average of 27-mpg and retailed for approximately $7,089 (base model).[18]

The Cordia's partner was the Tredia, an almost exact replica of the Cordia only in four-door sedan form.

At the top end of the Mitsubishi line was the Starion, a five-speed-only, 2 + 2 turbocharged hatchback coupe with a 2.6-liter, four-cylinder engine with throttle-body injection producing 145 horsepower and 185 ft-lb of torque at 2,500 rpm. The Starion LS had a number of standard equipment features such as power windows, six-way power seats, adjustable steering column, air conditioning, alloy wheels, premium stereo, and all-disc brakes. The most prominent extra was what was known as the "Technical Options Package" featuring electronic skid control on the rear brakes. The Starion was no larger than a Cordia or Tredia—in fact it had a one-inch-shorter wheelbase—but naturally its 22 mpg fuel economy was compromised due to its power, and its price was higher at between $12,000 and $14,000.[19]

The first Starion was a pleasant-looking car (to some) with wide triangular back windows through which ultra-thin roof pillars sloped down to the outer edge of the deck lid. Two side-by-side upright louvers fit between the back window and side window. The front end angled downwards with an elongated but non-functional scoop rising out of the hood between the hide-away headlights. The word "Turbo" was prominently displayed in white script along the car's rear-quarter flank. Mitsubishi's advertising boasted that they were "alone among manufacturers" in that they designed and built turbos specially for their own engines. The ad's tag-line read: "Mitsubishi takes you where you've never been before"[20]

*Car and Driver* kept up with Mitsubishi's doings in 1982, commenting: "Mitsubishi Motor Corporation (is) attacking U.S. market with an exclusive line of cars."[21] A few pages later they featured a review of the Cordia. First up for speculation was the car's name, true to the American penchant for criticizing Japanese car names. "'Cordia' sure is a nice name, all right. Maybe too nice. It's the verbal equivalent of vanilla ice-milk. It hits you with all the authority of a powder-puff. Still, Honda didn't do too shabby with the name 'Accord', did it?"

After that brain-teasing query, the thrust of the article was more interesting for its comments regarding the United States–Japan market than for its review, which was quite vanilla itself: "The Cordia's goodness, like the Accord's, lies in its ability to do all things with competence, if not brilliance."[22]

The sting was then being applied to Japanese manufacturers who now had quotas to deal with, as Michael Jordan, author of the above review, noted: "Mitsubishi's 1983 import quota of 30,000 cars restricts Cordia sales to just 15,000 examples."[23]

Model changes throughout the next few years included a larger 2.0-liter engine for the Cordia and a turbo model for the Tredia, while the Starion received antilock brakes as well as a few body modifications which included the elimination of the scoop and reworking of the front air dam. Mitsubishi sales for 1986 were 84,418 units (including trucks).[24]

The Starion came along in 1982 as the company's flagship sports coupe. This 1988 ESI-R came equipped with an optional sports handling package which featured adjustable shock absorbers (courtesy Mitsubishi Motor Corporation).

Two new models had arrived in 1985, the smallest of which was called the Mirage, encased in a body almost identical to the Dodge Colt. The normally aspirated Mirage was driven by a 68-horsepower, 1.5-liter engine, while its turbo version squeezed 102 horsepower out of a 1.6-liter motor. A sport package also came with this model, which included hatchback roof spoiler, 14-inch tires, firmer suspension, and sport seats.

The other new arrival was the Galant, which had been on the Japanese market for a number of years. The front-wheel-drive, mid-sized Galant was powered by a 2.4-liter, 101-horsepower engine and had a "lock-out" overdrive four-speed automatic transmission. By 1986 it had 110 horsepower and alloy wheels. The sport version of the Galant approached the Starion in style, but without its turbo power and extra luxuries.

The Starion had become even more powerful in 1985 with a new ESI model sporting an intercooled turbo with 25 extra horsepower. A year later the ESI had been usurped by the even-faster 176-horsepower ESI-R kit which featured a modified "racer" body. The ESI-R could travel from zero to sixty in 8.3 seconds and do the quarter-mile in 16.2 seconds.[25]

While *Consumer Reports* singled out the Cordia, Tredia, and Starion for their "sagging and hesitation" during acceleration, the Galant was reported to have "started and r[u]n well," although it was given only an average predicted reliability rating while the other three managed a "better than average" grade.[26]

***Top and bottom:*** Mitsubishi filled the economy gap with this little Precis. Both LS and RS models (as shown) were surprisingly well-equipped (courtesy Mitsubishi Motor Corporation).

In 1987 the fruits of an agreement between Mitsubishi and Korean automaker Hyundai appeared in Mitsubishi showrooms. The Precis was very much the mechanical twin of the Mirage with the same 1.5-liter engine, but in appearance it closely resembled the Hyundai Excel. *Auto Guide* magazine reviewed the latest car in the Mitsubishi stable and found it to be "a good set of cheap wheels" which could "be dressed up with a surprising amount of luxury."[27]

Despite what they referred to as the car's "rousing sales success" the *Auto Guide* editors nevertheless felt that Hyundai should further refine its product up to "world-class standards."[28] With the benefit of hindsight, it was probably an ill-advised decision to use the services of a virtually untried manufacturer when Mitsubishi itself

Before the Diamante appeared there was this top of the line luxury sedan, the Sigma. It was powered by a 3.0 liter V-6 engine and featured electronically controlled suspension as well as antilock brakes (courtesy Mitsubishi Motor Corporation).

was struggling to gain a reputation for quality vehicles. Sales were in fact far from "rousing" with a total of 113,482 (including trucks) sold in 1988, down from 119,816 in 1987.[29]

With five models now representing their name, Mitsubishi added a high-end edition to its Galant, introduced in 1988 as the Galant Sigma. This car was powered by a 3.0-liter V-6 engine that generated 142 horsepower. In 1989 the Galant appellation was dropped and the car was known simply as the Sigma. A "Eurotech" package was offered which included antilock brakes and electronically-controlled sport suspension. The Sigma was longer by two inches than the base Galant but they shared the same 102.4-inch wheelbase. As a top-of-the-line-car, the Sigma also carried a higher price of $17,069 to the Galant's $10,971 (base model).[30]

The Galant of 1989 was a completely new design and took the place of the Tredia. The sporty GS edition featured a twin-cam, 16-valve, 2.0-liter engine which drew 135 horsepower from its four cylinders. This car won *Motor Trend*'s Import Car of the Year award in its debut year, a fact Mitsubishi used in its advertising, quoting the magazine's glowing assessment that the Galant GS "brings to the growing party of accomplished touring sedans a vigor, style, and level of world-class technology that advances the benchmark, import or domestic."[31] During this period Chrysler was building an ad campaign of its own around their Mitsubishi-made Colt and Conquest.

In 1989 the Cordia had faded away and was replaced by the vastly more exciting Eclipse for 1990. The Eclipse was built as a collaborative effort at Mitsubishi's and Chrysler's newly-opened Diamond-Star factory in Normal, Illinois.

The new Eclipse was available in five versions, with the base models carrying a 92-horsepower, 1.8-liter engine, and the GS, GS Turbo, and GSX models a 2.0-liter plant which produced between 190 and 195 horsepower. The GSX also received an all-wheel-drive arrangement.

Initial sales were brisk for 1990–91 and even more so in 1992 when the car lost its passé hidden headlights and featured flush-mounted versions instead, although in 1993 *Consumer Guide* editors were saying the Eclipse "was looking a bit dated already next to the new Ford Probe and Mazda MX-6," adding "(the) Eclipse still rates as one of the best values among small sports coupes. Our favorites are the GS DOHC and all-wheel-drive GSX." "At the top line," the review continued, "the turbocharged models deliver ferocious acceleration, but torque steer (sudden pulling to one side in hard acceleration) is a problem."[32]

New for 1992 was the flat-selling Sigma's replacement, the luxuriously appointed (and named) Diamante. The larger (190.2 inches long) Diamante came with a twin-cam, 3.0-liter engine that created 202 horsepower and 199 ft-lb of torque at 3,000 rpm. The only transmission available was an electronically controlled four-speed automatic and standard brakes were antilocking all-discs. A driver-side airbag was also standard. Mileage averaged out at a none-too-efficient 19 mpg, but that was not unusual for a car weighing over 3,500 pounds.

Features included traction control and electronically controlled suspension, as well as a long list of power equipment and controls, or as *Consumer Guide* reviewers put it, the "interior is laden with electronic toys," which they found a drawback rather than a benefit. Also inspiring criticism was the loud exhaust and somewhat restricted visibility. Overall, the consensus was that "The Diamante is a big improvement over the Sigma, but our loaded LS test car had more gimmicks than substance." And most damning of all: "One car you should compare it to is the Nissan Maxima SE. It has more verve without any gimmicks—and costs less, too." The Diamante's price range of $16,800 to $25,135 did put it above the Maxima's $18,000 to $21,800 asking price.[33]

It's tempting to assume there was something of Chrysler's influence at work here. The car's overall size and weight, higher price, and Chrysler's tradition of adding "gimmicks" all seem to lead straight to Chrysler's door. Although the Japanese version of the Diamante earned Mitsubishi Japan's Car of the Year award for 1991, it did not achieve equal success in America. In fact, Mitsubishi couldn't seem to break that invisible barrier between it and its more celebrated compatriots and always seemed to suffer the humiliation of guide books that referred customers to competitors' showrooms before they decided on a Mitsubishi. The Galant came close to a breakthrough in 1996 when *Consumer Reports* favored it by remarking that "The Galant is an extremely competent car, scoring only a notch below the excellent Toyota Camry and Honda Accord." The only problem was that the review concluded with the discouraging, "Reliability has improved to average this year"—a comment which rather negated the opening sentiment.[34] As for the now–$35,000 Diamante, the same mag-

*Top:* When the Eclipse was introduced in 1989 for 1990, its daring styling caused a great stir. As it entered its third generation, it continued to draw an audience (courtesy Mitsubishi Motor Corporation). *Bottom:* One-upmanship. The 2003 Eclipse Spyder (courtesy Mitsubishi Motor Corporation).

The 2003 Galant displayed a newer and more refined technique from Mitsubishi and has drawn consistent praise from reviewers (courtesy Mitsubishi Motor Corporation).

azine reported that though the car was "capable," "it doesn't stand out against such high-line competitors as BMW and Volvo."[35]

The Eclipse, which had a new convertible edition for 1996, also got a black circle for its predicted reliability just as its Chrysler twin Eagle Talon was taking a battering in trade magazines.

Image problems continued to plague Mitsubishi throughout the 1990s. This was aptly illustrated by *Car and Driver*'s 1998 review of the Galant GTZ in which Don Schroeder tackled the issue forthrightly in the opening paragraph: "When it comes to getting publicity, being bigger is almost always better. Toyota had little problem getting the word out about its restyled Camry a couple of years ago. And Honda had no problem with the new Accord last year. These huge-selling cars are backed by commensurate ad budgets, and they draw lots of attention from the mainstream press. Mitsubishi, which sells less than a quarter as many cars here as Honda or Toyota does, isn't so fortunate. It is determined, though, not to let its new Galant go unnoticed."[36]

Schroeder's review was on the whole a positive one, with praise for the car's styling (though not the rear wing), as well as its convenient controls, comfortable seats, ample cabin and cargo space, and "exceptional handling." Of the two engines available, the base being a 2.4-liter, 145-horsepower four and the other being a 3.0-liter V-6 with 195 horsepower, the team chose the latter to test, finding it not quite "fleet of foot." Braking drew a "so-so" rating and Schroeder concluded, "The new Galant ... is a gallant effort from Japan's fourth-largest car seller. The GTZ can't

A head-turner. This 1992 3000 GT SL came loaded with extras and was propelled by an impressive 222 horsepower 24-valve V-6 (courtesy Mitsubishi Motor Corporation).

match the performance of many of its competitors, but it feels swift enough when you drive it. And the Galant does match the refinement of its competitors' products, wrapped in sportier, more distinctive styling, at a slightly lower price." And once again referring to the company's image problems, he added: "That's not a very clearly defined hook to hang your marketing hat on, is it?"[37]

Despite a lower brand profile, the Mitsubishi line stayed remarkably intact into the year 2000. The addition of two high-powered sports cars, the 3000GT back in 1991 and the more recent Eclipse Spyder GT convertible in 1999, helped boost the company's image as a performance builder but sales were still modest.

In 2001 the new Lancer appeared wearing sporty alloy wheels, a rear spoiler and a canary-yellow paint job. The Lancer was powered by a 2.0-liter, 120-horsepower four with a five-speed manual or four-speed automatic transmission. The LS models offered dual airbags and antilock brakes, while a special edition OZ Rally model paid tribute to the car's four rally championships and victory at the Pikes Peak hill-climb in 2001. *Consumer Reports* called this model "superficially sporty," but pinned more hopes on the soon-to-arrive Evolution model, expected to take on Subaru's Impreza WRX.[38] As for the Lancer's older sibling, the Galant, the magazine reported in 2002 that its "reliability has deteriorated, so we can no longer recommend this otherwise capable car."[39]

The Diamante, which had fallen in price and was now built in Australia, didn't fare much better than the Galant or the Eclipse. The Eclipse was labeled as "not very sporty" by *Consumer Reports*.[40]

*Top:* Starting its own revolution — the Mitsubishi Lancer. This 2003 OZ Rally model is a tribute to the car's four world rally championships, including the 2001 Pikes Peak hillclimb (courtesy Mitsubishi Motor Corporation). *Bottom:* The Diamante replaced the Sigma in the early 1990s as the company's luxury sedan. *Motor Trend* praised its "handsome Germanic styling" (courtesy Mitsubishi Motor Corporation).

It is interesting to note how frequently prominent trade magazines disagreed with the consumer journals. *Motor Trend* found all of the Mitsubishi vehicles praiseworthy in their 2001 Buying Guide edition. The Diamante was "a refined and smooth sedan with handsome Germanic styling"; the Eclipse had "show-car styling combined with sporting performance and refined ride"; the Galant "proved to be a revelation, becoming the first Mitsubishi to compete without apology against the best midsize family sedans from Japan," and the Mirage coupe was called a "simple and well-built coupe that delivers excellent value for (the) money."[41]

*Motor Trend*'s initial reports on the new Lancer Evolution VII with its 276-horsepower turbo engine have been positive, with Matt Stone opening his assessment by stating simply, "Yup, it's fast."[42]

Mitsubishi refers to themselves these days as the fastest-growing Japanese automaker in North America. Sales reached 345,111 by 2002, but have recently slipped again. Despite the roller-coaster ride, the company clearly has no intention of relinquishing its position as an automaker with one foot in Japan and the other in America, no matter what consumer magazines say about it.

# 13

## Advantage Japan — Environment, Embargo and Excellence

### *Environment*

In the early 1950s, California Institute of Technology chemist Dr. A.J. Haagen-Smit coined the term smog — a combination of industrial smoke and fog. By 1960, discussion had begun in California's state legislature on the benefits of using emission control devices on automobiles. The target areas of concern were lead, unburned hydrocarbons, carbon monoxide, and nitrogen oxides. In 1965, the new Motor Vehicle Air Pollution Control Act set the first federal standards which were to take effect by 1968. They required that a 72 percent reduction be made for hydrocarbons, a 56 percent reduction in carbon monoxide, and a 100 percent reduction of crankcase hydrocarbons. But by 1969, tests showed that more than half of American cars failed to meet the new standards, although they had been fitted with positive crankcase ventilation (PCV) valves in 1964.

When Haagen-Smit was interviewed by the *Los Angeles Times* in 1969, he declared that: "in a few years, the industry has to rethink and redevelop the automobile so that it drives as well as it does now but doesn't pollute the atmosphere while doing it."[1]

Easier said than done, protested the automotive engineers. Adding anti-pollution equipment as an after-thought as opposed to integrating it into the engine's design could not help but adversely affect its operation. Electronic ignitions, exhaust oxygen sensors, vacuum systems, modified carburetors, and evaporative systems were but a few of the requirements necessary to reduce emissions. These modifications not only caused such problems as engine run-on, or "dieseling," but also consumed much more fuel than an engine that was free of such devices. For each control added, a counter-measure had to be taken to keep the engine in balance and running properly. To ensure that the new emission-reduced engines would perform as required, an "LA4" test was set up using a special dynamo connected to a computer. The test was a simulation of driving conditions on a freeway in one of America's most polluted states—California. In fact the nation's smog index and most of its pollution research was centered around Los Angeles. In Japan, the densely populated city of Tokyo assumed the same position.

Japan's rapid industrialization had so dramatically increased air pollution that by the 1960s children were collapsing in the school-yard due to breathing-related problems. An increasing number of citizens were being admitted to hospitals with high levels of lead in their systems, and diseases like asthma and bronchitis were also on the rise. In 1964, newly elected Prime Minister Eisaku Sato assured the Japanese people that one of his first priorities would be to clean up the environment, calling industrial pollution "a distortion in economic growth."[2] One year later the Japan Environment Corporation was established, followed by the passing of the Motor Vehicle Exhaust Emissions Standard in 1966, which was buttressed a year later by the Basic Law for Environmental Pollution Control.

By 1970, a total of fourteen air- and water-pollution-related bills had been approved by the Japanese government. Simultaneously, work began to eliminate lead from gasoline. In 1971, the Environmental Agency was established and its leader was appointed a minister of state. In addition, the Health and Welfare ministry increased its budget in order to provide relief measures for those who had suffered physically as a direct result of pollution. The Pollution-Related Health Damage Compensation Law was enacted in 1973, providing increased medical care and disability benefits for people in designated high-pollution areas. The cost of these measures, decreed the high courts, was to come out of the pockets of those most responsible for major pollutants—namely industries and automobile companies. These stringent new laws set Japan apart as enforcing some of the toughest anti-pollution policies in the world.

By the mid-sixties, pressure was brought to bear on the Japanese automobile companies who fought the new laws just as vehemently as their American counterparts were doing in the United States. Senator Edmund Muskie's sponsoring of the Clean Air Act, or "Muskie Act," in 1970 meant that American automakers were challenged with reducing carbon monoxide and hydrocarbons to one-tenth of what they had been in 1970 by 1975. In Japan, the Environmental Agency was imposing even tougher standards for Japanese automakers. But the most difficult target goal of all was the call to reduce nitrogen oxide emissions to 0.25 grams per kilometer driven by 1978.

The cost to the automobile companies of implementing these emission controls was enormous. Particularly hard-hit were Toyota and Nissan, who each had a substantial number of automobiles to bring into compliance. Resistant Toyota executives demanded that the government offer hard proof that automobile emissions led to health problems before they would consider investing in re-engineering their vehicles. This concern for cost over health angered government officials whose only response was: "You can't buy health with money."[3] But continuing public outcry demanded that the emission controls proceed and high-profile companies like Toyota had no choice but to comply or risk being closed down.

Despite pleas for leniency, the target of date of 1978 was rigidly adhered to by the government. As an incentive, tax breaks were offered to any company who could meet the control standards ahead of time. The incentives sparked a fierce competition among automakers to be the first to meet the 1978 requirements. As a result they not only met them early, but also significantly earlier than the American automakers were able to. This is not to say there was no struggle involved. Indeed the process of producing emission-reduced vehicles was something of a baptism by fire, especially for Toyota and Nissan who became resigned to the fact that "what didn't kill them only made them stronger." Eiji Toyoda, although pronouncing that first period of emission controls "a disaster," nevertheless admitted that Japan's stringent policies prepared them well for the American market.[4] At the same time, he conceded that he had been undeniably angry at the cavalier manner in which the Japanese government had acted. "The Environmental Agency rode roughshod over the auto industry," he wrote in his autobiography.[5] In this view he echoed a sentiment General Motors' Bunkie Knudsen had once expressed in an interview: "One of the difficulties is that there are not too many people outside the automobile industry that understand the problems involved in the design and building of an automobile that will be sold in quantity. And so consequently it is difficult to understand that you just can't push a button and change anything that you wish to have changed at a moment's notice."[6] Eiji's more direct translation amounted to: "People who didn't know the first thing about emissions were making a lot of fuss."[7] Chrysler engineers would have agreed. When they installed a temperature control device to deactivate the exhaust gas recirculation (EGR) system at colder temperatures to help drivability, the EPA demanded they place it next to the radiator. When the device failed, as it naturally would being a heat-activated control, the EPA forced Chrysler to recall all vehicles so equipped.[8]

While the Big Three were calling the new standards impossible, Toyota and Nissan agreed, flatly stating that no Japanese company could possibly meet the strict regulations either. Their claim, however, was rendered inconsequential when representatives from Honda and Mazda declared they could not only meet but also surpass the guidelines, and do so as early as 1972. But because of Mazda's ensuing difficulties with blending an emission-free vehicle with a fuel-efficient one, it was the Honda Motor Company who rose to lead the industry in those difficult years with an engine that was both.

In 1968, Honda temporarily withdrew from auto racing to begin research on a unique new motor. By 1971, the compound vortex controlled combustion (CVCC) engine was being developed under the direction of engineer and future CEO Tadashi Kume. The CVCC used a stratified charge system and each cylinder had two combustion chambers—a pre-chamber and a main chamber. While a rich air/fuel mixture entered the pre-chamber, a lean mixture entered the main chamber. The spark plug fired the rich mixture, which in turn ignited the lean mixture resulting in a stable, slow burn with an even temperature. This leaner and cooler method of combustion lowered both carbon monoxide and hydrocarbons, as well as nitrogen oxide emissions. Since no catalytic converter was required, the automobile could run on low-lead or leaded gasoline. This meant that the CVCC was the most cost-effective of all the anti-pollution systems. The engine was placed into a slightly larger Civic and introduced in America in 1975 as the Civic CVCC. The latest Civic was an immediate success with both government and public. Honda's success as well as their cutting-edge technology made them the envy of other companies, who soon came knocking on their door to purchase licensing rights.

Before the advent of the CVCC, the latest in propulsion technology was found in Germany where Felix Wankel had invented the rotary engine. Toyota, along with 20 other automobile manufacturers including GM, Nissan, Ford, Suzuki, and Mazda, approached the NSU automobile company for rights to the Wankel engine. But when Toyota failed to develop a successful version of it, they turned to Honda instead. It was a humbling experience for such a large, dominant company to approach a small fringe automobile manufacturer for leading technology. Toyota executives airily dismissed the notion that Honda engineers had surpassed them with the observation that as a small motorcycle company, Honda held the advantage of long experience with tiny, efficient engines. Honda, however, was not ready to give up their lead and Toyota's first emission controls ended up consisting of an EGR system, a thermal reactor, and a catalytic converter. The Corona and Corolla were among the first vehicles to receive the new anti-pollution devices.

At Nissan, engineering research led them to the development of the Nissan Anti-Pollution System (NAPS), which used an air-injector pump and an evaporative system, and which included an exhaust gas recirculation circuit. They also utilized a catalytic converter.

Mazda's advantage stemmed from their success with the Wankel engine. A few of the beneficial features of rotary power were that it generated less vibration and had a more tightly controlled intake and exhaust system, thereby producing fewer emissions including NOx. To complement this system, Mazda added an air-injector pump and a thermal reactor which was encased in a metal shell. The air pump directed air into the reactor and out through a secondary tailpipe positioned next to the main tailpipe. It was a system that put them just behind Honda in the emission-control race.

One surprise came from Fuji Heavy Industry's Subaru automobile company. Their already unique dual-radiator, fan-less front-wheel-drive model was fitted with what they called the SEEC-T engine. It was equipped with a high-efficiency combustion chamber designed to reduce engine knock while still running on regular fuel. It managed to meet the emission standards while still producing above-average fuel efficiency.

But while Japanese automobile companies were meeting the new standards albeit with a few hiccups, American automakers were consistently missing deadlines. It wasn't necessarily for lack of technology, but rather, as they claimed, for lack of funding. They were still reeling from the safety implementations of the 1960s. But as an editorial in a 1971 edition of *Motor Trend* magazine pointed out: "Most people probably still believe the automakers are paying the high cost of their current massive emissions control and safety research programs. Not so. The bulk of these costs, as it has in the past, is passed directly to customer [sic] in the form of higher prices."[9]

In America in 1970, the requirement had been that 90 percent of emissions be controlled by 1975. The more difficult problem of controlling nitrogen oxides was given until 1976. Any manufacturer that failed to meet the requirements faced a $10,000 fine for each vehicle in violation of the laws. But by 1973 the Environmental Protection Agency was forced to grant a one-year extension for hydrocarbons and carbon monoxide, and a two-year extension for nitrogen oxides. In 1975, the year Honda was recording sales of 10,000 Civics per month in America, the EPA granted yet another year's extension for hydrocarbons and carbon monoxide. In 1977 the Clean Air Act was amended once again, and further extensions were granted for a new deadline of 1980. The restrictions on amounts of emissions allowed were also revised, with the troublesome nitrogen oxides amount allowed increased from 0.4 grams per mile driven to 1.0 gram per mile. The deadline for this requirement was moved to 1981 or "later." The deadlines continued to be extended until well into the 1990s as standards became more exacting and as demands for cleaner automobiles rose rather than declined. The present-day environmental and energy concerns have led to the development of such automobiles as the Toyota Prius and the Honda Insight, both hybrid models running on a combination of fuel and electricity. Fuel cell research continues to be a priority with automotive companies who are still being prodded by environmental agencies who are in turn gathering increasing public support.

While Detroit played a game of catch-up it just couldn't seem to win in the 1970s, the Japanese companies took advantage of the opportunity to expand their American, and indeed global, bases. In 1965, Japan had exported 100,716 passenger cars. By 1975, that number had grown to 1,827,286, most of those going to the United States.[10] *Car and Driver* editors wrote: "Now that the Japanese have successfully colonized the U.S., they are seeking to expand their empire."[11] Aside from conquering the stiff emission-control standards, the other essential advantage they possessed proved to be pivotal in the autumn of 1973.

## Embargo

In May of 1972, an Exxon Oil Company advertisement in *National Geographic* magazine read: "World energy relationships are now at a turning point. The earth is not running out of potential sources of energy, but it will take a major effort and considerable lead time to develop resources to meet our future needs."[12]

From that date forward it was not unusual to see many more such advertisements, some of them a full six pages long. One of these warned that "The United States is no longer in an era of abundant energy. Our needs for the future are critical."[13] The edition was dated February 1973. Ironically, directly across the page from the Standard Oil insert was an ad for the new Oldsmobile Ninety-Eight, one of the largest American cars ever made.

The oil crisis that came in October of 1973 and shocked the world should not have come as a surprise, according to author Jean-Jacques Servan-Schreiber. Servan-Schreiber, who devoted years of research to the petroleum industry, wrote that: "For fifty years, from 1920 to 1970, the West based its factories, transportation systems, cities, universities, laboratories—its industrial civilization and growth —*on cheap oil*. And the companies did this without considering the possibility of increasing payments to the producing countries."[14] The figures Servan-Schreiber produced bore this out. Oil, which had been $1.20 per barrel in 1900, had risen only sixty cents by the time the Organization of Petroleum Exporting Countries (OPEC) was founded in 1960. In fact OPEC was formed mainly for the purpose of establishing a stronger bargaining position with the oil companies. Simply put, OPEC felt they should be paid more for the oil that came from their land. But when the oil companies flatly refused their demand for $6.00 per barrel in 1973, the ensuing stand-off resulted in the halting of oil shipments to Europe, America, and Japan. The embargo was seen by many as the result of the Arab-Israeli war of October 1973, but Servan-Schreiber discounts that notion, claiming that: "…OPEC's decision to hike oil prices began long before."[15] He also noted that the embargo was "…just a spectacular episode within an irreversible trend."[16]

While Americans panicked after Nixon warned them of the coming "harshest energy curtailments that (America) has ever experienced,"[17] and rumblings of using force against OPEC echoed around Senate chambers, Japan, without any oil wells of her own, was faced with only a two-week supply of oil in reserve.

The government immediately called for a 10 percent reduction of oil provided to the automobile, rubber, and steel industries, among many others. It was obvious that Japan had to vote to capitulate to OPEC's demands, even if risking America's wrath by doing so. Europe was in a similar situation. But while Europe and Japan conceded, America, with her own modest stores of oil, refused to. This hard-line stance dealt a devastating blow to the nation's automobile industry. While boardroom politics were being played out, Americans recoiled from the skyrocketing gas prices—that is if they could even get near the pumps in the first place. Riots broke out in some areas and people began hoarding gas and constantly "topping up" in a state of frenzied paranoia.

No blow could have found a more vulnerable target than withholding oil from a nation of gas-guzzling automobiles. The repercussions to the automobile industry were felt immediately. As John DeLorean put it: "Big cars fell out of favor overnight because they were inefficient and wasteful. In some respects, it became un-American to drive a big car. This was a particularly unfortunate occurrence for the country because the rising imported car penetration contributed a substantial portion to the United States' balance of trade deficit–three or four billion dollars a year."[18] Yet Lee Iacocca took a different view of the situation. He insisted that the demand for large cars was still there even after the oil crisis, and reported that Ford was making "a ton of money."[19] Then, dismissing Japan's success in the United States as mainly serendipitous, he continued: "As for the Japanese, did they really anticipate the American demand for small cars? For thirty years, they've been building nothing else. *Whenever* the shift occurred, they would have been ready. It wasn't that Ford, GM, and Chrysler couldn't anticipate the American market. *Nobody* could."[20]

Iacocca and his American colleagues had reason to complain. As demand for imports rose an unprecedented 40 percent in 1974, GM sales had dropped 21 percent, while Chrysler's fell by a staggering 62 percent. The new Corporate Average Fuel Economy (CAFE) standards introduced in 1975 may not have posed a problem for the Japanese but for GM, who had the worst rating in the industry at only 12.2 mpg, it was something of a hardship to meet the first standard of 18 mpg by 1978. And while their advertisements spoke of power and luxury, Toyota, Nissan, Honda, and Subaru focused on the economy angle. A Subaru ad boasted of its 27.3-mpg rating which, as they said, was "more than double the national average."[21] Nissan turned away from their slogan of "Datsun Original" to "Datsun Saves," and Toyota claimed "We make 12 different economy cars. But it's how we make them that counts."[22] One Honda ad headlined "Onedownsmanship" claimed a mileage of close to 40 mpg for the Honda N600 model.[23]

The tripling of the price of gas combined with the cost of emission controls led to widespread experimentation in the area of alternative fuel and power sources in both Japan and America. Even steam propulsion was not discounted as could be seen from the automobile developed by Calvin and Charles Williams in 1967 and featured in a 1968 edition of *Life* magazine. Steam, however, proved to be almost as impractical as it had been earlier in the century and was quickly discounted.

Electric vehicles, however, received much more attention. General Motors had produced an experimental vehicle which author Ed Cray cynically observed was invented more to placate than to innovate. Accusing GM president Pete Estes of being more concerned that the company should *appear* to be reaching for solutions rather than actually finding them, Cray wrote: "If he (Estes) had any favorite project, it was the battery-powered automobile Chevrolet engineers sometimes trotted out to impress innocent reporters and congressmen."[24]

But GM was not alone in its attempts to "impress congressmen." The Electric Fuel Propulsion Company was at the time America's largest manufacturer of electric passenger cars. Among other models, they were responsible for the American Motors Corporation's electric Hornet, developed with a 20-horsepower electric motor which was fueled by 24 regular car batteries. The vehicle was impossibly heavy at 5,500 pounds and had to be recharged 11 times on a trip from Detroit to Chicago.[25] *Mechanix Illustrated* magazine reported in July 1973 that the United States Post Office was experimenting with a small electric van as was the Volkswagen company but no outcomes were predicted. The article concluded rather vaguely with: "So in special circumstances, the electric may yet find its own thing."[26] Toyota, Honda, and Mazda were among the Japanese companies who also experimented with electric vehicles in the 1970s.

But when experimental engines faded into the background, the problem remained of the surplus of full-size cars, which although enjoying a comeback between 1976 and 1978, spelled disaster when the second oil shock came in 1979. In addition to having to adapt to the CAFE rules, another "punishment" appeared in the form of a "gas guzzler" tax. It was applied on a graduated scale, according to a vehicle's fuel-economy rating and was applicable to passenger vehicles weighing under 6,000 pounds, excluding light trucks and sport utility vehicles. For instance, a car achieving less than 18.5 mpg would face a tax of $2,600.[27]

Ironically, when gas prices again began to fall after 1981, two of the American industry's most formidable adversaries— safety advocates and EPA officials— squared off against each other over the CAFE rules. In the article "The Effect of Fuel Economy Standards on Automobile Safety," Robert W. Crandall and John D. Graham asserted that the lower-weight, fuel-efficient automobiles were unsafe as compared to large vehicles when involved in crashes. As a result they claimed that: "the CAFE program may be increasing the number of deaths and injuries on U.S. highways compared to the number that would occur without CAFE. This is a real social cost of pursuing fuel efficiency that policymakers have been reluctant to acknowledge."[28] Others agreed. A *USA Today* analysis of previously unpublished fatality statistics produced in the 1990s claimed that 46,000 people died because of the "1970s-era push for greater fuel efficiency."[29]

This unusual turn of events did not help or hinder the American automobile industry — rather as usual, they were caught in the middle of the debate. They were also caught on the horns of a dilemma. The question was how to produce automobiles that were safe, emission-free, and fuel-efficient. And if they achieved that, the next challenge was to meet the rigorous standards of quality that had been set by the Japanese.

## *Excellence*

"Reports of high quality in Japanese cars were initially met with incredulity and contempt in Detroit. To some extent Detroit's memories were fixed on the little Honda 600s and Subaru 360s of the early 1970s, minicars that could barely get out of their own way and weren't safe in a collision."[30] So wrote author Doron Levin in *Behind the Wheel at Chrysler: The Lee Iacocca Legacy.*

There is no question that it was import quality that whetted consumer appetites and forced Detroit to reassess its definition of the word. As automotive analyst Maryann Keller wrote about General Motors' perceptions of quality concerning the Chevrolet Vega in particular: "Rather than face the fact that the Vega wouldn't achieve its targets, GM executives chose to ignore it. They didn't fix the car. They just changed the targets, and justified the higher cost and heavier weight by saying that the car was American-made and therefore had higher quality standards. This wasn't just public relations talk, either. They really *believed* that made-in-America meant higher quality, and this factor was enough to compensate for weight and price."[31]

It is difficult to find an automotive magazine of the times that didn't extol the virtues of Japanese cars, though some were quite blatantly patronizing. It was an about-face from the late fifties and early sixties when reviews for the Toyota and Datsun were thin on the ground.

In 1967, *Motor Trend* reviewed the Datsun 1600 saying they were "impressed with the well-thought-out details and little extras we found on the car." And also that: "it was built by people trying to make the best possible product, and that it was built to last a long time."[32] In 1968, *Car Life* magazine reported that: "The tactics the Japanese are using, too, are unmerciful: They are building quality automobiles, in styles and colors people want, at a price any car buyer can afford to pay."[33] The implication that producing a quality vehicle was "unmerciful" surely didn't speak well for the American manufacturers.

*Road Test* magazine praised the Datsun PL-510: "The Datsun incorporates a single overhead cam engine, fully-independent four-wheel suspension, front disc brakes, bucket-type seats, curved side windows, and a flow-through ventilation system. Many of these features would be considered luxury items for a domestically built car and therefore would be listed as extra-cost options, if they were available at all."[34] The same magazine also reviewed the Subaru FF-1, warning readers to "Hold back on your laughs until you've driven it."[35] *Car and Driver* reviewers concluded their praise of the Mazda RX-2 with the comment: "Ford's better-idea lightbulb says 'Mazda' on top."[36] In 1972, *Motor Trend* reported on the Toyota Celica, saying: "Look around the inside of the Celica and you see just how tough a row to hoe Detroit's got in order to match the ingredients *or* the way they're put together."[37] And although he labeled the Subaru FF-1G a "chipmunk chaser," the tough-talking reviewer Tom McCahill had this to say about Japanese cars in general: "...I haven't the slightest idea of how many Japanese cars are landing on these shores every month, but I do know most of them are well built and the quality is exceedingly good."[38]

The Japanese automakers proved they could not only produce quality, but also innovation (CVCC and rotary), while simultaneously advancing rapidly in other areas of technology.

When they first arrived in America, the Japanese imports were powered by heavy engines that typically had three main bearings, side or overhead valves, in-block camshafts, and cast-iron blocks and heads. By the mid-sixties these configurations had given way to overhead camshafts, aluminum blocks or heads, and five main bearings (seven for the six-cylinder 240Z).

These advancements were nothing new to the American automaker, but what had them most puzzled was how the Japanese could produce such high-efficiency engines in such a small package. The secret, if it could be called that, was simple — most of them produced what were known as "square" engines, where the bore and stroke are so close in dimension as to be almost square. This allowed for a higher displacement per cylinder, which in turn resulted in more horsepower per liter. Compression ratios were also consistently high for such physically small engines. The widespread use of aluminum in either the block or head, or sometimes in both, also increased efficiency by reducing the vehicle's overall weight. Mitsubishi went to new heights with its special "Silent Shaft" design that incorporated twin balance shafts to reduce noise and vibration. They also used special bearings on the camshaft to guarantee even smoother revolutions.

To complement these innovative engines the Japanese tended to use only highly efficient carburetors, of which they typically favored Hitachi, or in Honda's case, Keihin-Seiki. These were almost always two-barrel, sometimes three-barrel or even four, in the case of Honda's 1965 S500 sports car. Later dual carburetors became common on higher-end models until fuel injection took over. The fuel/air ratio provided by these units was typically on the lean side for better fuel economy, with various air-intake modifications to improve performance.

Fuel injection first began to appear on cars like the 1979 Toyota Celica Supra and Corona Mark II, which used an electronic system they referred to as EFI, then incorporated a special "L-Jetronic" system by 1983.

By the mid– to late 1980s throttle-body, multi-port, and programmed injection units had taken the place of carburetors completely. Also during this period extensive experimentation with multi-valve engines had begun, an early example of which was the Civic CVCC's three-valves-per-cylinder arrangement in 1975. Honda was very much a leader in valve-train technology, and their variable valve timing system (VTEC) became the latest word in 1986 when it was first used on the Acura line. By 1990 it was standard fare to read about some type of 12-, 16-, or 24-valve engine in Japanese imports.

The gears that gave these engines life were also quite advanced. Full synchronization of manual transmissions was complete by the early 1970s, and automatics had their origins in units like Toyota's two-speed Toyoglide that appeared around the mid–1960s, as well as Honda's semi-automatic Hondamatic which came with the 1969 N600.

By 1989 journalists were reporting on Subaru's advanced electronically controlled continuously variable transmission which ran on two hydraulically operated pulleys with "V" grooves upon which a drive belt rode. As speed increased or decreased, the pulleys accordingly widened or contracted to provide a continuously smooth transition of gear ratios. This system utilized an electromagnetic "powder" clutch which provided virtually no slippage whatsoever because of the fine-grain stainless-steel powder between the rotor and the drum. This unit was devised by Subaru in collaboration with Mitsubishi Electric.

Most unusual was Mitsubishi's mid–1980s "4 + 4" eight-speed manual transmission that featured a dual-gear arrangement. This system was soon found to be too complex and too costly to repair and did not remain in the line for very long. Mitsubishi's other noteworthy achievement was to be the first Japanese automaker to export a turbo-diesel-powered car to the United States.

Japanese cars became renowned for their mechanical engineering, but also for their drive-trains. Although the 1965–66 Oldsmobile Toronado was one of America's first front-wheel-drive passenger cars, front-wheel-drive really came into the spotlight with the introduction of such cars as the Honda N600 and Civic, as well as the Subaru 360 and FF-1 Star, all of which arrived between 1968 and 1973. Surprisingly, Nissan, Toyota, and Mazda were late to adopt the configuration, doing so in 1976, 1980, and 1981, respectively.

Subaru was also the pioneer of four-wheel-drive passenger cars, and now bases its entire image on being the sole provider of an entire line of all-wheel-drive vehicles. Others have been much less enthusiastic about utilizing four-wheel-drive systems, with half-hearted efforts in the early 1980s showing up on vehicles like the Tercel and Civic wagons, as well as Mazda's GLC. Naturally, as the trend toward SUVs began, it seemed less and less important to incorporate the drive system into passenger cars particularly since Subaru had first dibs on the market.

Early Japanese vehicle body-shells have drawn considerably less interest and often-times derision, but they were nonetheless important for their early use of monocoque or "frameless" bodies. Although the very first Toyotas and Datsuns to arrive in America were made of body-on-frame designs, by 1962 the Datsun PL310 series wore a steel "unitized" body. Toyota went to a unitized body in the mid–1960s, and those coming afterwards were also frameless.

But if exterior designs were not always viewed with pleasure, nothing drew more criticism than early Japanese car suspension systems, which were consistently rated as "too stiff" for American tastes, for reasons that have been described elsewhere in this book. The Japanese took these criticisms to heart and attempted to alter their designs to become more suitable to American tastes. The results were impressive, with most Japanese companies coming early (mid–1970s and before that for Subaru and Honda) to four-wheel independent suspension of some type. Honda also became famous in the mid-eighties for its double-wishbone arrangement, while Mazda's RX-7 carried the distinction of having one of the most complex suspension systems, especially at the rear, for its time.

Steering went from worm-roller types in the 1960s to sophisticated electronically controlled, variable speed systems by the 1990s. Between 1987 and 1989 Mazda and Honda introduced their versions of four-wheel steering, with Mazda's being electronically controlled while Honda's was purely mechanical. Nissan followed suit, but there was no great demand for the feature and by 1992 it was no longer included in equipment lists, although GM has recently revived it for their enormous pickup trucks.

There have been a host of other developments through the years which have taken place side-by-side with the American industry, such as experimental safety vehicles, diesel engine development, electric vehicles, and hybrids. But somehow it always seems that whatever the Japanese do stimulates more interest in the field. This fact has naturally become something of a thorn in the domestic manufacturers' sides, as their efforts seem to be consistently overshadowed.

To further exacerbate matters, American consumer journals and trade magazines seem to consistently rate Japanese cars above the domestics. When Japanese vehicles are new, they are usually considered excellent. And when they are used, they are said to have weathered extremely well, holding high resale values as well as customer loyalty.

That Japanese cars are held in such a high regard should not be surprising when their dedication to quality is considered. According to the Time-Life book *Japan,* quality is not just a word to the Japanese, it's a mantra. From an early age they are trained to search for only the best, both within and outside of themselves. This is evident in the way they shop: "Japanese consumers have become famous for their choosiness ... automobile buyers check the upholstery for proper stitching, examine the paint job inside the trunk and open the hood to inspect the welds."[39]

It was apparent that Japanese automakers did indeed take W. Edwards Deming's lessons on quality to heart, as the authors explained: "The Japanese seized upon Deming's message: Control of quality became a national passion."[40] It was that passion for quality that earned Toyota its five millionth sale in 1981.[41]

It may seem to some that the Japanese automakers have had an easy ride, but this would be a gross over-simplification. They have all had their share of troubles, some coming early as in the case of Toyota, and some more recent, as is true for Nissan,

Isuzu and Mitsubishi. During the mid-seventies Mazda nearly became extinct due to the oil crisis. In their book, *Working for the Japanese: Inside Mazda's American Plant*, authors Joseph and Suzy Fucini wrote: "With the exception of Chrysler, no automaker in the world had been wounded so deeply by the OPEC oil embargo of late 1973, and the subsequent rise in gasoline prices, as Mazda."[42] A sales drop of 50 percent in 1974 confirmed the extent of the damage. Subaru also suffered heavy losses in the seventies and eighties.

Bearing these and other factors in mind, it cannot be said that Japan has had all the advantages as some American automakers have claimed. Despite the fact that Eiji Toyoda readily admitted in his autobiography that luck and timing certainly played a part in Toyota's achievements in America, he made it abundantly clear that it was mostly due to hard work, determination, and sacrifice.

As ex–Vice-Minister for International Affairs Shohei Kurihara had once remarked, "During the 1970s, luck smiled on the Japanese automotive industry, with perhaps part of the industry's advantage not due to its own efforts."[43] Being a minister in the very department that interfered in practically every move the Japanese automakers ever made, it is understandable why Mr. Kurihara held such a view.

Aside from what many Japanese automakers saw as excessive government control, some also pointed to the lack of support from banks who showed an alarming lack of faith in those crucial early days. Certainly the Japanese had no advantage environmentally or financially speaking during their industry's formative years.

But by 1981 it was the American industry that felt put-upon. Blaming everything from outdated factories and equipment to unfair trade practices, the Detroit automakers could not escape the fact that consumers had grown weary of cars that required constant attention and frequent repairs. Even the normally loyal industry magazines took shots at American quality. In a tongue-in-cheek editorial in a 1972 edition of *Car and Driver*, Bob Brown wrote: "In what year did my 1967 (or 1972) Hornet, Impala, Skylark, Gremlin, Pinto, Camaro, Mustang, Colt, Maverick, Cutlass, Polara, Charger, Torino, Vega, Dart, Valiant, Toronado, Fury, Firebird, etc. etc. start to (the following are presented in order of frequency) rust out, fall apart, burn oil, send my mechanic to Nassau, BWI?"[44]

So far had American industry quality deteriorated that according to the Automotive Service Association (ASA), "rumblings for shop licensing began in 1965 because of widespread consumer discontent and concern about the automobile, its costs, ineffective warranties and poor repairability."[45] They further reported that: "…by the mid–1970s, American-made cars had taken a quality nose dive and consumer complaints increased to the point that German and Japanese vehicles had seized a significant share of the new car market."[46]

By 1980, the Ford Motor Company began to speak of quality in their advertisements. GM claimed to have the "Mark of Excellence," while Chrysler's Lee Iacocca went on television urging people to "buy a better car if they could find it." It was a risky statement to make and one that left Chrysler vulnerable to contempt from those who had been burned by the low-quality vehicles they had produced in the 1970s. But with the introduction of the K-cars—the Dodge Aries and the Plymouth Reliant—things began to look up for the scarred Chrysler Corporation in 1981. Ford could not say the same, while General Motors began its downward spiral that would find bottom in the late 1980s.

Quality is still, after three decades, a prominent word in the industry vocabulary, and most irritatingly it is most often associated with Japanese vehicles.

In September of 2001 *Business Week* magazine ran an article entitled: "Detroit is Cruising For Quality," which said in part: "Try as it might, the U.S. auto industry can't shake its karma for shaky quality — even though its cars and trucks are better than ever…. Detroit is finding, as it did back in the 1970s, that there is no better way to begin than with a close look at Japan."[47]

But if Detroit expected a return to its glory days, it was a lesson learned too late.

# 14

## This Yacht Is Sinking — Detroit Flounders

There has been no shortage of criticism of American automobile manufacturers during the past 30 years but no period saw more virulent condemnation than did the 1980s. During this decade a rash of books and articles appeared, most of which identified Detroit's problems as self-inflicted. An article in a December 1997 issue of *Business Week* magazine proved that opinion was still held well into the 1990s. The author wrote in part that: "...Detroit is notoriously shortsighted. In the 60s, the Big Three ignored the threat from Japan. In the 70s, they were caught without fuel-efficient cars."[1] In the interest of accuracy, it was not that Detroit failed to produce small cars, it was just that the cars they did produce failed.

In the late fifties and early sixties the VW Beetle satisfied a small but growing group of consumers who wanted something different. Other imports such as Fiat, Renault, Volvo, Peugeot, and Mercedes were also available but were far less popular and most could not be classified as economy vehicles. Toyota and Datsun didn't arrive in America until 1957–58, and were unable to produce a successful car until 1965. On the other hand plans for the compacts Chevrolet Corvair, Ford Falcon, and Chrysler Valiant had been laid as early as 1955. Pre-dating these models were the Rambler American and the Studebaker Lark, introduced in 1957 and 1959 respectively. With these Big Four economy cars available, American automakers considered the compact market sufficiently filled by 1960. And for those who preferred something with a European flavor, there were the Opel Kadett built in Germany for General Motors, the British-made Cortina for Ford, and the Bertone Simca, made in France for the Chrysler Corporation. Early advertisements for these cars clearly illustrate the fact that Detroit was quite aware of the compact market. In 1970 the domestic sub-compacts made their debut in the form of the Ford Pinto and Chevrolet Vega. Only Chrysler had no native-built compact, offering instead the Mitsubishi-made Dodge Colt and the Plymouth Cricket, first produced in England and later in Japan.

The great problem of course was that most of these cars were to some degree failures, but the fact that they existed at all proves that Detroit didn't miss the race entirely, it just finished in last place.

In light of the tremendous successes of imports today, it is easy to forget that no one could have possibly predicted their popularity back in the late 1950s. The most popular model of the time, the Volkswagen Beetle, could have gone either way, for a large majority of people simply didn't like the car, complaining that it was too noisy, underpowered, cramped, poorly heated, and that its round shape left it vulnerable to mud and slush sprayed from other vehicles.

Although the other European imports available at the time were generally of good quality, their more temperamental aspects were sometimes obscured by the element of novelty. But as one Mercedes-Benz owner testified: "Having just escaped 30 discouraging months as a Mercedes owner, ... I am not convinced that the people at Daimler-Benz are doing anything in an outstanding fashion.... I will confess that having been taken in by the M-B story, one is not quick to own up to having made a $5,000 blunder. Thus, I have found many Mercedes owners tend to minimize the unreliability of their cars, and in fact, have been known to fib about their obvious shortcomings. Let's be more tolerant of our own auto makers. They're doing a better job than we give them credit for."[2]

In 1960 the average American consumer didn't need much prompting to display loyalty—in fact most were more than eager to "buy American," as can be seen in the substantial sales figures later in this chapter. The effect of the arrival of the domestic compacts on imports was immediate and damaging. Before 1960, imports had captured almost 10 percent of the American market—afterward that number fell to 7.6 percent.[3] By 1962 their claim had been furthered reduced to only 4.9 percent.[4]

The Ford Motor Company was the first of the Big Three to offer a domestic compact. Preliminary plans for the Falcon had been drawn up in 1957 under the careful hand of soon-to-be Ford president, Robert McNamara. Over 400,000 Falcons sold in 1960, its first year. The ultra-conservative Falcon was, according to author Robert Lacey, McNamara's "...pride and joy, the triumph which bore him out of Detroit and into Kennedy's 1961 administration...."[5]

The Falcon rode on a 109.5-inch wheelbase, weighed 2,500 pounds, and was powered by a 144-cubic-inch, six-cylinder engine that produced 90 horsepower. Its gas mileage was estimated between 23 and 26 miles per gallon and it retailed from $1,975 to $2,300. Lee Iacocca mistakenly called it "...the first American compact...."[6] either forgetting about or simply choosing to ignore the AMC Rambler and Studebaker Lark. His pride in the Falcon's robust sales, however, was qualified. He lamented the loss of profit usually garnered from full-size vehicles. As he later wrote of the car in his autobiography: "As an economical small car, its profit margin was limited. Nor did it offer any options, which could have greatly increased our revenues."[7]

It was exactly this type of attitude that was to draw fire from critics. The myopic scrutiny of the bottom line, the shortsighted greed for short-term gain as opposed to sacrificing for long-term benefit, and the refusal to put quality above profit were identified as the pervasive cancers that disabled the American automobile industry.

Probably a measure of Iacocca's discontent with Falcon profits could be attributed to the fact that it had cannibalized sales from the company's full-size divisions. In fact, shortly after the Falcon was introduced Ford sales fell from 1.4 million to 917,000.[8]

In October of 1959, General Motors unveiled its new compact, the revolutionary Chevrolet Corvair. It was heralded as something completely different in an American automobile. Appearing under the leadership of engineer and later president, Ed Cole, GM spent $150 million developing the car which came available in 500 or 700 sedan model. The 500 retailed for approximately $2,000 while the 700 was slightly over one hundred dollars more. The prototype Corvair was powered by an unusual — at least for a domestic automaker — aluminum air-cooled, horizontally opposed, six-cylinder, rear-mounted engine which produced 80 horsepower. To trim costs the production Corvair was equipped with a half-aluminum, half-cast-iron engine. The aluminum content helped reduce the car's weight, which was around 2,300 pounds. There were conflicting reports about its gas mileage — some maintained that it could average as much as 27 mpg, while others rated it at closer to 23. Much to the discredit of General Motors it wasn't the vehicle's economy they focused on so much as its unique design features. As one advertisement boasted, the Corvair was: "The only American car with an airplane-type horizontal engine; The only American car with independent suspension at all four wheels;" and was "The only American car with an air-cooled aluminum engine."[9]

Consumers were divided on the pancake design of the car, which some found unappealing. Comparing the over 400,000 Falcons made in 1960 to the only 250,000 Corvairs shows that the car was not the stunning success GM had hoped for. Even the hype generated could not counteract its lukewarm reception. What the public didn't know was that any GM employees who refused to work on the car were told: "Get on the team, or you can find someplace else to work."[10]

Aside from handling problems linked to inadequate rear suspension, there were many other defects. Some owners reported that the car "...will ping severely when timed correctly and lug while using regular gas."[11] It was also a notoriously poor cold-weather starter. As an owner in Alaska commented about his 1961 model: "I must give them one point in their favor — they certainly are economical during the winter. They won't start and therefore use no gas!"[12] But if the odd-looking Corvair failed to find wide appeal, there was always the new offering from the Chrysler Corporation.

Chrysler designer Virgil Exner was responsible for appearance of the bold and stylish Valiant which also made its debut in 1960. Sharply flared body panels, an aggressive grille, and a spare tire outline on the trunk were a few of the features that set the car apart from its two main competitors in terms of style. The Valiant was also more powerful, driven by a 170-cubic-inch, 101-horsepower, slant-six engine that achieved an average of 23 mpg. Its wheelbase measured 106.5 inches, and it was heavier than the Falcon or Corvair, weighing 2,700 pounds. The Valiant was available as the V100, retailing for approximately $2,100, while the more luxurious V200 sold for $2,300. But sales of 106,515 in its first year put it well behind the Falcon and Corvair.[13]

Of all the American compacts at that time, the Rambler American held the record for best fuel mileage with an average of 31.1 mpg. Its success was evident in its healthy sales of 422,00 for 1960.[14] But while American Motors had always been a leader in the economy field, the Big Three could make no such claim and soon came under fire for their failure to meet expectations. Shortly after the Falcon, Corvair, and Valiant were released, journalists were already questioning their viability as economical compacts. *Motor Life* magazine editors voiced one of the earliest concerns in the March 1960 edition. Under the "Facts and Forecasts" section they wrote: "Disappointment with early economy figures of the new Big Three compacts (which may have been result of [sic] hasty preparations for fall introductions) is sparking drive for improved gas mileage. Only Falcon comes anywhere near claims."[15]

The editors observed that if the Big Three had intended to win sales from the imports and even from their own smaller sister American Motors, they had failed: "If anything, the compacts are stealing sales from their full-size cars, especially medium-price models."[16]

It wasn't long before other doubts began to surface. In a 1962 edition of *Motor Trend* magazine, one headline queried: "Are U.S. Compacts Rugged Enough for Real Heavy-Duty Service?" Apparently not, according to a survey of fleet owners in Baltimore who reported that it cost an average of 65 cents a mile to maintain a compact car, while it only cost 45 cents a mile to maintain a full-size vehicle. This conclusion did not bode well for the reputation of the compacts as an economical buy. The cost differential, concluded the piece, "...has caused many fleet users to switch back to big cars, with their extra space, comfort and performance."[17]

As the new compacts began to lose face in the economy arena, the gradual move to built them larger, heavier, and more powerful was underway. By 1965, an optional 180-horsepower "Turbo-Air" engine was available for the Corvair; for the Falcon there was a 289-cubic-inch 200-horsepower engine, and the Valiant came with a 225-cubic-inch 145-horsepower engine with an optional four-barrel carburetor, 148-horsepower "Hyper-Pack" edition.

But while Falcon and Valiant sales remained stable, the Corvair floundered as accident statistics related to its unstable handling began to pile up. In November of 1965, the same year Toyota won the Deming Prize for Quality, Ralph Nader published the book *Unsafe at Any Speed: The Designed-In Dangers of the American Automobile*. Nader took particular aim at the Corvair and thereby caught the attention of General Motors executives who immediately responded by having him investigated. He promptly retaliated by filing and winning a lawsuit against the corporation. As for the lawsuits related to the safety of the Corvair, company officials insisted that the suspension system was not at fault, but rather the problems were due to incorrect tire pressures. By 1968 it was obvious the Corvair could not survive the massive assaults and GM announced that it would be discontinued after 1969. Post-mortems on the car generally pointed to Nader's book as the cause of its death, but others disagreed. *Consumer Guide* editors felt it was a combination of factors, pointing out in the book *Cars of the 60s*: "...consumer advocates, who might have been expected to welcome such an automobile, disparaged it. This is not to say that Ralph Nader's book, *Unsafe at Any Speed*, single-handedly killed the Corvair. Rather, the ax had actually fallen six months before Nader's book appeared. But economics played a part also. For General Motors, the Corvair never made it because it failed to compete well with Ford's Falcon as an economy car."[18]

Years later, ex–Chevrolet president John Z. DeLorean verified that the car was deeply flawed, a fact he maintained GM officials were cognizant of before the car was even released: "...problems with the Corvair were well documented inside GM's Engineering Staff long before the Corvair ever was offered for sale." The car, he reported, had flipped over a number of times even on the test track.[19]

Regardless of how the story unfolded, it was a grim tale with the Corvair dying a slow and painful death despite a desperate attempt to revive it with the Monza Spyder edition. From its debut production of 250,000 units in 1960, only 6,000 Corvairs were produced in 1969, its final year. The vehicle that *Motor Trend* magazine voted "Car of the Year" in 1960 went the way of the Edsel. Some insist that the Corvair needn't have died in the first place. According to author Ed Cray, if General Motors would have invested an extra fifteen dollars per car for a much-needed anti-sway bar, the handling defects would have been eliminated.[20]

Meanwhile the debate about the importance of economy cars continued. In 1965 *Popular Science* magazine asked; "Who buys compact cars? During the first six months of this year, 656,330 people did. Why do people buy compact cars? ... I suspect that people who buy compacts do so because they *like* them."[21]

For a while at least, this suspicion seemed to be confirmed by early compact and import sales. But as these numbers fluctuated, American automakers concluded that consumers were somewhat fickle, not to mention unpredictable. For even as the trend seemed to be moving toward smaller cars, there was a simultaneous demand for full-size models. In March of 1966, *Motorcade* magazine reported that according to their dealer surveys "bigger was better": "Dealers this year are in a peculiar spot because of this ravenous appetite for luxury. A Lincoln-Mercury dealer in Los Angeles says that he has plenty of Comets but can't get enough Continentals to fill orders. And a Chevrolet dealer in Texas reports that his customers want everything. He says that 65 per cent of his sales are for loaded luxury models, the balance for what is now called an economy car."[22]

There were further indications that economy was not high on the consumer's priority lists, as the article continued: "From the way customers are adding on optional power equipment; ordering the biggest, hottest engines, one could logically assume that except for small imports, interest in operating economy is dead."[23] And some buyers fell somewhere in the middle, wanting the best of both worlds: "A surprising number of customers have discovered to their chagrin that they can't have their cake and eat it, too."[24]

These conclusions, taken together with the dawning of the muscle car era in the mid-sixties, indicated that Americans were still drawn by the seductive pull of speed, size, and power. All of these were readily available in cars like the Pontiac GTO with its 389 V-8, the Ford Fairlane with an optional big-block 427, and with Chrysler's also-optional hemi-head 426 V-8, rated at 425 horsepower, but in actuality closer to 575.[25] Even American Motors offered a special powerful Hurst edition of the American, rated at 315 horsepower. The horsepower limits imposed in the late fifties were cleverly circumvented by offering larger engines as optional equipment.

But the car that epitomized the ideal combination of horsepower, style, and comfort, was the Ford Mustang introduced in 1964 under Lee Iacocca's direction. The attractive little car ushered in the ponycar era that found a welcoming audience in the youth-driven America of the sixties. When the car was released it was so popular that tens of thousands of people turned out to see it at the New York World's Fair in the spring of 1964. Buyers were so eager to purchase a Mustang that one man even spent the night in a Ford dealer's showroom, sleeping in the car until his check cleared the next day.[26] For such an attractive sporty car, the reasonable price of approximately $2,350 allowed sales to reach 418,812 in the first year.[27]

By 1965 the American automobile industry had reached a pinnacle with over nine million vehicles produced in a single year. There is little wonder then that not much attention was being paid to Toyota and Datsun despite their steadily growing market-share. In the early 1960s, Japan had been the tortoise, Detroit the hare. Periodic checks over the hare's shoulder revealed that the tortoise was still well behind. Besides, the hare was far too busy wrestling with the new mandated safety measures to worry about the progress of a slow-moving Japanese tortoise.

The safety issue, which had been brewing basically since the invention of the automobile, was to spark some of the most heated debates in the industry's history, next to the enforcement of emission controls. From a grass-roots consumer movement led by activists like Ralph Nader, the matter of safety rose to feature prominently in the United States Congress. In turn, the government applied steady pressure on the automotive leaders. But while Senators Abraham Ribicoff and Robert Kennedy were asking why American automakers couldn't build safer cars, automotive journalists disparaged the move to what some called "wombs on wheels." While industry apologists pointed at driver error as the cause of most automobile accidents, the government pointed back toward Detroit, supporting its policies with statistics that concluded: "If our cars were built differently and certain safety devices were used, 43 percent of those killed in autos might be alive today."[28] It was an impossible argument to refute.

The new laws that evolved from the months and years of hearings and debates targeted automobile features such as door locks, body structure, braking systems, visibility, steering wheels, bumpers, and even the amount of windshield covered by wipers. In 1966 the National Highway Traffic Safety Administration was established, and its new leaders directly challenged automotive industry leaders. Henry Ford, II, speaking for himself as well as his competitors, strenuously objected to the new safety requirements, which he called: "...arbitrary, unreasonable and impractical."[29] Ford insisted that these changes would cause the downfall of the industry. But when Senator Kennedy mercilessly dug out the fact that automakers spent only 11 million of their 2.5-billion-dollar profits on safety in 1965, there was little sympathy for the automakers.[30]

Pleading that the incorporation of the safety measures would leave less time and fewer financial resources to develop competitive responses to the imports which had sold a combined total of one million vehicles in America by 1968, gained no pardon.[30] The regulations were not negotiable. Automakers were left to calculate their added costs per vehicle in comparison with lawsuits relating to injury or death. By the early 1970s, the liability to automakers for a human life lost as a result of a traffic accident caused by failing to meet safety requirements had been estimated by the NHTSA at $200,725.[31]

But as the industry struggled to meet the safety regulations, they were once again forced to think small, but this time not a scaled-down version of an intermediate, but an authentic sub-compact vehicle. The first of these, like the first American compact, came from the American Motors Corporation who were able to capitalize on their advantage as a small-car producer. The AMC Gremlin made its debut in April of 1970, riding on a 96-inch wheelbase and weighing a rather substantial 2,800 pounds. The Gremlin was powered by a six-cylinder, 128-horsepower engine that achieved approximately 24 miles per gallon. It was rated as a good buy at an economical $1,879,[32] which probably accounted for its quite strong sales. Certainly its weight and gas mileage strained the definition of sub-compact. In the meanwhile, both consumers and industry observers were waiting to see if the Big Three would match that definition a little more closely.

In September of 1970, *Car and Driver* editors asserted that: "Now Detroit is making its last stand. Ford and General Motors have anted up, not millions, but hundreds of millions of dollars to tool the Pinto and the Vega 2300 and no excuses or copouts are being made. Neither is a half-hearted, cut-down intermediate with 'broad appeal' instead they are the best, most import-beating sub-compacts that American technology knows how to build. If VW and the other small intruders survive this attack, they'll be deemed invincible."[33]

The Ford Pinto was introduced in the autumn of 1970 as a 1971 model. It was driven by a four-cylinder, 97.7-cubic-inch British-built Cortina engine rated at 75 horsepower. An optional 100-horsepower engine produced by Ford of Germany was also available. The transmission was a four-speed manual with an optional Select-Shift automatic. The Pinto's gas mileage was rated at 24.1 mpg. Lee Iacocca's goal of building a 2,000-pound, 2,000-dollar car was realized with the car weighing in at 2,030 pounds and retailing for approximately $1,950. Its wheelbase was 94.2 inches and it was available only in a hatchback model. But the eagerly awaited Pinto brought in disappointing sales of 350,000 in its first year, falling behind the more successful debut of the 1969 Ford Maverick by about 200,000.[33]

From General Motors came the Chevrolet Vega 2300, which was larger and heavier than the Pinto with a wheelbase of 97 inches and a weight of 2,190 pounds. Billed by General Motors as "the little car that grows on you,"[35] the Vega came in four models: a basic sedan, a hatchback coupe, a station wagon, and a small panel delivery truck. The Vega was powered by a four-cylinder, 140-cubic-inch, 90-horsepower engine, with a 110-horsepower engine optional. On tests the Vega rated between 23 and 25 mpg. Base price was $2,196. Unlike the Pinto, front disc brakes were standard equipment on the Vega.

Seeking to convince skeptics that GM meant business this time, one automotive journalist wrote: "In another attempt at being truly competitive with the imported subcompacts, Chevrolet has announced that there will be no styling changes to the Vega for at least four years.[36]

It is of course now widely known that these cars represented a humiliating failure for Ford and General Motors, and in the case of the Pinto, even posing a threat to life. Lee Iacocca, after condemning the Corvair and Vega as "terrible cars," had only this to say about the Pinto: "I can't talk about bad cars without a few words about the Ford Pinto." It was "…involved in a number of accidents where the car burst into flames after a rear-end collision. There were lawsuits—hundreds of them." But Iacocca was adamant that the deaths did not stem from deliberate callousness, writing that: "The guys who built the Pinto had kids in college who were driving that car. Believe me, no one sits down and thinks: 'I'm deliberately going to make this car unsafe.' In the end, we voluntarily recalled almost a million and a half Pintos. This was in June 1978, the month before I was fired."[37]

Aside from its tendency to explode into a fireball upon a rear-end collision, the Pinto was laden with an assortment of defects, including major engine faults, problematic carburetors, poor paint quality, and serious premature corrosion.

The Vega did not fare much better than the Pinto despite the 200 million dollars GM invested in it, and also despite winning the accolade of *Motor Trend*'s Car of the Year for 1971. The editors raved about the car's engine, calling it a "wonder motor, a SOHC, aluminum-block four, designed without iron cylinder liners…"[38]

General Motors chief designer Lloyd Reuss was responsible for the Vega which went from design to production in less than two years. Such a short time-span was afterwards pointed to as the cause for the car's many failings which included excessive oil consumption leading to engine failure, sticking accelerators, engine compartment fires, undersized axles, and extensive corrosion, particularly in the fenders. By 1972, 95 percent of all Vegas had been recalled. The glorious fanfare accompanying the release of the car soon died out as its poor reputation spread. As Ed Cray commented rather bitingly in *Chrome Colossus*: "The Vega was no more or no less a Chevrolet, a General Motors car after all, shoddy, tawdry, and eternally suspect."[39]

Similarly, Chrysler's captive imports held no salvation for their parent company. In the 1960s the Simca had made a dismal showing in America despite an extensive marketing campaign. And although the Dodge Colt and Plymouth Cricket available in the early 1970s fared somewhat better than the Vega and Pinto, neither car was able to compete with the high-flying Japanese imports. By 1972 it was becoming increasingly obvious that the American auto industry was in trouble. Toyota had sold its one-millionth automobile in America, and Nissan wasn't far behind.

The relentless rise of the imports combined with the new safety measures and the effects of the 1970 recession dealt a severe blow to the automakers. General Motors had also been plagued with a strike that year. The passing of the new Clean Air Act of 1970 seemed like the last straw for the besieged industry leaders who had resisted each new demand with equal vigor. A case in point was the positive crankcase ventilation valve which had been around since 1909, was recommended for use in 1961, but was only installed in American vehicles in 1964. Similar devices like the exhaust gas recirculation valve and various other engine emission controls were also reluctantly added. For these concessions horsepower and compression ratios had to be sacrificed, a bitter pill for companies that had built reputations on the race track.

The next major point of resistance came over the use of catalytic converters. An angry GM president Richard Gerstenberg was provoked into commenting that the two billion dollars required to install the converters might be better used to address "other more serious societal problems."[40] Automotive magazines loyally defended the industry with *Motor Trend* reprinting an *Automotive News* article which called the pollution issue a "Billion Dollar Smog Hoax." The article opened with a rather dramatic statement: "The automobile engine, a faithful servant to 90 million licensed American drivers today, may be legislated out of existence in one of history's worst miscarriages of justice."[41]

Blindsided and enraged, the automakers approached the government in 1971 for protection. Nixon's policies of wage and price freezes combined with a 10 percent surtax on imports provided temporary respite, a move which was substantially supplemented by his decision to take America off the gold standard. The vast gap between Japanese and American currencies immediately narrowed appreciably. Imports were suddenly more expensive to Americans, but the blow stunned the Japanese government and led to a conference between the two nations after which Nixon was persuaded to drop the 10 percent surtax.

There is no doubt that there were exceedingly expensive external factors contributing to the American industry's suffering, but neither can it be denied that these companies were riddled with inefficiency and waste. In the case of Ford, author Robert Lacey went so far as to conclude that many of its troubles could be attributed to only one man — Henry Ford II himself: "The history of the Ford Motor Company in the years after 1960 was, in many ways, a story of increasingly erratic and willful autocracy on the part of Henry Ford II."[42]

According to John DeLorean, one of General Motors' biggest problems was the fact that financial men had been running the company for too long: "The excessive emphasis on cost cutting has permeated the organization as the first, and sometimes the only, precept of management." But he also cited inefficiency as a factor contributing to its downfall: "We had task forces on everything ... a sure sign of failing management."[43] Of course, the generous bonus system GM had long practiced has been derided by many the automotive journalist.

As for Chrysler's troubles, Lee Iacocca wrote that the company in the seventies was quite simply a "sinking ship."[44]

By 1972, General Motors' production had dropped to 4,800,000, Ford's to 2,780,000, and Chrysler's to 1,550,000. AMC was struggling along with 258,000.[45]

By this time there were even more Japanese imports on the American scene. Fuji Heavy Industries' Subaru had arrived in 1968. The Honda Motor Company had followed in March of 1970, along with the Mazda Motor Company later that year. But if the appearance of still more imports combined with enforced safety and emission controls were painful shocks, they were but insignificant surges compared to the jolt that came in October of 1973 when the Arab Emirates took control of the oil fields.

The impact on the automobile industry was both swift and brutal. The embargo enacted by OPEC forced America to rely on its own inadequate oil stores and the shortages created long lines at the gas pumps and near-hysteria when many stations actually closed down. At one point Nixon even called for the voluntary closing of gas stations to discourage "Sunday drivers."

When it became obvious that the situation had reached crisis proportions, consumers turned away from full-size American cars to the better-made, more fuel-efficient imports. It wasn't until the embargo was lifted in March of 1974 and oil prices began to fall that intermediate and full-size car sales showed some improvement. By then Toyota was the number-one import in America, finally surpassing Volkswagen in 1975.

Detroit simultaneously tried to meet the small car challenge while still feeding, and hopefully creating, the demand for the higher-profit full-size models. On the first front they continued to offer the flawed Vega and Pinto, as well as their clones the Pontiac Astre and the Mercury Bobcat. Chrysler was relying on the mediocre sales of the Colt and Cricket, while hoping their new larger compacts Dodge Aspen and Plymouth Volare would raise sales until the release of their new L-body front-wheel-drive cars in 1978.

By 1976 it seemed that the effects of the oil crisis had dwindled into insignificance as evinced by Detroit's 22 percent sales increase that year. But they were still struggling to meet ongoing safety requirements and emission controls. It seemed that the new catalytic converters, which could operate with unleaded fuel only, were now emitting harmful sulfates. Horsepower devotees were trying to figure out how to disable their pollution control devices, and some mechanics helped them do it. Vehicles began to suffer from widespread stalling and rough-running problems. Bodywork suffered as the lion's share of funds and energy were devoted to mechanical engineering. And then in a double whammy, even sub-compacts failed to sell as the price of oil plummeted and imports gained recognition.

After General Motors unveiled its new sub-compact Chevette in 1975, it issued the ominous warning that they might have to shut down production for the 1978 year due to the rigid new emission control laws which they were finding impossible to meet. Similarly there was the new Corporate Average Fuel Economy law (CAFE) to contend with. Surprisingly though, full-size American cars were selling very well. Chevrolet reported that its top sales came from the Impala and Caprice. Another surprise came from Ford whose pickup truck was also a best-seller. But their triumph was to be short-lived.

The second oil crisis which struck in the spring of 1979 dealt the fatal blow to the American auto industry. The nation was immobilized by double-digit inflation combined with a stagnant economy which gave rise to the term "stagflation." Gas was up to 90 cents a gallon from 67 cents in 1978 and steadily rising. Imports had cornered 21.7 percent of the American market. Detroit, floundering in the long interim period between the two oil crises, was caught with 58 percent of their vehicles carrying V-8 engines and only 17.6 percent with four cylinders. One year later only 30 percent had V-8s, while four-cylinder vehicles had doubled, but it was too little too late.

General Motors lost $763 million, its first loss since 1921, Ford sustained well over a $1 billion loss, but it was Chrysler which took the spotlight with losses of more than $1.1 billion in 1979. Newly hired president Lee Iacocca plunged into the mess within the company that had been accumulating since the early sixties but soon found that nothing short of a massive infusion of cash could save it. For this he approached the federal government, a move that was derided as flying in the face of free enterprise and violating the "survival of the fittest" law. Citing the fact that saving Chrysler would help the economy and save thousands of jobs, Iacocca hotly defended the move in his autobiography, writing that: "By going to Congress did we really violate the spirit of free enterprise? Or has our subsequent success actually helped free enterprise in this country? I don't think there's any doubt about the answer. Even some of our opponents from 1979 now concede that the Chrysler loan guarantees were a good idea."[46]

But Ford's losses were also enormous, and as Alton F. Doody and Ron Bingaman wrote in *Reinventing the Wheels: Ford's Spectacular Comeback*: "Some industry observers felt that the government was rescuing the wrong company. A collapse of the much larger Ford organization would have been a far heavier blow to the U.S. economy and would have opened the gates even wider to the imports."[47]

Ford president Donald Petersen and CEO Philip Caldwell managed to slash 2.5 billion dollars from the company's expenses while simultaneously launching Ford's new slogan and philosophy — "Quality Is Job One."

It couldn't have been easy for the American industrialists to concede that perhaps they and their colleagues both past and present had made serious errors in judgment. The more arrogant of those never deigned to. But while the chasm between worker and management grew and executive bonuses escalated to new heights, no one was willing to admit there were not enough lifeboats aboard this *Titanic*. Once again, panic-stricken leaders led by Richard Gerstenberg and Lee Iacocca turned to the government asking for protectionist measures. The result culminated in the 1980 "Voluntary Restraint Agreement" with Japan which had been accused of "dumping" subsidized vehicles on the American market. This action had a huge effect on both the American and Japanese industry, and will be discussed in more detail in a later chapter.

Nineteen eighty was, by all accounts, a turning point for the industry, but the direction was downwards. The fact that imports now had 27 percent of the market stimulated something of a backlash, particularly in the Motor City, where protests had gone unheard since the late sixties. An increasing number of Detroit bumper stickers made such statements as: "Made in America by Americans" and "Buy American." Loyal UAW members had been complaining as far back as 1970, with one member warning his fellow Americans in a union newsletter: "That little Datsun on the freeway is a symbol of disappearing jobs in the automobile industry."[48]

But the hard truth that no one in Detroit wanted to face was that when once-loyal American consumers complained about everything from engine failure to poor fit and finish of domestic automobiles, Japanese automakers were only too willing to listen and turn the complaints into a "what-not-to-do" list. It was partly this simple strategy that helped them rise to become the world's largest automobile producer in that pivotal year, 1980.

It was time for Detroit to listen. Back in 1970, General Motors chairman James Roche had stated: "We no longer have a measurable edge in technology. Foreign manufacturers have the latest and best in manufacturing methods...."[49]

This concession was behind the move to finally agree to tie-ins with Japanese companies, which began that year with Chrysler buying a percentage of the Mitsubishi automobile company. This subject will also be dealt with in the next chapter.

The sand castles built from the profits created in America's more prosperous years now began to crumble as the tide from Japan swept over them. For all that had been said about Japan's tendency to copy America, it now seemed that America had something to learn from Japan. There were few options left available in the depressed city of Detroit in 1980. It seemed there was only one remaining way to fight the competition — and that was by joining it.

# 15

## If You Can't Beat 'Em…
## Japanese/American Tie-ins

### *Chrysler-Mitsubishi*

If Detroit was as oblivious to Japan as many have claimed it is highly unlikely that the mergers that took place between the two nations' automakers as early as 1970 would have occurred. The first company to go against the wishes of Japan's Ministry of International Trade and Industry (MITI) was Mitsubishi when it entered into talks with the Chrysler Corporation in 1969. Once Mitsubishi Motors split off from its parent company it immediately showed its independent streak by resisting MITI's pressure to merge with another Japanese automobile company. The Japanese government was anxious to strengthen Japan's automobile industry by taking the 12 existing companies and forming a group similar to America's Big Three. But Mitsubishi not only wanted to maintain its Japanese presence, but also to establish an American one. As a result, when Chrysler officials offered to purchase a 35 percent stake in the company, Mitsubishi's president Yoshizane Makita was eager to sign the agreement.

Although talks had begun in 1969, the merger wasn't announced until March of 1970 and it was another year before MITI would agree to approve the deal. The signed documents meant that Mitsubishi's American presence was guaranteed, while Chrysler would have a Japanese import of its own to compete with Toyota and Datsun. Unfortunately Chrysler's financial situation was so bad that they didn't have the funds to cover the agreed-upon 35 percent. It was an inauspicious beginning. As author Robert Sobel wrote in his book, *Car Wars*: "The euphoria was badly damaged when Makita was informed by embarrassed Chrysler representatives that the corporation lacked the funds to purchase all the shares agreed upon. In time the money was paid, but Chrysler's credibility had suffered a severe blow, and Mitsubishi got a taste of what was to come."[1]

A hastily revised agreement allowed Chrysler a 15 percent share instead.

The Chrysler-Mitsubishi union was the first major, albeit shaky, alliance between a Japanese and an American automobile company. Of course mergers are nothing new in the industry — they've been going on since its inception but usually occurred on a national rather than international scale. One of Japan's earliest mergers gave us the present-day Nissan Motor Company while in later years Toyota, pressured into it by MITI, purchased shares in the Hino Motor Company (1966), as well as Daihatsu (1967), of which it now owns 51.2 percent. In March of 2000 Toyota raised its stake in Hino to 33.8 percent. Nissan absorbed the Prince Motor Company in 1966 and later established ties with Fuji Heavy Industries. Mitsubishi had pre-dated their Chrysler venture with a deal with the Willys Company in order to market the Jeep in Japan.

By 1970 both Japanese and American automakers were coming to the conclusion that joint ventures between the two nations would be mutually beneficial. In particular, the smaller Japanese companies were worried about their larger counterparts' not only monopolizing the American import market but saturating it. It seemed the only way for a company lacking the strength of a Toyota or Nissan to gain entry to the U.S. market was to "piggyback" on an American company's shoulders. Joining forces was also a politically astute move in an increasingly hostile American sales environment.

From Detroit's perspective, Japan's newly respected industry seemed attractive in many respects. If Japanese cars were going to continue to be popular there was no better way to cash in on that popularity than by purchasing a slice of it for themselves. It was also deemed prudent to gain a foothold in companies whose growth at the time seemed immeasurable. Chrysler in particular had nothing to lose and everything to gain. Its deals with France's Simca and Britain's Rootes had soured by 1970. Simca sales had dwindled to only 17,000 in its final three years and it was discontinued in 1971.[2] The only consolation they could offer Simca owners was a $125 credit on a trade for another Chrysler product.[3] The Simca had not been a popular car and Chrysler officials felt it wasn't worth the investment involved to equip it with safety devices and emission controls. Interestingly, Chrysler's ownership in Simca came about through the Ford Motor Company who had exchanged Ford of France for 15 percent of Simca in 1952 which they in turn sold to Chrysler. According to Lee Iacocca it would have been better if Chrysler had spent its money elsewhere: "Instead of concentrating on good cars, Lynn Townsend and his group started to expand overseas. In their zeal to become an international company, they bought European firms that were dead on their feet — companies that were dogs, such as Simca in France and Rootes in England."[4]

The British Rootes alliance lasted somewhat longer than the Simca union and the Plymouth Cricket fared somewhat better, but it was apparent by 1973 that it too was failing on the American market. As *Motor Trend* editors put it: "The Plymouth Cricket may stop chirping in 1974."[5]

The Cricket had originated as the Avenger, a four-door sedan with a 98-inch wheelbase and a 91.4-cubic-inch, 69-horsepower engine. It weighed under 2,000 pounds, had front disc brakes and a four-speed synchromesh transmission. Despite its virtues the Cricket expired, and a little later so did the Rootes alliance.

The first car to come from the Chrysler-Mitsubishi arrangement was the Dodge Colt, produced in Japan by Mitsubishi. Chrysler marketed the car in America as the Colt and Mitsubishi sold it in Japan as the Galant. It was available in three versions— a four-door sedan, a two-door hardtop, and a station wagon. Its wheelbase was 95.3 inches, and it was powered by a four-cylinder, 97.5-cubic-inch, 83-horsepower motor. In 1971 36,000 Colts were imported from Japan. The car received quite good reviews from American automobile magazines, but positive reviews could not counteract the self-defeating statements emerging from Chrysler's own headquarters. Said Chrysler's Chairman, Lynn A. Townsend: "The subcompacts are just too small, the American people won't climb into them. They have to give up too much in creature comfort. Even a compact car is a little too small."[6] This opinion could not have helped either the Colt, trying to soar in the market, or the Cricket, which was nearing the end of its life. Chrysler's apparent confusion and scattered sense of direction had been noted even before the Colt arrived on the scene. In September of 1970, *Car and Driver* magazine reported that, "Chrysler's handling of its imports in recent years has been marked by clandestine intrigues—one year Plymouth has it, an autonomous division is formed the next; names are changed and corporations discorporate and few people buy the cars."[7] It was true that sales were down significantly. And when the Chevrolet Vega and Ford Pinto appeared, the question naturally arose of when Chrysler would produce its own subcompact. The Colt was never quite accepted as a truly American car and Chrysler was forced to release a statement that it had every intention of building its own model, but not in the near future. As one journalist noted it would be some time before America would see a homemade Chrysler subcompact: "Chrysler still has its own small car plans on the shelf and because of a money squeeze will not change its plans."[8]

While the Vega and Pinto were selling in the six-digit figures by 1974, Colt sales had reached only 42,295, hardly a competitive number. To fortify their tenuous position in the subcompact market, Chrysler released the Mitsubishi-made Plymouth Arrow in 1976. The car achieved modest success due in large part to the oil-crisis market. That either the Colt or the Arrow was successful at all is amazing considering the conditions under which they were marketed. As Sobel observed: "Potential customers reported having visited a Dodge dealer hoping to be shown a Colt, only to be shunted aside to a Dart, on which the salesman received a much higher commission. Mitsubishi must have known this—the sales figures alone would have given them a hint of what was happening—but the Japanese firm could do little but protest and fume."[9]

Despite the mounting tension between the two companies, Chrysler purchased approximately one million Mitsubishi engines in 1978 for use in what would become the K-car. By 1979 Chrysler finances were so over-extended that Mitsubishi was forced to give them credit to allow them to maintain their position in the partnership. The only cars Chrysler could sell during the lean seventies were the Arrow and the Colt but they failed to sell in large enough numbers to keep the company profitable. Iacocca wrote that Chrysler was forced to offer $1,000 rebates on the small cars and even then sales did not materialize. Ironically, Iacocca was engaged at the time in what he would later be accused of as "Japan-bashing"—while simultaneously trying to sell his made-in-Japan imports. As Maryann Keller noted: "Sometimes the most strident protectionists seemed to contradict their own words with their actions. For example, even as Lee Iacocca was delivering firebrand stump speeches decrying the evils of Asian imports, Chrysler was importing Asian cars and components and selling them in the United States as American-made Plymouths and Dodges."[10]

Mitsubishi, in the meantime, was trying to find a way out of the merger. They were dismayed by Chrysler's rapid downfall and not pleased with repeatedly having to extend them credit. Although they tended to blame both management and Chrysler's production system for the company's problems, it was clear that they were unimpressed with the Chrysler product as well. Japanese car dealer Makoto Nakajima was attempting to sell Chryslers in Japan but met with little success. He later looked back on the experience as a "nightmare." The Omni/Horizon twins and the Plymouth Valiants he had on offer were, as he put it, "very, very, bad."[11] He ended up losing his job when his company decided to close the showroom after only one year. Surprisingly, Nakajima went on to establish a Chrysler franchise in the 1990s— this time with considerably more success.

Although Mitsubishi had been discontented for some time, it wasn't until May of 1981 that Lee Iacocca released them from certain contractual clauses, allowing them to establish their own dealership network in the United States. Just when it seemed that a "divorce" was imminent between the two companies in 1981–82, the instant success of the K-cars solidified their bond and went a long way in repairing the rift. In 1985 they bound themselves even more tightly together with the formation of the Diamond-Star Motor Corporation. By this time Chrysler had suffered much public humiliation which forced them to learn some tough lessons— mainly that Japanese cars were in America to stay, and that consumers actually *liked* them. Accordingly, the chastened company leaders were forced to forego their arrogant ways and assume the position of student. As a result they were content to let Mitsubishi take the lead within the new operation.

The Diamond-Star Motor Corporation was set up in Bloomington, Illinois, and was very much a Mitsubishi-operated business, as Robert Sobel confirms: "Although Chrysler put up half the money for the Diamond-Star plant and its executives are present, Mitsubishi is in the driver's seat. The Chrysler executives are trying to learn how the Japanese do what they do, and to ensure that Chrysler has a supply of automobiles to market."[12] In fact Diamond-Star claimed their U.S. content was 60 percent, but with engines, chassis, and drive trains coming from Japan as well as many of their suppliers working under the Mitsubishi umbrella, the figure was closer to 25 percent.[13]

The $650 million plant was built to produce of an array of models— among them the Eagle Talon, Mitsubishi Eclipse, Plymouth Laser, Mitsubishi 3000GT, Dodge Stealth, and the Mitsubishi Galant. Also born at this plant were the company's first all-wheel-drive and anti-lock brake systems. Unfortunately both Chrysler and Mitsubishi were struggling not only as a united corporation, but also individually in their home territories. In 1991 Chrysler sold its equity in Diamond-Star to Mitsubishi and in 1996 the company announced that it would not be renewing its contract with Mitsubishi after it expired in 1999. But the merger that was fraught with difficulties from the beginning was destined not to die, but only to be reincarnated in another form. When Daimler-Benz sent a shock wave through the automotive community by merging with Chrysler in 1998, the new company soon announced plans to purchase 33.4 percent of Mitsubishi. But by the year 2000, both Mitsubishi and Chrysler were still the weaker links in the organization, and as such were drawn even closer together as they shared development and production in order to cut costs. Working on their own was no longer an option. Chrysler's struggles have been legendary despite periodic revivals in the form of the LH models released in the mid-nineties and the innovative PT Cruiser introduced in 2000. As for Mitsubishi, automotive analyst Steve Usher was quoted in the March 27, 2000, edition of *Business Week* as saying: "If Daimler walks away from this one (merger), Mitsubishi looks very vulnerable."[14] In 2002, DaimlerChrysler raised its interest in Mitsubishi to 37.3 percent, a move then-president of Mitsubishi Takashi Sonobe called: "...further proof for the ongoing progress of our successful alliance with DaimlerChrysler."[15] In May of 2002, the group also announced the formation of the "Global Engine Alliance"—a tie-in with Mitsubishi and Hyundai to produce in-line four-cylinder engines. Today DaimlerChrysler has plants in 37 countries with 382,558 employees who produce Mercedes-Benz, Jeep, Dodge, Chrysler, Maybach, Smart, and Mitsubishi. In addition, its commercial vehicle department sells Sterling, Setra, Freightliner, Mercedes-Benz, and Western Star. The situation at Chrysler is looking up as sales rose from 187,119 in 2001 to 200,421 in 2002.[16] The success of Daimler along with strict cost-cutting has helped Chrysler, as has the success of the Jeep, the Ram truck, and the PT Cruiser. Speculation as to where the DaimlerChrysler-Mitsubishi union was headed was still strong in 2002 as the massive restructuring continued.

## GM–Isuzu

In 1949 the Diesel Automobile Company of Japan became the Isuzu Motor Company. A pioneer in Japan's diesel truck industry, Isuzu made its name by supplying the Japanese military with vehicles. But when World War II ended so did the company's good fortune. For a brief period it appeared that Isuzu's existence was under threat but it managed to reinvent itself by adding small automobiles to its production. In 1953 Isuzu entered into an agreement with the British Rootes Company to produce Hillman trucks which was in effect until 1964–65. In 1961 the company had the distinction of building Japan's first diesel sedan, the Bellel, and by 1965 had captured a respectable 4 percent of the Japanese automobile market. Under heavy pressure exerted by MITI, Isuzu signed a deal with Fuji Heavy Industries to share production and technology. At the same time there was talk of an Isuzu-Fuji-Mitsubishi merger, but this never materialized. Like Mitsubishi, Isuzu desired an American alliance, and for the same reasons. With Chrysler already spoken for and Ford proving resistant to overtures from the heavyweight Toyota, they were forced to look elsewhere for a partner. An agreement had been entered into with Nissan to produce a small van, but Isuzu was hoping for something a little more substantial. In October of 1970 they got their wish when talks opened with General Motors.

In January of 1971, *Motor Trend*'s "Inside Detroit" column contained the following item: "General Motors may link up with Isuza [*sic*] Motors of Japan as a means of gaining a foothold in the Japanese market. GM had been 'discussing areas of possible cooperation covering technical assistance and the exchange of know-how with respect to exhaust emission controls, safety measures, automatic transmissions and heavy duty engines."[17] The agreement, which was finalized on July 16, 1971, was "both shocking and troubling to the Japanese automobile fraternity."[18] The idea of General Motors' staking out territory in a Japanese company sent the Japanese industry and government into a tailspin. The fact that GM now owned 34.2 percent of Isuzu was cause for concern among those who felt threatened by an "American invasion," but nothing could be done except to wait and see how the tide would turn.

The first vehicle to spring from the union was the small Light Utility Vehicle (LUV) pickup truck which was exported to the United States in 1972, and in 1976 the Gemini sedan went on sale in America marketed under the Buick division.

It wasn't long before the two companies expanded their operations to other parts of the world, the first being Egypt. Following that a commercial-vehicle venture under the name IBC Vehicles was established in the United Kingdom in 1987, and in 1989 GM–Isuzu moved into Australia.

By all accounts the GM–Isuzu relationship was a mutually beneficial one although at times there were signs of conflict. Certainly it ran much smoother than did the Mitsubishi-Chrysler arrangement, probably due in part to the fact that GM and Isuzu were not in direct competition with each other for the same markets. The predominant source of tension in the relationship was the fact that Isuzu wanted to sell automobiles under their own name in the United States. In 1982 GM granted this wish by allowing them to export their small truck and sell it under the Isuzu nameplate. In later years other models followed. As a return gesture Isuzu asked for permission to manufacture and market GM's Cavalier model in Japan. In the meantime, the heart of the venture continued to be centered around the production of diesel engines and large and medium-size trucks.

In 1994 General Motors' plant in Janesville, Wisconsin, began making the GM–Isuzu hybrid pickup truck. One year later in Shreveport, Louisiana, Isuzu's own pickup, the Hombre, went into production. The alliance continued to flourish and in 1999 GM raised its stake in Isuzu to 49 percent. The agreement included the production of a number of SUVs, light and heavy duty trucks, as well as passenger cars. Commenting on the new arrangement, GM CEO John F. Smith, Jr., remarked that the increase of GM's shares in Isuzu "...will enhance the ability of the two companies to work even closer. With this agreement, Isuzu assumes an even more important role as an equal partner within GM's global alliances."[19]

Kazuhira Seki, CEO of Isuzu, added his opinion: "This agreement will help us achieve our long cherished goal of becoming the world's leading commercial vehicle and diesel engine manufacturer. The new equity arrangement is symbolic of the increasing cooperation and presence of Isuzu with GM's global alliances."[20]

While GM was unquestionably the dominant partner, Isuzu was working to increase its strength in the market. In 1986, GM solidified its bond with Suzuki, of which it had purchased 5 percent in 1981, by establishing CAMI, a joint GM–Suzuki operation located in Canada to produce small sport utility vehicles. In 1987 a deal was signed with Fuji Heavy Industries to incorporate a joint production company in the United States under the name of SIA. General Motors' pursuit of globalization saw them purchase 50 percent of Sweden's SAAB company in 1989, and 10 years later they paid $1.4 billion for a 20 percent share in Fuji Heavy Industries (Subaru). By the year 2000 the company had purchased the remaining 50 percent of SAAB as well as 20 percent of Italy's Fiat Motor Company. GM still retains its ownership of Holden in Australia, Opel in Germany, and Vauxhall in England.

But of all GM's strategic moves, without a doubt its most ground-breaking alliance came in 1983 when they joined forces with the Toyota Motor Company to form the New United Motor Manufacturing Incorporated (NUMMI) automobile company.

Under the agreement, which was originally laid out to encompass a 10-year period, General Motors was to provide the plant facilities and handle the marketing while Toyota would offer management utilizing their famous Toyota Production System. The car chosen for production was the clone of the Toyota Corolla, the Chevrolet Nova. The plant is located in Fremont, California, and was a previously operating GM plant. But before NUMMI could commence countless details had to be sorted out—everything from labor relations to the design of the cafeteria. Negotiations began on the wrong foot when Toyota rejected out of hand any United Auto Workers (UAW) involvement, a fact that was unacceptable to General Motors. Maryann Keller summed up the differences between the two companies in respect to labor thusly: "American companies tend, fundamentally, to mistrust workers, whether they are salaried employees or blue-collar workers. There is a pervading attitude that 'if you give them an inch, they'll take a mile,' because they don't really want to work." In contrast, going to work for a Toyota-managed company was a shock. "At NUMMI, Toyota would demonstrate a business strategy based on trust, respect, and teamwork."[21] This new strategy meant there was a rather steep learning curve for the 80 percent ex–General Motors employees who had been among the five thousand laid-off Fremont workers. For one thing there were no rigid job descriptions. In fact everyone fell into the category of either an assembler or a technician of some type. There were no executive suites, bonuses, special dining rooms or reserved parking spaces. Employees were treated as a part of a team, and were expected to act as such. They were given the responsibility of stopping the assembly line if they detected a flaw or problem in the process. This process, known to the Japanese as *kaizen*, or "continuous improvement," was in direct opposition to the American practice of trying to correct the defects after the fact. In addition, employees had to adapt to the *kanban*, or "just-in-time" production system, whereby parts and supplies were delivered on an as-needed basis and not stored somewhere in a vast and expensive warehouse.

The employees, or team members as they were referred to, thrived on the new system and after a difficult first year NUMMI was running at peak efficiency by 1986, coming very close to the productivity of its twin factory in Japan. GM chairman Roger Smith was so impressed with what was happening at NUMMI that he tried to reproduce the atmosphere in other General Motors facilities. But his idea of a "team concept," as Keller noted: "...did not, as might have been expected, utilize experienced NUMMI-trained executives for this task; its approach was an Americanized version that mimicked the Japanese wisdom only on the most superficial level."[22]

Still, the establishment of two former adversaries working side by side towards one goal had an immeasurable impact on both Toyota and General Motors. The ultimate success of NUMMI could not help but alter both Japanese and American perspectives—not only those of company employees, but also those of the consumers who were forced to re-examine their purchasing biases. "Buy American" now took on a whole new meaning. Rank-and-file customers previously divided into sharply delineated patriotic lines suddenly discovered that their generals had joined forces. This is not to say that there was instant harmony—far from it. But when viewed through the passage of time it can be determined that on the whole NUMMI laid a cornerstone for the future globalization of the industry and had an overall positive effect. Teaming up with an American company had been a desire of Toyota since the 1930s. The partner they had in mind originally was the Ford Motor Company but it remained an elusive goal. The partner Ford had in mind by the late 1960s was not Toyota but Toyo Kogyo, the company that produced the Mazda.

As usual, MITI had to sanction the deal before it could be sealed, and in November of 1970 it did so, allowing Ford to purchase a 20 percent share of the Toyo Kogyo Company. The merger created the inevitable industry "buzz," as—like partners in a quadrille—Japanese and American automakers began pairing off.

In April of 1971 *Motor Trend* ran the following piece:

> We reported prematurely that Ford was buying a chunk of Toyo Kogyo of Hiroshima, the company that makes those neat little rotary-engined cars. It turns out that there were a few snags in the deal which have held it up. One is that the Ministry of International Trade and Industry in Japan did not dig the idea of Ford buying more than 20% of TK, although they let Chrysler buy 35% of Mitsubishi last year. The second problem is that since Toyo Kogyo only produces the Wankel rotary engine on a license from NSU of Germany, NSU might have to be included in the negotiations if Ford wants to end up producing their own Wankels. The third area of contention is the sudden discovery by other Japanese auto makers that the TK Wankel might be the only import engine able to beat the tough 1975 U.S. smog standards. Now Mitsubishi and Toyota are trying to buy rotary engines from TK and even Volkswagen brass has been seen pacing the floor in TK's lobby. "Deuce," the Detroit nickname for Henry Ford II, is supposed to have been in Japan last month to straighten it all out.[23]

Ford, together with Nissan, had been manufacturing automatic transmissions as part of a three-way joint venture with Toyo Kogyo as far back as October of 1969 when they formed JATCO, a 50 percent Ford, 25 percent Nissan, 25 percent Toyo Kogyo arrangement. Ford continued to work with Toyo Kogyo throughout the 1970s until it finally managed to claim 25 percent equity in 1979. By that time Toyo Kogyo was in dire straits after the failure of the Wankel as a fuel-efficient engine and was in need of support. In exchange for its support, Ford borrowed Mazda technology and established its own distribution channels in Japan to sell the re-styled Mazdas under the Ford name. One of these was the Ford Festiva, based on the Mazda 121. The Festiva was assembled in Korea by KIA, a company both Ford and Toyo Kogyo had a small stake in. Similarly, Toyo Kogyo had been supplying Ford with small trucks which were marketed in the United States as the Ford Courier. A later joint-production process produced the Mazda 323-Ford Escort combination.

Throughout the eighties Ford and Toyo Kogyo (which became the Mazda Motor Corporation in 1984) continued to work closely to share technology as well as parts, suppliers and marketing. In the early 1980s it was debatable as to who was in the worst shape — Ford or Mazda. Ford continued to suffer heavy losses and stood to gain if it could produce a subcompact of some value. Its production was suffering and its management chaotic. As James P. Womack, Daniel T. Jones, and Daniel Roos wrote in *The Machine That Changed the World: The Story of Lean Production*, Ford executives were obliged to travel to Japan in 1981 to observe Mazda's operations and learn why "Ford was taking such a beating in international competition."[24] According to the authors, "...the Ford executives and Ford's UAW leaders discovered the answer to Japan's success: lean production. Specifically, they found that Mazda could build its 323 model with only 60 percent of the effort Ford needed to manufacture its Escort selling in the same market segment. Moreover, Mazda made many fewer manufacturing errors in doing so. Equally striking, Mazda could develop new products much more rapidly and with less effort than Ford and worked much more smoothly with its suppliers to do so."[25]

In 1987 the two created another model, the Ford Probe, based on the Mazda MX-6/626 platform. These were produced at Mazda's new facilities in Flat Rock, Michigan, under the name of Mazda Motor Manufacturing USA Corporation (MMUC). Mazda invested over 100 billion yen to open the new plant which had previously been an old Ford metal-casting factory. Annual production capability was estimated to be 240,000 vehicles.[26] But Mazda, still trying to recover from the second oil crisis, found themselves operating under a constant deficit. The rise of the yen and the enforcement of local content regulations further hobbled the company which was also being adversely affected by labor-relations conflicts. Attempting to account for the company's troubles, president Kenichi Yamamoto remarked that: "...Americans have their own views on how to do things. Their individualism is strong, and when it came to starting up production lines, there were difficulties in attaining harmony in the workplace." Then as if anxious not to appear to be biased against Americans he added: "Japanese people aren't good at communication. They have curious views on the subject, invoking such sayings as 'silence is golden.'"[27]

Regardless of where the problem areas were, it was apparent in 1991 that Mazda again needed rescuing. Ford responded by purchasing 50 percent of MMUC and the venture became the AutoAlliance International Incorporated (AAII). In 1996 Ford spent 480 million dollars to acquire 33.4 percent of Mazda, enough to give Ford unilateral veto rights. In addition, Henry Wallace became the first foreign president of a Japanese automobile company. But it soon seemed that problems continued to dog the Ford-Mazda tie-in. In 2001 Mazda posted net losses of 458 million dollars. In an interview with *Business Week* magazine, Mazda's CEO Mark Fields attributed the company's problems to the unstable yen as well as "some structural issues," which he went on to identify as union-related. In addition a plant had to be closed in order to cut losses. Fields remarked that there was a definite need for a heightened marketing campaign, and he admitted that: "Our brand awareness is very low in many markets."[28]

Ford, which had rallied in the mid-eighties after the introduction of the Taurus/Sable twins, has faltered repeatedly since then. Jacques Nasser, who took over as CEO in 1999, attempted to build Ford into a company that would challenge General Motors. In doing so, he apparently alienated many of those who might have helped the company through its difficulties following the Firestone-tire-related accidents and ensuing lawsuits. And while Mazda seems to be recovering itself in the North American market, Ford continues to struggle with quality as well as damage control issues. However the essence of the Ford-Mazda merger remains, brought about by an integrated education system for managers, improved financial controls, technology sharing, and marketing upgrading. Ford may not have achieved equal status with General Motors, but as Womack et al. wrote in 1990: "It is sobering to realize that even with its limited progress in globalizing design and production, Ford is still the clear leader among all companies, including the Japanese, in establishing itself as a truly global organization with design and production facilities in three major markets." Ford also drew praise for at adopting at least some elements of lean production, which GM did not. General Motors was "too rich," wrote Womack, "to take the lessons of lean production to heart."[29]

In regards to Chrysler, the authors felt that its case was hopeless: "Why it [Chrysler] failed to learn much about its real problems in a time of crisis, despite its equity tie-in and access to Mitsubishi, is a tragic mystery."[30]

Another mystery of dramatic proportions was the temporary downfall of Nissan. The company suffered a declining market share that began in the 1980s. Some blamed the mid-stream name change from Datsun to Nissan in the mid-eighties, while others pointed to lackluster designs, half-hearted marketing and poor product planning. These have been identified by analysts as some of the real problems the company has labored under. In 1993 Nissan was forced to cut its workforce by 5,000, reduce its product line and close its historic factory in Zama, Japan. Relatively speaking the company has remained independent except for an agreement with Ford to produce minivans at its Tennessee facilities. Its historical rejection of the UAW may have had something to do with its stance on mergers, particularly with American firms. But when the debt-load became unbearable, Nissan was forced to rethink its position. In 1999, it made a bid to save itself by agreeing to sell a 36.8 percent share to the Renault Automobile Company of France with an option to increase the share to 44.4 percent. Renault, a company that had struggled in the 1970s and 1980s, had found a footing predominantly in the European and South American markets and thereby was able to pay the 1.8 billion dollars to acquire part of Nissan. It began its purchasing in 1979 when it bought 50 percent of the American Motors Corporation.

The deal with Nissan gave Renault minority control rights as well as operational capabilities. In return Nissan bought shares in Renault and announced in 2002 that it would be increasing those to 15 percent. The company also received some badly needed funds as well as fresh strategies. The problems with the models were bluntly summed up by Nissan's new leader, Carlos Ghosn, who went on record admitting that Nissan's cars have been "blandly styled."[31] Former chairman Yoshifumi Tsuji acknowledged in 1998 that it was mismanagement that brought about the company's enormous debts. *Business Week* reported in 2001 that the debt was rumored to be 21 billion dollars, and more importantly: "Nissan is running out of financiers willing to feed its debt habit." The piece concluded on a pessimistic note: "Debt is smothering Nissan. And cash alone from Renault may not save it."[32]

Nissan is now almost fully recovered after Ghosn closed down five plants and trimmed the global workforce. The company has recently been posting profits and sales continue on an upward trend. Ironically it is now Renault who is struggling. Undoubtedly Nissan has been helped not only by the merger, but also with the introduction and successes of the new boldly styled Nissan Frontier pickup, Pathfinder, Altima, and 350Z, all of which have won critical acclaim and piqued consumer interest.

While Nissan and other Japanese companies have been forced to seek protection in mergers, there is one company that has no plans to do so, nor does it need to. The closest the Honda Motor Company has come to merger was in 1999 when it signed a strategic alliance with General Motors to provide engines for a GM vehicle built in North America. Despite that, Honda has always been, and remains, an independent venture. Its formula has been so successful that it seems unlikely that it will ever seek to join another company, which would mean compromise and the adoption of another's technology and/or methodology. So far there is no need to change what works, and works well.

In the mid-seventies Lee Iacocca spoke of a union between Chrysler, Mitsubishi, and perhaps Volkswagen. He named this imaginary conglomerate Global Motors. In this vision he has often been credited as being ahead of his time but in fact the industry trend was already moving strongly towards globalization. It continues to evolve with no predictable outcome. There is much debate over whether or not mergers have been beneficial or harmful to the industry. In a 1998 edition of the *Los Angeles Times*, Peter F. Cowhey and Jonathan D. Aronson raised the question: "Do mergers threaten nations?" Citing difficulties with establishing multinational governmental policies that are equitable to all parties, the authors maintain that mergers do pose a threat unless "…there was a sharing of the burden of corporate governance among nations."[33] Differing views on antitrust is a prime example of the challenges that face the global auto industry. How big is too big, and who gets to decide? A "somewhat large" corporate merger in America may be considered outlandish by Japanese or European standards. Should the strong be allowed to overtake the weak? Should two strong entities be allowed to become one even stronger one? And more importantly, as Cowhey and Aronson queried, "Who makes the rules of a global enterprise?"[34]

There are countless other questions that remain unanswered. Can any company maintain its unique qualities if taken over, even in small increments, by another company? Will a troubled company bring down its supposed savior? And how will the consumer view the union, particularly in the brand-conscious culture we now live in?

Taking it one step further, if a Japanese company builds and invests in America, and hires American labor, is that company not an American enterprise? The answer to that is yes and no. In the end, it is ultimately the parent company in Japan that stands to gain (or lose) from its operations in America. Earnings are folded back into headquarters and are dispersed in a multitude of directions, not all of them back into America. On the other hand jobs are created, satellite organizations supported, and an economy boosted. So America gains. But this type of operation need not be related to a merger. While Diamond-Star and NUMMI sprang from Japanese-American alliances, there is also the establishment of wholly owned Japanese companies in America to be considered, or as they are sometimes known, transplants—the subject of the next chapter.

# 16

## The New American
## Automotive Community

"When Honda built its first plant in the United States, no other Japanese companies were here. Its margin for error was very thin, but its timing was superb."[1] So wrote David Gelsanliter in *Jump Start: Japan Comes to the Heartland*. Honda's timing had indeed been ideal but it was by no means serendipitous. Plans had been laid as far back as 1974 when discussion began about building a manufacturing plant in the United States. At the time the yen was weak against the dollar, Volkswagen was the only foreign manufacturer in America, and talk of export restraints against Japan had not yet been brought to the table.

When word got out that Honda was planning to build in America the news was met with considerable skepticism and even hostility in both the United States and Japan. No large Japanese automobile company had dared to make such a move and it was almost inconceivable that a small company like Honda would have the nerve or the wherewithal to do so. What was even more difficult to digest was that the company was planning to go it alone, without benefit of an American partnership to facilitate its entry to the country.

But once the decision was made, Honda stuck by it and plans quickly followed. An investment of $30 million was the initial requirement to build the 260,000-square-foot plant which at first would produce only motorcycles. The American press got wind of the story and reported on the anticipated arrival without naming the company. As David Gelsanliter relates, when developer James Duerk alerted Ohio Governor James Rhodes to the fact that a Japanese company was planning to build in the United States, Rhodes agreed to make a trip to Japan. Wishing to cover all the bases, they met with Toyota, Nissan, and Honda executives. A year later they got a call from Honda officials requesting a meeting to take place in Ohio. The state of Ohio was attractive to Honda not least because it contained one of the world's largest test track and research facilities. After touring the area, Honda leaders chose a site of a little over 200 acres, 8 miles south of the small community of Marysville. The site was within reasonable distance of both the Dayton and Columbus airports, as well as being in a rural area with a strong work ethic. It was also nowhere near Detroit and the United Auto Workers union. Labor relations were the furthest thing from James Rhodes' mind. Instead he envisioned a boost to the area's economy that he and others felt was well worth the $2.5 million incentive package he planned to offer Honda. The money was mostly earmarked for road and services improvements, with a portion going towards training and development.

In October of 1977 an agreement was reached between the Ohio government and the Honda Motor Company. Its ratification signaled the commencement of Phase I of the new Honda of America Manufacturing Operations—namely a motorcycle plant. But the company approached with caution, and according to Gelsanliter, was extremely sensitive to the community it was moving into: "Conscious of Marysville's resistance to change, Honda moved ahead with great care and deliberation in those early years. It drilled its own wells and built its motorcycle and first auto plant with union construction workers."[2] The company was apparently equally deliberate about its hiring practices: "For its assembly line jobs, Honda restricted hiring to one person per family, to high-school graduates (the younger the better) and to people with preferably no manufacturing — and almost certainly no automobile manufacturing — experience.... Honda hired from a radius of twenty miles, later expanded to thirty, with the formula for developing managers much the same."[3]

Kazuo Nakagawa was appointed president of the new firm and he reported back to Japan that over 3,000 job applications had been received. Applicants were thoroughly screened and narrowed down to 100 or so potential candidates. Those hired were to be known as associates rather than employees. On September 10, 1979, the 64 chosen associates worked together to produce 10 model CR250 dirt bikes on the company's first day of operation.[4]

Two months later Honda announced its intention to build an automobile factory next to the motorcycle facility, and in December of 1980 construction began on the 1-million-square-foot, $250 million plant. Two years later almost to the month, the second-generation Honda Accord rolled off the line at the new factory. It seemed that Honda had found a fool-proof way to circumvent the 1981 Voluntary Export Restraints agreed upon by America and Japan.

Once the company was established it continued to expand at a rapid rate. In 1984 Honda Power Equipment was opened in Swepsonville, North Carolina, and in 1985 a 235,000-square-foot plant was raised in Anna, Ohio. Initial production was Goldwing motorcycle engines, but the plant was eventually tooled to produce Honda Civics. In 1986, the Marysville facility was expanded to 2.2 million square feet and Accords as well as Civics were produced there. Also that year a plant was opened in Alliston in the province of Ontario, Canada. It seemed that Honda had pulled off a feat it hadn't been able to manage back home — it usurped the dominant position of Toyota and Nissan, and on American soil. Honda's president made it quite plain that he wanted there to be no doubt that the company would be an American operation. In an interview shortly after Honda's initial successes, Tetsuo Chino stated that: "Ultimately, we would like to see Honda accepted as an American company."[5] By 1987 it seemed like that visualization was becoming a reality when 738,000 Hondas sold in the United States, exceeding its sales even in Japan. The strong demand for the Honda automobile soon prompted yet another expansion — this time Honda had its eye on the Transportation and Research Center. But before they could purchase the land, it had to be rezoned as industrial rather than agricultural. It took delicate nego- tiations to convince the local farmers the move would not pose a threat to them or the land around them. In the end, despite some resistance, Honda purchased the 7,000-acre site and added it to its list of American properties.

In March of 1988, ground was broken for a new factory to be located in East Liberty, Ohio. Production was set for 150,000 cars a year, but this figure, as at other plants, was expected to be exceeded. By 1989, Honda's U.S. investment totaled more than $1.5 billion. It was also responsible for moving Ohio, formerly near the bottom of America's job-growth statistics, to fourth place on the list.

But it was not all sunshine and roses. It wasn't long before Honda hit turbu- lence when it was accused of unfair hiring and labor practices. Lawsuits were filed against the company for, among other things, discrimination against minorities and older persons. While not admitting to any wrongdoing, Honda paid a $6 million set- tlement. It also paid $450,000 in damages to settle the age-discrimination case.[6]

But these were but mere ripples when compared to the battle the UAW waged against Honda. It had been attempting to organize at Honda since the very begin- ning without success. The threat of a large public demonstration drew from Honda the concession that it would not actively stand against the union, but rather it would let its associates decide for themselves. Those associates formed a group of their own in reply to the UAW. Calling themselves the Honda Associate Alliance, the group made it abundantly clear that the UAW was not welcome at the plant. Their main argument, and one that was difficult to refute, was that they required no union inter- vention. Honda was treating them more than fairly, they claimed. Wages were more than satisfactory, the work environment was pleasant and clean, and on the whole they had no quarrel with the company.

On Honda's part, they did all they could to build a reputation as a benefactor in the community, making it public knowledge that their American corporate phil- anthropy dated back to 1964 when it supported a Los Angeles youth center. They also contributed relief after Hurricane Camille struck in 1969. In 1981, they went one bet- ter and established the Honda of America Foundation which covers everything from food-bank donations to education grants. Today Honda's commitment to the com- munity is widespread and deeply rooted. In the interests of brevity, only a few of its charitable actions include: providing vehicles for the disabled; contributing over $13 million to the United Way since 1982; matching associate donations for such causes as arts and culture as well as education; supporting scout troops and senior citizen groups, and occupying positions on the boards of numerous non-profit organiza- tions; an outreach program that helps the YWCA, the Children's Hospital, and the Ohio Hunger Task Force; funding for the Ohio State University College of Engi- neering and the Martin Luther King Complex, as well as many other worthy causes. It also sponsors a Ride for Kids program, funds the Center for Earth and Planetary Studies, Little League baseball, the Jazz Festival, and the African Marketplace and Culture Fair. In its Honda Heroes program, associates and their spouses are rewarded with "Dollars for Doers" grants to help the charities of their choice. Since 1995, $175,000 has been awarded under this program.[7]

To date, Honda has spent many millions of dollars in the United States. As of 2001, it has 8 plants operating in America which are fed by hundreds of suppliers. It employs over 15,000 people in its plants alone, not to mention its dealerships, parts companies and headquarters in California. It has been producing in America for 23 years and its successes can be attributed in part to its company philosophies, most of which originated with founder Soichiro Honda. The company follows these major tenets: Strive for harmonious flow of work; value research and endeavor; enjoy your work and encourage open communication; develop fresh ideas and use time effectively; respect sound theory; and proceed always with ambition and youthfulness.[8]

All valuable lessons to be learned, even for larger and older companies who ended up following the trail Honda blazed in the United States. The first of these was Japan's once-largest automobile company, the Nissan Motor Corporation.

In October of 1980, Nissan Motor Manufacturing Corporation USA (NMMC) became the second Japanese automobile company to establish operations in America when it announced it would be building in Smyrna, Tennessee. Nissan spent $760 million developing the 778-acre site which was 20 miles south of Nashville. When the plant was ready to open in 1983, 1,736 employees were hired to build a projected 120,000 vehicles annually.[9] Initially all of these would be small trucks.

Like officials at Honda, Nissan executives carefully considered the location of their first American plant. But unlike Honda who professed to assume a neutral position on the UAW, Nissan stood firmly and vocally against it. Finding a relatively union-free southern state in fact had been a factor in the decision to build in Tennessee. The issue of labor soon became a fly in the ointment of Nissan's American plan. Matters were not helped when Nissan's president in Japan, Takashi Ishihara, publicly expressed doubts about the wisdom of building in the United States, worrying that American labor would not meet the standards that were currently being met in the Japanese facilities. It was partly for this reason that he decided this shop should be highly automated and union-free. The company had a long and bitter history concerning labor relations and had something of a reputation as a union "tamer." At the time however, these clouds remained hidden at least from the governor of Tennessee's perspective.

Competing against 24 other states for the chance to boost their economies and employment rates, Tennessee ultimately won out. Its closest competitor had been another southern state, Georgia. What finally swayed Nissan toward Tennessee had been a promise to spend $14 million to connect the plant to the nearby interstate highway and an additional $7.3 million to help train workers. But Nissan proved it was anxious to show itself as an eager contributor as well when it spent to help build a new highway, to make improvements to water and sewage facilities, and for employee training. Including its plant and other expenses, Nissan's initial investment in Tennessee totaled around $500 million.[10]

Despite Nissan's wariness of American labor, it was decided that the U.S. facility should be headed by an American and be seen to be as pro–American as possible. In accordance, ex–Ford V.-P. Marvin Runyon was hired to head NMMC USA. Runyon was chosen in part because he was in agreement with Nissan's non-union philosophy. Still, Nissan took pride in the number of Americans at the plant, and of their employees who were to be known as technicians. The company also ensured that the majority of its suppliers and parts companies would be American as well. But as David Gelsanliter noted, doing so was sometimes a challenge: "It was not always easy. In the early years, Runyon rejected parts from U.S. suppliers at least twice as often as parts from Japanese companies."[11]

Unfortunately Nissan's fresh new page was blotted by the stain of its anti-union stance which earned them much negative publicity. In time this publicity worked against the UAW whose behavior soon caused the tide of sympathy to turn toward Nissan. To deflect the slings and arrows from a public that kept a close eye on the "foreign" company, Nissan pointed to all it was doing for the American community. Good public relations combined with the indisputable quality of the little trucks they were producing won them approval and allowed them to expand operations by 1985. That year the Sentra was added to the production line, boosting production to 250,000 vehicles annually. In 1989, a further investment of $490 million was added to build another 1.7 million square feet on the site.

In 1997, Nissan established another plant in Tennessee — this time in the small community of Decherd which was about 70 miles south of Smyrna. An additional 380 employees were hired to build 200,000 engines and 300,000 transaxles a year at the 230,000-square-foot factory.[12] Meanwhile, operations at Smyrna also continued to expand. By 1998, the Frontier truck, Sentra, Altima, and 200SX sports coupe were being produced there, in addition to engines, axles, and bumpers. Some of these were to be used on Nissan's joint vehicle project with Ford, the Nissan Quest/Mercury Villager minivan.

It seemed clear that choosing Tennessee had been a sound choice, and NMMC president Jerry Benefield wanted Tennessee to know it appreciated the support and was giving back in kind: "This presence is not just about vehicle production. It's also about Nissan giving back to the community. We have plenty of motivation: a beautiful place with so many great people. It's no wonder NMMC so eagerly serves its role as a good corporate neighbor in Middle Tennessee."[13]

The "good neighbor" theme was a focal point in Nissan's American philanthropy. The "Nissan Neighbors" program supports a wide variety of organizations and causes including culture and the arts, youth involvement in science and technology, and the environment. Non-profit organizations are invited to apply for funding for their community outreach programs. Hand-in-hand with the Neighbor program runs the Nissan Foundation, a $5 million endowment bestowed by the company to help stimulate economic growth in south-central Los Angeles. In addition, numerous charities, including Martha's Table, the Los Angeles Urban League, the American Red Cross, Women Escaping a Violent Environment, the Boys and Girls Club, Sacramento START, Hands on San Francisco, the National Hispanic Scholarship Fund, and others are supported.[14]

In the year 2000, Nissan announced it would be investing an additional $1 billion to expand its Tennessee facilities. And in the February 2002 edition of *Industry Week* online, it was reported that the company would be building a $930 million, 2.6-million-square-foot manufacturing plant in Canton, Mississippi, that will produce an estimated 250,000 units annually built by a 3,500-strong workforce.[15]

Nissan's other American operations include Nissan Research and Development, located in Farmington Hills, Michigan, and employing around 500 people; Nissan Design International, founded in 1979 and located in La Jolla, California; and the hub around which everything operates—its U.S. headquarters, centered in Gardena, California. All together, Nissan has created thousands of jobs in the United States and has contributed greatly to the American economy and community. Yet as impressive as its contributions are, it still plays second to its long-time rival, the Toyota Motor Corporation.

"Until Toyota and its parts and suppliers arrived and began creating a new middle class, Scott [county] and some of its neighboring counties resembled a Third World country with extremes of wealth and poverty and little in between."[16] David Gelsanliter's assessment of the area surrounding Georgetown, Kentucky, is debatable. But there is no question that Toyota's presence in the area dramatically altered the landscape both literally and figuratively. The company seemed to have a penchant for locating in rural, out-of-the-way, somewhat humble surroundings. Its home base in Aichi prefecture in Japan was chosen for just those attributes.

The risk of locating in the United States had been much reduced when Toyota joined forces with General Motors to create NUMMI. In many ways it was an exercise in "testing the waters" for the company, whose leaders were cautious in the extreme and did not share Honda's more devil-may-care attitude. When NUMMI proved to be a success, and Honda and Nissan had already cleared a path, Toyota decided it was time to perform solo in America. But while Honda and Nissan had pioneered and taken considerable risks to battle the unknown, Toyota had the benefit of valuable American production experience to draw upon. Most importantly, it had already dealt with the UAW and knew more or less what to expect. This is not to say it welcomed the union—it did not. But by choosing a southern state like its compatriots, Toyota was able to avoid a large population of pro-unioners. In the end, it was not its rejection of the UAW that caused problems, but rather the controversial incentive package offered by Kentucky governor Martha Layne Collins that almost kept the budding empire from being built. When it was made public that Toyota was to receive at least a $125 million enticement, protests and demonstrations plagued the enterprise from the very beginning. Even the press assumed a stance against what everyone perceived as an overly generous offer. To add salt to the wound, Toyota's imperious manner of negotiating made it clear that they did not consider the offer particularly generous. The ensuing chaos stirred the attention of activist Ralph Nader who demanded that disciplinary action be taken against Collins for her mishandling of taxpayer dollars. There were allegations that the money was "padded" and was more of a bribe than an incentive.

Construction, which was slated to begin in 1986, was continually held up by one protest or another. The UAW accused the company of unfair hiring practices when it was discovered that Toyota was bringing in cheaper out-of-state labor to build the plant. A nasty public demonstration drew a concession from Toyota to use union labor for the construction. Needless to say, Toyota's welcome to the community was a rather frosty one. Toyota tried to smooth the ruffled feathers by boosting its investment to $1.16 billion, and by increasing hiring to 3,500 people.[17] And although many seemed to feel put out by Toyota's presence, it didn't stop over 100,000 people from submitting applications. This process instigated even further unpleasantness when the UAW accused Toyota of screening out union sympathizers. Yet there was little they could do other than protest, since the company was offering above-scale wages and other perks. But Toyota caused more irritation when, unlike Nissan, it imported its management from Japan and made it clear it would be following its time-honored Toyota Production System to the letter. In essence, Toyota's American facility was to be a clone of its Japanese operations. There was no room for UAW concessions at this plant. It was soon difficult to dispute Toyota's business acumen, for the plant eventually grew to produce a staggering 495,000 units per year by the year 2000.[18]

But Toyota did not ride roughshod over the American community as some union sympathizers liked to believe. Its record of American investment and philanthropy has been impeccable and impossible to ignore. From its humble beginnings in a tiny building in Hollywood in 1957 when it could not even afford proper advertising, it grew to plant many millions of dollars in American soil. Toyota's philanthropic activities are far too numerous to list in full here, but a few of these include: the Toyota USA Foundation, which provides $1 million per year in awards for innovative math and science programs; the Toyota Mobility program, which provides up to $1,000 to equip vehicles for the disabled; the Toyota Volunteer program, which includes contributions to the United Way, mentoring, and the Special Olympics; the Toyota Education Support program; the L.A. Urban League; grants for math and science teachers; educational television; scholarships; arts and culture funding; child care; homelessness; fire departments, as well as their considerable environmental work.[19]

In addition to its headquarters in Torrance, California, the company also has a presence in Indiana, Kentucky, West Virginia, Michigan, Maryland, Colorado, Illinois, New Jersey, Ohio, and Oregon. Private distribution companies are located in Florida and Texas. Toyota produces not only automobiles, but forklifts, industrial equipment, aviation equipment, and marine sports equipment, and has its own aluminum plant. In addition, it operates a Research and Development facility, a Logistics Service company, a financial services branch, a business development service, a productivity assistance service, a technical center, a design center, and Toyota Racing Development USA, Inc.

In 2001, Toyota announced its intention to build a 300,000-square-foot plant in Huntsville, Alabama, to be in operation by 2003. The plant would build V-8 engines for their full-size pick-up truck, the Tundra. Alabama's governor, Don Siegelman, was quoted as saying: "Toyota brings to Alabama not only its international reputation as a first-class manufacturer of automobiles, but it also brings high-skilled and high-paying jobs to Alabamians."[20] Toyota's president Fujio Cho was equally gracious when he replied that the company appreciated a chance to set up operations in

Alabama: "We know we will find people of the highest caliber here, who have the skills, the intelligence and the enthusiasm to become a successful Toyota team."[21] And just in case there were any doubts as to Toyota's intentions, the new president of the Huntsville plant went on record saying: "You will find us a willing participant in organizations that help improve the quality of life in the state and community. And let me assure you, Toyota is making a long-term commitment to this community. We're not just passing through. We're here to stay! That is the Toyota way."[22]

The Huntsville facility will bring Toyota's production capacity up to 1.45 million vehicles a year, with 1.16 million engines also being produced.[23] This quite substantial production is more than enough to earn the company "Big Three" status—a status they have long been striving for in their drive to become a major global enterprise.

One company that entertains considerably more modest aspirations in the United States is the Mazda Motor Corporation. Although its U.S. operations are technically a 50/50 split with the Ford Motor Company, Mazda has in its own way contributed greatly to the American economy and community. With $780 million invested in the Mazda/Ford plant, now called the AutoAlliance International Incorporated (AAI), Mazda is responsible for its own research and development, sales and marketing, as well as parts and service of its own vehicles. Quite naturally, as a partner of Ford, Mazda's North American operations are in cooperation with the UAW. Nonetheless, the company has been plagued with labor relations difficulties which will be examined in more detail in the following chapter.

Mazda of Japan had been hit hard by the Voluntary Export Restraint agreement between the United States and Japan, as well as the instability of the nation's currency, but it managed to rebound to a degree by exporting its small B2000 pickup truck which was exempt from the agreement. As has been noted in a previous chapter, the only way Mazda could have established a North American manufacturing presence was by joining an American company. But the protection from Ford came at a price — it meant abandoning some of their most treasured production methods and doing things the Ford way.

As the years passed and Ford gradually assumed more and more control of Mazda, changes in its operations reflected that control. In 1988, the Japanese paper *Chugoku Shimbun* ran a story entitled: "Winds of Change at Mazda: Japanese-Style Production System Diminishing at AAI." In part the article said: "…the Japanese practice of 'kaizen,' bottom-up quality and efficiency improvement efforts involving all the workers, is followed to a lesser extent. Mazda introduced this system into the U.S. plant during MMUC days and generated as many as 8,000 improvement proposals annually. But now that figure is down by half."[24]

Despite this turn of events Mazda continues to rise in the United States, aided by its public relations endeavors and the quality of its vehicles. Working conditions have improved since 1988, and so has the company's image. This was helped by the creation of the Mazda Foundation in 1990. Through it, Mazda has helped advance youth literacy, set up scholarships, promoted cross-cultural relationships between the United States and Japan by sponsoring a student-exchange program, established an In-Care Network to help American Indian children and youth, worked to preserve the environment, and set up a program to grant wishes to children suffering from life-threatening illnesses. The company also takes part in a Matching Gift program where it matches employee donations to various charities.[25]

It is clear that Mazda plans to retain its independence, bolstered by the fact that Mazda of Japan's two plants have been quite successful with 800,000 vehicles produced in 1999. The company has an AutoAlliance in Thailand, and assembles vehicles in fourteen other countries. In the United States it is located in California, where it is headquartered, and in Michigan, where the manufacturing facility is located.

Confirming that Mazda would continue to work to raise its profile, its American president, Mark Fields, stated: "Mazda must continue to stake out its turf as a unique Japanese brand within the Ford group of brands. Just being Japanese has positive connotations in terms of product quality and manufacturing expertise."[26]

These four major Japanese automotive companies have all etched out a place for themselves in America and gained acceptance in sometimes-not-quite-welcoming communities. They have all made a substantial impact on America's economy as well as having changed the face of its automotive industry, bringing a global flavor and offering a wider variety of choice to the American consumer. It is to be expected that Detroit has viewed these enterprises with some trepidation, but how has the average American reacted to the transplants? According to one study, a full 30 percent said they still would not buy a Japanese car.[27] And yet there are even more Japanese automobile companies to be considered, particularly Subaru and Subaru-Isuzu of America (SIA).

Subaru has dramatically risen to prominence within the past few years, as well as having increased its product line and boosted its image. Subaru teamed up with Isuzu in 1989 to create Subaru-Isuzu of America and began manufacturing out of a base in Lafayette, Indiana. Subaru's parent company, Fuji Heavy Industries, owns 51 percent of the venture while Isuzu controls 49 percent. In total, approximately $850 million was invested in the facility which occupies 2.3 million square feet and initially employed around 1,700 workers. Production of 60,000 Subaru Legacys and 60,000 Isuzu pickups and sport utility vehicles began in September of 1989.[28]

Like other Japanese companies, SIA was offered generous incentives to build in Indiana by Governor Robert Orr. By some estimates the amount offered was equal to $50,000 per job created.[29] Again the Japanese facility was to be nonunion, a condition that would stir up some of the same troubles the other companies experienced. They were problems the company could scarcely afford, since independently they were both struggling in the U.S. market. Ultimately both were to end up under the General Motors umbrella.

Thanks to a raised brand awareness, particularly for Subaru, SIA announced in 2000 that it would be expanding its operations in Lafayette. By then the company employed 3,100 with an additional number expected when the new plant was built. The company also took pains to portray themselves as community players, and in this they were assisted by Governor Joe Kernan who called SIA's community contributions "significant." "On top of the job creation, they've been involved with everything from a new playground in a local park to a productive partnership with Ivy Tech's automotive program. Subaru-Isuzu has been a great asset to the community, as well as the state as a whole, and we're pleased to support this latest investment."[30] That new investment was to total an estimated $167 million. In return, Indiana offered $380,000 in the form of a training grant, along with up to $3.5 million in tax credits as well as other assorted incentives.[31]

Some of SIA's contributions to the community include a Volunteer Program; "TEECAP"— Teacher Education Exchange Cultural Awareness Program; United Way funds totaling over $1 million from 1997 to 2000; the SIA Foundation which has a Matching Gift section; various grant programs; March of Dimes contributions; and assistance given to Purdue University. Started in 1997, the SIA Foundation had given over $1.4 million by the year 2000. In addition, the company also supports culture and the arts in the community.[32]

Another up-and-coming Japanese automobile company in the United States is the American Suzuki Corporation. Paired with GM back in 1981, Suzuki up until then had been known only for its motorcycles. In 1985 that changed when it produced the first compact sport utility vehicle, the Samurai. It has since added small cars to its production line and has upgraded its SUVs to include the popular Vitara and Grand Vitara models. With GM owning nearly 10 percent of the company, it will be interesting to see how Suzuki will progress in America.

In a 1999 edition of the *International Automobile Dealer* newsletter, Lori Weaver Barnes wrote: "There is no question about it. The international automobile industry is a vital part of the American economy and the American way of life. The industry provides American jobs, supports American businesses, invests in our nation's economy and offers American consumers the freedom to choose from a multitude of quality vehicles to meet their transportation needs."[33]

Detractors of Japanese "transplants" cannot dispute the figures—more than 300,000 Americans are directly involved in producing "Japanese" cars in America, and even more are employed in satellite industries. Japanese companies have invested some $18 billion in their American operations and in the American economy, while producing over 2.4 million vehicles a year (1998 data). In 1998, 90,000 of these were exported overseas.[34]

Undoubtedly these companies' contributions to the American automotive community are laudable—unfortunately the same cannot be said for their labor-relations record and history. And while matters have improved over the past few years, it is inevitable that some eggs would be broken in order to create the omelet, particularly as the two cultures adjusted to one another's method of operation.

# 17

## American Labor — Japanese-Style

"The Toyota method of production appears to the outside world as the systemization of the 'relationship of a community bound together by a common fate'... But truthfully, it's nothing more than the absolute determination to make all movement of goods and people in and out of these plants subordinate to Toyota's will."[1] This declaration was part of perhaps the most damning indictment of Japanese management ever to be recorded in print. *Japan in the Passing Lane: An Insider's Account of Life in a Japanese Auto Factory* was published in 1980 and documented journal-style how the celebrated Japanese management appeared from the worker's perspective.

Professional writer Satoshi Kamata spent a season at a Toyota factory solely for the purpose of finding out if the Japanese system was really as harmonious as it was being portrayed by the automakers. Clearly it was not. From long work hours and poor safety measures, to guarded barracks-style living quarters, Kamata's account is both fascinating and moving — a tale so finely detailed it's difficult to believe it could have been fabricated. One journal entry for instance contains a complete breakdown of Kamata's assembly-line duties, with every single movement carefully recorded.

Yet another passage speaks of the sense of exhaustion and despair the workers have come to feel: "On the night shift. By 5:00 A.M. I'm completely worn out. I've lost the power to think and simply move my hands absent-mindedly. Yesterday I slept only one hour during the day. I ask the others, and they all say they can't sleep during the daytime. The Monday night shift is the hardest because you can't suddenly change your sleeping and waking rhythm. I walk home with Ogi, the 'Red Line.' 'Hey!' I say. 'You've still got thirty-nine years to go before you can retire.' He answers with his usual smile, 'I'll be dead before I stay here that long.'"[2]

It seemed to Kamata and others that producing more cars at a faster rate was all that Toyota cared about. The fact that the company had increased its production from 2,930,000 vehicles in 1978 to 3,070,000 in 1979 with only 30 additional workers seemed to prove his point.[3] A later entry confirms this: "Later Kudo (a colleague) returns to the room furious: 'The company sure cares a lot more about production than it does about our health.' He says the daily output of the drive shafts has been increased from 600 to 700. The workers, though, have to fill the new quota in exactly the same time—from eight in the morning to seven at night. Last year his job was done by three workers, but now he's left to do the entire job alone."[4]

Stories such as Kamata's were not unique to the time. For all the talk of *kanban* (just-in-time production), and *kaizen* (continuous improvement), it seemed that Japan's stunning advancement in the automotive industry was gained in large part the old-fashioned way—through the back-breaking labor of its workers. The situation was in many ways similar to that which existed in America's auto plants before the UAW entered the scene. Unions had been present in Japan since the MacArthur era but most were, up until very recently at least, company unions rather than a separate entity that answered only to its members.

The predominant functions of a Japanese union were to maintain a peaceful existence between management and labor, ensure that working conditions were satisfactory, and curtail any unfair or discriminatory practices. They did not negotiate wages, security, hours, or benefits. Such was the case at least when Kamata wrote his book on Toyota in the 1970s. Even today the Japanese Auto Workers union (JAW) does not operate the way the UAW does in America. Rather less adversarial, the JAW holds periodic sessions called *shunto*, a type of gathering where union leaders and employers meet to reach agreements, and rarely do conditions deteriorate to the point where strike action is necessary. In this way, Japanese automakers have been able to exercise more control over the labor force than have their American counterparts. In return for this control, they have endeavored to keep the workers satisfied by making them feel like part of the team and by engendering pride in the company. This type of doctrine says that if the company succeeds, the workers succeed. Loyalty is a trump card played by both employee and management. Dedication to your job in Japan is a requirement and has usually meant the promise of lifetime employment in return.

The other major factor in Japan's success is the strong work ethic of its people. The work ethic together with loyalty have traditionally been ingrained in the Japanese right from childhood. Individualism is frowned upon and workers and management alike are cautioned to leave their egos at the door. Some employees even take part in "truth exercises" where they are festooned with "ribbons of shame" and go before their colleagues to confess to weaknesses which may have led to errors. This self-abasement is meant as atonement and to relieve the real sense of guilt they feel if a product or service they have had a part in has been substandard. It is difficult to image the same type of exercise occurring in the United States where the expression "passing the buck" originated.

Rightly or wrongly, there is no doubt Japan's methods have catapulted it onto the world's stage, but with the collapse of its economy in the 1990s combined with increased exposure to other cultures, many Japanese are now rejecting the "company is all" philosophy. They no longer want to "live to work"—some now simply want to "work to live." At least this is the new outlook on the part of the workers—employers on the other hand are adhering to the more traditional principles and are nervous about the growing influence of countries like America on their labor force. It is for this reason that Japanese automakers have so persistently and defiantly rejected the UAW at their manufacturing plants in the United States. They also have no intention of abandoning their long-cherished production systems and adopting American methods. According to Lee Iacocca, the Japanese had good reason to be wary of the union. Describing what amounted to a stranglehold the UAW had on the auto industry, Iacocca began his criticism by first assuming part of the blame for the situation. "I was part of that system. Gradually, little by little, we gave into virtually every union demand. We were making so much money that we didn't think twice. We were rarely willing to take a strike, and so we never stood on principle ... our motivation was greed.... Today we're all paying the price for our complacency."[5]

The "killers" were, according to Iacocca, unlimited cost-of-living allowances; "thirty-and-out"— retirement after thirty years with a pension equivalent to 60 percent of the salary regardless of age; and "cradle-to-grave" medical benefits. He pointed out that when he first arrived at Chrysler the company was being billed more by Blue Cross/Blue Shield than by its rubber and steel suppliers.[6] And while Japanese autoworkers were wishing for a five-day work week, American workers were agitating for a four-day work week. Although that never materialized, a consolation was offered in the form of what was known as a "paid personal holiday," where employees were paid to stay at home on days which were not sick days or public holidays.

Toyota, as the largest automaker in Japan, was particularly cognizant of the possible ramifications of a UAW presence. Aside from that, company leaders were thoroughly dedicated to the system that its founder Kiichiro Toyoda dedicated his life to and, as Eiji Toyoda wrote, nearly "...burned himself out working on..."[7] The now-famous Toyota Production System laid the path for what has since become known as "lean production"—a system incorporating the combined elements of *kanban*, *kaizen*, quality control and teamwork.

*Kanban* is a misnomer according to author Steven Schlossstein, who writes that it has been "erroneously translated by us as the just-in-time system. *Kanban* literally means signboard or shingle and refers to the *kanji* character signs that hang outside shops and stores all over Japan, identifying the proprietor or owner."[8] If this is correct, then Eiji Toyoda and many others seem to have ignored the proper translation, for they have continually equated *kanban* with just-in-time in the many books written about the Japanese auto industry. Since the word has been so frequently associated with just-in-time, it will be so used within this text.

The just-in-time method, brought to fruition by Taiichi Ohno and Eiji Toyoda, originally evolved from Kiichiro Toyoda's flow-through production method—a system born out of necessity. Deprived of materials, supplies, and warehouse space, Toyota set the wheels of production into motion only after an order for a vehicle was placed. Parts were produced on an as-needed basis and delivered to the assembly plant "just-in-time." This way no materials were wasted in overproduction, no energy was wasted moving the parts around, and no valuable storage space was wasted holding inventory. Obviously eliminating waste was the main objective of the *kanban* system.

*Kaizen*, or the process of continuous improvement, also came out of necessity. Cash-strapped Japanese plants simply could not afford to hire extra labor to repair defects after they had occurred, so assembly-line workers were enlisted to conduct their own quality control and correct any defects they found on the spot. If a problem required more extensive repair the worker was authorized to pull a cord stopping the assembly line, and then "...to trace systematically every error back to its ultimate cause (by asking 'why' as each layer of the problem was uncovered), then to devise a fix so that it would never occur again."[9]

This additional responsibility instilled a certain amount of pride in the workers who felt that they were a crucial part of the process, which of course they were. Workers were also encouraged to offer suggestions as to how to improve production methods. In fact Toyota took enormous pride in its annual "Good Ideas" contest which originated in the 1950s. Each year management posted the number of ideas received along with a selection of the chosen best in a bulletin each year. It is a practice that has since been adopted by many other Japanese companies.

Another major element of lean production is the cross-training of team members. Even those in top management are encouraged to specialize in more than one area of production. Workers are expected to be as flexible as possible and willing to learn a wide variety of tasks so that they might fill in for each other as needed. Team leaders are similarly cross-trained to perform each other's jobs. Therefore no set job description hindered anyone at a Japanese automotive plant as is the custom in American plants where the refrain "that's not my job" can be heard quite frequently.

According to authors James P. Womack, Daniel T. Jones, and Daniel Roos, lean production is far superior to America's system of mass production: "Mass-producers set a limited goal for themselves—'good enough,' which translates into an acceptable number of defects, a maximum acceptable level of inventories, a narrow range of standardized products. To do better, they argue, would cost too much or exceed inherent human capabilities. Lean producers, on the other hand, set their sights explicitly on perfection: continually declining costs, zero defects, zero inventories, and endless product variety."[10]

But as the authors acknowledge, lean production also carries a down side—for one thing there is substantially more stress placed on both team leader and team member. A lack of a defined job description, while beneficial to those wanting to get the most out of a single employee, is not so desirable to the individual who is forced to learn many different tasks, perform them as ordered and without benefit of extra compensation.

Having no extra labor on hand can also be disastrous should the unexpected happen, such as a shortage of workers due to illness, or a sudden surge in demand. Similarly, waiting until the last minute to order parts can also result in catastrophe if it is discovered the parts are defective or were made to the wrong specifications. But most importantly, it is the constraints on the human element of a company's resources that have caused a growing number of Japanese to become disenchanted with the lean production system. The system that caused the world to take notice also invited unwelcome scrutiny from those whose mandate was to protect the rights of the worker, as well as the workers themselves. There is no doubt of the efficiency of the lean production system, but there is also no doubt that it is somewhat at odds with a union such as the UAW which stands for the employee and not the employer.

When Japanese companies moved into America, they quite naturally brought their production systems with them. Also quite naturally, American laborers did not take kindly to the restrictions they suddenly found themselves under. It wasn't long before problems arose, some of which were documented in books published during the late 1980s and early 1990s. Professor Laurie Graham contributed her experiences as a factory worker at the Subaru-Isuzu plant in Indiana. *On the Line at Subaru-Isuzu: The Japanese Model and the American Worker*, is a critical account of SIA's non-union shop and of the *kaizen* system. Graham maintained that SIA routinely violated workers' rights, particularly concerning injuries, and was also guilty of racial prejudice. In addition, the book contained an assertion that SIA management had coerced some employees into being "anti-union."

Joseph and Suzy Fucini, after working at Mazda's Flat Rock plant in Michigan, recorded some of the many difficulties there in *Working for the Japanese: On the Line at Mazda*. These were identified as inadequate safety measures, discriminatory practices, loss of personal freedom, and excessive work-related stress.

"It was clear that not everyone was entranced by the Mazda system. After viewing a video of Japanese factory workers racing from one car to the next, not even pausing to wipe the sweat off their foreheads, one Mazda applicant commented that if that's the way he'd have to work, he'd rather 'take the highway'—'The more they [the Mazda trainers] talked, the more it sounded like this whole team thing was just a way to squeeze more work out of every worker, with a good dose of old-fashioned paternalism thrown in to keep everybody happy.'"[11]

Heated arguments were also witnessed between team leaders, while some workers resented the fact they had to learn someone else's job — particularly skilled workers who felt insulted by having to learn a job that was "beneath" them. American workers also had a problem displaying the loyalty taken to such extremes by their Japanese co-workers. As the Fucinis noted: "Japanese and Americans had very different ideas about the degree of loyalty and obedience a company should expect from its employees."[12] They also wrote that Mazda was "...no place for anyone who did not share his team leader's intensity..." and that "Workers who were injured trying to keep up with this intense work pace were often ridiculed and harassed by Mazda managers."[13] Employee claims for work injuries were commonly dismissed by Mazda, even after they were confirmed as being work-related by the company's own doctors.

Summing up the situation at Mazda in 1990, the authors wrote: "Despite the magazine articles and television specials that praised the Japanese system for treating workers with dignity and respect, and despite the noble promises made by Mazda during its orientation, workers at Flat Rock were not happy."[14] At the same time, they qualified this pessimistic observation by concluding that: "The Japanese are not hostile toward Americans or American values, they are simply taking a management system that has worked well for them at home and exporting it...."[15]

The system had probably worked so well at home because no union truly represented the worker and the workers themselves would not revolt on their own. In the United States the UAW took a stand against worker abuse, but still conditions were such that Ben Hamper felt moved to write his account of life on the American assembly line. The book *Rivethead* paints a depressing portrait of an autoworker's daily grind and depicts the iciness of management at a GM plant, but one somehow is left with the impression that not all of Hamper's problems were related to poor working conditions or the work itself.

By comparison, when Satoshi Kamata and his colleagues at Toyota read about a revolt in General Motors' Lordstown facility, it was not the fact that some Americans walked off the line while others smashed windshields and slashed seats that caught their attention, but rather "...the most amazing part of the article is that the correspondent reported that he saw workers smoking and chatting while they worked on the line. Those with free time gathered at a table in a corner and played cards.... How could they smoke and play cards when the speed of the line was increased to raise productivity? The article says that the time allowed for one operation was reduced to thirty-six seconds, but that only ten seconds were actually needed. GM workers are well treated compared with Toyota workers. It's hard to believe."[16]

In fact while Americans were working five days a week, Japanese were working six, and for less money. One Toyota employee joked that "The labor productivity at Toyota is as good as that in the United States—and the pay is as low as that in Japan."[17]

As to the hours, Toyota's union issued a statement which contained the following message: "Since Toyota has developed rapidly and has entered into fair competition with overseas companies, and because international opinion has also asked us to establish proper and fair working conditions, the question of the five-day work week system must be faced up to and must be solved as quickly as possible by labor and management."[18] But Toyota's president at first resisted the change, citing severe sales competition, restrictions imposed by antipollution requirements, and the need to stay in first place as well as to expand operations overseas.[19]

According to some, conditions had been steadily deteriorating rather than improving over the years. One long-time Toyota employee recounted to Kamata his story about the changes he himself had witnessed: "Now the work is nearly three times tougher than when I came here six or seven years ago. Around 1965, they measured our work by stopwatch. Since then it's been getting tougher. But until a couple of years ago we still had enough workers, and the line used to stop ten minutes before finishing time.... You read in the papers that Toyota workers are quick and active. We're not quick. We're forced to work quickly. It's the ones up there who benefit by exploiting us down here."[20]

Translator Tatsuru Akimoto confirmed that this still held true in 1982: "This book depicts the realities of 1972–73. If the situation has changed at all, it is only in the sense that the work has become much more difficult, the levels of production greatly increased, and the workers' frustrations more widespread than ever. The only real difference is that the work situation is worse and the competitive power of Toyota stronger."[21]

Since 1982 working conditions have gradually improved in both Japan and America. Not much could be done about the heat, noise, and boredom, but as the Fucinis noted, some plants were more pleasant than others. When a group of American workers hired by Mazda were sent to Japan for training, they were astounded at the conditions they found at Mazda's Hofu plant. "The American plants that they were familiar with were Dickensian dungeons compared to the bright and spotless Mazda plant that greeted them at Hofu. There were no burned-out lightbulbs as there were at so many American plants, where every other light seemed to be out; no discarded equipment tossed into a corner away from the line to collect dust; no tools strewn about the work area like a child's toys; no metal scraps and shavings speckling the floor; no rivers of oil running down the sides of machinery gathering into greasy puddles."[22]

A similar story was recounted by Schlossstein in *Trade War: Greed, Power, and Industrial Policy on Opposite Sides of the Pacific*. After touring Nissan's Zama plant in Japan, the author recorded his impressions: "It was so quiet in the central assembly building that we could carry on a normal conversation without raising our voices. In Detroit, the first thing you notice when you enter an assembly plant is the incredible noise level…. You don't talk, you shout, in Detroit."[23]

The other negative aspect of factory work is the mindless repetition which wreaks havoc with mind, body, and soul. Some of that repetition was alleviated when robotics were introduced but initially, rather than acting as an aid to the human worker, robots ended up exerting pressure, creating a need for humans to work even faster. As Maryann Keller recorded, GM's first experiments with robotics proved to be disastrous: "Automation, it was suggested, was a ruthless direction; it created a salt mines environment, sapping dry creativity and pride from the American labor force and leaving workers deadened with boredom and unmotivated…. The problem wasn't with the robots, per se. The problem was designing a system that integrated humans and robots in a compatible work environment. GM thought it could reduce the number of workers by replacing them with robots; instead, the workers had to stay on the line because of frequent robot breakdowns."[24]

But breakdowns were only one side of the issue. There was also the question of safety. Workers were frequently injured by robots, and in 1987 this was tragically illustrated by the death of Donald Morris, a GM employee in a Delco Remy plant. Morris was crushed by a robot he was attempting to repair, an accident that, according to Keller, GM tried to keep quiet. Still the company pursued its automation policy, particularly under the directorship of Roger Smith whose fascination with robotics was well documented. Unfortunately, as Keller noted, the technological advances made by GM were still inadequate against the Japanese machine: "The Japanese system of continuous improvement on older equipment worked better than the typical American solution of investing in state-of-the-art technology that the workers were poorly trained to operate…. How different things were in the Japanese factory systems! It is ironic that we once feared the Japanese for their secret high-tech industrial weaponry when, in fact, they were slow to implement technology for the very reasons it was such a disaster at General Motors."[25]

And while General Motors was battling to conquer its own automation, Ford and Chrysler were almost relieved that they couldn't afford the problematic robotics. Japanese manufacturers also looked askance at the mounting difficulties at GM and approached robotics in their plants with extreme caution. This was increasingly difficult as joint ventures with American companies began to take place in the 1980s, forcing Japanese automakers to mesh with their new American partners.

But by far the most problematic area was that of labor relations. Toyota, however, had a substantial say in how labor was managed at the Toyota/GM plant (NUMMI) as officials at GM were anxious to learn Toyota's management secrets. The result was that labor relations were not nearly as acrimonious as they were at GM's other facilities. In an historic agreement between the UAW and NUMMI, NUMMI management agreed to pay American-scale wages and benefits if the UAW would accept the Toyota Production System — which they did. The first collective bargaining agreement was signed in June of 1985 between UAW Local 2244 and NUMMI. The contract contained a "no lay off" policy. Other elements of the agreement included non-confrontational problem resolutions; consultation in advance with the union on business issues; minimum job classifications; and a "no-strike" provision over production and safety standards. The NUMMI philosophy also carried over into the area of traditional American-style management perks. There were to be no executive dining rooms, no reserved parking spaces, and no private office suites.

In the late 1980s, NUMMI was selected as a model of labor-management relations by the then–Secretary of Labor William Brock and presented as a case study at the International Labor Organization Conference. Gary Convis, the first American to head a Toyota-operated plant, credited the success to the Toyota Production System which focused heavily on the involvement of the worker. When Toyota opened its plant in Georgetown, Kentucky, Convis commented that it was "...common for the production lines to stop hundreds of times during each shift.... It does affect production and may create more overtime, but we feel it's a legitimate tradeoff because it ensures that we are building quality into the cars."[26] It also forced the Toyota team members to work harder, as senior vice-president Jim Olson confirmed to *Time* magazine, calling the system the 'Toyota vise': There's this hatred of waste, and [you're] continually driving to get more for less. You're never happy. You're never allowed to be satisfied. Attacks and setbacks are only used as learning exercises."[27] Toyota trainer Randy Sinkhorn also spoke to *Time* writers, telling them that he is often asked if he "works like a dog for 15 or 20 hours a day"— to which he replies that he does not.[28]

But for the hours worked, Toyota has paid well — but not well enough according to some. In 2001 team members hired for Toyota's Buffalo, West Virginia, plant were offered $14.25 per hour to start. In 2000, Kentucky worker Steve Vincent agitated for wage parity with unionized workers and put up a website to foster pro-UAW feelings among Toyota workers. The *Detroit News* interviewed Vincent and commented on his mission to bring the UAW to Toyota: "If history is a guide, an organizing drive at Toyota would be an uphill battle for the UAW. Most auto factories owned by foreign manufacturers in the United States are non-union."[29] This was particularly true at Nissan, where the UAW was definitely not welcome.

In his 2001 Labor Day message, then–UAW president Stephen P. Yokich directly targeted Nissan as a company whose workers were in need of organizing. Yokich did not mince words when he spoke out against companies that treated their workers as less valuable than the machinery they operated. Neither did he have patience with what he perceived as insincere sentiments: "…they call their workers 'associates' or 'partners,' and use touchy-feely slogans like 'our people are our most important resource.' But let a few of their most important resources start talking about forming a union, and suddenly it's back to the '30s. In the vast majority of workplaces, workers who try to organize face intimidation, threats, harassment, and protracted legal maneuvering—all designed to break their spirit and shatter their solidarity."[30]

Mentioning Nissan, Yokich stressed the fact that many such non-union factories do pay wages equal to that of unionized shops, but that there is something more important than money. "Most employers," he said, "don't want their workers to have a seat at the decision-making table; they want to dictate, not negotiate. And while wages, benefits, and working conditions are obviously important to all workers, what inspires them to stand up for themselves and organize in the face of fierce employer resistance is their determination to have a voice in the decisions that affect their lives instead of letting a powerful few call all the shots."[31]

The fact remained, though, that Nissan workers voted 2 to 1 against the UAW in 1989, a humiliating defeat for the union. In fact it had been an exercise in futility before Nissan even built its first American plant. UAW president Doug Fraser traveled to Japan to meet with Nissan leader Takashi Ishihara. The mutually frustrating meeting gradually deteriorated into a war of words with Fraser accusing Nissan of being undemocratic and Ishihara denouncing American labor in general. He was blunt in his criticism of the UAW and the poor quality its workers produced. But the UAW/Ishihara conflict wasn't the only battle going on—there was fighting within the ranks at Nissan as well. Nissan's own union leader, Ichiro Shioji, thought allowing the UAW in would be a wise move and one that would endear them more to the American community they were about to enter. Ishihara's answer was to hire anti-unionist Marvin Runyon to head the new plant in Tennessee.

The blow to the UAW as a result of failing to organize at Nissan was a particularly harsh one in light of the fact that union membership had fallen from 1.5 million members in 1970 to only 733,000 in 2001.[32] The southern states were known for their anti-union leanings and therefore losing Nissan left the South virtually closed to the UAW. But it was not for lack of trying.

The petition filed by Nissan workers with the National Labor Relations Board in August of 2001 calling for a union election was the UAW's third attempt to organize the Tennessee facilities. Speaking to the *Detroit News*, UAW vice-president Bob King explained there was a difference in the latest bid to unionize, citing the fact that workers were "more aware of disparities between Smyrna and UAW plants in wages and benefits, retirement plans, layoff protections and workplace injury policies."[33]

One week later the same paper reported that "The United Auto Workers union blamed a lack of vocal supporters inside Nissan Motor Co.'s Smyrna, Tenn., plant for its stunning organizing defeat Wednesday. In a high-profile election, workers voted 3,103 to 1,486 to reject the union's bid to represent 4,800 employees at the plant."[34] One of the problems the UAW claimed they faced was the intimidation Nissan inflicted upon its workers along with hours and hours of "anti-union rhetoric." They also felt that the union was repeatedly denied access to Nissan workers, and King even went so far as to accuse the company of conducting illegal surveillance of

Nissan workers engaged in pro-union activities. But many still felt the writing had been on the wall all along.

Writing about the defeat in the *Labor Educator*, Harry Kelber offered an explanation as to why the UAW lost so heavily at Nissan: "Obviously, UAW organizers overestimated the value of the signed cards they had collected. There is no assurance that a card signer will cast a ballot for the union."[35] Probing deeper into the cause, Kelber continued: "Community support in the town of 25,000 was not only lacking — many residents were actually hostile toward the UAW. People in Smyrna are grateful to the Japanese company for revitalizing the local economy."[36]

Charles W. Baird, writing for the Smith Center for Private Enterprise Studies, had even harsher criticism for what he saw as King's naïveté: "He just doesn't get it. In 1989 the UAW lost its first certification election at Nissan by approximately the same decisive margin. It dropped attempts even to get an election in Smyrna in 1997 and again in 2000 for lack of worker interest. The message seems clear: Nissan workers in Tennessee want to remain union-free. They want the UAW to go away, but because it's so desperate, the UAW will probably continue to try to capture Nissan workers."[37]

It's difficult to "capture workers" when those workers are averaging $22 per hour and are receiving satisfactory benefits while working in a clean, bright environment. Union shops, on the other hand, must operate according to a myriad of regulations and complex structures which, as Baird summarized, renders them "...impaired by their lack of ability to adapt to rapidly changing market conditions that have become common due to globalization of competition."[38]

But the UAW show no signs of giving up where Japanese automakers are concerned. Even while digesting the bitter Nissan defeat, Bob King indicated his intentions to target the Honda Motor Company's American operations. He told *Detroit News* reporter Joe Miller that "Honda's a possibility. Workers at Honda have asked us to come down there."[39] But the UAW's history with Honda is not a promising one. The union attempted to organize the company when petitions for elections were filed in 1985 and again in 1989, but no elections ever took place. So adamant were Honda workers that no UAW presence was required that they formed their own anti-union group called the Honda Associates' Alliance. Working conditions, wages, and benefits were, according to Honda workers, quite satisfactory. In fact, the Honda management system has since become legendary due to its elements of team spirit and fair play. Writing in *Honda: An American Success Story*, Robert L. Shook stressed the positive approach Honda adopted with its team: "Honda cares. While critics may scowl at this statement and declare it a PR snow job, Honda's caring attitude is as much an integral part of its success story as its technological and marketing achievements."[40] Associates, Shook reported, were allowed to vote on issues that affected the company as well as themselves. Honda's philosophy was very much one of "there is less need for unions if employers treat employees well." "It's apparent," Shook wrote, "that the people who work for this company feel as though they, themselves, are winners. It's a rare spirit in our American business world."[41]

Associates are asked to contribute ideas for improving production methods and are rewarded when those ideas are chosen to be implemented. They are encouraged to participate in *waigaya*, or "chattering," a system of offering opinions, expressing concerns, or raising questions—in short, speaking freely. Like team members at Toyota plants, Honda associates are very much involved in quality control and take pride in their product. Typical of a Japanese-run operation, individualism is held in check, with all, including the president, wearing identical uniforms.

Not exactly a welcome mat for the UAW, or for that matter Teamsters Local 413, who were also attempting to organize at Honda. And in fact neither union could find a crack in a seemingly impenetrable wall—at least that is until Honda began to hire contract workers whose wages were half those of the full-time employees. There were also increasing complaints of inconsistent work rules and a lack of retirement benefits to go on. But these claims were refuted by Honda Associate Alliance member Angie Dowell in a letter to the editor of the *Columbus Free Press* in 1999.

Tackling the issues one by one, Dowell firmly reiterated Honda's anti-union stance, stating that the company "is not in need of any representation for associates by any union or other collective bargaining organization. Based upon our current wages, benefits and structure, our group maintains that such unionization would serve no meaningful purpose for associates. If anything, such an organization would strain the current communication between associates and management."[42]

Moving on to the complaint regarding the number of contract workers hired, Dowell offered her own statistics: "The Teamsters have grossly exaggerated the number of temporary workers at H.A.M. Initially, they claimed that H.A.M. employed 5,000 temporary laborers. Within days, they revised that figure to 3,000. The fact of the matter is that H.A.M. averaged less than 860 full time Temps during the last fiscal year which ended in March 1999."[43]

Addressing the criticism of lack of an early retirement package, Dowell pointed out that Honda had only been operating for 20 years—an insufficient time to employ a worker with more than 20 years' service.

Her final point focused on benefits, and to union supporters who protested that Honda reserved the right to change its benefits without notice, she cited the fact that most union contracts carry similar clauses. Dowell directed her conclusion to those Honda employees who were being made to feel guilty for voting against unionization: "You are not alone in your quest to remain in control of your own future: in fact you are part of the overwhelming majority."[44]

Recognizing sure defeat, the Teamsters withdrew their attempts to organize. The UAW, on the other hand, intends to persist, as Bob King indicated to the *Detroit News*. But with failures mounting in a heap around his feet, the prospects of organizing a Japanese-owned manufacturing plant seem dim at best. This is bad news for the UAW who are in need of a boost to their membership. They are also facing difficulties in Big Three plants due to massive layoffs and downsizing. Consequently they have been forced to concede on some key issues—contract workers being one of them. Some people are now even accusing the UAW of becoming more like Japanese unions—that is, on the side of the corporations rather than the workers.

Certainly there's not much that can be done about the increasing trend toward out-sourcing of labor and moving production to countries where lower wages are more readily accepted. Having much of the assembly work done by outside firms allows automakers to substantially reduce the number of their full-time workforce. But it is not a practice that sits well with unions and workers alike.

In 1997 GM felt the displeasure of its employees when they went on strike to protest these new cost-cutting strategies. But as was pointed out in the *Harvard Business Review*, Toyota had managed to pay its workers the highest rates in the industry at its NUMMI factory while offering job security and topping GM's productivity by 50 percent. "...General Motors apparently did not learn its lesson that what matters is not pay rate but productivity."[45] It was noted that it took General Motors 46 hours to assemble a car, Ford 37.92, Toyota 29.44, and Nissan 27.36.[46]

However, the situation at GM had improved by 2001 when the *Harbour Report* issued its annual production statistics for the automotive industry. While Nissan again topped the list in assembly productivity, followed closely by Honda and Toyota, GM was voted the company most improved. Ron Harbour attributed GM's improvements to the implementation of the Japanese style of operation: "For the past several years, GM has been working very hard on implementing lean manufacturing systems and processes throughout its operations...."[47]

But for all the changes taking place in the American auto industry, it seems unlikely that American workers will change very drastically. They will retain their individualism for it is a vital part of their culture. At the same time they will, for the most part and within reason, adapt to whatever principles management adheres to. In the end it remains the managers who must examine their production methods and effect any changes necessary to keep their company competitive in the global marketplace.

Now that Americans have been exposed to work Japanese-style and the Japanese have seen American-style concern for the individual, it seems likely that manufacturing production methods may eventually come out somewhere in the middle where neither can accuse the other of unfair labor practices or be suspicious of the other's methods. Until then, barriers will remain between American and Japanese companies and workers, barriers which will rank in importance alongside those of trade between U.S. and Japanese automakers.

# 18

## The Return of the Unequal Treaties—U.S.-Japan Trade

Japan's legendary rise as an economic power would have been inconceivable to Commodore Matthew Perry when he first encountered that distant and isolated nation in the 1850s. But even at that time there were indications of the formidable trading partner Japan would later become. While those initial treaties brought over by Perry were undoubtedly heavily weighted in favor of the United States, they nevertheless contained stipulations designed to protect Japan's innermost sanctity. The most important of these was the preclusion of foreigners from investing in any of its industries or financial centers. It was a Shogunate strategy that allowed them to sell without "selling out."

Initially textiles were Japan's main exports and from these commodities sprang the first inklings of the trade friction that would later become a major source of contention between it and America. If there were any doubts as to Japan's intention to become a worthy trading partner, they were quickly dispelled by Japan's rapid and prolific production. As former trade negotiator Clyde V. Prestowitz, Jr., noted in *Trading Places: How We Allowed Japan to Take the Lead*, by the 1930s "Japan dominated Asia's textile markets and was making such large inroads elsewhere that it was being condemned for unfair competition by Western countries that only eighty years before had demanded it enter into trade with them."[1]

But even with this harbinger of things to come, the West—and especially America—continued to view Japan's progress with an unconcerned and patronizing eye. After all, how powerful could a country roughly the size of Montana and almost totally bereft of natural resources become? From this perspective it is understandable that not only the United States but also the rest of the world underestimated what appeared to be a perpetually struggling nation. When viewed from afar, these struggles seemed desperately chaotic with the true nature of the activity hidden from Western eyes. Behind the scenes were shrewd and astute strategists mapping out the nation's road to success. One key strategy lay in the simple theory of "strength in numbers"—a concept that the Japanese put their considerable energy behind. To achieve this strength, the government supported industry, industry obeyed the government, and the worker obeyed the industry. Wealth was held by the powerful *zaibatsu* groups. In other words, it was a "one-for-all and all-for-one" society.

But this system couldn't function without certain basic components—a populace raised to devote themselves to the welfare of their country; determined, ambitious and industrious business leaders; financial groups interested in accruing power and wealth; and finally a protective and even domineering government. This solidarity allowed even as tiny a nation as Japan to run like a well-oiled machine while presenting a strong and unified front to the world. The homogenous nature of the country also assisted by keeping the internal conflicts common to many culturally diverse nations to a minimum.

This formula was enormously successful up until World War II when its own military drew it into catastrophic defeat by the United States. Facing widespread devastation, poverty, and famine, the Japanese were forced to rebuild once again, but this time under the strict control of the American occupying forces. The locomotive that had been steaming out of control was now derailed and new, more democratic tracks were laid.

General MacArthur's disbanding of the *zaibatsu* groups was done for a number of reasons, not least to attempt to control Japan's trade, as explained by John W. Dower in *Embracing Defeat: Japan in the Wake of World War II*: "Improving the lives of the working population by promoting higher wages, higher incomes, and a more equitable distribution of wealth, the argument went, would create a larger domestic market and inhibit the dumping of underpriced goods abroad."[2]

At that time Japan's exports were seen as cheap and certainly inferior to Western-world products, and as such contributed to America's view of Japan as a non-threatening presence in world trade. This is well illustrated by Dower, who wrote: "It was taken for granted that Japan's future markets lay primarily in the less-developed countries of Asia, not in the United States or Europe. At a cocktail party in Tokyo only days before the Korean War began, President Truman's special envoy John Foster Dulles blithely but typically told a high Finance Ministry official that the country should consider exporting things like, well, cocktail napkins to the United States."[3] But, as Dower wryly commented, "No one on the Japanese side focused on cocktail napkins."[4]

Far from it. In fact, the plan to rebuild now hinged on creating new and more viable exports, and because of Japan's lack of natural resources most of these would be value-added commodities which would lead to further problems between Japan and the United States. Ironically, many of Japan's so-called future trade advantages, such as the undervaluing of the yen, were created by American economist Joseph Dodge who was called to Japan by MacArthur to "help stabilize the economy."[5]

While the Japanese had no choice but to carry out the American reforms to their system, they had not abandoned their own ideas of how their country should be run. Practically from the moment the Americans departed in 1952, the Japanese commenced with their plans which included a revival of many traditional Japanese ways.

To begin with, the "strength in numbers" mentality once again prevailed, and the *zaibatsu* was reborn as the *keiretsu*. A typical *keiretsu* included a bank, one or more trading companies, an industry, as well as an assortment of businesses, the objective being to cover as many key sectors as possible. They were intricately organized and led by an elite group of financial executives. The strength of a *keiretsu*, and they are still in existence today, lies in the fact that each segment looks after the interests of the other. If one company flounders, its *keiretsu* partners will not let it go down. Such was the case in the 1970s when the Sumitomo *keiretsu* rescued one of its members, the Mazda Corporation, from near-bankruptcy.

In addition, the Ministry of International Trade and Industry (MITI) resumed its powerful hold over not only all trade and export issues, but also over how industries conducted their operations.

Aside from these seemingly impenetrable and financially sound groups, Japan also had the advantage of cheap labor — workers so grateful for employment that they agreed to work for much less than their Western counterparts, a situation that Americans saw as being unfair. Another sticking point stemmed from the "biting the hand that fed them" school of thought — the fact that America helped to rebuild Japan after World War II, providing factories and in some cases more modern equipment than certain American manufacturers had, did not sit well. That the Allied forces practically annihilated Japan in the first place has not been deemed relevant and in any case only degenerates into the "well they started it" type of argument.

Advantages and disadvantages in this case can be debated almost endlessly, but the fact remains that the Japanese were determined to gain a reputation as a serious trade partner and toward that effort they signed the General Agreement on Tariffs and Trade (GATT) in 1955. Only two years later that reputation was tarnished when the country was accused of "dumping" cotton onto U.S. markets.

America's charges of dumping were then and remain today probably the largest source of friction between it and Japan. Many Japanese believe it is impossible to dump a product into a country so large, strong, and diversified. They further believe that they are providing goods at reasonable prices to feed a demand that obviously exists. Their ideas of competing seem to differ widely from those of Americans. If they can produce something that is of good quality for less money then that is to their advantage. This is seen as only common sense and a necessary part of looking after their own interests. If their government protects them and assists them in producing these goods then that, too, is perceived as an intelligent strategy. Certainly their trade surplus bears this out. They wonder why America does not know how to compete in its own market.

Americans, on the other hand, see major ideological differences in how Japan operates as compared to their own style. Producing goods more cheaply can mean an infringement on human rights, which goes against American principles. Yet many American companies have moved production facilities to countries where they can save on wages and benefits. They also protest against the Japanese government which acts as a "mother hen" to the nation's industries by keeping imports at bay with all manner of regulations as well as both tariff and non-tariff barriers. What Americans may fail to realize is that this type of protection is to be expected from a nation of people trained to look after their own best interests. As Lee Iacocca pointed out, the Japanese only wonder why America doesn't do the same. In short, what is considered unfair by America is not considered unfair by the Japanese — but rather the only way to get ahead, which is their primary goal.

American responses to Japan's trade practices have varied historically depending upon who the president was at the time. The fierce protectionism which had taken root in America in the 1930s had gradually given way until John F. Kennedy sponsored the Trade Expansion Act in 1962 and called for a true system of free trade.

But the winds of change were fanned by fresh accusations of Japan's dumping of steel onto U.S. markets in 1969. This was followed by the mass exportation of televisions and electronics in the 1970s and continued until the government closed ranks once again by creating the new Trade Act in 1974 which was far more protectionist in nature. By that time the trade imbalance was growing uncomfortably large and American industrialists and business people insisted that what protection they had was inadequate, while the government clung to the shreds of free trade. In each case some sort of voluntary restraint went into effect without noticeable difference and not until the American electronics industry among others had taken a major body blow.

The next threat and the one most relevant to this text came from an unexpected sector of Japan's industry — automobiles. It hardly seemed possible after the Japanese had stumbled so badly in the American market in the early 1960s that less than 20 years later a glut of inexpensive and well-built Japanese automobiles was landing on American shores. Daniel Burstein commented on this turn of events in his book *Yen!: Japan's New Financial Empire and Its Threat to America*: "Based on the history of U.S.–Japan economic relations since the arrival of the Toyopets, it would be unwise to continue underestimating either Japanese ambition or abilities."[6]

Dedicating four pages of point-form examples of how Japan had come to dominate the United States in both trade and economy, Burstein left no doubt as to the results of the disparity between the two nations as of 1988. Predominant among these was the fact that "all ten of the world's ten largest banks (ranked by deposits) are today Japanese."[7] and "The total value of all stocks listed on the Tokyo Stock Exchange surpassed the total value of all stocks listed on the New York Stock Exchange early in 1987."[8]

These were shocking and impossible facts for Americans to digest. Particularly slow to accept the approaching realities in the 1970s were the Big Three automakers. Indeed up until 1979 there had been little reason to doubt America's supremacy as the world's largest producer of automobiles. This is mainly why, when the dam did burst, there were not enough buckets in the world to bail out the American auto industry. There were no sandbags, no retaining walls, no preparation for such a contingency. The only thing to do was to go to the government and ask for help. The best way to do this was to present the case as being entirely out of the control of the Big Three — which necessitated painting Japan as the villain.

Naturally one of the most vocal protesters was Lee Iacocca who by then had some experience in approaching the government for assistance. Claiming that Japan's auto industry had been "wrapped in a cocoon of protection,"[9] Iacocca insisted that

America do the same for its industry. His tirade against "the monster" he claimed America gave birth to began with accusations of unfair tax advantages, moved to cheap labor and ended with currency manipulation which was "enough to bring you to your knees."[10] Free trade, sneered Iacocca, was nothing more than an illusion. "We're the only country in the world that comes close to practicing free trade — and we're getting clobbered…. They've already taken electronics. They've taken sporting goods. They've taken copiers. They've taken cameras. They've taken a quarter of the automobile industry. Along the way, they've taken a quarter of the steel industry, too. The Japanese have a clever way of smuggling their steel into the United States. They paint it, put it on four wheels, and call it a car."[11]

With ranting like this, it's not difficult to see the nature of the pressure brought to bear on the government to "do something." But while the Big Three were hollering "unfair," they were conveniently forgetting the fact that their founding fathers had all but wiped out Japan's fledgling auto industry in the 1920s and 1930s. In fact until Japan enacted the Automobile Manufacturing Law in 1936, no Japanese automobile company had a fighting chance against Ford and GM.

The other factor that fell victim to the industry leaders' temporary amnesia was America's own history of protectionist policies. While accusing Japan of having a closed market and for erecting non-tariff barriers, Big Three proponents had neglected to mention some of America's non-tariff barriers which included something called the American Selling Price (ASP) which meant that exporters paid a tariff based not on the price of the commodity in their country, but rather on the price of that same commodity in the United States. And as Steven Schlossstein pointed out, there was also the U.S. measurement system to contend with which added cost for exporters forced to adapt their products to it. In addition, there was the fact that when the American government had a choice of buying either American or foreign-made goods, a 6 to 12 percent price preference was offered in favor of the American goods over the foreign ones.[12]

Perhaps it was for these reasons that the Carter administration was hesitant to even broach the subject with their counterparts in Japan. Carter's advisors felt that Detroit was responsible for its own downfall by not building successful small cars to compete with the imports.

In the end the decision was left for Ronald Reagan who was handed the issue after he took office in 1980. After reflecting on the nation's deep recession and record unemployment particularly in the automotive sector, Reagan finally succumbed to the pressure. This pressure emanated not only from the manufacturing sector, but also from the UAW who had been clamoring for protection almost from the moment Japanese cars started to be popular in the United States. This is aptly illustrated by the writings of one UAW member in 1970: "There is a need for immediate legislation to build a framework of true international economic cooperation — which could preserve two-way foreign trade and at the same time preserve American employment. The time is past due for federal trade arrangements which will call for built-in limitations on the use and importation of low-labor cost foreign products and services in order that our own industries and jobs can endure."[13]

Unfortunately the jobs did not endure and by the end of 1980 over 200,000 were unemployed, with the Big Three reporting record losses. It was enough to prompt Transportation Secretary Drew Lewis to assemble a task force to report on why import restraints should be imposed. Senators John Danforth and Lloyd Bentsen also supported the restraints and announced their intention to introduce a bill to that effect.

When Japanese government officials got the word that they would be asked to impose voluntary export restraints, they were displeased to say the least. They traveled to Washington to report that they would not "be squeezed out" of the American market.[14] But as David Halberstam indicated in *The Reckoning,* the trade imbalance could not be allowed to continue, despite Japan's ruffled feathers: "Trade with Japan was so one-sided as to smack of reverse colonialism: The Western nations shipped raw materials to the Japanese, who turned them into finished goods that they sold back to the West."[15] It was true that America's exports to Japan were non-value added goods, including soybeans, corn, lumber, coal and wheat.

The Japanese, being shrewd enough to realize that the Americans were in a near-panic state, conceded to the restraints against the wishes of the Japanese automakers themselves who were reportedly furious over their government's "betrayal." In his autobiography Eiji Toyoda commented on the situation thus: "The trade friction between Japan and the U.S. following the second oil shock is probably as close as we have come to a crisis."[16] Reflecting on the issue calmly and rationally, Toyoda wrote that: "It was only to be expected that if Japan did well in the American market, the U.S. would fight back."[17] His philosophy on trade in general was expressed in a laconic manner: "Trade friction always is going to be around wherever there's competition in business. Conflict of this sort will disappear only if one side accepts total defeat. But complete capitulation by Japan is out of the question, as is a total routing of our trade partners, because Japan relies on trade for its very existence, to give this up would be to roll over and die."[18]

Underscoring these sentiments were reports that officials at Toyota and Nissan were enraged by the trade conflict and voluntary export restraints.

Whatever the barely concealed feelings of the Japanese industrialists, in April of 1981 the two nations announced the voluntary export restraint agreement which was to be in effect for a period of three years. The limit on exports of Japanese cars was set at 1.68 million for the first year. The Japanese government duly doled out U.S. market-share allotments to the Japanese automakers, based on 1979 sales.

The limitations imposed meant that the average price in America of a Japanese car immediately rose by approximately 14 percent. This price rise in turn meant higher profits for the automakers since demand continued to grow despite the efforts to check it. The reaction in Japan was evident when the combined stock value of the six firms rose $915 million in just two days.[19]

Typically, the Japanese sensed further American irritation and, fearing more severe limitations, quickly implemented a new strategy to counterbalance the restraints—the penetration of the high-priced, high-profit luxury car market. In the meantime they still had the restraints to deal with.

By 1984, the total quota for Japanese cars was raised to 1.85 million cars and again raised in 1985 to 2.3 million. The new allotments brought disputes among those jostling for market share. General Motors, whose affiliation with Isuzu and Suzuki placed it in both the domestic and exporter categories, drew fire from Japanese automakers for requesting special concessions. Ford and Chrysler were also upset by these requests, contending that GM did not merit any special treatment.

Yet despite the restraints which were having no obvious negative effect on the Japanese, the U.S industry continued to struggle. Some consumers finding Japanese cars suddenly more expensive turned to American showrooms and expected to receive a hefty price break. This hobbled Detroit who had foreseen some rather juicy price increases of their own. Nevertheless, between 1986 and 1990 overall profits to the Big Three did increase by approximately $2 billion per year.[20] But as officials at the Political Economy Research Center noted, it was not a win-win situation: "The big losers were American car buyers.... After accounting for the higher profits of American automakers, the U.S. economy as a whole thus suffered a loss of some $13 billion due to the restraints on Japanese car exports."[21]

The other effect had to do with American protests of Japan's closed market. In 1986 Japan's Advisory Group on Economic Structural Adjustment for International Harmony issued the Maekawa Report. This report called for the expansion of imports and domestic demand in order to counteract Japan's rapidly increasing U.S. trade surplus. In addition, the rising value of the yen after 1985 prompted Japanese automakers to increase both investment and production facilities in the United States. It was still not enough. In 1989 the Japan–U.S. Structural Impediments Initiative talks commenced in a further effort to reduce trade friction and correct the imbalance. Still Japan's surplus continued to increase and in 1993 the Japan–U.S. Framework for a New Economic Partnership was established, achieving modest success. *Time* magazine reported in 1994 that the Big Three "expect to sell 37,000 imported cars in Japan, almost double last year's total. That still represents less than 1% of the 4 million cars sold in Japan annually...."[22]

But these small gains were insufficient to hold back the growing tide of American resentment and anti-Japanese feelings. On May 9, 1995, the U.S. Senate voted on a resolution to impose trade sanctions against Japan after talks collapsed on May 5 of that year. Those voting in favor of the sanctions contended that: "Japan closes its automotive markets to United States imports in order to charge artificially high prices to Japanese customers. It then uses its excessive profits to subsidize exports, making them artificially more competitive. Japanese cars and parts cost more in Japan than in the United States. The devastating result of this policy has been to increase greatly the trade deficit with the United States. In fact, 56 percent of the enormous $66 billion trade deficit we had with Japan last year was attributable to trade in cars and auto parts."[23]

Senator Chuck Hagel, Chairman of the Subcommittee on International Economic Policy, Export and Trade Promotion, called the deficit "a cause for worry in the long-term," adding that "We may find ourselves in trouble if we reach a point at which foreign claims on U.S. assets become so great that we have difficulty paying them off.... The correct approach to dealing with these continued high trade deficits is to open new foreign markets for American goods and services." The senator concluded that: "shutting down our markets...only hurts us."[24]

Much of the blame, according to other senators, belonged to the cliquish *keiretsu* system, which seemed to exclude Americans as well as others trying to export to and sell within Japan. Pointing out that Section 301 of the Trade Act allowed tariff retaliation against unfair trade practices, the senators vowed: "If Japan does not quickly relent and open its market, we strongly encourage imposing sanctions under Section 301."[25]

Scorning Japan's threat to take the United States before the World Trade Organization if it went ahead and imposed the sanctions, the senators declared: "We welcome such an action, the United States will defend its sanctions vigorously, and it should prevail because sanctions are justified."[26]

The results of the Senate vote were 90 percent for the sanctions and 10 percent against. Those opposing offered the argument that sanctions were bound to be counterproductive since they would leave the United States isolated if a trade war ensued. They also feared that the yen would be devalued and Japan might even switch its reserves from dollars to deutschmarks.

There were others who felt the Clinton administration mishandled the delicate situation. James P. Przystup and Robert P. O'Quinn wrote in the Heritage Foundation F.Y.I. Report that: "...the Clinton team was committed to applying intense external pressure to get its way. The final miscalculation was that, in the post–Cold War world, this pressure could be applied with little collateral political damage."[27]

Nevertheless, on May 16, U.S. Trade Representative Mickey Kantor announced that a 100 percent tariff on thirteen models of Japanese cars valued at over $30,000 would be imposed. The total value was estimated at $5.9 billion per year.

It was regrettable news for a Japan that was now battling through the effects of a major recession caused by the bursting of its "bubble" economy in 1991. Peak production for Japanese automobile manufacturers had reached 13.48 million automobiles in 1990, but from there it fell to 10.1 million in 2000 — a level which is considered a major watermark in the industry. Sales for 2000 were below six million units.[28]

Subsequently the two governments engaged in intense negotiations to resolve the dispute and on June 28, 1995, they reached an agreement which averted the proposed tariffs but ill feelings remained on both sides. Japan's automakers felt that it was America's own fault they could not compete in Japan's market, and American automakers still harbored resentment over Japan's continuing success in theirs.

There were many who concurred with Japan's view. Gil Bamford was one. Writing in the May 1998 edition of the American International Automobile Dealers Association (AIADA) newsletter *Showroom*, Bamford commented that: "The possibility that Japanese consumers may simply prefer Japanese and European cars to U.S. models was never seriously considered. Nor was the apparent futility of building a dealer network to sell cars consumers don't want."[29]

Steven Schlossstein devoted long passages in his book *Trade War* to what could only be labeled as American short-sightedness. Like many other industry analysts, Schlossstein pointed to an overpaid American workforce and a "sick" automobile industry. "Economists call this phenomenon 'declining international industrial competitiveness,' and it had nothing whatsoever to do with trade. Washington complained that Japan kept Detroit's large cars out of their market by means of various tariff and non-tariff barriers. But Detroit couldn't even sell its monsters in our domestic market, let alone overseas."[30] Part of this was due, as Schlossstein saw it, to the fact that Detroit didn't even bother to try to design the cars to fit the Japanese market: "...Detroit calmly rolls its Cadillacs and Continentals off the assembly line with steering wheels irrevocably positioned on the left-hand side, just as they drive them in Bloomfield Hills. And when the monsters get to Japan, assuming they make it through the rat's nest of custom procedures, they no doubt contribute to Japan's growing perplexity with America."[31]

Concerning the restraints, the author's conclusion was that "Everybody learned something. The United States learned the hard way that the Japanese had not been responsible for Detroit's problems, but it was simply unacceptable politically for the Japanese market share to expand further.... MITI learned they could no longer control their industry participants as had been the case twenty-five years earlier."[32]

How had the situation described in this chapter come about? *Were* Japan's policies unfair? Did America cut its own throat, so to speak? Certainly any protective measures it took seemed to backfire, as the 25 percent truck tariff which went into effect in the 1960s did. Japan got around the tariff simply by importing the trucks in pieces—and then assembling them in small shops in the United States. Eventually the truck tariff became a crucial element in the catalyst that drove Nissan and Toyota to begin manufacturing in the United States. Others like Isuzu and Mazda produced their vehicles under the safe umbrella of American companies. When protectionist sentiment reached fever pitch, the Japanese did not relinquish their hold on the American market, but rather quickly transplanted themselves onto American soil to avoid the fallout.

Their successes in America have surpassed all expectations and it seems that they rarely put a foot wrong. Japan has appeared as an agile mouse before a lumbering elephant, continually out-maneuvering the United States. Most of this can be attributed to their business strategies, which William J. Holstein perfectly summarized in *The Japanese Power Game: What It Means for America.* "Japanese companies are not passing their huge profits through to their shareholders, or giving their employees big bonuses as an American company might. They are reinvesting their profits in a new drive to commercialize new technologies, develop new products, improve their efficiency, expand their investments in the United States and around the world, and in general to move to the next phase of economic lift-off. Whereas an American or European might be tempted to relax or coast under these circumstances, the Japanese are accelerating."[33] Holstein went on to address some of the questions many Americans were asking: "How can this be? Isn't Japan supposed to be cracking? What's all this about Socialists and women and consumers? About the work ethic collapsing? The young rebelling? What about the stock market? Bad aging problem? Labor shortage? And what about the political crisis?"[34] The answer, according to the author, was that Japan was "dealing" with them. As we have seen, Japan tends to deal with their problems most efficiently, but their devastating recession and the trade friction with the United States have not been so easily solved.

America's trade deficit reached $43 billion in 2000, up from $29 billion in 1995, the year the U.S.–Japan Trade Act expired. American automobile exports to Japan have fallen flat while Japan's to the United States continue to rise. But now that the industry has become more globalized, trade lines have been blurred to a certain extent and the situation somewhat diffused by joint ventures and transplant operations. Japanese auto companies are increasingly relying on North American production and sales and are now, strangely enough, having to work to increase sales in their own country.

Detroit has had its hands full trying to compete on its own territory with Japanese companies that can now claim they are on their own territory as well. As AIADA reported in 2000, "Foreign automakers such as Toyota Motor Corp. and Nissan Motor Co. continue to snap up larger portions of the U.S. vehicle market, as the share collectively controlled by Detroit's automakers dropped below 70 percent for the first five months of 2000. Market share for General Motors Corp., Ford Motor Co. and DaimlerChrysler AG dropped from 70.3 at the end of 1999 to 67.4 percent." Toyota alone had captured 9.1 percent of the U.S. market.[35]

In February of 2002, *Newsday* magazine ran a piece by Tom Incantalupo which maintained that "The American car may be disappearing from the American road...."[36] Incantalupo further noted that: "Whatever its impact on the economy, the Big Three's declining market share of their home market is hurting them, with the recession piling on the pain. GM's profits fell from $5 billion in 2000 to $1.5 billion last year. German-based DaimlerChrysler's Chrysler unit is losing an undisclosed amount of money. Ford, which posted a staggering loss of almost $5.5 billion for last year, recently announced 35,000 job cuts and the closure of at least five assembly and components plants over the next two or three years."[37]

It is unknown which way the trade winds will blow in the automotive industry, but it is certain that trade in general continues to be a contentious issue between Japan and the United States. A degree of harmony has been achieved due to the downturn of Japan's economy, agreements in the semiconductor industry, the allowance of more American investment in Japan, and finally by the fact that the United States has begun to focus more on other trading partners, such as China and Korea.

Consul General of Japan Makoto Ito made an effort to emphasize the positive aspects of U.S.–Japan trade relations in a speech to Western Michigan University's School of Business, calling the relationship "the most significant in the world."[38] While admitting that Japan still held an approximate $82 billion trade surplus with the United States as of 2000, he pointed out that they were working to counteract criticism of unfair trade practices. Specifically, the area of automobile manufacturing was mentioned as one undergoing significant change. Addressing the criticism that U.S. automakers have long been using Japanese parts, he responded by stating that Japanese automakers have now increased their use of American suppliers, as indicated by a $36 billion or 12 percent increase in purchases between 1999 and 2000. Ito also informed his audience that General Motors had recently become the first non–Japanese member of the Japanese Automobile Manufacturers Association (JAMA). At the conclusion of his speech, Ito remarked on Japan's close ties with Michigan and also touched on the economic situation in his country, saying that it was in "severe shape," but that it was still a major "economic powerhouse."[39]

The same month Ito appeared in Michigan, a piece by Senator Ernest F. Hollings ran in the Op-ed section of the *New York Times* entitled "The Delusion of Free Trade."

Without directly mentioning Japan, Senator Hollings alluded to the issue of unfair trade practices. Speaking of the period following World War II, a period in which he said "foreign trade became foreign aid,"[40] Hollings stated: "We set an example by opening up the American market. But our competition refused to follow suit."[41] He also took issue with the 1979 Tokyo Round Agreements, after which he said "America has lost more than four million manufacturing jobs…"[42] Defending the American way, Senator Hollings concluded his piece: "Since the fall of the Berlin Wall, hundreds of millions of people have entered the world's workforce ready to accept a minimal standard of living. In contrast, America continues to protect or raise its standard of living with requirements for a minimum wage, Social Security, Medicare, Medicaid, safe workplaces and machinery, clean air and water, plant closing notice and unpaid parental leave."[43] What the senator failed to mention was that Japan has been attempting to achieve the same things only by different methods.

Those methods again fell under criticism in March of 2002 when the United States brought charges against Japan for dumping steel in the U.S. market. Japan's Ministry of Foreign Affairs fired back, calling for the United States to "exert even more leadership in promoting free trade."[44] That potentially provoking statement was followed by a veiled threat to take the United States before the World Trade Organization: "In this context, we are deeply concerned with the protectionist measures that the United States has taken, as we believe they are inconsistent with the obligations of the United States under the WTO Agreement, while criticizing trade practices of other countries…."[45]

And so the battle continues. It seems clear that to create even a semblance of free trade, nations must first thoroughly understand one another. Such understanding is not facilitated by remarks such as Senator Byron Dorgan's, who when protesting Japan's high tariffs on American beef, asked "How about more T-bones in Tokyo?"[46] Perhaps the senator was not aware that beef is not as high on the Japanese dietary list as it is on the American one and therefore is not as much in demand.

Just as Detroit failed to take into consideration Japanese needs and tastes in an automobile, so have many in the American government misjudged Japanese customs and character, to say nothing of its business and governmental practices. Clyde Prestowitz, Jr., felt that there was something to be learned from Japan's customs. In his concluding chapter he had this warning for America: "A country in which government and consumers perceive no stake in the success or the failures of producers, in which producers and workers perceive few common interests and few mutual obligations, which pays young corporate takeover artists twenty to thirty times what it pays veteran teachers, and which most often settles disputes in a court of law, is a country in trouble. No amount of policy tinkering will help it if the fundamental values are absent."[47]

There cannot be a more appropriate conclusion to this chapter.

# 19

## The Road Ahead — From Conquest to Concept

"These days the Japanese auto industry doesn't seem too interested in providing comic relief for American automotive journalists. The Honda Accord brought that era to a close." This quote from *Car and Driver*'s January 1978 edition was but a mere indication of the success about to be enjoyed by Japanese automakers.[1] With automotive analysts predicting more of the same for the future, it's easy to see who is enjoying the last laugh. Even the final bastion of American automotive dominance — that of trucks and sport utility vehicles — has recently been assaulted by the Japanese. The *Detroit News* reported in 2002 that: "While 2001 will go down as the second-best automotive sales year ever, the future appears precarious and uncertain for General Motors Corporation, Ford Motor Company, and the Chrysler unit of DaimlerChrysler AG."[2]

It seems that history is repeating itself with Detroit accusing Japan of not playing fair. In February of 2002, GM CEO Rick Wagoner, Ford CEO William Clay Ford Jr., and Chrysler's Dieter Zetsche wrote a joint letter of appeal to President Bush asking him to investigate the currency exchange rate which they claimed was being manipulated by the Japanese. The currency issue has historically been, and remains, a smoldering issue between the two nations.

Another factor American automakers claim is adversely affecting their business is that of rigid union demands. When interviewed by the *Detroit News*, Professor of Organizational Behavior Gerald Meyers of the University of Michigan was succinct in his assessment of the union's hold over the automakers, stating: "There's no question that the UAW has the Big Three auto companies in a straight jacket."[3]

This opinion is widely shared by both those within and outside of the American industry but there seems to be little that can be done to remedy the situation — at least for now. However with tough times continuing to dog Detroit it may be that changes are on the horizon. The *Detroit News* hinted as much when it reported that:

"Don't be surprised if General Motors, Ford Motor and Chrysler look to the United Auto Workers union for concessions during contract talks in 2003."[4] The question is are they likely to get them? Concessions would provide respite to the American automakers who have been battling for so long that the expression "something's got to give" seems appropriate.

While it's true that 0 percent financing has acted as a boon to sales, the situation in Detroit does not look very promising, especially since the same financing is continuing into 2004. It is a situation the Big Three cannot afford to tolerate, perhaps Ford least of all.

Between 2000 and 2002, Ford lost an estimated $5.4 billion, most of which went towards replacing faulty Firestone tires and settling lawsuits resulting from tire-related accidents. The company cut 35,000 jobs, closed five plants, and eliminated four models—the Mercury Cougar, Ford Escort, Mercury Villager minivan, and the Lincoln Continental from its product line. Regarding these hard-line changes, new CEO Bill Ford, Jr., said "We haven't come to these decisions easily."[5]

Mr. Ford's hands have been full overseeing massive internal restructuring while trying to rebuild the company's battered reputation. As part of this campaign, he personally appeared in a series of television commercials created to remind potential customers of the long and illustrious history of his family's company. But with a fresh set of problems cropping up in 2002 concerning the Ford Explorer and Escape SUVs as well as the subcompact Focus, there was renewed disenchantment with the product, further tarnishing the company's image. Ford hopes the arrival of the new retro Mustang in 2004 will help to brighten it.

In 2001 General Motors recorded a slight profit, yet it was still necessary to trim the workforce by 10 percent and implement other cost-cutting measures. In order to increase its market share beyond 2002, GM president Gary Cowger told the American International Automobile Dealers Association that "We are going to have to capitalize even more on the momentum from trucks while stabilizing our car share."[6] But with Toyota and Nissan producing outstanding pickups of their own, this was easier said than done.

GM's foreign affiliates have been both a burden and a blessing, with Fiat and Isuzu struggling while Subaru and Suzuki are growing stronger. In an effort to appeal to the younger buyer, GM has incorporated a new 1,000-strong high-performance team to boost its showing in the concept and sports car arenas. Among its newest offerings is the Pontiac Solstice, a rear-wheel-drive sports car built in the Corvette-Firebird tradition. New models for 2004 like the Chevrolet Maxx and Optra and the new Pontiac G6 are now giving GM executives reason to believe in a strong recovery.

Chrysler, after enjoying considerable success with its PT Cruiser, minivans, and Dodge Ram trucks, recovered somewhat from its losses of almost $2.5 billion in 2001. During that period it had been necessary to close plants and cut jobs, paying out early retirement incentives in order to save money. Rebates are still being offered on certain models. And like Ford and GM, its formerly lucrative truck and minivan segment is inexorably being drained away by the Japanese. Even the once-venerated Jeep has been overshadowed by the proliferation of high-quality SUVs now on the market.

Chrysler intends to keep current and in touch with the younger generation, a fact made evident at the 2003 Detroit Auto Show when superstar Celine Dion wooed the audience with her famous "Titanic" song, then blasted them with Chrysler's new theme, a "techno" version of Roy Orbison's romantic ballad "I Drove All Night."

Perhaps now that DaimlerChrysler has teamed up with Mercedes-Benz they are sharing more than just technology and components. The company did report a profit in the first quarter of 2002 but despite the introduction of new models like the Dodge Magnum and 300, sales continue to disappoint.

Currently the Big Three hold approximately 60 percent of the U.S. automobile market, a far cry from the glory days when it commanded nearly 100 percent. Unfortunately, the trio continue to be troubled by problems with quality and image. General Motors has embarked on an extensive advertising campaign that promises its people are "professional grade"—a claim that unfortunately sounds more like a protestation than a promise—rather like a child pleading that he's good enough to play with the big kids. Feeling the need to identify themselves as professionals doesn't seem, well, very professional. Bill Ford, Jr., points out that his great-grandfather hobnobbed with presidents, and Chrysler seeks to remind the consumer that it is still a mighty force on the automotive scene if not in reputation then by sheer size.

These advertising campaigns together with 0 percent financing bespeak of problems rooted in the 1970s that have yet to be resolved. Following September 11 there was a brief surge in patriotic car buying, which to some extent lingered into 2002, just as rebates and low interest continued to linger. This consumer boost bought time for the American automakers and may or may not sustain them until they can fortify their positions.

Meanwhile, questions persist that have pestered the companies since Toyota surpassed VW in the 1970s. The most important one of these revolves around customer perception of today's American automobiles In 1997, *Business Week* asked "Can Detroit Make Cars That Baby Boomers Like?"[7] The overall consensus was that they could not. "Winning over baby boomers won't be easy," the article stated. "The seeds of their defection were sown a quarter-century ago, when they started buying their first cars—and when Detroit was turning out some of its worst cars ever." And what about the new generation of buyers—Generation "X"? It seemed they would be "even less inclined than boomers to buy American."[8]

These discouraging words are unfortunately supported by the numbers. Statistics tell us that American automobiles continue to lag behind imported ones in popularity if not by volume. Jerry Flint writing in *Forbes* put the question bluntly, asking: "Can't Anybody in Detroit Play This Game?"[9] Flint referred to the fact that in recent surveys American cars have come out "behind even Hyundai." What's the problem? "Just about everything: exterior design, interiors, handling, engines." All of GM's cars, according to Flint, are behind the times. Noting that Ford "desperately needs a new Taurus" and Chrysler "needs engines with more punch and interiors that stand out," Flint despaired that the Big Japanese Three of Honda, Toyota, and Nissan "will give the 'Big Three' family cars their worst thrashing ever next year."[10]

Some speculate that part of the Big Three's problem is that they are much too diversified to commit to building high quality automobiles and are distracted from the job by other, unrelated enterprises. Others have pointed to the constant and chronic corner cutting where corners should not be cut. The old adage "you get what you pay for" is firmly entrenched in many consumer's minds, and higher-priced imports have imparted a sense of quality for the money, which domestic automobiles don't seem to convey. The Big Three have only recently caught on to this logic and have raised their prices on certain higher profile models accordingly.

Yet try as they might they can't seem to break that barrier of superior form, fit, and finish. Road noise, ill-fitting and low-quality trim, along with a multitude of squeaks and rattles continue to be a major source of customer complaints. Perhaps it is for this reason that some domestic engineers and designers have been known to go over Japanese cars with a fine-tooth comb, testing, measuring and assessing. They have managed to ascertain that customers want a vehicle that is built with precision, but they haven't so far been able to exactly replicate that precision while keeping to their budgets. Then too, there is a certain amount of assumption that a given number of Americans will remain loyal to the product no matter what, but this is a dangerous assumption at best. As one customer put it when asked about the importance of buying American, "To buy American was never a question I considered. The final product is the most important in my mind. Country of origin is secondary."[11]

If that indeed is the prevailing attitude, and people do want the best quality for their money, then American automakers have cause for concern. At least they should be concerned, especially since at the time of writing Japan's automakers are in control of over 27 percent of the U.S. market. When the healthy sales of the Japanese transplants are factored in, the remaining slice of pie is fast diminishing. Toyota alone has recently cornered 10 percent of the U.S. market share, and makes no secret that it is aiming for more. *Automotive News* reported that Toyota planned to "shift to a profit structure supported by three bases: Japan, North America, and Europe."[12]

The company is also making inroads in China, where an enormous market awaits. In addition there are plans for a new plant to be built in Baja, Mexico. Toyota's strong growth has been well served by consistently outstanding products such as the Camry, Corolla, Tundra, Sequoia, and the RAV4. Toyota's luxury line Lexus continues to do well and the company also has produced the gasoline-electric hybrid Prius which has sold well since its launch in 2000. The joint venture with GM is still on and the latest result has been the Toyota Matrix crossover vehicle which is a twin of the Pontiac Vibe. The two vehicles were introduced in the spring of 2002.

Toyota's success with trucks and SUVs has been a major blow to the Big Three and is well reflected in their profit statements. While Ford and Chrysler have been seeing red, Toyota has billions to work with.

From a tiny office in a decidedly unglamorous area of Hollywood, Toyota has grown to establish close to a dozen American plants, plus one joint factory with GM. Its U.S. assets total in the billions and do not take into account its major global presence. It continues to dominate Japan's auto industry, holding 40 percent of that country's market share. Part of Toyota's success has been attributed to its steady increasing of research and development investments. And, as we have seen throughout this book, the Toyota Production System and the Toyota "way" are also responsible for the company's rise. As Toyota president Fujio Cho said, "The Japanese corporate culture is to grow people. It does not allow companies to overhaul the way they have run businesses."[13]

But although Toyota's fundamental business practices haven't changed much since Kiichiro founded the company in 1937, one major factor has. Toyota's long-time rival, Nissan, has been plucked from its position by the Honda Motor Company.

With the success of the Honda Civic in the United States during the oil crisis years, followed by the rocketing of the Honda Accord into the top import spot in the late 1970s, Honda has achieved almost unbelievable status in the world's automobile industry. The Civic continues to be a bestseller, and has recently been re-cloaked in green — environmentally speaking, that is. The Civic Hybrid has evolved from the Honda Insight gas-electric hybrid introduced in the late 1990s and leads the pack in the race for the automobile of the future.

Models like the Accord continue to keep sales strong, while the Odyssey mini-van and the CR-V SUV have provided the company with an enormous boost. In 2003 came the larger SUV Pilot and the more compact SUV Element. Both of these vehicles were primarily aimed at the youth market. They were followed by a new luxury sedan for Acura, called the DN-X. There are rumors that Honda intends to produce pickup trucks as well.

In summing up Honda's operations, it can be seen that although they are not nearly as large an operation, they are approaching Toyota's status in many respects. Honda has 11 factories in North America, as well as over one hundred businesses throughout the world. In addition to automobiles it commands a hugely profitable motorcycle, marine sports, and power equipment industry. Its profits in its automobile division were $618 million for only one quarter of 2002.

Honda's president Hiroyuki Yoshino said Honda has been successful because it "builds small and grows big."[14] Its American investment exceeds $5.3 billion with 120,000 employed in Honda-related operations. But although the company is steadily rising, it may have to look over its shoulder for Nissan is beginning to recover its stride.

It can be said that the Nissan-Renault alliance has been mutually beneficial. Nissan contributed $435 million to Renault's 2001 profits for a total of $920 million. The *Detroit News* reported that: "Nissan Motor Company is pouring almost $2 billion into U.S. plants, its most aggressive capacity and model range expansion there for two decades...."[15] Nissan's recent record profits can be credited in large part to Carlos Ghosn's Nissan Revival Plan (NRP) which has so far been extremely effective. The totally redesigned Nissan Altima was part of that plan, as was the return of the Z car — known as the Nissan 350Z. Infiniti has also recently expanded its line to include the FX45 SUV and the M45 sedan. And in an all-out bid for market share, Nissan has announced it will be embarking on a product "blitz" over the next decade, introducing some 28 new models during that time. Said Mr. Ghosn: "We have a clear idea about our future. The new fiscal year started under the banner of Nissan 180; a plan that opens a new perspective for our company, a perspective of lasting profitable growth. Now we have to earn it."[16]

Part of that plan was the announcement that Nissan would be expanding its plant in Canton, Mississippi, investing a further $500 million and bringing production capacity up to 400,000 vehicles annually. In 2002 it was voted the most efficient manufacturer in North America for the eighth consecutive year by the Harbour Report. Obviously Nissan's plan is working and the results are reflected in the current health of the company.

Trailing Nissan but also undergoing major restructuring is the Mazda Motor Corporation. The company introduced new models for 2002–03, including the Mazda 6, a replacement for the long-popular 626 sedan. The car shares the same platform as the Ford Mondeo and is built at the AAI plant in Flat Rock. And just as Nissan brought back its racy Z car, so has Mazda upgraded its RX-7 to an RX-8 which was shown as a concept car at the 2001 Detroit Auto Show. Following the RX-8 was a revamped Miata arriving in 2003. One year later the company unveiled a freshly styled Protegé sedan and wagon, which shared components with the Ford Focus.

In May of 2002, Mazda announced its "best-ever year-on-year turnaround."[17] Its revenue had increased to $15.7 billion, up from $594 million in 2000. Mazda's then-president Mark Fields said: "Mazda's back in the black. We are meeting all our performance targets, and there is more to come as we introduce exciting new products in FY2002 — a new lineup which will deliver significant growth."[18]

That growth will now be handled by Lewis Booth who took over from Mark Fields as president in June of 2002. Mazda's U.S. production for 2001 hit 729,951 vehicles with 141,292 produced overseas. Its total exports for the same year were 484,632.[19]

Mazda has worked hard to re-create itself from a somewhat understated company with a staid product line, apart from the RX-7 that is, to a more adventurous and youthful enterprise. The popular "Zoom Zoom" campaign caught the attention of many younger buyers. With a newly designed product line, typical Mazda quality, and support by Ford, it's not difficult to imagine that the company will remain a strong figure in the industry.

Much of the same can be said for the smaller Subaru company, although it is difficult to project what would happen should GM take a larger share of it. As of 2001, Subaru held about 1 percent of the American automobile market, selling 185,944 units.[20] According to a press statement, the company plans to double that share in the near future, with the help of General Motors. The *Detroit News* quoted Subaru senior executive Hideo Wada as saying: "We have access to very important information that we didn't have. GM has been helping us a lot in the U.S."[21]

Subaru's Executive Vice-President Fred Adcock stated that "...we achieved our success by remaining true to our core philosophy of offering 100% all-wheel drive vehicles designed to complement the active lifestyle."[22] The Legacy accounted for 95,291 sales, the Outback for 70,625, the Impreza for 35,612, and the Forester for 55,041.[23]

The company now has over six hundred dealers in the United States with more on the way as it seeks to expand its exclusively Subaru dealership base. GM and Subaru are expected to jointly develop a new SUV to be released in 2005.

Suzuki, like Subaru, is a partner with General Motors. While its market is fair in the United States, America accounts for only 20 percent of its total sales. Including motorcycles, sales in Japan hit 934,000 in 2002.[24] In addition to bikes, the company is strong in Japan in the minicar segment — an asset in a country and an economy that has been severely constrained. Suzuki relies predominantly on its home-based operations and keeps a fairly low profile in the U.S automotive industry. Its small SUVs have recently been rivaled by Honda and KIA, although the Vitara and Grand Vitara have sold well in the past few years. The name Suzuki, however, at least for many Americans, remains synonymous with motorcycles.

Two companies that have not surged ahead on the American market as well as some of their compatriots are Mitsubishi and Isuzu.

Isuzu is now controlled by General Motors and as such can no longer be assessed as a solely Japanese-owned company in the United States. Its operations in Japan, however, are widely diversified and it also enjoys a strong world-wide presence particularly as a diesel equipment and truck manufacturer.

Mitsubishi's story is somewhat similar to Isuzu's in that it too is a long-standing Japanese company paired with one of the Big Three. The company is seeking ways to survive in an industry glutted with models and loaded with unforgiving competition from the likes of Toyota, Honda, and Nissan. One way to accomplish that would be to form an even stronger alliance. There is current speculation that Mitsubishi, DaimlerChrysler AG and Hyundai will merge to form Global Engine Alliance in an arrangement similar to the one Lee Iacocca envisioned in the 1980s.

Mitsubishi announced a return to profit in 2001 after heavy losses in 2000. Its American position is stronger, with record profits in 2001 after three fairly solid years. It hopes to claim a higher percent share of the market in the future by way of stronger brand identity and a wider appeal to the youth segment. According to a company press release, the Mitsubishi Turnaround Plan has been effective and there are indications of reduced losses on the Asian and European markets as a result of the new eK Wagon together with a restructured sales network and new distribution systems. It is also expected to benefit from its partnership with DaimlerChrysler, particularly in Germany where a new engine plant is currently being constructed. It will be interesting to see where an even stronger global alliance will lead.

There are no clear answers as to why Mitsubishi and Isuzu never really "took off" in America, although they both occupy a prominent and historical place in Japan's industry. One reason may be a simple lack of appeal to American tastes — the vehicles have not struck a major chord with American consumers. Styling has been more of an issue for Mitsubishi since it relies on cars for its sales in America whereas Isuzu's trucks and SUVs can get by on more practical and rugged designs.

To remedy Mitsubishi's problems Olivier Boulay, formerly of Mercedes-Benz, was brought in to "work his magic on Mitsubishi's dull designs...."[25] And as *Business Week* reported: "The game plan is to reinvigorate the company with daring concepts in three crucial models: sport-utility vehicles, minivans, and subcompact sedans. Boulay wants to shed Mitsubishi's image of producing Spartan vehicles popular with middle-aged men. That means it's time to get racy, at least by Mitsubishi's staid standards."[26]

As for Isuzu, it hasn't managed to break those invisible barriers, with even the new Axiom SUV failing to attract American buyers in a hot SUV market. With GM fighting its own battles and Subaru just gaining speed on the market, Isuzu has been left much to its own devices to survive in the United States. As Ted Evanoff of the *Indianapolis Star* wrote: "Staying healthy in the U.S. market ultimately will come down to developing fresh designs highlighted in new ads."[27]

Americans put much stock in image and are heavily influenced by advertising. Certainly American automakers have gone to great lengths and expense to create just the right image for their products, although not always with success. Eiji Toyoda was a firm believer in image, and even said that the name of a car was terribly important to the vehicle's success on the market. Perhaps there is something in a name.

A prime example of the importance of a name can be found in the case of Nissan switching its name from Datsun in the 1980s—some go so far as to say that decision marked the beginning of the downfall of the company in America. For a long time there was a sense of disappointment and even irritation, as people had gotten used to Datsun and seemed to prefer it over Nissan. There was also widespread confusion with some believing the Nissan was an entirely different product.

With such intense competition, a product needs everything going for it and nothing against it. When consumers begin to know and trust a name it can only mean tempting the fates to change it.

Some American consumers feel they have been burned by their own industry and have therefore turned away from it in numbers unforeseen in the 1960s. Japanese automakers realize there is no room for error and always room for improvement. American automakers have not always been so perceptive, and the same old mistakes lead inevitably to the same old complaints.

In addition to satisfying the customer, automakers are still obligated to satisfy government and public demands. Safety continues to be an issue as can be seen in the increasingly stringent crash and roll-over standards which have led to a proliferation of structural changes, restraint systems, and sophisticated computerized handling and braking systems now available.

There is also growing backlash against behemoth SUVs, not only because of their dominating and sometimes threatening presence on the highways, but also for their guzzling of precious fuels. It's ironic that what turned the American consumer away from American automobiles now seems quite acceptable from Japanese companies who are investing more and more in larger SUVs, full-size trucks, and more powerful luxury cars. The race for bigger and faster is again under way, just as it was in the 1950s, but this time the Japanese have joined in. Yet still Ford and GM lead the pack with the enormous Excursion and Denali models.

Another industry facet still targeted for criticism is the automobile's effect on the environment. After working for 30 years to clean up automobile emissions, the industry continues to be prodded by the government which put together the voluntary National Low Emissions Vehicle initiative in the 1990s with the first automobiles meeting it in 1999. The Alliance of Automobile Manufacturers claim that by 2009 American vehicles will be 80 percent cleaner than they are today and 99 percent cleaner than they were in the 1960s. The Alliance has recently reported that the auto industry "has traveled farther than any other industry toward a cleaner environment."[28]

To achieve this, it spends an estimated "$18.4 billion annually in research and development of new advanced technologies to make cars and light trucks cleaner, safer and more fuel-efficient than ever — more than any other manufacturing industry spends."[29] The prediction is that cars and light trucks will account for about one-fifth of emissions by 2005, down from one-quarter in 2001.[30]

Of course the issue that goes hand-in-hand with the environment is fuel efficiency. In February of 2002, a plan was released by the Senate which would require a substantial increase in fuel economy, provoking the ire of the automakers in an echo of the oil crisis years. The current Corporate Average Fuel Economy (CAFE) stands at 27.5 miles per gallon for cars and 20.7 miles per gallon for pickup trucks, minivans, and SUVs. Although there are discrepancies between what the Democrats and Republicans see as the ultimate target for the CAFE, the number falls at approximately 35 miles per gallon for cars by around 2013.

The *Detroit News* reported that those representing the automakers are angered by this new demand, claiming that building vehicles even smaller to make them more fuel-efficient will severely compromise safety, and as Michigan's Governor John Engler remarked, the new proposed mileage rate would be the equivalent of telling Michigan to "drop dead."[31]

Automakers feel that they have been working hard enough to develop alternative vehicles, and much to their frustration the Japanese have taken the lead there as well. Toyota and Honda have been the first to develop viable gas-electric hybrids that are actually being marketed as opposed to being shown as concepts. Nissan is currently working on direct-injection engines with a CVT, as well as direct-injection diesel engines. It has produced a hybrid vehicle but as yet it is not ready for the market.

The difficulties with hybrids is that they are complex and prohibitively expensive to build, forcing automakers to subsidize them in order to make them affordable. They typically operate with a high-efficiency internal combustion engine supplemented with a series of batteries. The electricity generated assists the vehicle during acceleration and under load and recovers energy from the brakes during deceleration and braking. However, they still emit pollution and require both fossil fuel and storage room for that fuel. They require fairly involved maintenance. Even so, they are much preferable to purely electric cars which have posed too many difficulties to be considered as viable transportation. But the most promising alternative power source thus far lies with fuel cell development.

Fuel cell technology is not exactly new — it's been around in some form or another for decades but gained attention when it was used in spacecraft in the 1960s. A fuel cell is basically a type of battery that can be refueled by gasoline, methane, ethanol or hydrogen. Electrons are chemically extracted from the fuel by the elements inside the cell and produce enough current to power the vehicle. There is no traditional engine as we know it but instead a series of connections leading from the cells and the fuel storage unit to a complex drivetrain.

The race to be the first to create a marketable fuel cell vehicle is under way with both Japanese and American automakers investing billions in research and development in order to be ready when the demand for the ultimate clean and fuel-efficient vehicle arises. Since the American government has been steadily pushing automakers into creating such a vehicle, it is naturally taking great interest in fuel cell development.

On January 9, 2002, government representatives and automakers alike met to discuss what is being called "FreedomCAR"— CAR standing for Cooperative Automotive Research. This program, undertaken jointly by government and the private sector, was established to fund research on hydrogen-powered fuel cells. The government's interest, besides cleaning up the atmosphere, is to reduce dependency on foreign oil.

A day before this meeting convened at which Energy Secretary Spencer Abraham addressed the assembly, General Motors unveiled its fuel cell concept car, the AUTOnomy, at the North American International Auto Show in Detroit. The vehicle, as CNN reported, looked like "a skateboard on steroids,"[32] and included radical new components that allowed the driver to operate the vehicle from any position within it.

Costs for developing these vehicles have so far been astronomical, forcing automakers to seek partnerships with energy companies. DaimlerChrysler and Ford for instance together own one-third of Ballard Power Systems and are working on fuel cell vehicles of their own. Ford announced it would have a fuel-cell-powered Focus by 2004, available for fleet sales only due to limited fuel availability.

On June 5, 2002, Chrysler's fuel cell powered DCX NECAR5 completed a cross-country trip from San Francisco to Washington, D.C., the first time such a vehicle traveled so far. The car was able to reach speeds up to 90 miles per hour and went 300 miles on one tank of methanol.

But while fuel cells are the vital component, they have been refined to suit the needs of automakers and are not the problem. It is now the fuel that feeds them that is the primary source of focus. Hydrogen has emerged as the preferred choice, not least because it is the cleanest and in the long term the most sustainable. The Honda Motor Company opened a hydrogen fuel station in Los Angeles in July of 2001, using solar power backed up by electricity to extract the hydrogen from water. The hydrogen is then compressed and stored in tanks. Honda has been a leader in fuel cell technology, with hydrogen-powered fuel cell vehicles such as the FCX V3 in operation since 1999. They are participants in the California Fuel Cell Partnership (CaFCP) program and their FCX V3 was used as the pace vehicle for the 2001 Los Angeles marathon.[33]

Now that nearly all of the automakers have some type of fuel cell vehicle in production, the final proving ground will be the marketplace. Consumers are still wary of the untried and are used to the internal combustion engine's speed, dependability, and convenience. Automakers and governments are expected to offer incentives to spark market demand as well as to subsidize the initial cost of the first low production runs. But if oil prices become more unstable as the volatile situation in the Middle East intensifies, breaking free of those ties may be enough to compensate for any lag between technologies.

The next question will be again one of competition — will American automakers regain dominance in the industry with this new fresh start? Or will the Japanese maintain the edge they won with internal combustion technology?

As the twenty-first century opens, Japanese automobile exports have increased by 25.6 percent since 2001. The yen now stands at around 109 to the dollar and even though the falling of the U.S. dollar makes it more difficult for Japanese companies, U.S. sales for May of 2002 still dropped by 5.7 percent.[34]

The situation today in corporate America is unstable to say the least, with scandals like Enron, WorldCom and Delphi rocking the stock market as well as shaking consumer confidence. General Motors was forced to submit to scrutiny of its accounting practices, but maintained it had nothing to hide. Suspicions of antitrust violations lie ever closer to the surface, and Japanese transplants in America are not immune.

The "streamlining" of the automotive industry seems to be the wave of the future, but although the number of companies will be reduced, those remaining will balloon as they absorb the others under one umbrella.

Some automotive analysts have predicted that by 2010 there will be only be three or four automotive companies left in the world. This theory is on its way to being proven by the "merger mania" that has been under way since the 1980s. Which company will reign supreme? A Big Three hybrid or a Japanese monopoly?

One thing is certain — Japanese automobiles have captivated American consumers in a manner that no analyst could have predicted. Early model Japanese cars are now considered collector's items and websites have popped up all over the internet devoted to Japanese car enthusiasts. The bond has been forged and even if relations between Japan and America were to deteriorate, that bond will not be broken, just as the history of Japanese cars in America can never be erased.

# Chapter Notes

## Chapter 1

1. *Saturday Evening Post Automobile Book* (Indianapolis, Indiana, Curtis Publishing Company, 1977), p. 112.
2. *Ibid.*, p. 112.
3. Joseph H. Wherry, *Automobiles of the World* (New York: Galahad Books, Chilton Books, 1968), p. 3.
4. *Ibid.*, p. 4.
5. Robert Lacey, *Ford: The Men and the Machine* (New York: Little, Brown and Company, 1986), p. 41.
6. *Ibid.*, p. 44.
7. Lacey, p. 64.
8. *Ibid.*, pp. 112, 194.
9. *Auto Topics*, October 1965, p. 70.
10. atlantabuick.com.
11. James M. Flammang, *100 Years of the American Auto* (Lincolnwood, Illinois, Publications International, Ltd., 1999), p. 58.
12. Lacey, p. 71.
13. Maryann Keller, *Rude Awakening: The Rise, Fall, and Struggle for Recovery of General Motors* (New York: William Morrow and Company, 1989), p. 42.
14. Ed Cray, *Chrome Colossus: General Motors and Its Times* (New York: McGraw-Hill Book Company, 1980), p. 149.
15. Alfred P. Sloan, *My Years with General Motors* (New York: Doubleday and Company, Inc., 1964), p. 31.
16. Lacey, p. 21.
17. Oscar Handlin, *The History of the United States*, vol. 2, (New York: Holt, Rinehart and Winston, 1968), p. 3.
18. Blake McKelvey, *The Emergence of Metropolitan America 1915–1966* (New Brunswick, New Jersey, Rutgers University Press, 1968), p. 4.
19. John Bell Rae, *The Road and the Car in American Life* (Cambridge, Massachussetts: MIT Press, 1971), p. 43.
20. Flammang, *100 Years*, p. 84.
21. Sloan, p. 42.
22. Arthur S. Link, William S. Link, and William B. Catton, *American Epoch: A History of the United States Since 1900*, 6th ed., vol. 1, *1900–1945* (New York: Alfred A. Knopf, 1987), p. 172.
23. Sloan, p. 162.
24. *Ibid.*, p. 163.
25. Flammang, *100 Years*, p. 126.
26. Michael Moritz and Barrett Seaman, *Going for Broke: The Chrysler Story* (New York: Doubleday and Company, Inc., 1981), p. 42.
27. Flammang, *100 Years*, pp. 132, 138.
28. Cray, p. 286.
29. *Ibid.*, p. 303.
30. Richard M. Langworth and Jan P. Norbye, *The Complete History of the Chrysler Corporation 1924–1985* (New York: Beekman House, 1985), p. 69.

## Chapter 2

1. "Owner's Report on the VW," *Popular Mechanics*, October 1956, p. 155.
2. *Ibid.*, p. 154.
3. *Ibid.*, p. 154.
4. *Ibid.*, p. 157.
5. Lacey, p. 534.
6. Keller, *Rude Awakening*, p. 50.
7. "America's Smallest Car — The Metropolitan," *Popular Mechanics*, April 1954, p. 262.
8. Langworth and Norbye, p. 141.
9. Flammang, *100 Years*, p. 343.
10. *Ibid.*, p. 301.

11. Lacey, p. 510.
12. *Ibid.*, p. 511.
13. Flammang, *100 Years*, p. 250.
14. *Ibid.*, pp. 254, 343.
15. *Ibid.*, p. 266.
16. *Ibid.*, p. 254.
17. David E. Davis, Jr., *The World of Collector Cars*, PBS, December 15, 2001.
18. Herbert Gold, "The Hipster," *Nation*, November 16, 1957.
19. "Mental Hygiene: The Dos and Don'ts of the Doo-Wop Age," *New York Times*, January 2, 2000.
20. Brock Yates, *The Decline and Fall of the American Automobile Industry* (New York: Empire Books, 1983), p. 81.
21. William H. Chafe, *The Unfinished Journey: America Since World War II* (New York: Oxford University Press, 1986), p. 119.
22. "Owner's Report on the VW," *Popular Mechanics*, October 1956, p. 159.
23. *Ibid.*, p. 169.
24. fiftiesweb.com.
25. *Popular Mechanics*, May 1953, Inside Front Cover.
26. Lee Iacocca, *Iacocca: An Autobiography* (New York: Bantam Books, 1984), p. 66.
27. Sloan, pp. 440, 441.

## Chapter 3

1. L. Johannes Hirschmeier and Tsunehiko Yui, *The Development of Japanese Business 1600–1973* (London: George Allen & Unwin Ltd., 1975), p. 75.
2. John W. Dower, *Embracing Defeat: Japan in the Wake of World War II* (New York: W.W. Norton and Company, Inc., 1999), p. 92.
3. *Ibid.*, p. 71.
4. David Williams, *Japan: Beyond the End of History* (London: Routledge, 1994), p. 71.
5. Yukichi Fukuzawa, *Conditions in the West (Occidental Affairs)*, Vol. 2 (Japan: 1868).
6. www.japanauto.com, Japanese Automobile Manufacturer's Association (JAMA).
7. *Ibid.*
8. *Ibid.*
9. *Ibid.*
10. *Ibid.*
11. *Petersen's Complete Book of Datsun* (Los Angeles, Petersen's Publishing, 1977), p. 7.
12. Eiji Toyoda, *Toyota: Fifty Years in Motion* (Japan: Kodansha International Ltd., 1985), p. 46.
13. *Ibid.*, p. 55.
14. *Ibid.*, p. 59.
15. Yukiyasu Togo and William Wartman, *Against All Odds: The Story of the Toyota Motor Corporation and the Family That Created It* (New York: St. Martin's Press, 1993), p. 71.
16. Marco Ruiz, *The Complete History of Japanese Cars 1907 to Present* (New York: Crown Publishers, Inc., 1986), p. 171.
17. Toyoda, p. 58.
18. *Ibid.*, p. 64.
19. Dower, p. 91.
20. Toyoda, p. 104.
21. www.japanauto.com, JAMA History of the Japanese Automobile Industry.
22. Dower, p. 542.
23. Toyoda, p. 105.
24. Andrea Gabor, *The Man Who Discovered Quality: How W. Edwards Deming Brought the Quality Revolution to America — The Stories of Ford, Xerox, and GM* (New York: Random House, Inc., 1990), p. 15.
25. *Ibid.*, p. 9.
26. *Ibid.*, pp. 92, 93.
27. Toyoda, p. 107.
28. Nissan Fact File, The Nissan Motor Company Ltd.

## Chapter 4

1. Toyota Motor Sales Archives.
2. Shotaro Kamiya, *My Life with Toyota* (Toyota City, Japan: Toyota Motor Sales Company, Ltd., 1976), p. 78.
3. *Ibid.*
4. Togo and Wartman, p. 113.
5. *Ibid.*, p. 144.
6. *Ibid.*
7. Toyoda, p. 121.
8. Seisi Kato, *My Years with Toyota* (Toyota City, Japan: Toyota Motor Sales, 1981), p. 69.
9. Mike Sullivan, Interview with author, November 3, 2001.
10. Toyota Motor Sales Archives.
11. www.rosetoyota.com.
12. *Ibid.*
13. *Ibid.*
14. *Ibid.*
15. Robert Krause, Interview with author, January 31, 2002.
16. *Ibid.*
17. *Ibid.*
18. *Ibid.*
19. *Ibid.*
20. *Ibid.*
21. *Ibid.*
22. *Toyota: 40 Years in America* (Toyota City, Japan: Toyota Motor Sales, 1997), Chapter One.
23. *Ibid.*
24. *Ibid.*
25. www.greghalpin.com.
26. "The Toyopet Crown," *Motor Trend*, October 1958.
27. www.zubup.com.
28. *International Automobile Dealer*, April 1997, Vol. 14, No. 3.
29. Toyota Motor Sales Archives.

30. *Toyota: 40 Years in America,* Chapter One.
31. Toyota Motor Sales Archives.
32. Toyoda, p. 130.
33. *Toyota: 40 Years in America,* Chapter One.
34. *International Automobile Dealer,* April 1997, Vol. 14, No. 3.
35. "Move Over World: Here Come the Japanese," *Car Life,* August 1968, p. 21.
36. *Toyota: 40 Years in America,* Chapter Two.
37. *Consumer Reports,* April 1966.
38. "The Toyota Corona," *Popular Mechanics,* January 1967, p. 38.
39. *Ibid.*
40. *Ibid.*
41. Toyota Motor Sales Archives.
42. "Move Over…," *Car Life,* August 1968, p. 23.
43. *Ibid.*
44. *Road Test,* August 1969, inside front cover.
45. Toyota Motor Company slogan, Copyright Toyota Motor Sales.
46. Toyota Motor Sales Archives.
47. www.rosetoyota.com.
48. Fred King, Interview with author, March 7, 2002.
49. Michael Bowler, *Classic Cars from Around the World* (New York: Smithmark Publishers, 1996), p. 86.
50. "Move Over…," *Car Life,* August 1968, pp. 19, 20.
51. *Ibid.*
52. "Advance News from Japan," *Road Test,* August 1969, p. 16.

## Chapter 5

1. "The Owner's Survey Rates the Foreign Car," *Road Test,* September 1968, p. 49.
2. "Move Over…," *Car Life,* August 1968, p. 19.
3. *Ibid.,* pp. 22, 23.
4. *Ibid.*
5. *Ibid.*
6. "For Your Information," *Car and Driver,* September 1971, p. 52.
7. *Ibid.,* p. 53.
8. *Ibid.,* p. 65.
9. "Move Over…," *Car Life,* August 1968, p. 19.
10. "The 12 Best Cars to Own in a Gas Shortage," *Science & Mechanics,* April 1974, p. 88.
11. Toyoda, p. 134.
12. Kamiya, pp. 80, 89.
13. *Showroom,* April 1997, Vol. 14, No. 3.
14. www.jdpa.com.
15. Doron P. Levin, *Behind the Wheel at Chrysler: The Lee Iacocca Legacy* (New York: Harcourt Brace and Company, 1995), p. 63.
16. www.jmfamily.com.
17. *Ibid.*

18. *Petersen's Complete Book of Japanese Import Cars* (Los Angeles: Petersen's Publishing Company, 1972), p. 9.
19. "Return of the Native," *Motor Trend,* August 1971, p. 52.
20. *Ibid.,* p. 50.
21. *Car and Driver,* May 1974, pp. 64, 65.
22. "Toyota Celica GT Liftback," *Car and Driver,* January 1978, pp. 57, 58.
23. *National Geographic,* September 1971, advertisement.
24. James M. Flammang, *Standard Catalog of Imported Cars 1946–1990* (Iola, Wisconsin, Krause Publications, 1994), pp. 605, 606.
25. *Ibid.,* p. 606.
26. Toyota Motor Sales Archives.
27. *Ibid.*
28. "Datsun 280Z vs. Toyota Supra," *Motor Trend,* August 1979, p. 52.
29. *Ibid.*
30. *Auto Guide. Car Preview* 1988, p. 99.
31. "Japan 1983: Charting the Changes," *Car and Driver,* November 1982, p. 69.
32. John DiPietro, *A Toyota Camry History,* www.edmunds.com.
33. "International Report," *Motor Trend,* May 1987, p. 70.
34. toyota.com.
35. *Consumer Guide. Automobile Book* 1993, pp. 236, 237.
36. Flammang, *Imported Cars,* p. 606.
37. "Road Test — Toyota MR2," *Motor Trend,* January 1985, pp. 26–34.
38. *Consumer Guide. Automobile Book* 1993, p. 242.
39. *Ibid.*
40. Flammang, *Imported Cars,* p. 607.
41. "Lexus ES 300," *Motor Trend,* November 2001, p. 61.
42. *Consumer Guide. Automobile Book,* pp. 149, 150.
43. *Ibid.,* pp. 151, 152.
44. "First Drive 2002: Lexus ES 300," *Motor Trend,* September 2002, pp. 96, 98.
45. www.edmunds.com.
46. www.toyota.co.jp.
47. Maryann Keller, *Collision: GM, Toyota, Volkswagen and the Race to Own the 21st Century* (New York: Doubleday, 1993), p. 72.
48. www.fortune.com.
49. www.themuseumofautomobilehistory.com.

## Chapter 6

1. *Petersen's Complete Book of Datsun,* p. 6.
2. David Halberstam, *The Reckoning* (New York, William Morrow and Company, 1986), pp. 293, 294.
3. *Ibid.,* p. 295.

4. *Ibid.*

5. "Nissan Is Back After Several Missteps Along the Way," *Detroit News*, January 10, 1958.

6. *Ibid.*

7. Halberstam, p. 301.

8. *Ibid.*, p. 425.

9. Flammang, *Imported Cars*, p. 162.

10. *Petersen's Complete Book of Datsun*, p. 2.

11. Nissan Motor Company Archives.

12. Robert Sobel, *Car Wars: The Untold Story of the Great Automakers and the Giant Battle for Global Supremacy* (New York: E.P. Dutton, Inc., 1984), p. 169.

13. Halberstam, p. 425.

14. *Ibid.*, p. 426.

15. Ruiz, pp. 53, 149.

16. *Ibid.*, p. 150.

17. Mike Lawrence, *A to Z of Sports Cars* (St. Paul, Minnesota: Bayview Books, 1996), p. 241.

18. Halberstam, p. 427.

19. *Ibid.*

20. www.1.shore.net, *Japan Car* magazine interview.

21. Flammang, *Imported Cars*, p. 163.

22. *Ibid.*, pp. 163, 164.

23. "Japan's Cars Are Getting Better and Better All the Time," *Car and Driver*, June 1964, pp. 64, 65.

24. "Datsun 1966… A New Power and Economy Package," *Auto Topics*, November 1965, p. 65.

25. "Detroit's Economy Car Gap," *Motor Trend*, March 1967, p. 56.

26. Flammang, *Imported Cars*, p. 163.

27. *Ibid.*, p. 165.

28. "Car Clinic," *Motor Trend*, September 1962.

29. Bob Hayes, Interview with author, April 11, 2002.

30. Yates, p. 166.

31. "Nissan Is Back…," *Detroit News*, May 4, 2001.

32. www.zhome.com.

33. www.1.shore.net.

34. *Ibid.*

35. Halberstam, p. 440.

36. *Ibid.*, p. 446.

37. *Ibid.*

38. Flammang, *Imported Cars*, pp. 165, 166.

39. "Engineering: Datsun PL510," *Road Test*, April 1968, p. 55.

40. *Ibid.*, p. 56.

41. *Ibid.*

42. "Datsun PL510: A Lot of Car for a Little Money," *Motor Trend*, April 1968, p. 87.

43. "Move Over World: Here Come the Japanese," *Car Life*, August, 1968, p. 29.

44. Halberstam, p. 441.

45. Nissannews.com.

46. *Road & Track*, January 2000.

47. Flammang, *Imported Cars*, pp. 165, 166.

## *Chapter 7*

1. Flammang, *Imported Cars*, p. 165.

2. Lawrence,, p. 242.

3. Flammang, *Imported Cars*, pp. 166, 167.

4. "Eighth Annual Reader's Choice Winners," *Car and Driver*, May 1971, p. 61.

5. *Car and Driver*, January, 1971, back cover.

6. "For Your Information," *Car and Driver*, September, 1971, p. 68.

7. *Petersen's … Datsun*, p. 18.

8. "Z/28 vs 240-Z: Great Expectations—Unconfirmed," *Motor Trend*, August 1972, pp. 99, 100.

9. *Ibid.*

10. *Petersen's … Datsun*, p. 18.

11. *Petersen's … Japanese Import Cars*, p. 56.

12. "International Report," *Motor Trend*, August 1971, p. 26.

13. nissannews.com.

14. *Petersen's … Japanese Import Cars*, p. 56.

15. *Ibid.*, pp. 12, 13.

16. Flammang, p. *Imported Cars*, 169.

17. "International Report," *Motor Trend*, December 1977, p. 23.

18. *Ibid.*

19. Flammang, *Imported Cars*, p. 169.

20. *Ibid.*

21. "International Report," *Motor Trend*, December 1975, p. 20.

22. *Petersen's … Datsun*, p. 14.

23. *Ibid.*, p. 15.

24. *Ibid.*, p. 23.

25. *Ibid.*

26. *Ibid.*, p. 22.

27. Flammang, *Imported Cars*, p. 171.

28. *Ibid.*, p. 170.

29. "1978 Import Car of the Year, the Nominees," *Motor Trend*, December 1977, p. 36.

30. *Ibid.*, p. 42.

31. Halberstam, p. 517.

32. Flammang, *Imported Cars*, p. 172.

33. "Datsun F-10," *Car and Driver*, June 1978, p. 115.

34. *Ibid.*, p. 30.

35. "'79 Import Buyer's Guide," *Motor Trend*, April 1979, p. 63.

36. Flammang, *Imported Cars*, p. 172.

37. *Ibid.*, p. 173.

38. Jack Gillis, *The Used Car Book 1981–1989*, p. 130.

39. Flammang, *Imported Cars*, p. 172.

40. Jack Gillis, *1994–1995*, p. 174.

41. "Japan 1983: Charting the Changes," *Car and Driver*, November 1982, p. 68.

42. Yates, p. 279.

43. *Consumer Reports, The 1996 Cars*, p. 232.

44. Gillis, *1994–1995*, p. 175.

45. "Nissan Sentra SE Sport Coupe," *Road & Track*, September 1986, pp. 46, 48.

46. *Consumer Guide 1993 Automobile Book*, p. 195.

47. *Consumer Guide 1994–1995 Car Guide*, p. 174.

48. "International Report," *Motor Trend*, May 1987, p. 24.

49. *Ward's AutoWorld*, www.wardsautoworld.com, "Managing Import Brands."

50. *Ibid.*

51. *Road & Track*, April 1989, advertisement.

52. *Consumer Guide Auto Report 1992*, pp. 66, 67.

53. *Ibid.*, p. 69.

54. *Consumer Guide 1993 Automobile Book*, p. 135.

55. *Ibid.*, p. 188.

56. www.1.shore.net.

57. Don Spetner, *Journal of Integrated Communication 1996-1997* (www.medill.northwestern.com).

58. *Asiaweek*, 1999, www.asiaweek.com.

59. *Ibid.*

60. *Motor Trend*, September 2001 (www.motortrend.com/roadtests).

61. *Consumer Reports New Car Buying Guide 2002*, p. 200.

62. "Used Car Buying Guide," *Motor Trend*, October 2001, p. 106.

63. "First Test: 2003 Nissan 350Z," *Motor Trend*, September 2002, pp. 60–64.

64. *Ibid.*, p. 64.

## Chapter 8

1. Copyrighted slogan, The American Honda Company.

2. Tetsuo Sakiya, *Honda: The Men, the Management, the Machines* (New York: Kodansha International, 1982), p. 49.

3. *Ibid.*, p. 53.

4. *Ibid.*

5. *Ibid.*, p. 55.

6. *Ibid.*, p. 56.

7. *Ibid.*, p. 66.

8. *Ibid.*, p. 71.

9. *Ibid.*, p. 88.

10. Robert L. Shook, *Honda: An American Success Story* (New York: Prentice-Hall, 1988), p. 11.

11. Yates, p. 168.

12. Sakiya, p. 72.

13. *Ibid.*, p. 123.

14. Shook, p. 30.

15. *Ibid.*, p. 35.

16. www.superhonda.com.

17. "Move Over World: Here Come the Japanese," *Car Life*, August 1968, p. 32.

18. *Ibid.*

19. "Honda 600 Sedan and Honda 600 Coupe," *Car and Driver*, April 1972, p. 43.

20. *Motor Trend*, August 1972, back cover.

21. *Petersen's ... Japanese Import Cars*, p. 114.

22. *Ibid.*

23. "International Report," *Motor Trend*, August 1971, p. 26.

24. *Road Test*, August 1969, p. 18.

25. *Ibid.*

26. "Editorial," *Car and Driver*, October 1972, p. 22.

27. Flammang, *Imported Cars*, p. 285.

28. Yates, p. 168.

29. "The 12 Best Cars to Own in a Gas Shortage," *Science and Mechanics*, April 1974, p. 48.

30. *Car and Driver*, May 1974, p. 47.

31. Flammang, *Imported Cars*, p. 285.

32. *Ibid.*

33. Shook, p. 38.

34. Sakiya, p. 161.

35. *Ibid.*, p. 162.

36. Yates, p. 42.

## Chapter 9

1. "International Report," *Motor Trend*, December 1975, p. 20.

2. Flammang, *Imported Cars*, p. 286.

3. Yates, p. 41.

4. *Ibid.*, p. 42.

5. www.hondahistoryau.com.

6. www.honda.com.

7. "Road Test: Honda Accord 4-Door," *Car and Driver*, March 1979, p. 41.

8. *Ibid.*

9. *Ibid.*

10. *Ibid.*

11. Yates, p. 42.

12. Shook, p. 64.

13. Flammang, *Imported Cars*, p. 287.

14. "For Your Information," *Car and Driver*, March 1979, p. 22.

15. *Ibid.*, April 1979, p. 54.

16. Flammang, *Imported Cars*, p. 286.

17. *Car and Driver*, April 1979, advertisement.

18. "Honda Prelude at 26,000 Miles," *Road & Track*, May 1983.

19. *Ibid.*, August 1986, p. 54.

20. *Ibid.*

21. Flammang, *Imported Cars*, p. 291.

22. *Consumer Reports, The 1988 Cars*, pp. 220–223.

23. *Consumer Guide, Auto Report '92*, pp. 60, 61.

24. Gillis, *1994–1995*, p. 136.

25. *Consumer Guide, Auto Report '92*, pp. 60, 61.

26. "Ten Best Cars," *Car and Driver*, January 1996, p. 51.

27. *Consumer Reports New Car Buying Guide 2002*, p. 132.

28. *Ibid.*

29. *Consumer Guide, Auto Report '92*, pp. 58, 59.

30. "Ten Best Cars," *Car and Driver*, January 1996, p. 51.

31. *Consumer Reports New Car Buying Guide 1996*, pp. 58, 59.

32. "Sport Compact Deathmatch: Four.

Played.," *World of Wheels*, September 2002, p. 41.

33. Flammang, *Imported Cars*, p. 292.

34. "Letters," *Motor Trend*, May 1987, p. 9.

35. *Consumer Reports, New Car Buying* Guide, 1996, p. 114.

36. "Used Car Buying Guide," *Motor Trend*, October 2001, pp. 76, 94.

37. www.motortrend.com.

38. *Consumer Guide Auto Guide 1988*, p. 87.

39. "Acura Legend Coupe," *Motor Trend*, May 1987, p. 105.

40. *Consumer Reports, 1988*, p. 238.

41. "Update: Long-Term Road-Test Acura Legend Coupe," *Road & Track*, April 1988, p. 78.

42. Gillis, *1994–1995*, p. 70.

43. Flammang, *Imported Cars*, p. 290.

44. "New Cars," *Popular Mechanics*, March 1992, p. 90.

45. "Ten Best Cars," *Car and Driver*, January 1996, p. 48.

46. "Miscellaneous Ramblings," *Road & Track*, April 1989, p. 41.

47. "Honda Inside Out," *Sport Compact Car*, July 2000, p. 144.

48. www.nsxprime.com.

49. www.auto.consumerguide.com.

50. *Consumer Reports, 1996*, p. 105.

51. Gillis, *1994–1995*, p. 71.

52. "Firsts: Honda Hybrid," *Motor Trend*, February 2002, p. 32.

53. "How Honda Thrives," *Industry Week*, December 5, 1998, www.industryweek.com.

54. "Honda's Yorhino: Traditionally, We Build Small and Grow Big," *Business Week*, July 5, 1999, www.businessweek.com.

55. *Ibid.*

56. David Gelsanliter, *Jump Start: Japan Comes to the Heartland* (New York: Kodansha International, 1992), p. 20.

## *Chapter 10*

1. www.monito.com.

2. www.chugoku-np.co.jp.

3. *Ibid.*

4. *Ibid.*

5. www.rx7uknet.dircon.uk.

6. Flammang, *Imported Cars*, p. 392.

7. "Import Report," *Motor Trend*, April 1971, p. 12.

8. "Mazda Wankel vs. Comet 302," *Motor Trend*, May 1971, pp. 76, 87.

9. *Ibid.*

10. *Ibid.*

11. "Eighth Annual Reader's Choice Winners," *Car and Driver*, May 1971, pp. 38, 39.

12. *Ibid.*

13. "Import Car Buyer's Guide," *Motor Trend*, August 1972, p. 37.

14. Petersen's ... *Japanese Import Cars*, pp. 82, 83.

15. "Import Car Buyer's Guide," *Motor Trend*, August 1972, p. 37.

16. Flammang, *Imported Cars*, p. 394.

17. *Motor Trend*, December 1977, advertisement.

18. Flammang, *Imported Cars*, p. 394.

19. *Ibid.*, p. 395.

20. "Short-takes: Mazda GLC," *Car and Driver*, February 1977, p. 30.

21. "Mazda GLC Sport," *Motor Trend*, December 1977, p. 74.

22. Flammang, *Imported Cars*, p. 395.

23. *Ibid.*, p. 396.

24. American International Automobile Dealers Association (AIADA), www.aiada.org.

25. Flammang, *Imported Cars*, p. 396.

26. *Ibid.*

27. www.rx7.org.

28. *Car and Driver*, March 1979, advertisement.

29. "Showdown of the Sudden Samurai," *Motor Trend*, June 1982, p. 30.

30. Flammang, *Imported Cars*, p. 396.

31. *Ibid.*

32. "Showdown...," *Motor Trend*, June 1982, p. 30.

33. "For Your Information," *Car and Driver*, March 1979, p. 26.

34. *Ibid.*

35. *Ibid.*

36. "Import Report," *Motor Trend*, April 1979, p. 12.

37. "Japan 1983: Charting the Changes," *Car and Driver*, November 1982, p. 68.

38. Flammang, *Imported Cars*, p. 398.

39. www.chugoku-np.co.jp.

40. *Ibid.*

41. *Ibid.*

42. "Trends," *Motor Trend*, January 1985.

43. Flammang, *Imported Cars*, p. 399.

44. *Consumer Reports, The 1996 Cars*, pp. 231, 232.

45. "Letter from Japan: 4WD Craze," *Road & Track*, August 1986, p. 88.

46. *Auto Guide, 1988 Car Preview*, p. 89.

47. *Road & Track*, April 1988, advertisement.

48. *Consumer Reports, The 1988 Cars*, p. 228.

49. *Consumer Reports, 1996*, p. 62.

50. "First Test: Mazda MP3," *Motor Trend*, September 2001, p. 103.

51. *Consumer Reports New Car Buying Guide 2002*, p. 178.

52. Flammang, *Imported Cars*, p. 399.

53. "Mazda 626 GT," *Road & Track*, September 1986, p. 72.

54. *Consumer Guide Automobile Book 1993*, p. 163.

55. *Consumer Reports, 1996*, p. 96.

56. "Used Car Buying Guide," *Motor Trend*, October 2001, p. 102.

57. *Consumer Guide Auto Report '92*, p. 86.

58. Flammang, *Imported Cars*, p. 401.
59. Gillis, *1994–1995*, p. 153.
60. *Consumer Guide, 1993*, p. 83.
61. "Used Car Buying Guide," *Motor Trend*, October 2001, p. 102.
62. "Mazda 929," *Road & Track*, April 1988, p. 142.
63. *Consumer Reports '92*, p. 91.
64. Sam Mitani, "Long-Term Test: Mazda Millennia S," *Road & Track*, December 1995, p. 112.
65. *Consumer Reports, 1996*, p. 122.
66. *Consumer Reports*, 2002, p. 175.
67. "Used Car Buying Guide," *Motor Trend*, October 2001, p. 102.
68. *Consumer Guide, 1993*, p. 161.
69. "New Cars," *Popular Mechanics*, March 1992, p. 88.
70. "Ampersand," *Road & Track*, December 1995, p. 32.
71. "10 Best Winners and Losers," *Car and Driver*, January 1996, p. 67.
72. www.motortrend.com.
73. *Ibid.*
74. www.chugoku-np.co.jp.
75. *Ibid.*

## Chapter 11

1. Ruiz, p. 162.
2. www.subaru.ca.
3. "Move Over World: Here Come the Japanese," *Car Life*, August 1968, p. 32.
4. "Newer and Bigger: Subaru FF-1," *Road Test*, November 1969, p. 66.
5. *Ibid.*
6. *Petersen's ... Japanese Import Cars*, p. 130.
7. "Newer and Bigger...," *Road Test*, October 1969, p. 62.
8. "You Can Get More Than You Pay For," *Motor Trend*, February 1971, p. 75.
9. *Motor Trend*, April 1971, back cover advertisement.
10. Flammang, *Imported Cars*, p. 588.
11. *Ibid.*, p. 589.
12. "Winter Windercar," *Motor Trend*, December 1975, pp. 97, 99.
13. *Ibid.*
14. "Jeep Wagoneer & Subaru DL," *Motor Trend*, April 1979, p. 123.
15. Flammang, *Imported Cars*, p. 589.
16. "Jeep Wagoneer...," *Motor Trend*, April 1979, p. 123.
17. Flammang, *Imported Cars*, p. 589.
18. *Ibid.*, p. 590.
19. "Road Test Summary," *Road & Track*, September 1986, p. 28.
20. *Ibid.*, advertisement.
21. *Comsumer Reports, The 1986 Cars*, p. 233.
22. "International Report," *Motor Trend*, May 1987, p. 26.
23. Flammang, *Imported Cars*, p. 590.

24. *Road & Track*, April 1989, advertisement.
25. "Subaru Justy ECVT," *Road & Track*, pp. 62, 67.
26. *Auto Guide Preview 1988 Cars*, p. 96.
27. *Consumer Reports New Car Buying Guide 1996*, pp. 102, 103.
28. *Ibid.*, pp. 65, 85, 102.
29. "Used Car Buying Guide," *Motor Trend*, October 2001, p. 112.
30. *Motor Trend,* July 2001, www.motortrend.com.
31. *Consumer Reports New Car Buying Guide 2002*, p. 225.
32. *Ibid.*, p. 224.
33. *Showroom*, 1998, Vol. 15, No. 6, www.aiada.org.
34. *Ibid.*
35. *Ibid.*
36. www.suzuki.com.
37. Ruiz, p. 168.
38. "Now! Second-Generation ATVs," *Mechanix Illustrated*, September 1971, p. 89.
39. *Petersen's ... Japanese Import Cars*, p. 159.
40. *Ibid.*
41. Ruiz, p. 168.
42. "Trends," *Motor Trend*, January 1985, p. 14.
43. "Suzuki X90," *Car and Driver*, January 1996, p. 115.
44. Gillis, *1994–1995*, p. 206.
45. *Road & Track*, April 1989, advertisement.
46. Flammang, *Imported Cars*, p. 597.
47. *Comsumer Guide, The 1993 Automobile Book*, pp. 234, 235.
48. "Road Test Summary," *Road & Track*, December 1995, p. 161.
49. *Ibid.*, advertisement.
50. "Suzuki X90," *Car and Driver*, January 1996, pp. 115–117.
51. *Consumer Reports New Car Buying Guide 1996*, p. 66.
52. www.auto.consumerguide.com.
53. "One-Year Test Update," *Motor Trend*, November 2001, p. 140.
54. www.suzuki.com.
55. *Ibid.*

## Chapter 12

1. "Japan 1983: Charting the Changes," *Car and Driver*, November 1982, p. 33.
2. *Motor Trend*, May 1987, p. 14, advertisement.
3. www.isuzu.co.jp.
4. "Japan 1983...," *Car and Driver*, November 1982, p. 33.
5. Flammang, *Imported Cars*, p. 308.
6. *Motor Trend*, May 1987, p. 14, advertisement.
7. *Consumer Reports, The 1986 Cars*, p. 231.
8. *Ibid.*, p. 235.
9. *Ibid.*, p. 235. *Ibid., The 1988 Cars*, p. 232.

10. Flammang, *Imported Cars*, p. 309.
11. Gillis, *1994–1995*, pp. 141, 142.
12. "News, Views and Hype," *Road & Track*, April 1988, p. 120.
13. *The Used Car Book*, p. 141.
14. *Ibid*.
15. *Consumer Guide, The Automobile Book 1993*, p. 136.
16. Ruiz, p. 118.
17. *Ibid*.
18. Flammang, *Imported Cars*, p. 445.
19. *Ibid*.
20. "Japan 1983: Charting the Changes," *Car and Driver*, November 1982, p. 84.
21. *Ibid*., pp. 68, 69.
22. *Ibid*., p. 71.
23. *Ibid*.
24. Flammang, *Imported Cars*, p. 446.
25. "Road Test Summary," *Road & Track*, August 1986, p. 24.
26. *Consumer Reports, The 1986 Cars*, pp. 232, 236, 240.
27. *Auto Guide 1988 Car Preview*, p. 93.
28. *Ibid*.
29. Flammang, *Imported Cars*, p. 447.
30. *Ibid*.
31. *Road & Track*, April 1989, p. 106.
32. *Consumer Guide Automobile Book 1993*, p. 180.
33. *Consumer Guide Auto Report '92*, pp. 100, 101.
34. *Consumer Reports New Car Buying Guide 1996*, p. 98.
35. *Ibid*., p. 125.
36. "Road Test: Mitsubishi Galant GTZ," *Car and Driver*, December 1998, p. 73.
37. *Ibid*., p. 77.
38. *Consumer Reports New Car Buying Guide 2002*, p. 194.
39. *Ibid*.
40. *Ibid*., p. 193.
41. *Motor Trend, Used Car Buying Guide*, October 2001.
42. www.motortrend.com.

## Chapter 13

1. Rae, p. 344.
2. Edwin O. Reischauer, *Japan: The Story of a Nation*, 4th ed. (New York: McGraw-Hill, 1990), p. 274.
3. Toyoda, p. 139.
4. *Ibid*.
5. *Ibid*., p. 140.
6. "There's a Ford in My Past," *Mechanix Illustrated*, February 1970, p. 45.
7. Toyoda, p. 140.
8. www.motorage.com.
9. "Editorial," *Motor Trend*, February 1971.
10. www.japanauto.com, JAMA.
11. "Special Report Now: Japanese Empire," *Car and Driver*, April 1972, p. 88.
12. *National Geographic*, May 1972.
13. *National Geographic*, February 1973.
14. Jean-Jacques Servan-Schreiber, *The World Challenge* (New York: Simon and Schuster, 1980), p. 18.
15. *Ibid*., p. 39.
16. *Ibid*.
17. *Ibid*., p. 59.
18. J. Patrick Wright, *On a Clear Day You Can See General Motors* (New York: Avon Books, 1979), p. 212.
19. Iacocca, p. 109.
20. *Ibid*., p. 194.
21. *Popular Mechanics*, July 1974.
22. *National Geographic*, January 1972, advertisement.
23. *Car and Driver*, April 1972, p. 23, advertisement.
24. Cray, p. 499.
25. "The Next Sound You Will Hear Will Be Your Electric Car," *Motor Trend*, August 1971, p. 95.
26. "A New Switch for Electrics," *Mechanix Illustrated*, July 1973, p. 97.
27. www.apecsec.org, Automotive Fact File February 28, 2002.
28. www.fortfreedom.org.
29. "Death by the Gallon," *USA Today*, July 2, 1999, www.serve.com.
30. Levin, pp. 63, 64.
31. Keller, *Rude Awakening*, p. 54.
32. "Detroit's Economy Car Gap," *Motor Trend*, March 1967, p. 55.
33. "Move Over World: Here Come the Japanese," *Car Life*, August 1968, p. 17.
34. Engineering Datsun PL510," *Road Test*, April 1968, p. 17.
35. "Newer and Bigger: Subaru FF-1," *Road Test*, October 1969, p. 62.
36. "Eighth Annual Reader's Choice Winners," *Car and Driver*, May 1971, p. 84.
37. Return of the Native," *Motor Trend*, August 1971, p. 50.
38. "MI Tests the Subaru FF-1G," *Mechanix Illustrated*, October 1971, p. 74.
39. Time-Life, *Japan*, p. 120.
40. *Ibid*.
41. Toyota Motor Sales Archives.
42. Joseph J. Fucini and Suzy Fucini, *Working for the Japanese: Inside Mazda's American Plant* (New York: MacMillan, Inc., 1990), p. 27.
43. Robert E. Cole, *American Automobile Industry: Rebirth or Requiem?*, Michigan Papers in Japanese Studies, No. 1B. (Ann Arbor: University of Michigan, 1984)
44. "Editorial," *Car and Driver*, April 1972, p. 4.
45. Automotive Service Association, www.asashop.org.
46. *Ibid*.
47. "Detroit Is Cruising for Quality," *Business Week*, September 2001, www.businessweek.com.

# Chapter 14

1. "Can Detroit Make Cars That Baby Boomers Like?," *Business Week*, December 1997, www.businessweek.com.

2. "Letters," *Motor Trend*, September 1962, p. 10.

3. "Import Report," *Motor Trend*, April 1971, p. 12.

4. *Ibid.*

5. Lacey, p. 514.

6. Iacocca, p. 47.

7. *Ibid.*, p. 48.

8. Flammang, *100 Years*, p. 351.

9. *Ibid.*

10. Wright, p. 66.

11. "Letters," *Motor Trend*, September 1962, p. 9.

12. *Ibid.*

13. Flammang, *100 Years*, p. 358.

14. *Ibid.*, p. 81.

15. "Facts and Forecasts," *Motor Life*, March 1960, p. 8.

16. *Ibid.*

17. "Facts, Forecasts, and Rumors," *Motor Trend*, September 1962, p. 14.

18. *Consumer Guide, Cars of the 60s*, p. 25.

19. Wright, p. 65.

20. Cray, p. 409.

21. "Comparing the Compacts," *Popular Science*, November 1965, p. 91.

22. "Economy Motoring, Anyone?," *Motorcade*, March 1966, p. 53.

23. *Ibid.*

24. *Ibid.*

25. Flammang, *100 Years*, p. 401.

26. Iacocca, p. 77.

27. *Ibid.*, p. 79.

28. "Why Can't We Make Cars Safer?," *Popular Science*, November 1965, p. 64.

29. www.nader.org.

30. "Why Can't We Make Cars Safer?," *Popular Science*, November 1965, pp. 64, 67.

31. Lacey, p. 608.

32. Flammang, *100 Years*, p. 452.

33. "For Your Information," *Car and* Driver, September 1970, p. 25.

34. Flammang, *100 Years*, p. 457.

35. "1971 Cars: Detroit's Minis Challenge the Imports," *Canadian Motorist*, Fall 1970, p. 17.

36. *Ibid.*

37. Iacocca, p. 171.

38. "1971 Car of the Year: Chevrolet Vega 2300," *Motor Trend*, February 1971, p. 38.

39. Cray, p. 474.

40. *Ibid.*, p. 443.

41. "Detroit's Economy Car Gap," *Motor Trend*, March 1967, p. 68.

42. Lacey, p. 532.

43. Wright, p. 254.

44. Iacocca, p. 161.

45. Flammang, *100 Years*, p. 474.

46. Iacocca, p. 240.

47. Alton F. Doody and Ron Bingaman, *Reinventing the Wheels: Ford's Spectacular Comeback* (Cambridge, Mass., Ballinger Publishing, 1988), p. 23.

48. www.local95.org.

49. "Import Report," *Motor Trend*, February 1971, p. 24.

# Chapter 15

1. Sobel, p. 199.

2. "For Your Information," *Car and Driver*, September 1971, p. 68.

3. *Ibid.*

4. Iacocca, p. 164.

5. "International Report," *Motor Trend*, August 1971, p. 28.

6. Moritz and Seaman, p. 117.

7. "For Your Information," *Car and Driver*, September 1970, p. 75.

8. *Ibid.*

9. Sobel, p. 214.

10. Keller, *Collision*, pp. 215, 216.

11. Scott Latham, *Grinding Gears: The Japanese Automobile Dealer Network and American Trade Complaints*, (Chester Springs, PA: Latham and Associates, 1998).

12. William J. Holstein, *The Japanese Power Game: What It Means for America* (New York: Pengiun Books USA, Inc., 1991), p. 203.

13. *Ibid.*, p. 205.

14. "Union News," *Business Week*, March 27, 2000, www.businessweek.com.

15. www.dc.com.

16. *Ibid.*

17. "Inside Detroit," *Motor Trend*, January 1971, p. 13.

18. Sobel, p. 200.

19. "Isuzu, GM Agree to Strengthen Partnership," PRNewswire, December 18, 1998.

20. *Ibid.*

21. Keller, *Rude Awakening*, p. 136.

22. *Ibid.*

23. "Import Report," *Motor Trend*, April 1971, pp. 12, 14.

24. James P. Womack, Daniel T. Jones, and Daniel Roos, *The Machine That Changed the World: The Story of Lean Production* (New York: Harper Perennial, 1989), p. 237.

25. *Ibid.*

26. www.chugoku-np.co.jp.

27. *Ibid.*

28. "Mazda's Mark Fields," *Business Week*, January 16, 2001, www.businessweek.com.

29. Womack et al., p. 238.

30. *Ibid.*

31. "Globalization: Do Mergers Threaten Nations?," *Los Angeles Times*, June 27, 1998.

32. "Mazda's Mark Fields," *Business Week*, January 16, 2001, www.businessweek.com.

33. "Globalization…," *Los Angeles Times*, June 27, 1998.
34. *Ibid.*

## Chapter 16

1. Gelsanliter, p. 15.
2. *Ibid.*, p. 26.
3. *Ibid.*, p. 28.
4. *Ibid.*, p. 49.
5. Shook, p. 44.
6. www.autonews.com.
7. www.honda.com.
8. *Ibid.*
9. www.autointell.com.
10. "Foreign Direct Investment in Tennessee," *Global Commerce*, Fall 1995, Vol. 1, No. 2, www.mtsu.edu.
11. Gelsanliter, p. 56.
12. www.autointell.com.
13. American International Automobile Dealers Association, *Showroom*, May, 1998, Vol. 15, No. 4.
14. www.nissandriven.com.
15. "Locations — Canton, Miss.," *Industry Week*, February 2002, www.industryweek.com.
16. Gelsanliter, p. 72.
17. *Ibid.*, p. 130.
18. www.toyota.com.
19. *Ibid.*
20. *Ibid.*
21. *Ibid.*
22. *Ibid.*
23. *Ibid.*
24. www.chugoku-np.co.jp.
25. 2000 Annual Report, Mazda Motor Company, p. 5.
26. *Ibid.*
27. www.autonews.com.
28. www.subaru.net.
29. www.hartford-hwp.com.
30. www.ai.org.
31. *Ibid.*
32. www.subaru.com.
33. *Showroom*, Nov./Dec., 1997, Vol. 14, No. 8, www.aiada.org.
34. JAMA, www.japanauto.com.

## Chapter 17

1. Satoshi Kamata, *Japan in the Passing Lane: An Insider's Account of Life in a Japanese Auto Factory*, (New York: Pantheon Books, 1983), p. 200.
2. *Ibid.*, p. 147.
3. *Ibid.*, p. 198.
4. *Ibid.*, p. 71.
5. Iacocca, p. 320.
6. *Ibid.*, p. 323.

7. Toyoda, p. 166.
8. Steven Schlossstein, *Trade War: Greed, Power, and Industrial Policy on Opposite Sides of the Pacific* (New York: Congdon and Weed, Inc., 1984), p. 35.
9. Womack et al., p. 57.
10. *Ibid.*, p. 13.
11. Fucini and Fucini, p. 210.
12. *Ibid.*, p. 104.
13. *Ibid.*, p. 182.
14. *Ibid.*, p. 210.
15. *Ibid.*, p. 224.
16. Kamata, p. 64.
17. *Ibid.*, p. 78.
18. *Ibid.*, p. 126.
19. *Ibid.*
20. *Ibid.*, p. 144.
21. *Ibid.*, Translator's Note, p. viii.
22. Fucini and Fucini, pp. 80, 81.
23. Schlossstein, p. 32.
24. Keller, *Rude Awakening*, p. 55.
25. *Ibid.*, p. 203.
26. "Toyota Alters the Face of Production," *Industry Week*, August 13, 2001, www.industryweek.com.
27. "Toyota Road USA," *Time*, October 7, 1999, Vol. 148, No. 17.
28. *Ibid.*
29. "Toyota Hearing Talk of Unions," *Detroit News*, February 18, 2000.
30. 2001 Labor Day Message, www.uaw.org.
31. *Ibid.*
32. Charles Baird, "The Pursuit of Happiness — Unions on the Run," *The Freeman: Ideas on Liberty*, February 2002.
33. "Lack of Access Tied to Defeat of UAW," *Detroit News*, September 28, 2001.
34. *Ibid.*
35. www.laboreducator.org, October 8, 2001.
36. *Ibid.*
37. Baird.
38. *Ibid.*
39. "Lack of Access…," *Detroit News*, October 4, 2001.
40. Shook, p. 100.
41. *Ibid.*, p. 110.
42. "Honda Workers Oppose USW Representation," *Columbus Free Press*, May 15, 1999.
43. *Ibid.*
44. *Ibid.*
45. "Six Dangerous Myths About Pay," *Harvard Business Review*, May/June 1998, Vol. 76, No. 3.
46. www.manufacturingcenter.com.
47. *Ibid.*

## Chapter 18

1. Clyde V. Prestowitz, Jr., *Trading Places: How We Allowed Japan to Take the Lead* (New York: Basic Books, Inc., 1988), p. 9.

2. Dower, p. 537.

3. *Ibid.*

4. *Ibid.*

5. *Ibid.*, p. 540.

6. Daniel Burstein, *Yen! Japan's New Financial Empire and Its Threat to America* (New York: Simon and Schuster, 1988), p. 36.

7. *Ibid.*, p. 37.

8. *Ibid.*, p. 38.

9. Iacocca, p. 332.

10. *Ibid.*, p. 333.

11. *Ibid.*, p. 336.

12. Schlossstein, p. 113.

13. www.local95.org.

14. *The Japanese Auto Cartel*, www.cato.org.

15. Halberstam, p. 684.

16. Toyoda, p. 167.

17. *Ibid.*

18. *Ibid.*

19. *The Japanese Auto Cartel*, www.cato.org.

20. Political Economy Research Center, www.perc.org.

21. *Ibid.*

22. "A Tokyo Head Twister: Look Who's Buying U.S. Cars!," *Time*, October 17, 1994, Vol. 144, No. 6.

23. 104th Congress, 1st Session, www.senate.gov.

24. *Ibid.*

25. *Ibid.*

26. *Ibid.*

27. *Heritage Foundation F.Y.I.*, Report No. 95, April 11, 1996.

28. www.fpcj.jp.

29. www.aiada.org.

30. Schlossstein, p. 19.

31. *Ibid.*, p. 33.

32. *Ibid.*, p. 22.

33. Holstein, p. 169.

34. *Ibid.*, p. 171.

35. www.aiada.org.

36. "Taking a Back Seat," *Newsday*, February 2002.

37. *Ibid.*

38. www.detroit.us.emb-japan.go.jp.

39. *Ibid.*

40. "The Delusion of Free Trade," *New York Times*, April 25, 2002.

41. *Ibid.*

42. *Ibid.*

43. *Ibid.*

44. "2002 National Trade Estimate Report," www.mofa.go.jp.

45. *Ibid.*

46. www.usembassy.it, April 15, 2002.

47. Prestowitz, p. 332.

## Chapter 19

1. "Toyota Celica GT Liftback," *Car and Driver*, January 1978, p. 51.

2. "Do Americans Feel Compelled to Buy American?," *Detroit News*, January 7, 2002.

3. *Ibid.*

4. *Ibid.*

5. "Axe Falls on Ford's Oakville Truck Plant," *Financial Post*, January 12, 2002.

6. www.aiada.org, December 13, 2001.

7. "Can Detroit Make Cars That Baby Boomers Like?," *Business Week*, December 1, 1997, www.businessweek.com.

8. *Ibid.*

9. "Can't Anybody in Detroit Play This Game?," *Forbes*, December 3, 2001.

10. *Ibid.*

11. "Do Americans Feel…," *Detroit News*, January 7, 2002.

12. "Toyota Eyes 15% Global Market Share by Early 2010s," *Automotive News*, April 01, 2002, www.autonews.com.

13. "Toyota Achieves Record High Sales and Profit," Japan *Weekly Post*, November 19, 2001.

14. "Honda's Yoshino: Traditionally, We Build Small and Grow Big," *Business Week,* International Edition, July 5, 1999, www.businessweek.com.

15. "Nissan Adds More Models, More Capacity to Spur U.S. Growth," *Detroit News*, May 8, 2002.

16. www.nissanglobal.com.

17. www.mazdausa.com, May 15, 2002.

18. *Ibid.*

19. *Ibid.*

20. www.subaru.com.

21. "Weak Yen May Cut Jobs in U.S.," *Detroit News*, February 12, 2002.

22. www.subaru.com, January 3, 2002.

23. *Ibid.*

24. "Suzuki Expects Sales to Rise 7 Percent in 2002," *Bloomberg News*, January 22, 2002.

25. "Mitsubishi Gets a Makeover," *Business Week*, November 5, 2001, www.businessweek.com.

26. *Ibid.*

27. "Isuzu Struggles with Sales, Image," *Indianapolis Star*, February 7, 2002.

28. Auto Industry and the Economy Fast Facts, www.autoalliance.org.

29. *Ibid.*

30. *Ibid.*

31. "Senators Seek Better Fuel Economy," *Detroit News*, February 9, 2002.

32. http://money.cnn.com.

33. www.cartrackers.com.

34. "Exports Soar but Not All Rosy for Japan Carmakers," *Automotive News*, June 28, 2002, www.autonews.com.

# Bibliography

## Books

Bingaman, Ron, and Doody, Alton F. *Reinventing the Wheels: Ford's Spectacular Comeback*. Massachusetts: Harper and Row Publishers, Inc., 1988.

Bowler, Michael. *Classic Cars from Around the World*. New York: Smithmark Publishers, 1996.

Burstein, Daniel. *Yen! Japan's New Financial Empire and Its Threat to America*. New York: Simon and Schuster, 1988.

Chafe, William H. *The Unfinished Journey: America Since World War II*. New York: Oxford University Press, 1986.

Cole, Robert E. *American Automobile Industry: Rebirth or Requiem?* Michigan Papers in Japanese Studies, No. 1B. Ann Arbor: University of Michigan, 1984.

*Consumer Guide. Cars of the '60s*. New York: Beekman House, 1979.

Cray, Ed. *Chrome Colossus: General Motors and Its Times*. New York: McGraw-Hill, 1980.

Dower, John W. *Embracing Defeat: Japan in the Wake of World War II*. New York: W. W. Norton, 1999.

Flammang, James M., and the Auto Editors of *Consumer Guide. 100 Years of the American Auto*. Millennium Edition. Lincolnwood, Illinois: Publications International, Ltd., 1999.

_____. *Standard Catalog of Imported Cars 1946–1990*. Iola, Wisconsin: Krause Publications, 1994.

Fucini, Joseph J., and Suzy Fucini. *Working for the Japanese: Inside Mazda's American Plant*. New York: MacMillan, 1990.

Fukuzawa, Yukichi. *Conditions in the West (Occidental Affairs)*. Vol. 2. Japan: 1868.

Gabor, Andrea. *The Man Who Discovered Quality: How W. Edwards Deming Brought the Quality Revolution to America — The Stories of Ford, Xerox, and GM*. New York: Times Books, Random House, 1990.

Gelsanliter, David. *Jump Start: Japan Comes to the Heartland*. New York: Kodansha International, 1992.

Graham, Laurie. *On the Line at Subaru-Isuzu: The Japanese Model and the American Worker*. Ithaca, New York: ILR Press, 1995.

Halberstam, David. *The Reckoning*. New York: William Morrow, 1986.

Hamper, Ben. *Rivethead: Tales from the Assembly Line*. New York: Warner Books, 1986.

Handlin, Oscar. *The History of the United States*. Vol. 2. New York: Holt, Rinehart and Winston, 1968.

Hirschmeier, Johannes L., and Tsunehiko Yui. *The Development of Japanese Business 1600–1973*. London: George Allen & Unwin, 1975.

Holstein, William J. *The Japanese Power Game: What It Means for America*. New York: Penguin Books U.S.A., 1991.

Iacocca, Lee. *Iacocca: An Autobiography*. New York: Bantam, 1984.

*Japan*. By the editors of Time-Life Books. Alexandria, Virginia: Time-Life Books, 1985.

Kamata, Satoshi. *Japan in the Passing Lane: An Insider's Account of Life in a Japanese Auto Factory*. New York: Pantheon Books, 1983.

Kamiya, Shotaro. *My Life with Toyota*. Toyota City, Japan: Toyota Motor Sales, 1976.

Kato, Seisi. *My Years with Toyota*. Toyota City, Japan: Toyota Motor Sales, 1981.

Keller, Maryann. *Collision: GM, Toyota, Volkswagen and the Race to Own the 21st Century*. New York: Doubleday, 1993.

_____. *Rude Awakening: The Rise, Fall, and Struggle for Recovery of General Motors*. New York: William Morrow, 1989.

Lacey, Robert. *Ford: The Men and the Machine*. New York: Little, Brown, 1986.

Langworth, Richard M., and Jan P. Norbye. *The Complete History of the Chrysler Corporation 1924–1985*. New York: Beekman House, 1985.

Latham, Scott. *Grinding Gears: The Japanese Automobile Dealer Network and American Trade Complaints*. Chester Springs, Pennsylvania: Latham and Associates, 1998.

Lawrence, Mike. *A to Z of Sports Cars*. St. Paul, Minnesota: Bayview Books, 1996.

Levin, Doron P. *Behind the Wheel at Chrysler: The Lee Iacocca Legacy*. New York: Harcourt Brace, 1995.

Link, Arthur S., William A. Link, and William B. Catton. *American Epoch: A History of the United States Since 1900*. 6th ed. Vol. 1, *1900–1945*. New York: Alfred A. Knopf, 1987.

_____, and William B. Catton. *American Epoch: A History of the United States Since the 1890s*. New York: Alfred A. Knopf, 1987.

McKelvey, Blake. *The Emergence of Metropolitan America 1915–1966*. New Brunswick, New Jersey: Rutgers University Press, 1968.

Moritz, Michael, and Barrett Seaman. *Going for Broke: The Chrysler Story*. New York: Doubleday, 1981.

*Petersen's Complete Book of Datsun*. Los Angeles: Petersen's Publishing Company, 1977.

*Petersen's Complete Book of Japanese Import Cars*. Los Angeles: Petersen's Publishing Company, 1972.

Prestowitz, Clyde V. *Trading Places: How We Allowed Japan to Take the Lead*. New York: Basic Books, 1988.

Rae, John Bell. *The Road and the Car in American Life*. Cambridge, Massachusetts: MIT Press, 1971.

Reischauer, Edwin O. *Japan: The Story of a Nation*. 4th ed. New York: McGraw-Hill, 1990.

Ruiz, Marco. *The Complete History of the Japanese Car 1907 to Present*. New York: Crown Publishers, Portland House, 1986.

Sakiya, Tetsuo. *Honda Motor: The Men, the Management, the Machines*. Translated by Kiyoshi Ikemi. Tokyo: Kodansha International, 1982.

*Saturday Evening Post Automobile Book*. Indianapolis, Indiana: Curtis Publishing, 1977.

Schlossstein, Steven. *Trade War: Greed, Power, and Industrial Policy on Opposite Sides of the Pacific*. New York: Congdon and Weed, 1984.

Servan-Schreiber, Jean-Jacques. *The World Challenge*. New York: Simon and Schuster, 1980.

Shook, Robert L. *Honda: An American Success Story*. New York: Prentice Hall, 1988.

Sloan, Alfred P. *My Years with General Motors*. New York: Doubleday, 1964.

Sobel, Robert. *Car Wars: The Untold Story of the Great Automakers and the Giant Battle for Global Supremacy*. New York: E. P. Dutton, Truman Tally Books, 1984.

Togo, Yukiyasu and William Wartman. *Against All Odds: The Story of the Toyota Motor Company and the Family That Created It*. New York: St. Martin's Press, 1993.

Toyoda, Eiji. *Toyota: Fifty Years in Motion*. Tokyo: Kodansha International, 1985.

*Toyota: 40 Years in America*. Toyota City, Japan: Toyota Motor Sales, 1997.

Wherry, Joseph H. *Automobiles of the World*. New York: Chilton Books, Galahad Books, 1968.

Williams, David. *Japan: Beyond the End of History*. London: Routledge, 1994.

Womack, James P., Daniel T. Jones, and Daniel Roos. *The Machine That Changed the World: The Story of Lean Production*. New York: Harper Perennial, 1989.

Wright, J. Patrick. *On a Clear Day You Can See General Motors: John Z. DeLorean's Look Inside the Automotive Giant*. New York: Avon Books, 1979.

Yates, Brock. *The Decline and Fall of the American Automobile Industry*. New York: Empire Books, 1983.

## Consumer Buying Guides

*Auto Guide. 1988 Car Preview*
*Consumer Guide. Automobile Book 1993*
_____. *Auto Report '92*
_____. *The 1986 Cars*
_____. *The 1988 Cars*
_____. *The 1989 Cars*
*Consumer Reports.* The 1988 Car Book
_____. *New Car Buying Guide 1996*
_____. *New Car Buying Guide 2002*
Jack Gillis, *The Used Car Book 1981–1989*
_____. *The Used Car Book 1990*
_____. *The Used Car Book 1992*
_____. *The Used Car Book 1994–1995*

## Periodicals

### AUTO TOPICS

"Auto Topics Historical Section: Model T Humor." Clymer, Floyd. October 1965, p. 70.
"Datsun 1966...A New Power and Economy Package." November 1965, p. 65.

### AUTOMOTIVE NEWS

"Exports Soar but All Not Rosy for Japan Carmakers." June 28, 2002.
"Toyota Eyes 15% Global Market Share by Early 2010s." April 1, 2002.

### BLOOMBERG NEWS

"Suzuki Expects Sales to Rise 7 Percent in 2002." Inoue, Kae. January 22, 2002.

### BUSINESS WEEK

"Can Detroit Make Cars That Baby Boomers Like?" Kerwin, Kathleen, and Keith Naughton. December 1, 1997.
"Detroit Is Cruising for Quality." Muller, Joann, and Katie Kerwin. September 3, 2001.
"Honda's Yoshino: 'Traditionally, We Build Small and Grow Big.'" International Edition, July 5, 1999.
"Mazda's Mark Fields: 'This Isn't Just a Restructuring Plan.'" Harbrecht, Douglas, ed. January 16, 2001.
"Mitsubishi Gets a Makeover." Dawson, Chester. November 5, 2001.
"Too Many Models, Too Little Focus." Vlasic, Bill. December 1, 1997.

### CANADIAN MOTORIST

"1971 Cars: Detroit's Minis Challenge the Imports." Fall 1970, p. 17.

### CAR AND DRIVER

Advertisement. January 1971, Back Cover.
_____. May 1974.
_____. March 1979.
_____. April 1979.
_____. November 1982.
"Datsun F-10." Cook, Terry. June 1978, p. 115.
"Datsun P410-U: Japan's Cars Are Getting Better and Better All the Time." June 1964, p. 64.
"Editorial." April 1972, p. 4.
_____. Yates, Brock. October 1972, p. 22.
"Eighth Annual Reader's Choice Winners." May 1971, p. 57.
"For Your Information." September 1970, p. 75.
_____. September 1971, p. 68.
_____. March 1979, pp. 22, 26.
_____. April 1979, p. 54.
_____. November 1982, p. 33.

"Honda 600 Sedan and Honda 600 Coupe." Bedard, Patrick. April 1972, p. 43.

"Japan 1983: Charting the Changes." Ceppos, Rich. November 1982, p. 69.

"Mazda 626." Sherman, Don. March 1979, p. 26.

"Road Test: Honda Accord 4-Door." Davis, David E., Jr. March 1979, p. 41.

"Road Test: Mitsubishi Galant GTZ." Schroeder, Don. December 1998, p. 73.

"Short-Takes: Mazda GLC." February 1977, p. 30.

"Special Report Now: Japanese Empire." April 1972, p. 88.

"Suzuki X90." Gregory, Fred M. H. January 1996, p. 115.

"Ten Best Cars." Csere, Csaba. January 1996, p. 51.

"Toyota Celica Liftback." January 1978, p. 57.

"Upfront." Smith, Steven Cole. December 1998, p. 31.

"Winners and Losers." Phillips, John. January 1996, p. 59.

## Car Life

"Move Over, World: Here Come the Japanese." Hamilton, Jim. August 1968, p. 16.

## Columbus (Ohio) Free Press

"Honda Workers Oppose UAW Representation." Dowell, Angie. May 15, 1999.

## Consumer Reports

"Review of the Toyota Corona." April 1966.

## Detroit News

"Do Americans Feel Compelled to Buy American?" January 7, 2002.

"Lack of Access Tied to Defeat of UAW." Miller, Joe. October 4, 2001.

"Nissan Adds More Models, More Capacity to Spur U.S. Growth." Ohnsman, Alan/Bloomberg News. May 8, 2002.

"Nissan Is Back After Several Missteps Along the Way." Higgins, James V. January 10, 1958, reprinted quote in the *Detroit News*, May 4, 2001.

"Senators Seek Better Fuel Economy." Pickler, Nedra. February 9, 2002.

"Toyota Hearing Talk of Unions." Associated Press. February 18, 2000.

"Weak Yen May Cut Jobs in U.S." Carney, Susan. February 12, 2002.

## The Financial Post

"Axe Falls on Ford's Oakville Truck Plant." Brieger, Peter. January 12, 2002.

## Forbes

"Can't Anybody in Detroit Play This Game?" Flint, Jerry. November 30, 2001.

## Freeman: Ideas on Liberty

"The Pursuit of Happiness—Unions on the Run." Baird, Charles. February 2002.

## Global Commerce

"Foreign Direct Investment in Tennessee." Vol. 1., No. 2, Fall 1995.

## Harvard Business Review

"Six Dangerous Myths about Pay." Vol. 76, No. 3, May/June 1998.

## Heritage Foundation

F.Y.I., Report No. 95, April 11, 1996.

## Indianapolis Star

"Isuzu Struggles with Sales, Image." Evanoff, Ted. February 7, 2002.

## Industry Week

"How Honda Thrives." Clark, Tanya. December 5, 1998.

"Locations—Canton, Miss." Jusko, Jill. February 1, 2002.

"Toyota Alters the Face of Production." Strozniak, Peter. August 13, 2001.

## Journal of Integrated Communication

"How We Made Public Relations a Critical Strategic Weapon at Nissan." Spetner, Don. 1996-1997.

Los Angeles Times

"Globalization: Do Mergers Threaten Nations?" Cowhey, Peter F., and Jonathan D. Aronson. June 27, 1998.

Mechanix Illustrated

"MI Tests the Subaru FF-1G." McCahill, Tom. October 1971, p. 72.
"A New Switch for Electrics." July 1973, p. 97.
"Now! Second-Generation ATVs." September 1971, p. 89.
"There's a Ford in My Past." February 1970, p. 45.

Motor Life

"Facts and Forecasts." March 1960, p. 6.

Motor Trend

"Acura Legend Coupe." May 1987, p. 105.
Advertisement. December 1975.
_____. April 1979.
_____. September 1986.
_____. May 1987.
"Car Clinic." Spencer, Doane. September 1962, p. 90.
"Datsun PL510: A Lot of Car for a Little Money." April 1968, p. 86.
"Datsun 280Z vs. Toyota Supra." August 1979, p. 52.
"Detroit's Economy Car Gap." Schilling, Robert. March 1967, p. 55.
"Editorial." February 1971, p. 12.
"Facts, Forecasts and Rumors." September 1962, p. 14.
"First Drive 2002: Lexus IS 300." Walton, Chris. September 2002, p. 96.
"First Test: Mazda MP3." Walton, Chris. September 2001, p. 103.
"First Test: 2003 Nissan 350Z." Sessions, Ron. September 2002, p. 60.
"Firsts: Honda Hybrid." Schifsky, Chuck. February 2002, p. 32.
"Honda Prelude." Nerpel, Chuck. April 1979, p. 51.
"Import Report." April 1971, p. 12.
"Inside Detroit." January 1971, p. 12.
"International Report." August, 1971, p. 26.

_____. December 1975, p. 20
_____. December 1977, p. 23.
_____. May 1987, pp. 24, 26, 70.
"International Report." Bingham, Phillip. May 1987, p. 24.
"Jeep Wagoneer & Subaru DL." Stafford, Fred. April 1979, p. 123.
"Letters." September 1962, p. 910.
_____. May 1987, p. 9.
"Lexus ES 300." Smith, Kevin. November 2001, p. 61.
"Mazda GLC Sport." Hall, Bob. December 1977, p. 74.
"Mazda Wankel vs. Comet 302." Wyss, Wally. May 1971, p. 76.
"The Next Sound You Hear Will Be Your Electric Car." August 1971, p. 95.
"1971 Car of the Year: Chevrolet Vega 2300." February 1971, p. 38.
"1978 Import Car of the Year, the Nominees." December 1977, p. 36.
"One-Year Test Update." Stone, Matt. November 2001, p. 140.
"Return of the Native." Wyss, Wally. August 1971, p. 50.
"Road Test — Toyota MR2." Assenza, Tony. January 1985, p. 26.
"'79 Import Buyer's Guide." April 1979, p. 63.
"Showdown of the Sudden Samurai." June 1982, p. 30.
"The Toyopet Crown." October, 1958. Excerpt from *Fifty Years of Motor Trend*. Minnesota: MBI Publishing, 1999.
"Trends." January 1985, p. 14.
"Used Car Buying Guide." October 2001, Insert.
"Winter Wondercar." Carlton, David. December 1975, p. 97.
"You Can Get More Than You Pay For." Koch, Chuck. February 1971, p. 72.
"Z/28 vs 240-Z: Great Expectations — Unconfirmed." Christy, John. August 1972, p. 96.

Motorcade

"Economy Motoring, Anyone?" Thoms, Wayne. March 1966, p. 53.

## NATION

"The Hipster." Gold, Herbert. November 16, 1957.

## NATIONAL GEOGRAPHIC

Advertisement. September 1971.
_____. January 1972, Back Cover.
_____. May 1972.
_____. February 1973.

## NEW YORK TIMES

"The Delusion of Free Trade." Hollings, Senator Ernest F. April 25, 2002.
"'Mental Hygiene': The Dos and Don'ts of the Doo-Wop Age." Smith, Ken. January 2, 2002.

## NEWSDAY

"Taking a Back Seat." Incantalupo, Tom. February 2002.

## POPULAR MECHANICS

Advertisement. May 1953, Inside Cover.
_____. July 1974.
"America's Smallest Car — The Metropolitan." Railton, Arthur. April 1954, p. 88.
"New Cars." Chaikin, Don. March 1992, p. 90.
"Owner's Report on the VW." Chaikin, Don. October 1956, p. 154.
"The Toyota Corona." Markovich, Alexander. January 1967, p. 38.

## POPULAR SCIENCE

"Comparing the Compacts." Norbye, Jan P. November 1965, p. 90.
"Why Can't We Make Cars Safer?" November 1965, p. 64.

## PRNEWSWIRE

"Isuzu, GM Agree to Strengthen Partnership." December 18, 1998.

## ROAD & TRACK

Advertisement. *Road & Track,* April 1988.
_____. *Road & Track,* April 1989.
_____. *Road & Track,* December 1995.
_____. *Road & Track,* January 2000.
"Ampersand." Homan, Richard. December 1995, p. 32.
"ASAP — News, Views and Hype." April 1988, p. 120.
"Honda Prelude at 26,000 Miles." August 1986, p. 54.
"Letter from Japan: 4WD Craze." Yamaguchi, Jack. August 1986, p. 88.
"Long-Term Test: Mazda Millenia S." Mitani, Sam. December 1995, p. 112.
"Mazda 626 GT." September 1986, p. 72.
"Mazda 929." Albrecht, Peter L. April 1988, p. 142.
"Miscellaneous Ramblings." April 1989, p. 41.
"Nissan Sentra SE Sport Coupe." September 1986, p. 46.
"Review of the Datsun 210." 1960.
"Road Test Summary." August 1986, p. 24.
_____. September 1986, p. 28.
_____. December 1995, p. 161.
"Subaru Justy ECVT." Kott, Douglas. April 1989, p. 62.
"Update: Long-Term Road-Test Acura Legend Coupe." April 1988, p. 78.

## ROAD TEST

"Advance News from Japan." August 1969, p. 16.
Advertisement. August 1969, Inside Front Cover.
"Engineering:Datsun PL510." April 1968, p. 17.
"Newer and Bigger: Subaru FF-1." October 1969, p. 62.
"The Owner's Survey Rate the Foreign Car." September 1968, p. 49.
"The $2,000 Package." April, 1968, p. 8.

## SCIENCE AND MECHANICS

"The 12 Best Cars to Own in a Gas Shortage." April 1974, p. 46.

Showroom (Automobile International Dealer's Association)

Vol. 14, No. 3, April 1997.
Vol. 14, No. 8, Nov./Dec. 1997.
Vol. 15, No. 6, 1998.

Sport Compact Car

"Honda Inside Out." Stengel, Marc. July 2000, p. 144.

Time

"A Tokyo Head Twister: Look Who's Buying U.S. Cars!" Desmond, Edward W., with Irene M. Kunii. October 17, 1994.
"Toyota Road USA." Greenwald, John. October 7, 1999.

USA Today

"Death by the Gallon." Healey, James R. July 2, 1999.

Weekly Post (Japan)

"Toyota Achieves Record High Sales and Profit." November 19, 2001.

World of Wheels

"Sport Compact Deathmatch: Four. Played." La Fave, Michael. September 2002, p. 35.

## Internet Websites

www.ai.org
www.aiada.org
www.apecsec.org
www.asashop.com
www.asiaweek.com
www.atlantabuick.com
www.autoalliance.org
www.auto.consumerguide.com
www.autointell.com
www.autonews.com
www.businessweek.com
www.cartrackers.com
www.chugoku-np.co.jp
www.dc.com

www.detroit.us.emb-japan.go.jp
www.edmunds.com (DiPietro, John. "A Toyota Camry History.")
www.fiftiesweb.com
www.fortfreedom.com
www.fortune.com
www.gm.com
www.greghalpin.com
www.hartford-hwp.com
www.honda.com
www.hondahistoryau.com
www.industryweek.com
www.isuzu.co.jp
www.japanauto.com
www.jdpa.com
www.jmfamily.com
www.laboreducator.org
www.local95.org
www.mazdausa.com
www.medill.northwestern.edu
www.mofa.go.jp
www.money.cnn.com
www.monito.com
www.motorage.com
www.motortrend.com
www.nader.org
www.nissandriven.com
www.nissanglobal.com
www.nissannews.com
www.nsxprime.com
www.1.shore.net
www.perc.org
www.rosetoyota.com
www.rx7uknet.dircon.uk
www.subaru.ca
www.subaru.com
www.subaru.net
www.superhonda.com
www.suzuki.com
www.themuseumofautomobilehistory.com
www.toyota.com
www.usembassy.it
www.zhome.com
www.zubup.com

## Archives

Mazda 2000 Annual Report
Nissan Fact File, The Nissan Motor Company, Ltd.
Toyota Motor Sales, Archives

## *Interviews by the Author*

Alexander, Nick. November 10, 2001.
Hayes, Bob. April 11, 2002.

King, Fred. March 7, 2002.
Krause, Robert. January 31, 2002.
Sullivan, Mike. November 3, 2001.

# Index